INSIGHT GUIDE

THAILAND

APA PUBLICATIONS

Part of the Langenscheidt Publishing Group

ABOUT THIS BOOK

Editorial

Managing Editor
Scott Rutherford
Editorial Director
Brian Bell

Distribution

UK & Ireland
GeoCenter International Ltd
The Viables Centre, Harrow Way
Basingstoke, Hants, RG22 4BJ
Fax: (44 1256) 817988

United States
Langenscheidt Publishers, Inc.
46–35 54th Road
Maspeth, NY 11378
Fax: (718) 784-0640

Australia & New Zealand
Hema Maps Pty. Ltd
24 Allgas Street, Slacks Creek 4127
Brisbane, Australia
Tel: (61 7) 3290-0322
Fax: (61 7) 3290-0478

Worldwide
APA Publications GmbH & Co.
Verlag KG Singapore Branch, Singapore
38 Joo Koon Road
Singapore 628990
Tel: (65) 865-1600

Printing

Insight Print Services (Pte) Ltd
38 Joo Koon Road
Singapore 628990
Tel: (65) 865-1600

CONTACTING THE EDITORS Although
every effort is made to provide
accurate information in this
publication, we live in a fast-
changing world and would
appreciate it if readers would call
our attention to any errors or
outdated information that may
occur by writing to us at:
Insight Guides, P.O. Box 7910,
London SE1 8ZB, England.
Fax: (44 171) 403-0290.
e-mail:
insight@apaguide.demon.co.uk

This guidebook combines the interests and enthusiasms of two of the world's best-known information providers: Insight Guides, whose titles have set the standard for visual travel guides since 1970, and Discovery Channel, the world's premier source of non-fiction television programming. Editors of Insight Guides provide both practical advice and general understanding about a destination's history, institutions, culture, and people. Discovery Channel and its internet Web site, www.discovery.com, help millions of viewers explore their world from the comfort of their own home and also encourage them to explore their world firsthand.

This 13th edition of *Insight Guide: Thailand* journeys to one of Asia's most accessible nations and long-lived kingdoms. Our writers and photographers will help reveal it all – epic history, exquisite food, Buddhist foundations, and the rich and varied destinations, from the chaotic boulevards of Bangkok to the often serene solitude of its beaches and villages.

The chief places of interest are coordinated by number with specially drawn maps.

◆ The Travel Tips listings section, with an orange bar and at the back of the book, offers a convenient point of reference for complete information on travel, accommodation, restaurants and other practical aspects of the country. Information is located quickly using the index printed on the back-cover flap, which also serves as a handy bookmark.

The contributors

This edition was supervised by **Scott Rutherford**, who oversees Apa's Asian and Pacific titles. A considerable amount of the updating was done by three associates of CPA in Chiang Mai: **Andrew Forbes**, with a doctorate in Asian history; **Simon Robson**, who lives in Mae Sa; and **David Henley**, who has lived in Thailand for over a decade.

Bangkok was updated by **Susan Cunningham**, who has worked on previous editions and also updated Ko Samui and Nan, and **Paul Hicks**, who has also contributed to Apa's Hong Kong guide. **Jerry Hopkins**, a best-selling author, wrote on architecture, arts, and the *Ramakien*. **Ken Scott** updated Phuket and Krabi, while Bangkok-based **Sandy Barron** covered the Gulf Coast and west Thailand. Overhauling the extensive Travel Tips was **Katja Thomas**, who also updated areas just outside of Bangkok.

Wat Sri Mongkran, Mukdahan.

Using this book

The book is carefully structured to convey an understanding of Thailand and its culture, and to guide readers through its sights and attractions:

◆ The Features section, with a yellow colour bar, covers the country's history and culture in lively authoritative essays written by specialists.

◆ The Places section, with a blue bar, provides full details of all the sights and areas worth seeing.

Map Legend

▬ ▪ ▬	International Boundary
⊖	Border Crossing
▬ ▪ ▬	National Park
▬ ▬ ▬	Ferry Route
✈	Airport
🚌	Bus Station
P	Parking
❶	Tourist Information
✉	Post Office
∴	Archaeological Site
⋒	Cave
⚊	Statue/Monument
★	Place of Interest

The main places of interest in the **Places** section are coordinated by number with a full-color map (e.g. ❶), and a symbol at the top of every right-hand page tells you where to find the map.

Contributors

Forbes

Robson

Cunningham

Rutherford

INSIGHT GUIDE
THAILAND

CONTENTS

Limestone formations, Phuket area.

Travel Tips

Insight on....

Information panels

Places

KINGDOM OF THAILAND

Imagine a place that defines graciousness, tolerance,
and aesthetic ideals. You've just imagined Thailand

Land of the free, land of smiles. The former is a literal translation of *Thailand*, while the latter is a promotional slogan that carries considerable truth. Both define the Thai people. Beneath their graciousness, the Thai have a strong sense of self and a humanity without subservience. It is this pride in themselves, and in their monarchy, that underlies the Thai sense of identity and an ability to smile at the vicissitudes of life.

The Kingdom of Thailand – ruled by an elected government but inspired by the world's longest-reigning monarch, who celebrated 50 years on the throne in 1996 – has a population of over 60 million. It is nearly the size of Central America or France, or is twice that of England. Its climate is tropical, with three seasons: hot (March–June), monsoonal (July–November) and cool (December–February). The capital city of Bangkok, called Krung Thep in Thai, has at least 10 million people (accurate estimates are by definition dubious) and lies at the same latitude as Khartoum, Guatemala City and Manila.

Just inland from the apex of the Gulf of Thailand, Bangkok is the country's international gateway, and its seat of government, business and the royalty. It is almost a city-state unto itself and bears little similarity to the rest of the nation. When a Thai says that "I'm heading upcountry tomorrow," she or he could mean anywhere outside of Bangkok's city limits. Anywhere is upcountry. Indeed, the second-largest city in Thailand is perhaps one-fortieth the population of Bangkok. Most of Thailand is rural, a patchwork of rice fields, villages, plantations and forests.

Thailand is commonly divided into four regions: the central plains, of which Bangkok is a part; the north, including Chiang Mai and Chiang Rai; the northeast; and the south, extending from Bangkok down to the Malaysian border. Each region has its own culture and appeal.

Since the East first encountered Siam a millennium ago and the West began trickling in during the 16th century, Thailand has been a powerful magnet for adventurers and entrepreneurs. An abundance of resources, a wealth of natural beauty, a stunning cultural tradition revealed in dazzling architecture and art, and a warm, hospitable people have proved irresistible lures.

Thailand's traditional charms form only one side of the picture, of course. It is a country in transition, rapidly changing from a developing to a developed country in a roller-coaster of a ride. In the 1990s, it went from being one of the fiercest of Asian economic tigers to nearly becoming an economic disaster, a precursor of the economic doldrums that hit Asia at the end of the 1990s. But true to the peo-

PRECEDING PAGES: centuries-old illustration of elephants from a temple mural; architectural detail from Bangkok's Grand Palace; *nang yai*, the shadow-puppet; young girl and her father, protected from evil and misfortune by body tattoos and amulets. **LEFT:** Buddha images of Wat Mahathat, in Phetchburi, south of Bangkok.

ple's spirit, consistent throughout the country's history, Thailand reversed course quickly and regained stability.

Throughout its history, Thailand has shown a stubborn maverick streak and a sense of pragmatism, both of which have created a determination to chart its own course. The result is a country that has never been colonised by a foreign power, has never sought to conquer a neighbour, and one that has intentionally retained its past while moving ahead into the future.

It is hard to ignore the changes taking place, yet there is much that sets Thailand apart from nations on similar paths. The natural beauty is still there in superb beaches, seas of green rice, and forested hills, somewhat safe now that logging is illegal (although it still happens). And even in the most modern towns, the past continues to shine through as temples, palaces and cultural presentations. This uniqueness is not always apparent, especially in a chaotic city like Bangkok that pounds on the senses, all of them, unceasingly. *This is not the exotic Thailand I was promised,* the visitor whines. *This is a nightmare.* Well, Bangkok is a nightmare. It is also a repository of some of the world's most exquisite architecture and historical artifacts. But it is a city that is vibrantly alive.

The Thai enjoys life. Something that fails to give personal satisfaction, whether in work or in play, is not worth doing. Any activity must have something of this quality within it, something that gives value to life. Part of this is distilled from holding on to one's traditions. This may change in Thailand, but for the moment, it is firmly intact in Thailand. The traveller can't help but notice it.

About spellings of place names

The transliteration of Thai pronunciation into a roman alphabet has proved to be a quagmire of phonemes and good intentions. The traveller will encounter several, not just one or two, possible spellings for a single place name. Leaps of linguistic creativity are in order as one negotiates street signs (often romanised), maps and guide books, including this one. As much as possible, this book has sided with common sense and common usage, along with a dose of consistency.

When the letter *h* follows a consonant, it makes the consonant's sound less explosive, softer. Just as Thailand is pronounced *tai-land,* not *thigh-land,* so too with the *ph* sound. The pronunciation of *Wat Po* is the same as *Wat Pho,* and, in fact, they are the same temple in Bangkok. Similarly, the wonderful island of *Phuket* is always spelled thusly, but it is pronounced, always, like *poo-ket,* not *foo-ket* or in other less gracious ways. Other common variations of place-name spellings include *ratcha* and *raja,* and *chom* and *jom.*

The rule of thumb regarding spellings is to be like a Thai when in Thailand: adaptable and tolerant, and with a sense of humour. ❐

RIGHT: the canals in and around Bangkok are still vital to commerce.

Decisive Dates

Pre-Thai civilisation

3600–250 BC: Ban Chiang culture flourishes in north-eastern Thailand.

circa 250 BC: Suvannabhumi trading with India

4th–8th centuries AD: influence of Mon and Khmer empires spreads into Thailand.

9th–13th centuries: Khmer Empire founded at Angkor. Thai peoples migrate south from Yunnan Province of China into northern Thailand, Burma, and Laos. Lopburi becomes an important provincial capital in Khmer Empire, later tries to become independent.

Sukhothai era

1238: Khmer power wanes. Kingdom of Sukhothai founded under Intaradit.

1281: Chiang Saen kingdom founded in north.

1296: Lanna Kingdom founded at Chiang Mai. Mangrai controls much of northern Thailand and Laos.

1280–1318: Reign of Ramkamhaeng in Sukhothai. Often called Thailand's "Golden Age," the period saw the first attempts to unify the Thai people, the first use of the Thai script, and flourishing of the arts.

1317–1347: Lo Thai reigns at Sukhothai. The slow decline of the Sukhothai kingdom starts.

1438: Sukhothai is now virtually deserted; power shifts to the Kingdom of Ayutthaya, to the south and along the Chao Phraya River.

Kingdom of Ayutthaya

14th century: Area around Ayutthaya settled by representatives of the Chiang Saen kingdom.

1350: City of Ayutthaya founded by Phya U-Thong, who proclaims himself Ramathibodi I. Within a few years he controls the areas encompassed by the kingdoms of Sukhothai and the Khmer empire.

1369: Ramesuen, son of Ramathibodi, becomes king.

1390: Ramesuen captures Chiang Mai.

1393: Ramesuen captures Angkor in Cambodia.

1448–1488: Reign of King Trailok, who finally unites the Lanna (Chiang Mai) and Ayutthaya kingdoms.

1491–1529: Reign of King Ramathibodi II.

1549: First major warfare with Mon Kingdom of Pegu

1569: Burmese capture and destroy Ayutthaya.

1590: Naresuen becomes king, throws off Burmese suzerainty. Under Naresuen, Ayutthaya expands rapidly at the expense of Burmese and Khmer empires and flourishes as a major city.

1605–1610: Ekatotsarot reigns, begins significant economic ties with European traders and adventurers.

1610–1628: Reign of King Songtham. The British arrive and obtain land for a trading factory.

1628–1655: Reign of Prasat Thong. Trading concessions expand and regular trade with China and Europe is established.

1656–1688: Reign of King Narai. British influence expands. Reputation of Ayutthaya as a magnificent city and a remarkable royal court spreads in Europe.

1678: Constantine Phaulkon arrives at Narai's court and gains great influence; French presence expands.

1688: Narai dies, Phaulkon executed.

1733–1758: Reign of King Boromakot. Ayutthaya enters a period of peace, and of arts and literature.

1767: Burmese King Alaungpaya captures and sacks Ayutthaya, destroying four centuries of Thai civilisation. Seven months later General Phya Tak Sin returns and expels the Burmese occupiers. He moves the capital from Ayutthaya to Thonburi, near Bangkok.

Beginning of the Chakri dynasty

1767: Phya Tak Sin crowned as King Taksin.

1779: Generals Chao Phya Chakri and his brother Chao Phya Sarasih conquer Chiang Mai, expel the Burmese from what is now Thailand and so adding most of the Khmer and Lao kingdoms to the Thai kingdom. The Emerald Buddha brought from Vientiane, Laos, to Thonburi.

1782: The now-erratic Taksin deposed and executed, and Chao Phya Chakri is offered the throne, founding the Chakri dynasty and assuming the name Ramathibodi and later Rama I. Capital is moved across the river to the city that becomes known to the west as

Bangkok. Under Rama I, the Siamese Kingdom consolidates and expands its strength. Rama I revives Thai art, religion, and culture.

1809–1824: Reign of Rama II; best known for construction of Wat Arun and many other temples and monasteries. Rama II reopens relations with the West, suspended since the time of Narai.

1824–1851: Reign of Rama III, who left as his trademark the technique of embedding Chinese porcelain fragments as decorations on temples.

1851: King Mongkut (Rama IV) ascends the throne. He is the first Thai king to understand Western culture and technology. Before becoming king he spends 27 years as a monk, studying Western science.

1868: Chulalongkorn (Rama V) ascends the throne, reigning for the next four decades, the second-longest reign of any Thai king. Chulalongkorn ends the custom of prostration in royal presence, abolishes slavery, and replaces corvee labour with direct taxation. Schools, infrastructure, military and government modernised.

1910–1925: Reign of Vajiravudh (Rama VI), Oxford-educated and thoroughly Westernised.

1925–1932: Reign of Prajadhipok (Rama VII). Economic pressures from the Great Depression encourage discontent.

End of the absolute monarchy

1932: A coup d'etat ends the absolute monarchy and ushers in a constitutional monarchy.

1939: The name of the country is officially changed from Siam to Thailand, "Land of the Free." King Ananda (Rama VIII) ascends the throne.

1942: Japan invades Thailand with the acquiescence of the military government, but a spirited if small resistance movement thrives.

1946: King Ananda is killed by a mysterious gunshot, and Bhumibol Adulyadej (Rama IX) ascends the throne. The tireless royal family quickly becomes a symbol of national spirit and unity.

1973–1991: Bloody clashes between army and demonstrating students brings down the military government; political and economic blunders brings down the resulting civilian government just three years later. Various military-backed and civilian governments come and go for almost 20 years.

1991: Another clash between military forces and civilian demonstrators brings the unusual sight of the leaders of both factions kneeling in contrition in front of the king; as a result, the military leaves government to the civilian politicians.

1992: Thailand begins five years of unprecedented economic growth. The face of Bangkok changes, much of it climbing skyward in skyscrapers and middle-class condominiums. Growth reaches 9 percent annually.

1996: King Bhumibol Adulyadej celebrates his golden jubilee of 50 years on the throne, the longest-reigning monarch in the world.

1997: Thailand's banking system and economy begin a free-fall as the baht loses half of its value. Other regional economies also falter.

1998: Thailand successfully hosts the Asian Games despite the region's economic uncertainties.

1999: Following IMF guidelines, Thailand begins to resuscitate and stabilise its economy.

LEFT: Ayutthayan general mounts battle elephant.
RIGHT: portrait of King Chulalongkorn, or Rama V.

CHAKRI MONARCHY

Since 1782, a single royal dynasty – known as Chakri – has lorded over Thailand.

Rama I (Chakri)	1782–1809
Rama II (Phutthalaetia)	1809–1824
Rama III (Nangklao)	1824–1851
Rama IV (Mongkut)	1851–1868
Rama V (Chulalongkorn)	1868–1910
Rama VI (Vajiravudh)	1910–1925
Rama VII (Prajadhipok)	1925–1935
Rama VIII (Ananda)	1935–1946
Rama IX (Bhumibol)	1946–

THE RISE OF SUKHOTHAI

Sukhothai, the "dawn of happiness", was the first independent Thai kingdom.

Many consider it to be the golden era of Thai history, and of Thai culture

The Thai people have fiercely defended their country's independence for more than 800 years, and can boast the distinction of being the only country in Southeast Asia never to have been a European colony. Nor has the country been divided by serious civil war, as tumultuous as modern Thai politics can be. Indeed, Thai shrewdness in international diplomacy has won them the admiration of nations far more powerful and influential.

The name *Thai* means "free." Although the country was called *Siam* by foreigners from the 12th to the 20th centuries, to its citizens it always carried the name of its capital – Sukhothai and Ayutthaya, for example. In the 19th century. Siam was adopted as the official name of the kingdom, but this was changed to Thailand in 1939.

In the beginning

The origin of the ethnic Thai has been hotly debated for decades. Popular tradition claims that the first people fled to Siam from China to escape the depredations of Kublai Khan's hordes sweeping southward out of Mongolia. The theory might explain Thai empathy with later immigrants. Other theories suggest they originated in Thailand a millennium or two ago; Thais found in today's China are said to have emigrated north from Thailand about 1,000 years ago. Whichever conjecture is correct, it is accepted that the Thais' first home in Thailand was in the northern hills. As the centuries passed, they shared the country with ethnic Laotians, who populated the northeast, bringing a similar language and culture. The southern isthmus linking Thailand (from Bangkok south) with the Malay Peninsula became the home of Muslims. Over the centuries, the population was augmented by Hindu and Sikh Indians, who arrived as merchants, and by Chinese.

PRECEDING PAGE: two terracotta figures from the Sukhothai period. **LEFT:** sculpture from Sukhothai of a Hindu deity. **RIGHT:** illustration of two early indigenous Thai men.

Ban Chiang culture

But long before the Thai people migrated into today's Thailand, the Chao Phraya valley was inhabited by a high civilisation. The first discovery of their prehistoric relics was made during World War II, by a Dutch prisoner of war forced to work on the Siam–Burma "Death

Railway." He uncovered Stone Age implements at Ban Kao, in the western province of Kanchanaburi, which led to the discovery of Paleolithic and Neolithic caves, and to cemeteries containing pottery, tools and other artifacts.

The most important site, however, is the tiny village of Ban Chiang, near Udon Thani in the northeast. Excavations have uncovered painted pottery, jewelry, and bronze and iron tools. If thermoluminescent dating is correct, the Bronze Age in Thailand corresponds to – and according to some, may even predate – that of the Tigris-Euphrates Valley civilisation, which preceded the Bronze Age in Europe. The idea remains controversial, however.

The identity of the Ban Chiang people is a mystery. According to archeological timetables, the existence of pottery normally suggests a culture already 2,000 years along the road to civilisation; Ban Chiang's pottery dates from about 3600 BC. Settlement seems to have lasted until 250 BC, after which the people mysteriously faded from history. While they thrived, they farmed rice, domesticated various animals, and developed highly original pottery-decorating skills, with each design unique to that pot alone and not

OTHER ORIGINS

The Ban Chiang findings illustrate a high level of culture and technology. They also suggest, but not without debate, that China may not be the sole origin of East Asian civilisation.

fied as Southeast Asia. By the beginning of the Christian era, maritime trading between India and the south of Thailand had begun. Hindu statues found at settlements in southern Thailand suggest habitation from about the 4th century. In later centuries, Buddhism and Hinduism – along with Indian ceremonial rites, iconography, law codes, and cosmological and architectural treatises – were adopted *en bloc* by the Southeast Asian ruling elite and modified to suit local requirements and tastes. Sanskrit became the court lan-

repeated in others. Their red-painted jars, decorated with fingerprint whorl patterns, were buried in funeral mounds as offerings. Glass beads and semiprecious stones were also included in the mounds.

Indian influence

Archeological evidence is scant, but ancient texts discuss the presence of people in the region from India around the 3rd century BC.

The Sinhalese Buddhist chronicle, the *Mahavamsa*, relates that India's great Emperor Ashoka (ruled 268 to 232 BC), the first royal patron of Buddhism, sent two missionaries to Suvannabhumi, the "land of gold" now identi-

guage, while Pali was the language of the Buddhist canons. Native chiefs wanting to consolidate power and increase their prestige may have been responsible for this diffusion of culture, calling in Brahman priests (Indians of the priestly caste) to validate and consecrate their rule.

This transmission at court level had a vital and permanent impact, especially in nearby Cambodia. The Mons and Khmers were the first Indianised peoples to form settlements in present-day Thailand. Mon influence is evident in the Buddhist art of the Dvaravati period (6th to 11th centuries); the Khmers, famed as the builders of Cambodia's Angkor Wat, left many temples in Thailand's northeastern provinces. There is also archeological evidence of Mon religious settlements at Lopburi and Nakhon Pathom, from the 7th century onwards.

Arrival of the Thais

As noted earlier, there are several theories to explain the early habitation of Thailand. The most persuasive one says that from perhaps as early as the 10th century, a people living in China's Yunnan region migrated down rivers and streams into the upper valleys of the Southeast Asian river system. There, they branched off. The Shans, also known as Thai Yai (Great

Mai, in 1296. Long after the main group of Thais moved farther down the peninsula to establish more powerful states, Chiang Mai continued to rule more or less autonomously over the northern region, maintaining a distinctive culture of its own. By the 13th century, the Thais had begun to emerge as the dominant rulers of the region, slowly absorbing the weakened empires of the Mons and Khmers. Their rise to power culminated around 1238, when (according to inscriptions) the Khmers were expelled from Sukhothai.

The history of peninsular Thailand is lesser known than that of the north. It was once under

Thais), went to Upper Burma. The Ahom Thais established themselves in Assam. Another group settled in Laos, and yet another occupied the island of Hainan, off the Vietnamese coast.

The greatest number of Thai Noi (Little Thais) first settled in the north of modern Thailand, around Chiang Saen and valleys to the south. They formed themselves into principalities, some of which later became independent kingdoms. The first was in 1238, at Sukhothai, at the southernmost edge of Thai penetration. Then came Chiang Rai, in 1281, and Chiang

LEFT: perhaps from India, terracotta figures found in central Thailand. **ABOVE:** Sukhothai stone engraving.

the control of the mighty empire of Srivijaya, which existed from the 7th to 13th centuries. Ancient chronicles state that in the Srivijayan capital, "a man at noon cast no shadow". This suggests an equatorial location, but there is serious disagreement where that might be. There are competing schools of thought, each claiming Palembang in Sumatra, or Chaiya in southern Thailand. A site in Borneo has also been postulated. The proof of claim forwarded for Chaiya is the discovery of an 8th-century inscription of a Srivijayan king, at Chaiya, near the Kra Isthmus. The empire disintegrated during the 13th century and its dependencies were absorbed by Sukhothai.

Dawn of Sukhothai

The name *Sukhothai* translates into "the dawn of happiness", and if early inscriptions are to be believed, its people enjoyed considerable freedom to pursue their livelihoods. This first independent Thai kingdom is considered the golden era of Thai history, and is often looked back upon with nostalgia as the ideal Thai state. It was a land of plenty, governed by just and paternal kings who ruled over peaceful, contented citizens. Sukhothai represented early Thai tribal society in its purest form.

Siamese tradition attributes the founding of the kingdom to Phra Ruang, a mythological

containers, which arrived in Angkor intact. This success aroused the suspicion of the Khmer king. His chief astrologer said the ingenious Thai inventor was a person with supernatural powers who constituted a threat to the empire. The king at once dispatched a gifted general – who had the magic ability to travel swiftly underground – to eliminate the Thai menace.

Phra Ruang perceived the danger and went to Sukhothai, where he concealed himself at Wat Mahathat as a Buddhist monk. The Khmer general, who coincidentally surfaced in the middle of the *wat*, was turned into stone by Phra Ruang. From then on, Phra Ruang's fame spread far and

hero. Prior to his time, according to historical legend, the Thai people were forced to pay tribute to the Khmer rulers of Angkor. This tribute was exacted in the form of sacred water from a lake outside Lopburi; the Khmer god-king needed holy water from all corners of the empire for his ceremonial rites, a practice later adopted by Thai kings.

Every three years, the water tribute was sent by bullock carts in large earthenware jars. The jars inevitably cracked en route, compelling the tribute payers to make second and third journeys to fill the required quota. When Phra Ruang came of age, he devised a new system of transporting water in sealed woven bamboo

wide. He left the monkhood, married the daughter of Sukhothai's ruler, and when that monarch died, he was invited to the throne by popular mandate. He assumed the title Sri Indraditya, sovereign of the newly-independent Kingdom of Sukhothai. Fact and fiction are inseparable in this popular account.

Rule of Ramkamhaeng

The most famous king of Sukhothai was the founder's second son, Ramkamhaeng. He was the first Thai ruler to leave detailed epigraphical accounts of the Thai state, beginning with his own early life. He earned his title at age 19 on a campaign with his father against a neighbouring state, in which he defeated the enemy leader in a Thai form of medieval jousting: hand-to-hand combat on elephant-back. As a result, he was named Phra Ramkamhaeng (Rama the Brave) by his father.

Around the time of Ramkamhaeng's accession, the Sukhothai kingdom was quite small, consisting only of the city and surrounding areas. By the end of his reign, he had increased its size tenfold – from Luang Prabang in the east, in modern-day Laos, through Thailand's central plains to the

BUDDHIST BEDROCK

Since the ancient days of Sukhothai, Buddhism has been deeply rooted in the Thai way of life. Together with the monarchy, it provides a continuity for both Thai society and the individual.

bition of slavery and guaranteed inheritance. However, some experts now doubt its authenticity and believe the inscription to be a much later work.

The king was a devout and conscientious Buddhist of the Theravada school that was practiced in Sukhothai. Exchanges were initiated with Sri Lankan monks that resulted in a purification of texts and an adoption of Sinhalese influences in *chedi* design.

There remained, however, a trace of animism in Thai Buddhism. Ramkamhaeng wrote

southern peninsula. The Mon state in lower Burma also accepted his control.

Ramkamhaeng was noted as an administrator, legislator and statesman – and sometimes as an amorous king. He is credited with the invention of Thai script, which he achieved by systematising the Khmer alphabet with Thai words. A stone inscription bearing the date 1292 and employing the new script has been attributed to Ramkamhaeng. In the inscription, he depicted the idyllic conditions of his kingdom: fertile land and plentiful food, free trade, prohi-

LEFT: detail of Khmer ruins, Prasat Phanom Rung.
ABOVE: Wat Mahathat, in old Sukhothai.

about a mountain-dwelling ghost named Phra Khapung Phi, a spirit "above all others in the land." If correctly propitiated, he would bring prosperity to the country. The idea of a superior spirit looking after the Thai nation survives today, in the image of Phra Siam Devadhiraj, Siam's guardian angel.

One of the keys to Ramkamhaeng's success lay in his diplomatic relations with China. The Mongol court in northern China pursued a "divide-and-rule" policy and supported the Thais' rise, but at the expense of the Khmers. Ramkamhaeng was said to have gone to China himself in 1299, and the *History of the Yuan* records seven missions from Sien (Sukhothai) between 1282 and 1323. Chinese craftsmen came to teach the Thais their secrets of glazing pottery, resulting in the production of the famous ceramic ware of Sawankhalok, whose kilns still remain and whose products were shipped to China aboard Siamese junks.

In the same year, 1287, that Pagan fell to the armies of Kublai Khan, Ramkamhaeng formed a pact with two northern Thai princes, Mangrai of Chiang Rai and Ngam Muang of Phayo. The three agreed not to transgress, but instead to protect each others' borders against common enemies. The alliance was maintained throughout their lifetimes.

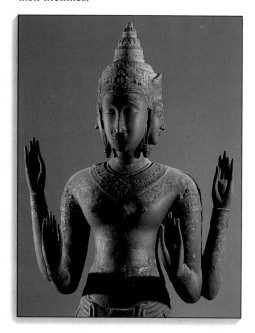

Founding of Chiang Mai

Mangrai completed Thai political ascendancy in the north by annexing the last Mon kingdom of Haripunjaya, in about 1292. He first sent an agent provocateur to sow discord, and when the time was right, his army "plucked the town like a ripe fruit."

Wishing to found a new capital, Mangrai invited his two allies to help him select a site. The location they agreed upon as truly auspicious was one where two white sambars, two white barking deer, and a family of five white mice were seen together. On that spot by the river Ping, Mangrai laid the foundation of Chiang Mai (New Town) in 1296, supplanting his

former capital at Chiang Rai and giving him a more centralised location from which to administer the southern portion of his newly-expanded kingdom. Thus, Chiang Mai became the capital of the Kingdom of Lanna, which translates as "Land of the Million Rice Fields."

Tradition says Ramkamhaeng drowned in the rapids of the Yom River at Sawankhalok. His son, Lo Thai (ruled 1318–1347), preferring religion to war, lost the feudatory states as fast as he had gained them. He was called Dharmaraja, the Pious King, an epithet his successors also bore. The relationship between Sukhothai and Sri Lanka, the centre of orthodox Buddhism, intensified during his rule; Lo Thai recorded that he built many monuments to house sacred relics of the Buddha obtained from Sri Lanka.

Lo Thai's son, Li Thai, was as pious as his father. As heir to the throne, he composed a famous treatise on Buddhist cosmology, the *Traibhumikatha*, or *Tales of the Three Worlds*. When he became king in 1347, he ruled according to the ten royal precepts of Buddha. He pardoned criminals, for example, as he wanted to become a Buddha, "to lead all creatures beyond the oceans of sorrow and transmigration."

The prioritising of religion over military affairs might have permitted the meteoric rise of one of Sukhothai's former vassal states, Ayutthaya. This kingdom expanded rapidly, extending its control over the Chao Phraya valley, until Li Thai was forced to acknowledge its hegemony. Deprived of his independence, the pious king took deeper refuge in religion, eventually assuming the yellow robe.

His family ruled for three more generations, but in 1378, power shifted to Phitsanulok, and Sukhothai's population followed. By 1438, Sukhothai was nearly deserted.

The Sukhothai period saw the Thai people, for the first time, develop a distinctive civilisation with their own administrative institutions, art and architecture.

Sukhothai Buddha images, characterised by refined facial features, linear fluidity, and harmony of form, are perhaps the most beautiful and the most original of Thai artistic expressions. Many authorities and Thais say that the Sukhothai aesthetic has been the high point of Thai civilisation. ❐

LEFT: Sukhothai Hindu deity. **RIGHT:** ruins of Wat Chetupon, Sukhothai.

AYUTTHAYA

Ayutthayan kings adopted Khmer cultural influences from the very beginning. Unlike those of Sukhothai, the rulers of Ayutthaya were absolute and inaccessible monarchs

History is ignorant regarding the ancestry of Ayutthaya's founder. But Thai folklore fills the lacuna. The king of Traitrung unhappily discovered that his unmarried daughter had given birth to a child after eating an eggplant, which a vegetable gardener had fertilised with his own urine. The culprit – Nai Saen Pom,

kings. During the reign of Phya U-Thong, a cholera outbreak forced the ruler to evacuate his people to the site of Ayodhya (Ayutthaya), an ancient Indianised settlement named after Rama's legendary kingdom in India.

The location of Phya U-Thong's new capital was blessed with several advantages. Situated

or Man With a Hundred Thousand Warts – was summoned and promptly banished from the city, along with the princess and her new son.

The god Indra, with his divine eye, saw the misery of the trio and decided to grant the gardener three magic wishes. Saen Pom first asked for his warts to disappear. Next, he prayed for a kingdom to rule over. And lastly, he wanted a cradle of gold for his son. The child was known as Chao U-Thong, Prince of the Golden Crib.

Rise of Ayutthaya

Historically, U-Thong was an independent principality in today's Suphanburi. Its rulers were members of the prestigious line of Chiang Saen

on an island at the confluence of the Chao Phraya, Lopburi and Pasak rivers, not far from the sea and surrounded by fertile rice plains, it was an ideal centre of administration and communications. Phya U-Thong officially established the city in 1350, after three years of preparation, when he assumed the title Ramathibodi I, King of Dvaravati Sri Ayodhya. Within a few years, the king united the whole of central Siam – including Sukhothai – under his rule, and extended control to the Malay Peninsula and lower Burma. He and his successors pursued expansionist campaigns against Chiang Mai and the Khmers in Cambodia. No longer the paternal and accessible rulers that the kings of Sukhothai had been, Ayutthaya's sovereigns were absolute monarchs whose positions were enhanced by trappings of royalty reflective of a Khmer *devaraja* (god-king).

The devaraja concept was, however, tempered by the tenets of Theravada Buddhism, wherein the king was not actually divine, but was the protector and supreme head of the religion. Nevertheless, Khmer court rituals and language were emulated at the Ayutthaya court. Brahmans officiated with Buddhist monks at state ceremonies.

KHMER INFLUENCES

Although the Thais were responsible for the decline and eventual collapse of the Angkor empire, the Ayutthayan kings adopted Khmer cultural and artistic influences from the very beginning.

Angkor three years later, and according to the *Pongsawadan*, the Annals of Ayutthaya, some 90,000 prisoners of war were taken. Given the economics of the time, people for labour were more precious than gold.

The death blow to the Khmer capital was delivered in 1431 when forces entered Angkor. The Khmer king abandoned his ancient capital in favour of Phnom Penh. The Siamese army returned from the campaign with booty and many prisoners, including artists and Brahmans.

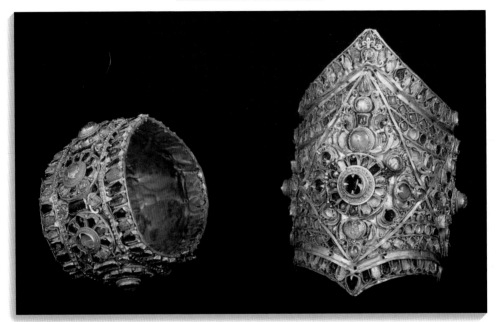

Ramathibodi I divided his administration into ministries of royal household, finance, interior and agriculture. This, and his subsequent legislation, provided a strong foundation for the kingdom, which survived for 417 years, with Ayutthaya as its capital.

Ramathibodi died in 1369. His son, Ramesuen, captured Chiang Mai in 1390, reportedly with the use of cannon, the first recorded use of this weapon in Siam. Ramesuen's army sacked

PRECEDING PAGE: 17th-century adventurers immortalised on a lacquer cabinet. **LEFT:** crypt mural detail, Wat Ratchaburana, Ayutthaya. **ABOVE:** Ayutthayan royal jewellery found at Wat Ratchaburana.

Reign of King Trailok

Two centuries of wars between Chiang Mai and Ayutthaya reached a climax during the reign of King Boroma Trailokanath, more popularly known as Trailok, who ruled from 1448 until 1488. In his campaigns against Maharaja Sutham Tilok, guile and the occult complemented military might.

Envoys sent from Ayutthaya to Tilok were discovered to have buried seven jars containing ingredients which, it was feared, would magically bring doom upon Chiang Mai. The jars were cast into the river, followed by the envoys themselves, their feet tied to rocks. The fighting between these rival kingdoms led to the transfer of Ayutthayan power, from the capital to Phit-sanulok during the last 25 years of Trailok's reign. The war, however, ended in a stalemate.

Trailok is important for having introduced reforms that shaped the administrative and social structures of Siam up until the 19th century. He brought Ayutthaya's loosely controlled provinces under centralised rule, and regulated *sakdi na*, an ancient system of land ownership that stratified society, dictated responsibilities of both overlord and tenants, and determined salary levels of the official hierarchy.

Trailok also defined a system of corvee labour, under which all able-bodied men were required to contribute labour during part of each working year to the state. This system indirectly heightened the status of women, who were responsible for the welfare of their families in the absence of the men.

Portuguese and Burmese

The 16th century was marked by the first arrival of Europeans, and by continual conflict with the Burmese. The Portuguese had conquered Malacca in 1511, and soon thereafter their ships sailed to Siam. King Ramathibodi II (ruled 1491–1529) granted the Portuguese permission to reside and trade within the kingdom, in return

PALACE PROTOCOL

Trailok's Palace Law of 1450 spelled out the relative ranks of members of the royal family, prescribed functions of officials, and regulated official ceremonies.

It also fixed punishments: death for "introducing amatory poems" into the palace and for whispering during a royal audience, and amputation of the foot of anyone kicking a palace door.

Royalty was not spared punishment, although no menial hands could touch royal flesh. It was therefore the executioner's task to beat the condemned royalty at the nape of the neck with a sandalwood club.

for arms and ammunition. Portuguese mercenaries fought alongside the king in campaigns against Chiang Mai and taught the Thais the arts of cannon foundry and musketry.

But this did nothing to stem the rising tide of Burmese aggression against Ayutthaya, already weakened by wars with Chiang Mai. In 1549, the Burmese laid siege to Ayutthaya. The Ayutthayan king, Mahachakrapat, led a sortie against them. Not only his sons, but his wife and daughter accompanied him into battle mounted on elephants. The queen, disguised as a warrior, galloped her mount between the king and his Burmese foe when she saw her husband in trouble, saving his life, but losing her own.

The Burmese invasion of 1549 was doomed to failure. They withdrew, and Ayutthaya's defenses were fortified with Portuguese help. Three hundred wild elephants were captured and trained for further wars against Burma.

Seven of the new war elephants were white ones. When Burma's new king heard about this, he launched another invasion of Ayutthaya.

In 1569, Ayutthaya fell to Burmese forces. The invading Burmese thoroughly ransacked and plundered the city, and forcibly removed much of Ayut-

WHITE ELEPHANTS

Buddhist kings of Southeast Asia treasured white elephants, considered to be auspicious, thus enhancing royal prestige and ensuring the country's prosperity.

Naresuen had gained an insight into Burmese armed strength and strategies during his formative gears in Burma. He trained his troops in the art of guerrilla warfare; their hit-and-run tactics earned them the nicknames of Wild Tigers and Peeping Cats. Naresuen's opportunity to restore Siamese independence came following the death of the Burmese king in 1581. Revolts in the Burmese empire were tying down the new king at home when Naresuen declared Ayutthaya's freedom, in 1584. During the following nine years,

thaya's population to Burma. The king was among the captives of the Burmese; he died before arriving in Pegu.

The defeated king's leading deputy was appointed by the Burmese to rule Siam as a vassal state. His eldest son, Naresuen, was brought to Burma by the Burmese king as a guarantee for the new vassal's good conduct. Naresuen was repatriated to Siam at the age of 15. Together with his younger brother, Naresuen began to gather armed followers.

LEFT: mural image of a 17th-century European adventurer. **ABOVE:** European impression of Ayutthaya in the 17th century.

the Burmese made several attempts to resubjugate Siam, but Naresuen had taken thorough defensive measures and repulsed all invasions. On one of these occasions, he killed the Burmese king in single combat, both of them mounted on elephants.

Naresuen assumed full kingship upon his father's death in 1590. He reconsolidated the Siamese kingdom, then turned the tables on Burma with repeated attacks that contributed to the disintegration of the Burmese empire. The Khmers, who had been whittling away at Siam's eastern boundary during Ayutthaya's period of weakness, were also subdued. Under Naresuen, Ayutthaya prospered.

Door to the east

The reign of Naresuen's brother, Ekatotsarot, between 1605 and 1610, coincided with the arrival of the Dutch in Siam. Ekatotsarot was not interested in pursuing Naresuen's militaristic policies. Instead, he sought to develop Ayutthaya's economy. To these ends, he decreed several measures to increase state revenue, among them the introduction of taxes on commerce. This gave him a reputation as a "covetous man" among Europeans.

The Dutch opened their first trading station at Ayutthaya in 1608. Keen to promote commercial relations, Ekatotsarot sent emissaries to a demand in Thai society for luxury items like porcelain and silk. The Japanese, who already had established a sizable community of traders at Ayutthaya, paid in silver for local Siamese products such as hides, teak, tin and sugar.

The Dutch established maritime dominance in the Far East when they drove the Portuguese out of Malacca, in 1641. Seven years later, they made a show of naval force in the Gulf of Siam, thereby persuading the Thai court to agree to certain trade concessions and giving the Dutch virtual economic control in Siam. A new king, Narai (ruled 1656–1688), despised the Dutch and welcomed the English as a European ally to

The Hague, the first recorded appearance of Thais in Europe. Later, during the reign of Songtham (ruled 1610–1628), the English arrived bearing a letter from King James I. Like the Dutch, they were welcomed and allotted a plot of land on which to build.

Europeans were primarily attracted to Siam as a door to the China trade. The nature of seasonal monsoons made direct sailing to China impossible, so Ayutthaya and its ports became entrepots for goods travelling between Europe, India and the East Indies, and China and Japan.

The Siamese home market was also quite substantial. The peace initiated by Naresuen had given rise to a surplus of wealth, which created

JAPANESE MERCENARIES

Under the Japanese adventurer Yamada Nagamasa, who earned himself an official rank in the Thai court, many Japanese gained employment as the king's guards.

In 1628 they helped the future king Prasat Thong establish himself as regent to a boy-king, and subsequently to depose the rightful ruler. Unfortunately, the shogun in Edo (modern-day Tokyo) refused to recognise him as the Thai monarch, prompting Prasat Thong to take his revenge on the Japanese settlement in Ayutthaya. Several of the Japanese residents were killed, while the remainder made their escape into Cambodia.

counter Holland's influence. But another Dutch blockade, in 1664, this time at the mouth of the Chao Phraya River, won them a monopoly on the hide trade and, for the first time in Thai history, extraterritorial privileges.

Greek favourite

It was the French who gained greatest favour in King Narai's court. Their story is interwoven with that of a fascinating character, a Greek adventurer named Constantine Phaulkon.

French Jesuit missionaries first arrived at the court of Ayutthaya in 1665. The king's friendliness and religious tolerance were taken by the bishops as a sign of his imminent conversion. Their exaggerated accounts excited the imagination of Louis XIV, who hoped that the salvation of Siamese heathens could be combined with French territorial acquisition. Narai was delighted to receive a personal letter from the Sun King in 1673.

Enter Phaulkon. Son of a Greek innkeeper, he began his career with the East India Company as a cabin boy. He worked his way east with the British, arriving in Siam in 1678. A talented linguist, he learned the Thai language in just two years, and with the help of his English benefactors, he was hired as interpreter within the court. Within five years, Phaulkon had risen through Thai society to the rank of *Phya Vijayendra*. In this powerful position, he had continual access to the king, whose confidence he slowly and surely cultivated.

The previous year, Phaulkon had fallen out of favour with the British East India Company. As Phaulkon moved firmly into the French camp, so did Narai. He sent two ambassadors to Louis's court, and the French reciprocated with a visit to Ayutthaya in 1685. Phaulkon, of course, served as interpreter during the French visit. He secretly outlined to visiting Jesuit priests his plans to convert the entire country of Siam to Catholicism. To effect this, he said, he would need civilians and troops from France. Following another exchange of embassies between the courts of Louis and Narai, a French squadron accompanied French and Thai delegations aboard warships to Siam. The small, but disciplined and well-equipped, French force of 500 soldiers was given landing rights by Narai,

under Phaulkon's advice. For his pains, Phaulkon was created a Count of France and a Knight of the Order of St Michael.

Then the tables began to turn against Phaulkon. A number of high-ranking Siamese officials had become increasingly alarmed by the influence of the "Greek Favourite" on the king. Phaulkon's extravagant lifestyle was considered proof of his blatant robbery of the country. His unpopularity was fuelled not only by the ominous French military presence, but also by a rumour that Phaulkon had converted King Narai's adopted son to Christianity, intending to secure succession to the throne.

When Narai fell gravely ill in 1688, a nationalistic, anti-French faction took immediate action. Led by Phra Phetracha, a commander of the Royal Regiment of Elephants, the rebels confined the ailing king to his palace. Phaulkon was arrested for treason, and in June was executed. Narai died the following month, and Phra Phetracha mounted the throne, declaring as his top priority the immediate withdrawal of French troops. The French eventually removed their soldiers from Thailand.

The presence of Europeans throughout Narai's reign gave the West most of its early knowledge of Siam. Voluminous literature was generated by Western visitors to Narai's court.

LEFT: Naresuen engages the Burmese in a sea battle.
RIGHT: Thai manuscript showing royal parade, 1600s.

Their attempts at cartography left a record of Ayutthaya's appearance, though few maps exist today. Royal palaces and hundreds of temples crowded the area within the walls around the island on which the capital stood. Some Western visitors called it "the most beautiful city in the east."

The kings who succeeded Narai ended his open-door policy. A modest amount of trade was maintained and missionaries were permitted to remain, but Ayutthaya embarked on a course of isolation that lasted about 150 years. This left the rulers free to concentrate mainly on religious and cultural affairs.

Burmese invasion succeeded in capturing Ayutthaya after a siege of 14 months.

The Burmese killed, looted and set fire to the whole city, thereby expunging four centuries of Thai civilisation. Showing complete disregard for their common religion, the Burmese plundered Ayutthaya's rich Buddhist temples, melting down all the available gold from Buddha images. Members of the royal family, along with 90,000 captives and the accumulated booty, were taken to Burma.

Despite their overwhelming victory, the Burmese didn't retain control of Siam for long. Attacks on Burma's northern borders compelled

Ayutthaya's golden age

The reign of King Boromakot (1733–1758) began with a particularly violent struggle for power, but Boromakot's 25-year term was an unusually peaceful one and became known as Ayutthaya's Golden Age. Poets and artists abounded at his court, enabling literature and the arts to flourish as never before.

The tranquil days proved to be the calm before the storm. Boromakot's son Ekatat ascended to the throne in 1758, surrounding himself with female company to ensure his pleasure. Meanwhile, the Burmese empire had regrouped, but invading Burmese armies were repelled in 1760. But seven years later, a second

the Burmese to withdraw most of their forces, and Thai tenacity shortened the period of Burmese domination.

Giving meaning to an ancient proverb that "Ayutthaya never lacks good men," a young general named Phya Tak Sin gathered a small band of followers during the final Burmese siege of the Thai capital. He broke through the Burmese encirclement and escaped to Chanthaburi, on the southeast coast of the Gulf of Thailand. There, Phya Tak Sin assembled a large army and navy. Seven months after the fall of Ayutthaya, the general and his forces sailed up the Chao Phraya to Ayutthaya and expelled the Burmese occupiers.

Move to Bangkok

Taksin, as Phya Tak Sin is popularly known, immediately moved the capital. A site nearer to the sea would facilitate foreign trade, ensure the procurement of arms, and make defence and withdrawal easier.

In the 17th century, a small fishing village downstream had become an important trade and defence outpost for Ayutthaya. Known as Bangkok, "village of wild olive groves," it contained fortifications built by the French. The settlement straddled both

> **DREAMY ORDERS**
>
> Taksin told his troops that the old kings had appeared in a dream and told him to move the capital. Strategic considerations were probably more important than those of the supernatural sort.

Taksin ruled until 1782. In the last seven years of his reign, he relied heavily on two trusted generals, the brothers Chao Phya Chakri and Chao Phya Sarasih, who were given absolute command in military campaigns. They liberated Chiang Mai and the rest of northern Thailand from Burmese rule, and brought Cambodia and most of present-day Laos under Thai suzerainty. It was from the victorious Laotian campaign that the Thai kingdom obtained the famous Emerald Buddha.

banks of the Chao Phraya, at a place where a short-cut canal had widened into the main stream. On the west side of the river, called Thonburi, Taksin officially established his new capital and was proclaimed king.

Taksin's reign was not an easy one. The lack of central authority after the fall of Ayutthaya had led to the rapid disintegration of the kingdom, and it fell upon Taksin to reunite the provinces. At the same time, he contended with a number of Burmese invasions that he resolutely repulsed.

At Thonburi, Taksin's personality underwent a slow metamorphosis from strong and just to cruel and unpredictable. He came to consider himself a *bodhisattva* or future Buddha, and flogged monks who refused to pay obeisance to him. He tortured his officials, his children, and even his wife to make them confess to imaginary crimes. When a revolt broke out in 1782, Taksin abdicated and entered a monastery. A minor official who engineered the revolt offered the throne to Chao Phya Chakri, who assumed the kingship on 6 April and established the still-reigning Chakri dynasty. Taksin, regarded by a council of generals as a threat to stability, was executed in a royal manner. ❐

LEFT: King Narai, and Constantine Phaulkon.
ABOVE: wat mural of foreigners.

ERA OF THE CHAKRI MONARCHY

For a century and a half, Thailand was under the rule of an absolute monarchy.
A coup d'etat ended it in 1932 while the king was at the royal beach in Hua Hin

Upon assuming the throne, General Chakri took the name of Ramathibodi. Later known as Rama I, he ruled from 1782 until 1809. His first action as king was to transfer his administrative headquarters from the marshy confines of Thonburi to the more spacious Bangkok, east across the river.

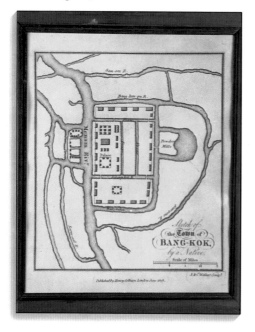

Understanding the value of traditions and symbols, he set about restoring the confidence of his war-shattered people. Buddha images were transported to Bangkok from Sukhothai and Ayutthaya, architects were instructed to design buildings in the Ayutthayan mode, and even bricks from ruined Ayutthaya were floated by barge to Bangkok for the city's new wall.

He assembled surviving master craftsmen from the old city and had them design the first permanent building in the new capital: Wat Phra Kaeo, constructed to house the Emerald Buddha. An elaborate ceremony marked the movement of the Buddha image from Thonburi to the new temple.

One of Rama I's chief concerns was to secure the borders of his kingdom. Early in his reign, King Bodawpaya of Burma had launched a series of military expeditions involving the largest number of troops in the history of Thai-Burmese wars. Siamese troops boldly counterattacked the invaders at strategic border points, routing the Burmese before they could do serious harm. After Bodawpaya, Burma became embroiled in British colonial conflicts and Thailand was left more or less in peace.

Modern Thailand is indebted to Rama I for his assiduous cultural revival program. He appointed experts to review and assemble fragments of historical and religious treatises, few of which had survived the destruction of Ayutthaya in 1767.

Rama I perpetuated another Ayutthaya tradition by appointing his brother as *Maha Uparaja*, a "second" or deputy king, with powers almost equal to his own. The deputy king's home, the Wang Na or Palace at the Back, now houses the National Museum and once extended across the northern half of Sanam Luang.

Because the royal regalia had been destroyed with everything else during the siege of Ayutthaya, Rama I had a new crown and robes commissioned for his coronation. Similarly, in his old age, he commissioned a golden urn to be prepared for his body, in accordance with ancient court protocol prescribing that the bodies of high-ranking royalty be placed in urns between the times of death and cremation.

Rama II and Rama III

Rama I's successors, Rama II and Rama III, completed the consolidation of the Siamese kingdom and the revival of Ayutthaya's arts and culture. Best remembered as an artist, Rama II (ruled 1809–1824) was responsible for building and repairing numerous Bangkok monasteries. His most famous construction was Wat Arun, the Temple of Dawn on the opposite bank from the Grand Palace, and which was later enlarged to its present height by Rama IV. He is said to have carved the great doors of Wat Suthat, throwing away the special chisels so his work could never be replicated.

During his father's reign, Rama II had gained renown as a great poet. His classic version of the *Ramakien*, the Thai interpretation of the Indian classical saga *Ramayana*, was completed during his reign, with large sections composed by the king himself. At his court, Rama II employed *khon* and *lakhon* dance-drama troupes to enact his compositions, just as in the courts of Ayutthaya. Rama II reopened relations with the West and allowed the Portuguese to

PORCELAIN LEGACY

Virtually any temple with porcelain-decorated gables, such as Wat Arun, can immediately be ascribed to the reign of Rama III.

Mongkut (Rama IV)

With the help of Hollywood, Rama IV (ruled 1851–1868) became the most famous king of Siam. Commonly known as Mongkut, he was portrayed in *The King and I* as a frivolous, bald-headed despot. But nothing could have been further from the truth. He was the first Thai king to understand Western culture and technology, and his reign has been described as the bridge spanning the new and the old.

The younger brother of Rama III, Mongkut spent 27 years as a Buddhist monk prior to his

open the first Western embassy in the Bangkok capital.

Rama III, who ruled from 1824 to 1851, continued to open Siam's doors to foreigners. The ready availability of Chinese porcelain led him to decorate many temples, including Wat Arun, with ceramic fragments. This vogue did not survive his lifetime. An extremely pious Buddhist, Rama III was considered to be "austere and reactionary" by Europeans. But he encouraged missionaries to introduce Western medicine.

PRECEDING PAGE: procession of royal barges at Prajadhipok's 1925 coronation. **LEFT:** early map of Bangkok. **ABOVE:** Bangkok khlong, late 19th century.

accession to the throne. This gave him a unique opportunity to roam as a commoner among the populace. He learned to read Buddhist scriptures in the Pali language; missionaries taught him Latin and English, thus enabling him to read European texts. As a monk, Mongkut delved into many subjects: history, geography and the sciences, especially astronomy.

Even as an abbot, he established himself as a reformer, ridding the Buddhist scriptures of their superstitious elements and founding a sect, the Dhammakaiya, which stressed strict adherence to Buddhist tenets. Today, these monks can be recognised by their brown robes. Mongkut realised that traditional Thai values would not save his country from Western encroachment. On the contrary, he believed that modernisation would bring Siam in line with the West and reduce hostilities with foreigners.

England was the first European country to benefit from this policy, when an 1855 treaty – not gained entirely without coercion by the British – granted extraterritorial privileges: a duty of only three percent on imports, and permission to import Indian opium duty-free. Other Western nations, including France and the United States, followed suit with similar treaties. And when Mongkut lifted the state monopoly on rice, that crop rapidly became

Siam's leading export. Mongkut wanted his children to gain the same benefits from the English language as himself. For this purpose, he engaged Anna Leonowens as an English teacher. The self-elevated governess greatly exaggerated her role in the Thai court in her autobiographical writings, misrepresenting the king as a cruel autocrat permanently involved in harem intrigues.

In fact, her five years in Siam are hardly mentioned in Thai chronicles. The book, as well as the movie and play based on it, are regarded as insulting to the deeply revered institution of the monarchy and are seldom mentioned by most Thais nowadays.

Mongkut's beloved hobby, astronomy, was the indirect cause of his death. From observatories at his favourite palaces, the Summer Palace at Bang Pa-In and the Palace on the Hill, at Phetchaburi, he successfully calculated and predicted a total eclipse of the sun in 1868.

European and Asian sceptics joined him on the southeastern coast of the Gulf of Thailand to await the event. As the moon blocked the sun's light, both the Europeans and the scoffers among the royal astrologers raised an exclamation of admiration, raising the king's esteem among both parties.

But his triumph was short-lived. The king contracted malaria during the trip, and died two weeks later from it.

Chulalongkorn (Rama V)

Mongkut's son, Chulalongkorn, was only 15 years old when he ascended the throne. But he reigned over Siam as Rama V for over four decades – longer than any Thai king until the present King Bhumibol, who has been on the throne for over half a century.

The farsighted Chulalongkorn immediately revolutionised his court by ending the ancient custom of prostration, and by allowing officials to sit on chairs during royal audiences. He abolished serfdom in stages, giving owners and serfs time to readjust to the new order, and replaced corvee labour with direct taxation.

His reign was truly a revolution from the throne. When Chulalongkorn assumed power, Siam had no schools and few roads, railways, hospitals, or well-equipped military forces.

To achieve the enormous task of modernisation, he brought in foreign advisors and sent his sons and other young men abroad for education. He also founded a palace school for children of the aristocracy, following this with other schools and vocational centres for the common people. Until then, the only previous schools in Siam had been the monasteries.

Chulalongkorn's brothers were leading figures in his government, especially Prince Devawongse, the foreign minister, and Prince Damrong, the first interior minister and a historian who has come to be known as the father of Thai history. Chulalongkorn's elder children returned home from their European schools in the 1890s, contributing to the modernisation of the army and navy. The first hospital, Siriraj, was opened in 1886 after years of unrelenting opposition. Most of the Thai common people preferred herbal remedies to *farang* (foreign) medicine. Besides, there was a shortage of doctors. Eventually, the obstacles were overcome.

In foreign relations, Rama V had to compromise and give up parts of his kingdom to protect Siam from foreign colonisation. When France conquered Annam in 1883 and Britain annexed upper Burma in 1886, Siam found itself sandwiched uncomfortably between two rival expansionist powers. Border conflicts and gunboat diplomacy forced Siam to surrender

WESTERN-FREE ZONE

Thailand is the only nation in Southeast Asia that has never been subjected to Western colonial rule.

during his reign, in 1897 and 1907. These led him to seek more spacious surroundings than those of the Grand Palace, so he built a palace on the site of a fruit orchard to the north, in Dusit. It was directly connected to the Grand Palace by the wide Thanon Ratchadamnern. At the Dusit palace, he held parties and even fancy-dress balls, often cooking the food himself. No doubt the food was royal.

The many reforms of Chulalongkorn bore fruit within his lifetime. The economy of the country flourished, and Thai peasantry – by comparison with

to France its claims to Laos and the western part of Cambodia. Similarly, certain territories on the Malay Peninsula further south were ceded to Great Britain in exchange for renunciation of British extraterritorial rights in Siam.

By the end of Chulalongkorn's reign, Siam had given up 120,000 square kilometres (50,000 sq mi) of fringe territory. But that seemed a small price to pay for maintaining the peace and independence of Siam.

Chulalongkorn made two European tours

its counterparts in French Indochina and British Burma – were very well-off. It is no wonder that Chulalongkorn was posthumously named *Piya Maharaj*, the Beloved Great King.

As Rama V, Chulalongkorn was conscious of worldwide democratic trends, not to mention the implications of technology, but he judged his country as yet unprepared for such rapid change. It is said that he brought progress to Siam through the judicious exercise of his absolute power.

Today, there is considerable adulation for King Chulalongkorn and his efforts at reform and innovation, not to mention his down-to-earth attitude.

LEFT: Rama IV (Mongkut) and his queen. **ABOVE LEFT:** Rama V (Chulalongkorn) and his entourage in Europe. **ABOVE RIGHT:** a son of Chulalongkorn.

Vajiravudh (Rama VI)

King Chulalongkorn's successor, Vajiravudh, began his reign (1910–1925) with a lavish coronation. Oxford-educated and thoroughly anglicised, his Western-inspired reforms to modernise Siam affected modern Thai society.

One of the first changes was a 1913 edict commanding his subjects to adopt surnames. In the absence of a clan or caste system, genealogy was virtually unheard of in Siam. The law generated much initial bewilderment, especially in rural areas, and Vajiravudh

FIND ANOTHER NAME

Before the reign of Rama VI, Vajiravudh, most Thais had used only first names, a practice that the king considered uncivilised.

Under a pseudonym, he also wrote essays extolling the virtues of the nation.

At the outbreak of World War I, Siam remained neutral, but late in the war, Vajiravudh joined the Allies in 1917 by sending a small expeditionary force to fight in France, thereby securing Siam's admittance to the League of Nations. The flag of Thailand, a white elephant against a red background, was flown with others at Versailles, but the pachyderm was unfortunately mistaken for a small domestic animal. The incident greatly dis-

personally coined patronymics for hundreds of families. To simplify his forebears' lengthy titles for foreigners, he invented the Chakri dynastic name, Rama, to be followed by the proper reign number. (A common name is also used, such as Chulalongkorn.) Primary education was made compulsory throughout the kingdom; Chulalongkorn University, in Bangkok and the first in Siam, was founded, and schools for both sexes flourished during his reign.

Rama VI's most significant political contribution was to promote the concept of nationalism. An accomplished author, he used literature and drama to foster nationalism by glorifying Thai legends and historical heroes in plays.

comfited the king, who then changed the flag to red, white and blue stripes to represent the nation, the religion and the monarchy – elements regarded by Thais as essential to the structure of modern Thailand.

Vajiravudh preferred individual ministerial consultations to summoning his appointed cabinet. His regime was therefore criticised as autocratic and lacking in coordination. Members of his family were dissatisfied because he rarely saw them, enjoying more the company of his courtiers. His extravagance soon emptied the treasury built up by Chulalongkorn. Towards the end of his reign, the national treasury met deficits caused by the ruler's personal expenses.

Vajiravudh married late. His only daughter was born one day before he died in 1925. He was succeeded by his youngest brother, Prajadhipok, who reaped the consequences of his brother's brilliant but controversial reign.

Prajadhipok (Rama VII)

The early death of his elder brother propelled Prajadhipok to royal succession, although being an old Etonian, he would have preferred a soldier's career to that of a ruler. Once king, however, he stressed economy and efficiency within the government. Unlike his brother, he tried to cut public expenditure by drastically reducing

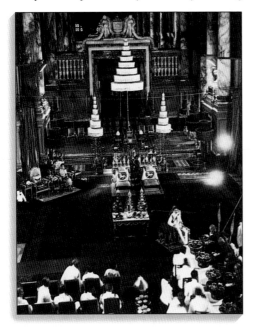

the civil service and royal household expenses. Prajadhipok's economic policies, combined with the blessings of increased revenue from foreign trade, amply paid off for the kingdom.

In the early years of his reign, communications were improved by a wireless service, and the Don Muang Airport began to operate as an international air centre. It was also during his reign that Siam saw the establishment of the Fine Arts Department, the National Library and the National Museum, institutions that continue

LEFT: Chulalongkorn's widow and family; Vajiravudh and Prajadhipok are at centre top and lower right.
ABOVE: Prajadhipok delivers the new constitution.

today as important preservers of Thai culture.

Hard-working and conscientious, Prajadhipok was personally concerned with improving the welfare of his subjects. He was aware of the rising demand for greater participation in government by a small foreign-educated faction, but felt that the Thais were, on the whole, not ready for democracy. In 1927, he publicly commented that the people must first be taught political consciousness before democracy could effectively be introduced.

The worldwide economic crisis of 1931 affected Siam's rice export. By the time Prajadhipok dropped the gold standard, linking the Thai baht to the pound sterling, it was too late to stem the financial crisis. The government was forced to implement further economies by cutting the salary of junior personnel, and by resorting to a retrenchment of the armed services. Discontent brewed among army officials and bureaucrats, who felt promotions were due.

Coup d'etat

Rumours and speculation were rampant during the 150th anniversary celebrations of the Chakri dynasty in 1932. Prajadhipok was the last regal representative of traditional Thai kingship to preside over grand pageantry, which featured a royal barge procession.

Two months later, a coup d'etat ended the absolute rule of the Thai monarchs. The coup was staged by the People's Party, a military and civilian group masterminded by foreign-educated Thais. The chief ideologist was Pridi Panomyong, a young lawyer trained in France. On the military side, Capt. Luang Pibulsongram (Pibul) was responsible for gaining the support of important army colonels. With a few tanks, the 70 conspirators sparked off their "revolution" by occupying strategic areas and holding the senior princes hostage. Other army officers stood by as the public watched.

At the time, the king was in Hua Hin, a royal beach retreat to the south. Acknowledging the writing on the wall and to avoid bloodshed, he accepted a provisional constitution by which he "ceased to rule but continued to reign."

Since then, the Thai constitutional monarchy has nevertheless become a beloved institution and a symbol of continuity and stability, not to mention a moral anchor, while civilian and military governments have come and gone with great frequency. ❑

CONTEMPORARY THAILAND

Thailand's modern history has been peppered with intrigue and punctuated with violence. The monarchy, however, has provided a stabilising anchor

Originally motivated by idealism, the People's Party soon succumbed to internal conflicts. A National Assembly was appointed, but universal suffrage was postponed while the public was to be tutored in the rudiments of representative democracy. The Thai people didn't show much interest, however, and they wouldn't voluntarily attend the party's educational rallies. Other parties were outlawed.

The party's military factions quickly outmanoeuvred the civilian factions. They had greater cohesion and more extensive connections with traditional royal power brokers. The officers exercised their influence when Pridi presented a vague and utopian economic plan in 1933. It called for the nationalisation of land and for the creation of peasant cooperatives. When his opponents attacked the plan as communistic, Pridi slipped into his first overseas exile. The power of Pibul and the army was further strengthened in October of 1933 by the decisive defeat of a rebellion led by Prince Boworadet, who had been Prajadhipok's war minister.

The king had no part in the rebellion, but he had become increasingly dismayed by quarrels within the new government. He moved to England in 1934 and abdicated in 1935. In a farewell message, he said that he had wished to turn over power to the entire people and not to "any individual or any group to use in an autocratic manner." Sadly, a subsequent history of coups, aborted coups and blood-baths has caused the king's words to be often quoted.

Ananda Mahidol (Rama VIII), a 10-year-old half-nephew, agreed to ascend the throne, but he remained for some time in Switzerland to complete his schooling.

The governments of the 1930s had some achievements. Most notably, public primary education, totalling four years, was extended to many rural areas. Indirect and, later, direct elec-

tions to the lower house meant that for the first time representatives from provincial areas had a voice at the national level. After a series of crises and an election in 1938, Pibul became prime minister. His rule grew authoritarian.

While some Thai officers favoured the model of the Japanese military regime, Pibul admired

and sought to emulate Hitler and Mussolini. Borrowing many ideas from European fascism, he attempted to instill a sense of mass nationalism. With tight control over the media and a creative propaganda department, Pibul whipped up sentiment against Thailand's Chinese residents. Chinese immigration was restricted, Chinese were barred from certain occupations, and state enterprises were set up to compete in industries dominated by Chinese firms.

By changing the country's name from Siam to Thailand in 1939, Pibul intended to emphasise that it belonged to Thai (or Tai) ethnic groups and not to Chinese, Malays, Mons or any other minorities.

PRECEDING PAGE: Royal Barges on Bangkok's Chao Phraya; their last appearance was in 1996 for the king's grand jubilee. **LEFT:** King Bhumibol's coronation. **RIGHT:** book showing coup d'etat leaders.

World War II

When Hitler invaded France in 1940, French hold over its Indochinese colonies was seriously weakened. Anticipating that Japan might make a claim, Thailand made its own by invading southern Laos and parts of western Cambodia, in November 1940. Then on 7 December 1941 (8 December in Asia) the Japanese bombed Pearl Harbour and launched invasions throughout Southeast Asia. Thailand was invaded at nine points. Resistance lasted

DEMOCRATIC FOCUS

Bangkok's Democracy Monument was built in 1939 to commemorate the 1932 revolution. In the 1970s, 1980s, and 1990s, it was the focus of numerous pro-democracy protests, and of bloodshed.

reached the stage of operating a guerrilla army.

By 1944, Thailand's initial enthusiasm for its Japanese partners had evaporated. The country faced runaway inflation, food shortages, rationing and black markets. The assembly forced Pibul from office. When the war ended in 1945, Britain demanded reparations and the right to station troops in Thailand. The Thais argued that due to the work of Seri Thai, they were in fact allies. The United States supported the Thai position, partly

less than a day. Pibul acceded to Japan's request for "passage rights," but Thailand was allowed to retain its army and political administration.

Popular anecdote has it that the Thai ambassador to Washington, Seni Pramoj, single-handedly prevented war between Thailand and the United States by hiding the declaration in a desk drawer. Thailand in fact declared war against the Allies. But it is also true that Seni immediately offered his services in Washington to set up an underground resistance movement, Seri Thai.

Starting with overseas Thai students, Seri Thai linked up with a network in Thailand headed by Pridi. The resistance supplied Allied forces with intelligence, but it never quite

because it was then trying to blunt British and French efforts to repossess their Asian colonies.

The next three years were marked by a series of democratic civilian governments. Pridi served behind the scenes, drafting a constitution, and briefly served as prime minister. In 1948, under threat of military force, Pibul took over once again. In the early years, his power was contested. Two coup attempts, supported by the navy, resulted in fierce battles on the streets of Bangkok and along the Chao Phraya River. In the 1950s, Pibul's grip grew tighter. Police power was abused, newspaper editors were beaten, critics disappeared. Pibul had also rid himself of Pridi. After attempting a coup in

1949, Pridi fled into exile. (After years in China, he died in France in 1983.) Pibul sealed Pridi's fate by convening an inquiry that implicated him in the death of King Ananda.

In 1946, on a visit to Thailand from school in Europe, the young Ananda was found dead of a gunshot in his palace bedroom. Pridi believed that the king accidentally shot himself. The charge now seems absurd. Ananda was succeeded by his younger brother, Bhumibol Adulyadej (Rama IX), the present monarch. However, he returned to Switzerland to complete law studies and did not take up active duties as monarch until the 1950s.

enterprises. Private firms were also encouraged to appoint officers to their boards of directors.

In 1957, a clique of former proteges overthrew Pibul. These generals ran the government until 1973. While Pibul had retained some trappings of democracy, such as a constitution and legislature, the generals employed martial law.

Unadorned dictatorship did not hinder official relations with the United States. By the end of the 1960s, the war in Vietnam was raging and Thailand was America's staunchest ally. American funds built the first roads in the northeast of the country, where air bases and other military facilities proliferated. From here, U.S. air-

Vietnam War

In addition to renewed anti-Chinese campaigns, Pibul vigorously hunted out Communists. Many of the leaders of the small, outlawed Communist Party of Thailand were Sino-Thais. Pibul's anti-Communist credentials helped win both economic and military aid from the United States. The resulting American largess, with too few strings, has been blamed as cause for the corruption that permeates the police and military to this day. Another cause was Pibul's practice of placing military officers to run state

Left: coronation of King Bhumibol Adulyadej.
Above: Bhumibol at crown prince's investiture.

ROYAL SUCCESSION

In the 15th century, King Trailok decreed that the king's eldest son, then brother, is heir apparent. The current king and queen have three daughters and one son. Thus, Crown Prince Maha Vajiralongkorn, born in 1952, is heir to the throne. If for some reason he can't ascend the throne, the oldest daughter, Princess Ubol Ratana, born in 1951, is technically next in line. However, after marrying an American and settling down in the U.S., it's doubtful she'd rule. The popular choice is Princess Sirindhom (b. 1955), a woman of considerable academic and social accomplishments, and highly respected.

craft bombed Vietnam and Laos. The northeast was also the Thai base for forays into Laos.

Meanwhile, Thai Communists had turned to armed conflict in 1965. The original strongholds were in the impoverished northeast, but by the early 1970s, there were Communist areas throughout, including the Muslim south, and especially along the northern frontiers. It would be some time before they were not a threat.

The ruling generals used their power to accrue enormous personal fortunes, but they also improved health standards. Construction boomed, while the business sector expanded. A middle class began to emerge.

The October revolution

In a mystifying burst of generosity, the government issued a constitution and held elections in 1969. The ruling party naturally won most seats, but the generals nonetheless quickly bored of slow parliamentary processes. In November 1971, parliament was dissolved and the generals reverted to their old ruling habits. Many Thais felt betrayed, but only students kept up low-key protests, despite grave personal risk.

With reasonable demands for a constitution and popular elections, students were able to harness public support. The final straw against the government was the arrest of 13 student leaders and professors who had made demands for pop-

ular elections. On 13 October 1973, a demonstration to protest the arrests attracted 400,000 people to Bangkok's Democracy Monument. The next day, the protest turned violent and at least 100 students were shot by riot police. Discovering that their army had deserted them, the ruling generals fled to the United States.

Political parties, labour unions and farming organisations sprang to life with very specific grievances. The press has never again been so unfettered as then. Right-wing and paramilitary organisations sprang up in response. The middle class was originally strongly supportive of the student revolution, as were parts of the upper class. But they came to fear that total chaos or a Communist takeover was at hand.

The 1976 return of one of the previously exiled generals, ostensibly to become a monk, sparked student protests.

On 6 October, police and paramilitary thugs stormed Thammasat University, in Bangkok just north of the Grand Palace. Students were lynched and their bodies burned on the spot. A faction of army officers seized power. Self-government had lasted three years.

The civilian judge appointed to be prime minister, Thanin Kraivichien, outlawed political parties, unions and strikes, and he ordered arrests of anyone "endangering society." A curfew was strictly enforced. Teachers suspected of left-wing leanings were required to attend anti-Communism indoctrination. Many students and other dissidents joined the Communists in the countryside. Yet another military coup took control in 1977. For the next decade, two comparatively moderate generals headed the government, endorsing amnesties for Communists.

Fragile democracy

The prospects for any sustained democracy remain uncertain, especially given the stormy economic situation of the late 1990s.

A former general was elected in 1989, but deposed two years later in a bloodless military coup. The junta, the self-dubbed National Peacekeeping Council, installed a businessman and ex-diplomat, Anand Panyacharun, as a caretaker premier, but were startled when he exhibited an independent streak and earned Thais' lasting affection for running the cleanest government in memory.

As expected, the junta's new party won the most parliamentary seats in 1992 elections.

Unexpected, however, was the public discontent when the coup leader, Gen. Suchinda Krapayoon, assumed the prime minister's post without having stood for election. In the following weeks, students, professors, social workers, maverick politicians, entertainers and the curious public convened in a series of outdoor rallies. On 17 May, more than 70,000 gathered at Sanam Luang, the grassy expanse near the Grand Palace and Democracy Monument. Late in the evening, soldiers

THE KING'S POWER

While avoiding the free-for-all of Thai politics, the king of Thailand retains an immense amount of moral authority, and power. Even the most ruthless of bickering generals and politicians yield to his authority, as in 1992.

erage. Unrepentant, Suchinda stepped down.

The Democrat Party and other prominent junta critics prevailed in September elections. A rarity in Thai politics, newly elected Prime Minister Chuan Leekpai was not personally corrupt and lived modestly. He prevailed for three years, setting a record for a civilian, elected government. He can be credited with diluting the power of military officers in many state enterprises, such as Thai Airways and the Tobacco Monopoly. But by the end,

fired on the unarmed demonstrators assembled there. The number of casualties is uncertain.

Shootings, beatings, riots, arson and mass arrests continued sporadically for three days. Broadcast media, which were controlled by the government or military, enforced a nationwide news blackout. But owners of satellite dishes, in Thailand and around the world, were glued to footage of "Bloody May." At Democracy Monument, vendors began hawking pirated news videos of the international television cov-

---

LEFT: remembering pro-democracy protesters killed by the army, 1992. **ABOVE:** waiting for national election results in Bangkok.

Chuan had lost much of the goodwill of the democracy forces that had lifted him to office. For many, he was too passive and reactive.

No one was prosecuted, punished or held responsible for carrying out the May crackdown. As with the massacres of 1973 and 1976, the numbers and identity of those who died or disappeared in May 1992 are still in dispute. Corruption flourished. Most disappointing, Chuan had been deflected in his efforts to push through a law that would have relegated more power to local governments. The final coalition collapsed in 1995 when wealthy members of Chuan's own party were discovered profiting from the latest land reform program.

Two subsequent elections brought a provincial businessman, Banharn Silpa-archa, and a former general, Chavalit Yongchaiyudh, to the highest office. Both had unsavoury reputations for their business dealings and campaign expenditures. And both were lambasted by the public and the press for their incompetent handling of the economy. In fact, the rot had set in much earlier. Kick-started by a massive influx of Japanese assembly plants in the late 1980s, for almost a decade Thailand had been one of the fastest growing economies in the world. Per capita income doubled, to US$ 2,000 per year. More than 4 million rural people migrated to

urban jobs. Thailand seemed on the course to becoming an industrialised nation.

Even as economic growth was slowing down, liberalisation of the financial sector in the early 1990s enabled Thai companies to borrow cheap money. Property firms in particular went on a borrowing binge. Visitors today can readily spot the empty hotels, apartments and office blocks that, together with abandoned construction sites, stand as monuments to profligacy.

The first cracks opened in mid-1996 when two officials at the venerable Bangkok Bank of Commerce fled after embezzling more than US$ 2 billion. The central bank stepped in with bail-outs that eventually extended to cash-strapped finance companies. More than US$ 16 billion later, the central bank had covertly carried out the biggest bank bail-out in world history. There was no end in sight.

IMF rescue

Faced with capital flight, currency speculation and a deteriorating balance of payments, in the summer of 1997 the baht was floated from its dollar-weighted peg. It quickly dropped 25 percent in value, dropping even more later.

The Thai government finally sought the help of the International Monetary Fund (IMF). In the following days, on IMF advice, 42 more finance companies were ordered to suspend operations. In sum, 56 of the nation's 91 finance companies were declared insolvent. IMF loans and credit guarantees came only after stringent conditions were met. Chavalit and finance officials reluctantly agreed to halt bail-outs of shareholders, raise income and value-added taxes, cut the state budget, practice strict monetary discipline and accelerate the privatisation of a large number of state enterprises.

As the economy ground to a halt in Thailand, the IMF was blamed for just about every problem in the country. Expensive European automobiles were pawned at bargain prices. Bankers and corporate managers found themselves driving taxis and waiting in restaurants.

Numerous public works projects have been suspended or cancelled. Bangkok has a half-completed rapid-transit system cluttering up its boulevards; overhead tracks and supporting pylons remain uncompleted. There is no guarantee that they will ever be finished.

Chuan Leekpai, who had been prime minister in the early 1990s, returned to office in 1998. More pro-active this time, he appeared to have learned the lessons of the heady 1990s and made internationally applauded moves to resuscitate Thailand. While many Asian economies continued to falter in the late 1990s, Thailand's economy was held up as an example of an economy that was diligently working its way out of the abyss, but still ever so slowly.

Symbolically if not pragmatically, Prime Minister Chuan continued to live in his modest house, in the shadow of an overhead expressway in central Bangkok. ❐

LEFT: suspended construction projects litter Bangkok.
RIGHT: the king and queen at a ceremony.

The King

In a cynical world, it is difficult to imagine the depth of respect that the Thai people have for their monarch, King Bhumibol – Rama IX in the Chakri line. Sceptical outsiders may think it contrived or quaint, but Thais have a profound respect for the king – no mere ceremonial figurehead – and for his moral authority that has offered sanctuary during Thailand's turbulent past 50 years.

Originating in the distant past, in the ancient city of Sukhothai, the royal symbol has endured through wars, revolutions, the fall of dynasties, the smashing of traditions and governments – both dictatorial and democratic – and through times of tribulation and prosperity. During the political turmoil in 1992, Bhumibol ended a political crisis between the prime minister and his chief political opponent, which had threatened civil war. The two men prostrated themselves at the king's feet, on live television, where they stayed silent as the king instructed them on how to bring the country back to a peace. Violence in the streets, which killed dozens, ceased, and there were free elections.

King Bhumibol was born in Cambridge, Massachusetts, in 1927, where his father, Prince Mahidol of Songkhla, was studying medicine at Harvard University, and his mother, nursing. His father, a son of King Rama V and later regarded as the father of modern medicine in Thailand, was a minor member of the royal family. At his birth, there seemed little chance of Prince Bhumibol becoming king. Between him and the throne, according to the laws of succession, stood Bhumibol's own father and Bhumibol's elder brother, Prince Ananda. (Rama VII had borne no sons to take the throne.)

Bhumibol came to the throne in 1946, the latest monarch in the Chakri dynasty, which has produced several enlightened monarchs in the 19th and 20th centuries. The abolition of the absolute monarchy in 1932 had exerted unprecedented strain on the system; the royalty seemed to lose contact with the people, along with their confidence. There were doubts if the monarchy could survive the turmoil of World War II, when 18-year-old Bhumibol ascended the throne unexpectedly after the fatal shooting of his elder brother, King Ananda, in the Grand Palace, in Bangkok. The king's death was never fully explained publicly, but much later, two royal servants were executed for his murder.

In the 50 years since his coronation, the king has proved himself a worthy successor to his celebrated ancestors. With Queen Sirikit, he has travelled to every part of Thailand, the first monarch to visit some parts of the country. He rarely travels outside of Thailand.

He has also turned over his palace grounds to agricultural purposes. Behind the walls of Chitralada Palace, where the king lives (the Grand Palace is for ceremonial and state occasions), the king has transformed gardens into an agricultural research station, with a dairy farm, rice fields, and orchards. His involvement with agriculture began with a concerted effort to find new crops for the hill tribes in order to wean them from opium cultivation. He then focused this experience into farm programs.

The monarchy costs the Thai treasury nothing, at least directly, since the royal family pays its own way with income from vast property holdings and investments. The king's mother, who died in 1995, founded the Flying Doctors program to provide medical and dental services in remote areas. Queen Sirikit works to preserve the arts and crafts, and the techniques of the ancient crafts, and to provide skills and income for rural people.

In addition, the king and queen take part in the numerous royal ceremonies that punctuate the year – the seasonal robing of the Emerald Buddha, the various Buddhist holy days, the opening of Parliament. A skillful musician, King Bhumibol plays jazz on clarinet and saxophone. ∎

NATURAL HISTORY

Although Thailand's wild lands have diminished from excessive logging over the past couple of decades, it is still endowed with some unique flora and fauna

Thailand's biological treasures and diverse land forms derive from its geographical position as the crossroads of Southeast Asia. Just as the nation has accommodated many peoples and cultures, so it has served as a conduit dispersing plant and animal life.

Roughly the size of France, Thailand covers 513,115 square kilometres (198,115 sq mi). The overall shape resembles an elephant's head with the southern peninsula forming the trunk. The most conspicuous landscape features are striated mountains enclosing cultivated valleys, but there are great contrasts in six geographical regions. In the north, extending along the borders of Burma and Laos, parallel mountains run north to south, generally reaching over 2,000 metres (6,500 ft) in height. The valleys have been cultivated for centuries, but until 50 years ago – with the proliferation of slash-and-burn farming – there was considerable forest cover in the higher altitudes.

To the south, the vast valley called the Central Plain stretches 450 kilometres (300 mi) to the Gulf of Thailand. The overflowing tributaries traditionally deposited rich silt that created an agricultural rice bowl. The farms nowadays are supported by intensive irrigation, courtesy of a network of highly controversial big dams. The western region consists mostly of mountain ranges, the source of tributaries of the Mekong, Chao Phraya and Salween rivers. Sparsely populated by humans, this region is the richest repository of wildlife.

The northeast encompasses the broad and shallow Khorat Plateau, which lies less than 200 metres (650 ft) above sea level. This is a land of poor soils, little rain, too many people, and a bit of grass and shrub. The sandstone base has weathered into strange shapes.

The small, hilly southeast coast is bordered on the north by the Cardomom Range, which protrudes from Cambodia. It includes 80 rocky,

forested islands. Intense heat and violent underground pressures created the rubies and sapphires mined here. Endowed with the heaviest rainfall and humidity, the south covers the isthmus down to the Malay peninsula. Coastal forests were cleared for rubber and palm plantations. But 275 islands, especially in the west-

ern Andaman Sea, support unique species and are surrounded by coral reefs.

The limestone rock so common on the Andaman side was once seabed. Soft and easily eroded, it is limestone that is the basis of the crumbly mountains and jutting islets. Underground streams in limestone also created the many spectacular caves.

Flora

Sixty years ago, forests covered about 70 percent of Thailand's land area. In 1960, the figure had dropped to 50 percent. Today, probably only about 15 percent of undisturbed forest remains, although perhaps another 15 percent of it has

---

PRECEDING PAGE: bats take flight as a setting sun takes the day. **LEFT:** yellow bittern fishing from lotus leaf. **RIGHT:** waterfall in Khao Yai National Park.

been replanted, often with non-indigenous species, or else turned into plantations growing the likes of palm-oil trees or eucalyptus. Aside from tiny Singapore, the scale and rate of forest loss in Thailand is the greatest in Southeast Asia. Following fatal landslides, logging was finally outlawed in 1989, but trucks ferrying contraband logs are still a common sight.

The nation's forests can be classified as either evergreen or deciduous; the latter shed leaves seasonally. There are many sub-categories, and a single habitat may contain both types of trees. Evergreen forests, of course, are green year-round. They are most abundant in the uplands

of both the south and southeast, where rainfall is plentiful and the dry season brief. Rain forests are classified as evergreen forests.

Contrary to many preconceptions, all tropical forests are not evergreen, and all evergreen forest is not rain forest. A rain forest is a four-layered forest harbouring the world's densest concentration of species. Herbs, shrubs, ferns and fungi form the bottom layer. A relatively open layer of palms, bamboos and shrubs is above ground level. Mid-level trees, festooned with vines, mosses and orchids, create a 25-metre-high (80 ft) canopy. The well-spaced trees of the upper-most canopy soar as high as 60 metres (200 ft). Healthy rain forests can be

found in the Khao Luang, Koh Surin, Tarutao and Thale Ban national parks, all in the south.

More common than rain forest is the broad-leaved evergreen forest, which is found at higher elevations. Here are found temperate-zone laurels, oaks and chestnuts, along with ferns, rhododendrons and the yew-like podocarps. Varieties of orchids proliferate. Usually the ground level consists of shrubs and grasses that attract larger mammals. The leaves of the taller dipterocarps turn yellow and red before shedding in the dry season. A few weeks later, they burst into purple, pink, orange and red flowers.

One hundred years ago, deciduous forests of the north were thick with teak trees, but virtually all were cut long ago.

Fauna

Of the world's 4,000 species of mammals, 287 can be found in Thailand: 13 species of primates, 18 hoofed species, nine of wild cats (including tigers and clouded leopards), two of bear, two of wild dogs and eight of dolphins. Bats are abundant, with 107 species identified so far. Tigers and the larger deer could soon join the list of mammals that have vanished this century – rhinoceros, several species of deer, two otter species, and the *kouprey,* wild cattle that were discovered in Thailand in the 1930s.

Declared the country's first protected species back in 1921, the Asian elephant is the national mascot, but nonetheless is perilously close to extinction. From well above 20,000 a century ago, fewer than 8,000 survive in Thailand today. Most of these are domesticated, many begging on Bangkok's hard streets. Khao Yai National Park offers the best chance of observing some of the few thousand remaining wild elephants.

Thailand also harbours four types of reptiles and three types of amphibians. Among 175 species of snakes are deadly cobras, kraits and vipers. No doubt most of the insect species haven't been identified yet, but there are 1,200 variegated butterflies. Beetle species may number in the tens of thousands, but have been so little studied that amateurs occasionally discover a new one.

Visitors of national parks and sanctuaries may not see any large animals, but they will be compensated with sightings of birds. There are around 900 species that are permanent residents of the region. In the north are the colourful montane birds with Sino-Himalayan affinities. The birds of the south are similar to those of Malaysia. There are also about 240 wintering and non-breeding migrants that pass through.

Marine life

Off the west coast, the flora and fauna of the Andaman Sea are characteristic of the Indian Ocean. Off the east coast, in the Gulf of Thailand, they are characteristic of Indo-Pacific seas. Coral reefs off both coastlines have been little surveyed, but they support at least 400 species of fish and 30 of sea snakes. The corals them-

> **LITTLE ENFORCEMENT**
>
> The country in fact does have environmental and wildlife protection laws, but they are poorly enforced.

habitats, be they forests or coral reefs, so could disappear many more species of flora and fauna, not only from Thailand, but from the world.

The Forestry Department, which includes the Parks Service, is underfunded and understaffed. In the past few decades, at least 40 rangers have been murdered in the line of duty. Earning less than a factory worker, many rangers also collude with poachers of logs and animals. The country's poorest people inadvertently contribute to the degradation by farming on protected lands. The demands of Chinese-Thais and Chinese vis-

selves come in almost 300 species, with the Andaman Sea boasting a far greater diversity. Intact reefs survive only in areas far from human habitation, such as the vicinity of the Surin and Similan islands.

Environment at risk

As many of the aforementioned remarks concerning habitats and wildlife indicate, Thailand's ecology is an environment in danger of irreversible damage. With the destruction of

itors, for both medicinal purposes and gourmet "jungle" dining, further threaten the endangered populations of tigers, bears and deer.

Tourism undoubtedly plays a part in the degradation of Thailand's ecosystems, most visibly when seaside hotels spew untreated sewage. There are also signs that tourism might conceivably become a positive force in the preservation of what remains of Thailand's ecology. There are encouraging signs that a few Thais – among them trekking guides and local green groups, and even a few progressive politicians – are becoming aware that environmental caretaking will sustain tourism longer than continued destruction. ❑

LEFT: *Burmannia disticha*, a flower endemic to Khao Yai National Park. **ABOVE:** decreasing in numbers, the Asian elephant, such as this youth, can still be seen.

PEOPLE

It will be readily apparent that the Thai people expect life and its experiences, large or small, to be fun and comfortable. Otherwise, what's the point?

Travelers to Thailand are generally struck by the ubiquity of smiles, warmth and friendliness. There are always amiable questions – not to be interpreted as nosiness – and an openness seldom found elsewhere. The standard greeting is *pai nai*, or "Where are you going?" But this is not meant to be interpreted literally, but rather it is the approximate equivalent of "Hello" or "How are you?"

The key focus for understanding the Thai is *sanuk*, a word that can be translated as "fun" or "enjoyable." Indeed, the quantity – and quality – of sanuk, whether in work or play, determines if something is worth pursuing. Almost as important is the concept of *sabai*, best translated as "comfortable" or "contented". As far as Thai people are concerned, in the best of all possible worlds life should be both sanuk and sabai, for visitors to the kingdom as much as for its inhabitants. The antithesis of sanuk is *seriat* – a borrowing from the English word serious. Life just isn't meant to be taken too seriously.

Background

Thailand's lifestyle traditionally has been centred on agriculture, an activity that nurtures a sense of community, especially during planting and harvest. All over the country, ethnic Thais inhabit lowland valleys or plains, growing rice in irrigated paddy fields. They leave the hills and mountains to other peoples – the *chao khao*, or hill tribes, like the Akha and Hmong.

Today, most Thais still live in the country or in small towns, although Bangkok, the archetypical primal city, is now home to more than 10 million people, nearly 20 percent of the national population. The demands of city life have changed much of the countryside's casual ways, but even in Bangkok it is a rare Thai who does not enjoy getting together with friends. Indeed, the notion that one might go off solo to a dinner or on a holiday is considered *mai sanuk*, or not

PRECEDING PAGE: a net fisherman on Ko Lanta, south of Krabi and Phuket. **LEFT:** a woman working on a farm in Thailand's northeast. **RIGHT:** Thai sailor, Chanthaburi.

fun. Similarly, office life must contain a certain amount of chatting and passing around of snacks for it to avoid being mai sanuk.

Generally speaking, Thais hate to be alone, and most are puzzled by the average foreigner's need for occasional solitude. There is a sense of family about Thai activities, a gathering that

does not exclude outsiders. For the visitor invited to join, there is no automatic expectation of reciprocation, although it would always be much appreciated. It is not unusual for a visitor to stray into a small city lane and be invited to join a partying group. Such activities are usually accompanied by music, alcoholic drinks and small snacks. Drunkenness is frowned upon, but a certain tipsiness is acceptable in such circumstances.

When a visitor encounters a tense situation, it is usually because of differences of language and custom. In such instances, it is best to adopt another Thai attitude, *jai yen*, or cool heart, to deal calmly with the problem. It is difficult to stir a Thai to real anger. A smile and an apology should deflate almost any tense situation. Anger, demonstrated by physical violence or raised voices, can provoke serious hostility, however, and an angry Thai can be aggressive indeed. For example, touching a Thai (especially on the top of the head), shouting, or threatening the strong feeling of independence that Thais have may effect an immediate and often hostile response.

Visitors should also avoid pointing their feet at Thais, for example, when crossing their legs, as the foot is considered

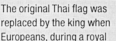

MISTAKEN IDENTITY

The original Thai flag was replaced by the king when Europeans, during a royal visit to Europe, mistook the elephant for a rodent.

without breaking, then snapping back into place and swaying in the breeze.

The population

Thailand's population is around 60 million. Most people (95 percent) are Theravada Buddhists. About 80 percent of the population are ethnic Thai. There is a small percentage of Thai Malays living in the south who are Muslim. Islam is Thailand's second religion, accounting for perhaps 5 percent of the population, and Thai-speaking Muslims may be

unclean, and pointing it at someone is thought to be a great insult.

Closely allied with jai yen is a concept that provides the answer to all of life's vicissitudes: *mai pen rai,* a phrase best translated as "never mind." Most Thai would rather shrug their shoulders in the face of adversity than risk escalating a difficult situation. Solutions that contribute to restoring or maintaining calm are welcomed. In fact, one reason the Thais have survived intact as a sovereign nation is by adopting a superb sense of compromise, putting trifling or trivial matters in perspective, or else ignoring them. Truly, this aspect of the Thai character may be likened to a bamboo, bending

found in every province of the country, from Chiang Rai in the north to Yasothon in the far northeast. The 2 percent of the population who are Confucianist or Mahayana Buddhist are mainly urban, living in the Chinatown areas of cities like Bangkok, Khorat, Hat Yai and Nakhon Sawan. Some 10 to 15 percent of Thailand's total population are of Chinese descent.

Hill-tribe people living in the north and west total about half a million, and many of the tiny group of Christians in Thailand are concentrated among them. Catholicism made some inroads in Chanthaburi in the south-east, due mainly to French influence. Christians in the north have been strongly influenced by the Protestantism of American Presbyterian missionaries. The main hill-tribe groups include Lisu, Lahu, Akha, Karen, Hmong and Mien (Yao). The smallest and least known peoples living in Thailand are the Mlabri, or "Spirits of the Yellow Leaves", about 250 of whom survive in the Phrae-Nan borderlands, and the Moken, or sea gypsies, who live on islands in the Andaman Sea between Phuket and Ranong

Bangkok's population is thought to exceed 10 million; an accurate census is virtually impossible due to the semi-permanent migrant population. The city functions as the epicentre of the country's political, business and religious life.

The Thais

Whilst all Thai-speaking, Buddhist inhabitants of Thailand consider themselves part of the Thai family, considerable regional differences exist. Basically, Thailand can be divided into four regions – central plains, north, northeast and peninsular south. All educated Thais – and literacy is estimated to run as high as 96 percent – can speak and understand Central Thai, the language of Bangkok, and of the radio and television. Yet Central Thai is far from being the mother tongue of the other three regions. In the northeast, people speak Lao at home, whilst in the north the people speak *kham muang*, or "the language of the Principalities".

Southern Thai is closer to the Central variant, but is spoken much faster and with an economy of terms. Thus, the simple word "tasty" or "delicious" is pronounced *aroi* in Central Thai, *roi* in the snappy southern dialect, *sep* in northeastern Lao, and *lam* in the kham muang of the north. In Central Thai, "Do you speak Thai" emerges as *khun pud phasa tai dai mai?* In kham muang it's *oo kham muang zhang ko?* Quite a difference, but the visitor has no need to worry, as Central Thai is universally spoken and understood throughout the country.

There are also considerable differences in regional cuisine. The Thai restaurants of London and Los Angeles – indeed all over the world – generally serve central Thai cuisine, which has become justly famed internationally.

Northeastern cuisine, by contrast, favours sticky rice (*khao niu*) instead of the more common long-grain rice, which is eaten with the fin-

gers rather than a spoon or chopsticks. Northerners are unique in Thailand in serving cooked tomatoes. The cuisine of Chiang Mai owes much to the culinary influence of neighbouring Burma and Yunnan, in China. Southerners like to use the ubiquitous coconut in their dishes, and the creamy effect of coconut milk helps to tame the otherwise fiery heat of the dishes found in the deep south.

The Chinese

Like every country in Southeast Asia, Chinese merchants have been active in Thailand since the earliest days of commerce. When King

Rama I selected Bangkok as his new capital, the site upon which he wanted to build the Grand Palace was occupied by Chinese shops. He asked the owners to move a kilometre down the riverbank to Sampeng, where they settled in what is today Bangkok's Chinatown.

Throughout the 19th century and the first half of the 20th, immigrants from China poured into the country. As in other Asian countries, these immigrants were denied ownership of land and participation in government, so they naturally drifted towards trade and commerce. One thing, however, has long distinguished the Thai Chinese from their counterparts in most other Asian countries: they have assimilated to a remarkable

LEFT: expressway toll-booth workers, north of Bangkok. **RIGHT:** Thai sneaker factory, near Bangkok.

degree into the life of their adopted land. In part this has been due to government policy.

All children, Chinese or otherwise, are required to learn the Thai language in primary school. (The Chinese language was not even taught at the university level until a few years ago.) Moreover, the Chinese were encouraged, sometimes pressured, into taking Thai names when they wanted a passport, a government scholarship, or an official document. As a result, Chinese and Thais have inter-married freely, so that today, especially in the cities, it is dif-

> **UBIQUITOUS UNIFORMS**
>
> The wild card in modern Thai politics has always been the military, involved in business and banking as well.

has been, and still is, some jealousy over the eth-nic Chinese command of the Thai economy, but the Thai response has been to intermarry with, rather than to isolate, the Chinese. It's a policy that has worked, resulting in little racial tension.

Flag, royalty and Buddhism

At eight o'clock each morning, the Thai national flag is ceremoniously raised in every Thai town and city. The modern flag – intro-duced in 1917 to replace an ear-lier red flag emblazoned with a white elephant, the flag of the

ficult to point to anyone and say with assurance that he or she is "pure" Thai or Chinese.

There is no deep-rooted anti-Chinese bias in Thailand, nor have there been any of the seri-ous racial conflicts marring the recent histories of neighbouring countries. Only among the older generation are there people who think and speak of themselves specifically as Chinese. The younger generation thinks of itself as Thai, speaks the language, voices loyalty to Thailand, and has only cursory interests in affairs in China – though pride in Chinese origins remains strong amongst Sino-Thais.

All Thais consider Chinese to be canny busi-nessmen – not without reason. To be sure, there

absolute monarchy – is composed of five hori-zontal bands of white, red, and blue. The white symbolises the purity of Buddhism; red, the land and its people; and blue, the monarchy as the force that binds the other two together. The central elements of the Thai polity – what makes Thailand Thai – have traditionally been per-ceived as the Buddhist religion, the Thai lan-guage and the monarchy. In recent years, this has changed somewhat, as recognition of other constituent elements of the Thai people, most notably the Malay-speaking Muslims of the deep south, have been brought into the equation. Still, to most Thai, religion, language and king still constitute a unique definition of being Thai.

The three colours, and the flag itself, are revered as symbols of enduring qualities amidst changes, values that were evoked in 1992 when Thais rose up against the military's grip on political power. For the first time, Thailand's burgeoning middle class exerted their influence on political issues; extensive civil unrest, if not civil war, loomed.

Using the moral authority that the monarchy possesses in Thailand, King Bhumibol lectured the prime minister and his primary opponent on live television, as the two men prostrated themselves silently at the king's feet. The crisis immediately evaporated. Since that historical turning point, the changes in government and politics have been enormous, and are continuing to this day.

Since the constitutional revolution of 1932, the king does not govern the country, but he retains considerable influence in government and in society, serving as a beacon of high moral standards and a bellwether in troubled times.

Thais regard the royal family with a reverence unmatched in other countries, and people will react strongly if they consider any member of royalty to have been insulted. Ill-considered remarks or refusing to stand in a cinema for the royal anthem before the start of a movie will earn some very hard stares, or even knocks.

A similar degree of respect is accorded the second pillar of society, Buddhism. Disrespect towards Buddha images, temples or monks is not taken lightly.

Such insults may be unintentional – for example, climbing or clambering about on Buddha images for purposes of photography – so visitors should exercise discretion at all times, remove shoes before entering temples (or also mosques in the south), and behave politely, including the wearing of proper dress. When visiting a temple, it is acceptable for both sexes to wear long pants but not shorts. Unkempt persons or those wearing what might be considered immodest clothing are frequently turned away from major temples.

Monks observe vows of chastity that prohibit their being touched by women, even their mother. When in the vicinity of a monk, a woman should try to stay clear to avoid accidentally brushing against him.

LEFT: walking under an elephant for good luck.
RIGHT: amulets protect from misfortune and evil.

Public behaviour

From the Hindu religion has come the belief that the head is the fount of wisdom and the feet are unclean. For this reason, it is insulting to touch another person on the head, or to point one's feet at or step over another person. Kicking in anger is worse than spitting.

When wishing to pass someone who is seated on the floor, bow slightly while walking and point an arm down to indicate the path to be taken. It is also believed that spirits dwell in the raised doorsills of temples and traditional Thai houses, and that when one steps on them, the spirits become angry and curse the building with

bad luck. Remember this especially in temples.

The Thai greeting and farewell is *sawasdee*, spoken while raising the hands in a prayer-like gesture called the *wai*, with the fingertips touching the nose while bowing the head slightly. It is an easy greeting to master and one which will win smiles.

Thais believe in personal cleanliness. Even the poorest among them bathe daily and dress cleanly and neatly. Thailand is a hot country, and the Thai people very fastidious. They frown on those who do not share this concern for hygiene. The lax care that some foreign travelers bring with their backpack ramblings win few points. Shower and change often, for your own comfort and to receive respect. Toilet paper is not generally provided except in hotels, airports and other tourist-oriented institutions. Look for the tap and water bowl, or a spray-hose.

Twenty years ago, Thai couples showed no intimacy in public. That has changed due to Western influence on the young, but intimacy still does not extend beyond holding hands. As in many traditional societies, displaying open affection in public is a sign of bad manners.

Old people in Thailand are treated with great respect, as are teachers, doctors and other professionals. Mishaps or accidents – such as a small traffic crash – are best met with smiles

but sometimes confusing way of saying "no".

As noted earlier, jai yen, or "cool heart," an attitude of remaining calm in stressful situations, is a trait admired by Thais. Getting angry or exhibiting *jai ron* (hot heart) is a sign of immaturity and lack of self-control. Reacting to adversity or disappointment with a shrug of the shoulders and saying "mai pen rai" (never mind) is the accepted response to most situations.

Thais converse readily with any stranger who shows the least sign of willingness. They may be shy about their English language ability but they try nonetheless: speak a few words of Thai and they respond even more eagerly. Be pre-

and apologies. Violence or rude language should be avoided at all times. The average Thai driver will respond positively to a smiling apology which defuses any delicate situation.

Thais strive to maintain equanimity in their lives and go to great lengths to avoid confrontation. The concept is called *kriengjai* and suggests an unwillingness to burden someone older or superior with one's problems. In many cases, it means not giving someone bad news until too late for fear it may upset the recipient.

Thais don't liking saying "no" too directly for fear of causing offense. In a common manifestation of kriengjai, giving no answer to a question, or evading a direct answer, is a considerate

pared, however, for questions considered rather impolite in Western societies, such as: How old are you? How much money do you earn? How much does that watch (camera, etc.) cost? Thais regard these questions as part of ordinary conversation and will not understand a reluctance to answer them.

If, however, one is reticent about divulging personal information, a joking answer delivered with a smile will usually suffice; for example, to the above question of "How old are you?", answer with "How old do you think?"

Be warned, however, that Thai people can be extraordinary flatterers. Speak a few words of Thai, and you will likely be pronounced *geng*, or "excellent", not to mention handsome or pretty, as the case may be. Smile, appreciate the compliment, and respond in kind. Remember that life is meant to be sanuk.

Government

Executive power is wielded by a prime minister selected by the majority party or a coalition of parties. He or she formulates and executes policies through a cabinet of 13 ministers.

While the prime minister and the parliament might seem far removed from the population,

protests. In part, it reflects the sense of family that constantly appears in Thai conversations, and in exhortations to stand together against common enemies. Although Thai leaders are regarded paternalistically, they are increasingly held accountable for their actions.

Provincial governors are still appointed by the government in Bangkok, but most other local officials must now be elected for a fixed term, a change made to the constitution in 1995. Previously, they were elected for life, or else obtained posts through dubious means.

> **GETTING ALONG THE THAI WAY**
>
> Although there is a significant Chinese population, not to mention the hill tribes, Thailand has little racial tension.

except perhaps at election time, they are, in fact, usually quite responsive to the electorate. It is not unusual for a delegation of disgruntled citizens to rent a fleet of buses to personally lodge a noisy protest in front of the parliament building or local government office against officials or a decree with which they disagree.

Ministers, even the prime minister, often talk with these delegations to remedy problems, although with the clamour generated by the surprisingly vocal and independent local press, it would be difficult for leaders to ignore their

LEFT: getting around in a set of modern wheels.
ABOVE: sisters along a canal (*khlong*) in Bangkok.

Military

For the first time in recent memory, the elected parliament has moved to the peak of political power in Thailand. After the turmoil of 1992, the constitution was changed to make it mandatory for the prime minister to be an elected member of parliament.

Previously, Thailand had generally been governed by generals, who traditionally had seized power by force or had been appointed to office by some of their fellows. Changes in the constitution since 1992 have weakened the political role of the military, but how the military will accept its diminished status over the long run has yet to be seen.

The military's role is vastly different from that in the West, but it is a role that has its roots in Thai history by which rulers and leaders rose out of the ranks of the military. In fact, the traditional avenue for advancement in all sectors of society has been the military. The Thai soldier, like the civil servant, belongs to a sprawling and complex organisation whose activities have most often gone beyond national defence. Thai conscripts serving obligatory two-year terms fill most of the lower ranks and perform duties of defending borders. The upper ranks, however, have been intimately involved in the business and government of Thailand.

SIZE MATTERS

Bangkok is over 35 times larger than the country's second- and third-largest cities, Khorat and Udon Thani.

has been further weakened by the financial crisis and currency devaluation that enveloped Thailand in 1997.

Women

The constitutional changes of 1995 also spelled out the equality of men and women. The constitution also says that a woman may now be the monarch, previously a forbidden possibility. Granted, true equality is by no means the norm in daily life, as in any society. But the improved status of women, and their greater share

ranks, however, have been intimately involved in the business and government of Thailand.

High-ranking military officers sit on the boards of banks, own hotels, and take part in business even as they actively pursue military careers. It is one of the few occupations in which a bright but poor young man can achieve advancement on merit.

The military establishment is now such an integral part of Thai society that it is difficult to imagine life without it. Its meddling in government over the years, however, has been problematic and increasingly unpopular with the Thai people. Since 1992, the Thai military has promised to stay out of government, and its role

of power in society, has been one of the most remarkable changes of the past few decades. However, Thai women still suffer discrimination in land ownership, marriage, and citizenship. (In fact, however, women obtained the vote at the same time as men, in 1932.)

But in many ways, Thai women have generally been powerful and influential behind the scenes. A 15th-century Chinese visitor reported that "it is their custom that all affairs are managed by their wives, both the king and the common people. If they have matters that require thought and deliberation... all trading transactions great and small, they all follow the decision of their wives."

In big business, women have been at the top for generations, as it has been customary for men to go into government and the military. Today, women are particularly prominent in the hotel business, tourism, real estate, advertising, export trade, banking, and law. Women helm major companies and own several of the largest hotels in Bangkok. Women also head villages and occupy top positions in the civil service and medicine. The university population is almost equally male and female. If renting a house in Thailand, the rent is paid to a woman, no matter whose name is on the title to the property.

In Thailand, lower-class women have less power but often control the family purse strings and moral upbringing of the children. Women with lower levels of education can be found on construction sites, cleaning offices, running small businesses, and driving buses. On the other hand, lapses in enforcement combined with years of tradition have contributed to the exploitation of women in the sex industry.

Sexual attitudes

Most unfairly, Thailand has acquired a something of a reputation as a sexual playland in the West. Much emphasis has been placed on the exploitation and degradation of women and especially children.

To be sure, prostitution exists and to some extent has been established for many centuries. But less than 1 percent of the female population is involved in the commercial sex business, and child prostitution is in fact a rare phenomenon. Most Thais – the overwhelming majority of Thais – are conservative and indeed almost puritanical where sex is concerned. Outside of a few urban venues like Bangkok's Patpong, Soi Cowboy and Nana Plaza, or the Russian- and German-dominated bar scene of Pattaya, Thai society is usually the epitome of respectability and propriety where sex is concerned.

This said, Thai people are generally open-minded and sympathetic in their attitude towards people's sexuality. Sex is seen as a normal human function and, if practiced between consenting or married adults, it is definitely sanuk – who could doubt it? Attitudes towards consensual adult homosexuality are sympathetic, and this extends to a peculiarly Thai (or

Southeast Asian) phenomenon: transvestism. Thailand has more than its share of *katoeys*, or "lady men", transvestite men who are accepted for what they are, treated with understanding and respect, and generally addressed as women. In fact, the most popular nationally-ranked kickboxer in 1998 was a transvestite.

Terms of address

Thais are addressed by their first, rather than their last, names. The name is usually preceded by the word *khun*, a term of respect. Thus, Silpachai Krishnamra would be addressed as Khun Silpachai when someone speaks to him. You

will find some Thais referred to in newspapers with the letters M.C., M.R. or M.L. preceding their names. These are royal titles normally translated as "prince" or "princess." The five-tier system reserves the highest two titles for the immediate royal family. After that comes the nobility, remnants of the noble houses of old. The highest of these three ranks is Mom Chao (M.C.), followed by Mom Rachawong (M.R.) and Mom Luang (M.L.). The title is not hereditary, thanks to a system that guarantees Thailand will never become top-heavy with princes and princesses. Each succeeding generation is born into a lower rank. Thus, the son or daughter of a Mom Chao is a Mom Rachawong. ❐

LEFT: bargaining in a Nonthaburi market.
RIGHT: saffron-robed monk, near Surat Thani.

HILL TRIBES

One of Thailand's prime tourist draws, the hill tribes of the north – less than 2
percent of the population – have both benefited and suffered from this attention

The tribal people of Thailand make up less than two percent of the total population, but account for a significant degree of interest with visitors to Thailand. (This is in striking contrast to neighbouring Laos and Burma, where the shares are at least 30 percent and 15 percent, respectively, but without the

tice slash-and-burn (swidden) agriculture. In March, at the height of the dry season, they set massive fires to burn the undergrowth on the mountain sides. (Unfortunately, there's no longer much forest left to burn.) The ashes at first provide a rich fertiliser, but over the years the process depletes the soil. Villagers used to

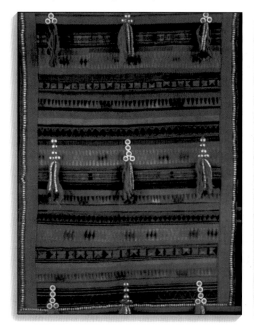

tourist obsessiveness.) Thousands of foreigners annually trek to the tribal people's mountain villages. The average Thai views tribal people as foreigners, if not illegal aliens, and thus not entitled to the same rights as Thais. Most tribal immigration – from Burma or Laos – has occurred only in the past 100 years. In fact, only in the past decade have significant numbers of tribal people been granted Thai citizenship. They cling to the bottom rung of the steep Thai economic and social ladder.

Thailand is home for up to 20 tribes, but there are six principal groups: Karen, Hmong, Mien, Lahu, Lisu and Akha. Living in villages at higher elevations, most hill tribe farmers prac-

then move their villages to a new site, but there's no place to move nowadays. With poorer soil and less of it, villagers often rely on the opium poppy as a cash crop.

Karen

The 265,000 Karen form by far the largest tribe. In Thailand, they comprise two sub-groups, the Sgaw and Pwo, whose dialects are not mutually intelligible. (The karenic language belongs to the Tibeto-Burman linguistic group.) Karens have settled in Thailand since the 18th century and they are still (illegally) trickling in. In Burma, there are between 3 million and 4 million Karens, a Karen rebel state, and a Karen rebel army that has been fighting the Burmese government for over four decades.

Karens were early converts to Christianity when Burma was a British colony. Some Thai Karens are Baptists or Seventh-Day Adventists. But whether of Christian, Buddhist or animist beliefs, the Karens place a great emphasis on monogamy, look down on premarital sex, and can trace ancestry through the mother. Unlike other Thai tribes, they have long practiced lowland wet-rice farming.

NORTHERN HOMES

With the exception of the Karen, who extend down to Kanchanaburi and Tak provinces, most hill tribes live in the three northwestern provinces of Chiang Mai, Chiang Rai and Mae Hong Son.

Opium use is somewhat common. Kinship is patrilineal and polygamy is permitted. Like Thai, Hmong is an Austroasiatic language, meaning that its roots have been traced to southern China. In fact, four million Hmong live today in China's Yunnan Province. The White Hmong and Blue Hmong can be identified by their dialects and clothing: Blue Hmong women wear indigo, pleated skirts and their hair in huge buns. White Hmong women wear white hemp skirts and black turbans.

Hmong

The most recent arrivals in Thailand, Hmong are the second-largest hill tribe, numbering about 80,000. The majority immigrated in the 1950s and 1960s, fleeing from the long civil war in Laos. Ever on the alert for communists, the Thai military then regarded Hmong as subversives, and Hmong relations with Thai officialdom still remain edgy. Ironically, Hmong are renowned for their fierce independence and, in Laos, for anti-communism. Indeed, they were American allies during the Vietnam War.

LEFT: hill-tribe textile, and a White Hmong woman.
ABOVE: Hmong with clothing of heavy black cotton.

Mien

Like Hmong, most Mien (Yao) probably came to Thailand from Laos, but there are large numbers in Burma, Vietnam and China's Yunnan Province – as well as Laotian Mien refugee communities in San Francisco and Seattle. Many Chinese elements, such as ancestor worship and Daoism, are evident in their animist religious beliefs. Kinship is patrilineal and polygamy is practiced. Mien place great emphasis on the peaceful resolution of conflict. Of all the hill tribes, they probably have the smoothest relations with Thais. Mien, including women, are often outgoing. Mien have also taken to the Thai dress of T-shirts, sarongs and jeans, but traditionally women wear black jackets and trousers, red fur-like collars and large blue or black turbans. Their dense, intricate embroideries are valued on bags and clothing. The language is Austroasiatic.

Lahu

Like the Karen, some of the 60,000 Lahu are Christian. Also like the Karen, traditional Lahu mix animism with millennial myths that have led them to be receptive to messianic movements; some hope for the return of a man-god called Geusha. Besides the usual opium, corn and rice, Lahu have successfully cultivated

chilli peppers as a cash crop. The traditional dress of the four groups – Red Lahu, Black Lahu, Yellow Lahu and Lahu Sheleh – is slightly different, but red and black jackets are common. Lahu are skilled makers of baskets and bags. Lahu languages are Tibeto-Burman.

Lahu are famed for their hunting prowess with both rifles and crossbows. Although leopards and tigers no longer roam the northern hills, Lahu continue to hunt bear, wild pigs, deer, squirrels, birds and snakes. Several hundred thousand Lahu live in Burma, where a small Lahu army, aligned with the Karen separatists, has fought the Burmese government since the 1970s.

Lisu

Although there are only about 25,000 Lisu, they are easily identified by their penchant for bright colours. Women wear long green or blue cotton dresses with striped yokes. Men wear baggy loose pants of the same colours. Lisu are good silversmiths and make jewelry for Akha and Lahu. Lisu are regarded by other tribal people as sharp businesspeople. Animist beliefs are combined with ancestor worship.

Lisu have a strong sense of self-esteem and will eagerly cite the reasons for the pre-eminence of their family, clan or village. Yet unlike other tribes, Lisu have an organisation that extends across villages. Lisu are a sub-group of the Kachins, a large minority group in the Kachin state in the far north of Burma. The Kachin languages are Tibeto-Burman.

Akha

Probably the poorest and the shyest of the hill tribes, the Akha have been the most resistant to assimilation by the Thais. Ironically, the 34,000 Akha are the people that most tourists want to see. The draw is the heavy ornate head-dress worn by the women. It consists of silver disks festooned with old coins, beads and feathers. And unlike other tribal women, who save their finery for ceremonies, Akha wear this even while tending the fields. Animists beliefs are mixed with ancestor worship; Akha can recite their ancestry back 20 generations.

An Akha village is extended by one of two gateways, which separate the domain of people and rice from that of spirits and wild animals. Akha neither farm nor consume opium. The language is Tibeto-Burman.

Other minorities

Strictly speaking, they are not Thai hill tribes, but two other groups, the Shan and Kayan, deserve mention, as their villages are frequent stops on trekking tours.

In their settled communities, rice-growing practices and Theravada Buddhism, the Shan are very similar to Thais. In fact, they are an ethnic Tai (Thai) group, also known as Thai Yai (Big Thai). Their language is similar to the northern Thai dialect, although not intelligible to central Thai speakers. Many Shans have immigrated to Thailand in recent times to escape the upheavals in Burma, but Shans may have been the first Tai inhabitants of northern

Thailand, in the 9th or 10th century. In the large area of Burma bordering the northern tip of Thailand is the home of 4 million Shans and several armies battling for autonomy. One of these was headed by the notorious opium trafficker, Khun Sa.

The Kayan (Padaung) are a Karennic people residing in the southern Shan areas. Until a few years ago, tours from Mae Hong Son would ferry tourists across the border to view Kayan women whose necks had been elongated by layers of heavy

DEADLY NECK RINGS

As successive rings are added to the necks of the so-called Kayan "giraffe women", the collar bone is pushed down and the neck muscles weaken. Removing the rings can thus be fatal.

Loss of culture

The cultures of Thailand's hill tribes are very much in danger of extinction. The chief culprit is not tourism. Greater threats are posed by a shortage of land, loss of land, resettlement, lack of land rights and citizenship, illiteracy and poor medical care. Official Thai hill-tribe policies have been shaped by the desire to discourage swidden farming and the cultivation of opium. Some of the crop substitution programs sponsored by the Thai government, United Nations and

brass rings. Kayan leaders, many of them Catholic, had long discouraged the practice and it had virtually died out. But the tourist attraction was so great that Thai officials allowed three villages to set up west of Mae Hong Son. Many Kayan women have since donned the rings and initiated girls beginning at age five. Tours to view the "Giraffe Women" have been heavily promoted in Bangkok. The 1,000 tourists daily are thus responsible for the reintroduction of a barbaric practice.

LEFT: distinctive headdress of an Akha woman, which are worn even in the fields. **ABOVE:** Mien women in their traditional – and daily – attire.

foreign governments have been very successful. Tribal people are marketing coffee, tea and fruit. But as trekkers amongst the hill tribes can observe, such projects have not penetrated to villages distant from roads and transport.

Some farmers have also resisted switching to non-opium cash crops because of the capital investment involved. They already know how quickly one can get into a crippling debt with (the usually Chinese) moneylenders.

According to development experts, wiser policies would attempt to ensure that villagers can grow enough to feed themselves. If they could do that, they wouldn't need to grow and sell opium to buy rice. ❑

CUSTOMS AND FESTIVALS THROUGHOUT THAILAND

Many festivals and feasts are held throughout the year and visitors should be able to attend at least one celebration during their stay. Loy Krathong, Bun Bang and Songkran are especially worth seeing.

Songkran, one of the most important festivals in the Thai calendar, comes from the Sanskrit and means the beginning of a new solar year. During this festival, people wear new clothes and visit their local *wat* to offer food to the monks. Housewives clean their homes on the eve of the festival and throw out anything old or broken so it will not bring bad luck. On the afternoon of April 13, Buddha images are bathed as part of the ceremony. Young people pour scented water into the hands of their elders and parents as a mark of respect and ask for their blessing. The Songkran custom of throwing water is thought to derive from a rain-making ceremony. According to myth, *naga* (mythical serpents) brought rain by spouting water from the seas. The more seawater they spouted, the more rain there would be, which is why, apart from it being good fun, Thai people throw water at this time of year.

Another custom during this time is the releasing of caged birds and live fish, which are sold in the markets for this occasion. This part of the festival remembers the time when the central plains of Thailand were flooded during the rainy season. After the earth had dried, little pools of water were left which often trapped young fish. Farmers caught the fish and then released them back into the water on Songkran, thereby gaining merit and preserving a food source.

FESTIVAL OF LIGHTS

Loy Krathong is one of the most beautiful Thai festivals. *Loy* means "to float" and a *krathong* is a leaf cup traditionally made of banana leaf. The festival is not strictly Buddhist, but the floating of krathongs is thought to bring good luck. When the full moon rises, the krathongs are taken to the banks of waterways, and small candles and incense sticks inside them are lit. A prayer is said as they are launched into the water. Children often swim out to collect coins that are put inside the krathongs.

PLANTING TIME ▷
The Royal Ploughing Ceremony takes place in the Sanam Luang at the time of rice planting, in May. Monks bless rice seeds that are scattered over the fields.

◁ WINTER FESTIVALS
Nearly all of the country's temples and provinces have festival days, which tend to occur during the cool season.

◁ SPRING FLOWERS
The Chiang Mai flower festival takes place on the first weekend in February. The town has a parade of floral floats and marching bands, holds beauty contests, and produces beautiful displays of the town's cultivated flora.

▽ AUTUMN CANDLES
Loy Krathong is held on the night of the full moon in the 12th lunar month (usually mid November). Small leaf boats contain candle, incense, and often a coin.

WHEN THE MOON SHINES BRIGHT

As Thailand is a Buddhist country, several religious holidays are attached to the lunar calendar and held on nights of the full moon. Visakha Puja (above) is a nationwide public holiday. It falls on the 15th day of the waxing moon in the sixth lunar month, which is May. This is the date of Buddha's birth, enlightenment and entry into *nirvana*.

On this night, devout Thais and their families gather at *wat* to hear a sermon on the life of Buddha given by the chief monk. As the moon rises, they hold a candle, incense stick and flowers between their hands, which are placed in a position of prayer. The monks of the wat then lead a procession three times around the temple *bot* (ordination hall), and the candles and incense are placed in a tray at the front of the bot. It is a solemn and moving ceremony that only a few foreign visitors will be invited to attend.

Visakha Puja has been celebrated in Thailand since 1300 AD. The ceremony was revised in 1817 and its observance was strengthened by Rama IV. During his reign, three nights were devoted to reading the *Life of Buddha*. Today, reading from this text is limited to one evening; however, several temples hold religious ceremonies that last until the dawn of the following day.

◁ NEW YEAR SPLASH
Songkran is the Thai new year festival, celebrated from 13 to 16 April. It involves lots of good-natured water throwing – so be prepared to get rather wet, if not drenched.

MAY MAYHEM ▷
The Bun Bang Fai or rocket festival is celebrated in the northeast, especially in Yasothon. Rockets are fired into the sky to bring rain at the end of the dry season.

RELIGION

A sense of spirituality sifts through most every aspect of Thai daily life. At its foundation is Buddhism, with a distinctly Thai texture

*I*n the pale light of early morning, a young saffron-robed monk walks with grave dignity along a city street, a cloth bag over one arm, a metal alms bowl cradled in the other. Silently, he opens his alms bowl to receive the offerings – not handouts – of rice and curries placed in it by ordinary Thais, who have stood for a long while before their homes awaiting his arrival. He says not a word of thanks, because, according to Buddhist tenets, he is doing them a favour, providing them a means to make merit so they can be reborn in the next life as higher beings. Turning, he continues to walk on bare feet to the next set of alms givers, following the steps of monks before him for 2,000 years.*

Buddhism – a philosophy, rather than a religion – has played a profound role in shaping the Thai character, particularly in the people's reactions to events.

The Buddhist concept of the impermanence of life and possessions, and of the necessity to avoid extremes of emotion or behaviour, has done much to create the relaxed, carefree charm that is one of the most appealing characteristics of the people. Tension, ulcers, nervous breakdowns and the like are not unknown in Thailand, at least not in places like Bangkok. But they are still fairly uncommon, in no small way due to the influence of Buddhism.

Buddhism first came to Southeast Asia from India as early as the 4th century, and was passed to the Thais by way of the Mon and Khmer kingdoms between the 10th and 12th centuries. King Ramkamhaeng introduced Theravada Buddhist influence to Thailand from Sri Lanka (Ceylon) in the 13th century, after he invited Ceylonese monks to reform the Khmer-influenced Buddhism then being practiced in his Sukhothai kingdom.

The basic form of Buddhism now practiced

PRECEDING PAGE: nearly every Thai male spends time as a monk, at any age. **LEFT:** lighted candles and lotus buds at Bangkok's Wat Benchamabophit. **RIGHT:** the golden glow of a temple's Buddha image.

in Thailand is Theravada, sometimes also called Hinayana, or "lesser vehicle". Originating in India, Theravada is also practiced in neighbouring Burma, but even a casual visitor to temples in both countries will quickly perceive differences between them. As they have done with most outside influences – Khmer temple

decorations and Chinese food, for instance – over the centuries the Thais have evolved a Buddhism of their own.

In addition to Theravada Buddhism, there is the Mahayana (Greater Vehicle) Buddhism practiced by those of Chinese descent. Their shrines can be found throughout Bangkok, and in most towns of Thailand. To the visitor stepping into a *sanjao,* or shrine, it is immediately evident that Mahayana is observed with more vigour. Incense smoke clouds the air, sticks are shaken out of canisters to tell fortunes, paper money is burned for use by deceased ancestors, bells are rung and the din of piety permeates every corner.

Temple life

Thailand's 300,000 monks typically live in a *wat,* practicing and teaching the rules of human conduct laid down by the Buddha more than 2,500 years ago. There are literally hundreds of Buddhist wat in the cities and suburbs, usually sited in serene pockets of densely-packed neighbourhoods and serving as hubs for spiritual and social life.

The term wat defines a large walled compound made up of several buildings, including a *bot* or hall where new monks are ordained, and one or more *viharn* where sermons are delivered. It may also contain a belltower, a *ho trai* (library), and *guti,* or monk meditation cells, as well as stupas, called *chedi* in Thailand. Chedi contain the ashes or relics of wealthy donors, or of important persons, emulating the Buddha whose ashes and relics were placed, by his instruction, in a mound of earth.

There may even be a school on the premises to educate the local children. And if there is any open space in temple the grounds, it is a sure bet that it will be filled with happy kids playing soccer or *takraw.*

The total number of monks in residence at Thailand's 28,000 wat varies from season to season, swelling during the rainy season, the

THE KING AS COMMONER

Not only is Buddhism deeply imbedded in the facets of daily life, but it is also intrinsic to the monarchy and the respect of it by the people.

Many of Thailand's monarchs have served as monks. King Mongkut (Rama IV) spent 27 years as a Buddhist monk prior to ascending the throne. The current king, Bhumibol, was a monk. Time spent as a monk not only strengthens the monarchy's legitimacy, but it also gives the king a commoner's experience and an understanding of how the people live. Bhumibol, for example, has long devoted himself to improving agriculture and rural quality of life.

normal time for a young man to enter the priesthood. Thai tradition requires that every Buddhist male enter the monkhood for a period ranging from seven days to six months, or even a lifetime. Regulations require that government offices and the military give a man time off to enter the monkhood; companies customarily grant leave time with pay for male employees entering the monkhood.

The entry of a young man into monkhood is seen as repayment to parents for his upbringing, and as bestowing special merit on them, particularly his mother. Since women cannot be ordained, it is the son, as monk, who also makes merit for his mother and other female relatives.

That merit advances her along the road to *nirvana*, which is attained for her, as for all Buddhists, when she acquires so much merit that she vanishes from the painful cycle of earthly death and rebirth.

Prior to being ordained, the would-be monk is shorn of all his hair. He then answers a series of questions put to him by the abbot to assure that the newcomer is in good mental and physical health. He then moves to a monks' dormitory, or to a small *kuti* or meditation house.

SIGNIFICANT NAMES

Wat that were founded by Thai royalty, or perhaps hold a special sacred status because something revered is kept within, often have names that begin with *Maha-, Rat-,* or *Ratcha-*.

in a group separate from the men, and receive whatever food has not earlier been consumed by the monks. A Buddhist monk must not only abstain from stealing, lying and idle talk, taking life, indulgence in sex, intoxicants, luxuries and frivolous amusements, he must also obey no fewer than 227 rules that govern the minutiae of daily conduct and manners. Except amongst the Dhammakaiya sect, in practice the monk usually observes ten basic rules. He can have no possessions except the yellow robe, the

While in the temple, he listens to sermons based on the Buddha's teachings, studies the *Tripitaka,* or *Three Baskets* (the teaching of Buddha in Pali), practices meditation, and learns the virtues of an ascetic life. He shares in the work of the monastery: washing dishes, keeping the quarters clean. He goes out at dawn to receive his daily food.

There are nuns who wear white robes, but they do not share the same rights as the monks, as there is no provision for the ordination of women. They live in side areas of the wat, chant

LEFT: monk's quarters at Wat Arun, Bangkok.
ABOVE: morning offerings, Wat Benchamabophit.

alms bowl and a few personal necessities. He eats two meals a day, the first early in the morning and the second before noon. A monk is forbidden to touch money, sleep on a comfortable bed, sing or dance.

Communal centre

For all its Spartan life, however, a Buddhist wat in Thailand is by no means isolated from the real world. Most wat have schools of some sort attached to them; in fact, for centuries, the only schools in most of Thailand were those run by monks. The wat has traditionally been the centre of social and communal life in the villages, with monks serving as herbal doctors, psychological counsellors, and arbitrators of disputes. Monks also play an important part in daily life, such as the blessing of a new building, or a birthday or funeral.

Except during the period of Buddhist Lent, from July to October, monks are free to travel about from one temple to another at will. Moreover, the wat are open to anyone who wishes to retire to them.

On *wan phra,* a day each week determined by the lunar calendar, Thais go to the wat to listen to monks chant scriptures

> **FOOLISH BELIEFS?**
>
> King Mongkut (Rama IV), who welcomed Christian missionaries to Siam and learned English from them, said to them: "What you teach us to do is admirable, but what you teach us to believe is foolish".

as are many funeral rites. The rites of statecraft pertaining to the royal family are presided over by Brahman priests. One of the most popular and impressive of these, the Ploughing Ceremony, takes place each May in Bangkok to signal the beginning of the rice planting season. A team of sacred oxen is offered a selection of grains. Astrologers watch carefully, as the grains that the oxen choose will determine the amount of rainfall and the degree of success or failure of the year's crops. Afterwards, the

and deliver sermons. In addition to providing monks with food, the laity earns merit by making repairs on the temple or, even better, replacing an old and derelict building with a new one. At the end of the Lenten season, groups of Thais board boats or buses and travel to distant villages to make donations, an occasion filled with as much riotous and festive celebration as solemn ceremony.

Brahman influences

Many of the Thais' non-Buddhist beliefs are Brahman in origin, and even today Brahman priests officiate at major ceremonies. The Thai wedding ceremony is almost entirely Brahman,

oxen draw a gilded plow around the field and seeds are symbolically sown (and afterwards eagerly collected by farmers to bring them luck). The head priest, after complex calculations, makes predictions on the forthcoming rain and bounty of the next harvest.

Spirits and spirit houses

The variety of *phi* (spirits) in Thailand is legion, outnumbering the human population many times over. A seductive female phi, believed to reside in a banana plant, torments young men who come near. Another bothersome one takes possession of her victims and forces them to remove their clothes in public. (The most destructive spirits apparently are only female.)

A very common sight in any town in Thailand, including sophisticated Bangkok, is a small house, generally set atop a post on a site selected after complex astrological consideration. In ordinary residences, the house may resemble a Thai dwelling; in hotels and offices, it may be an elaborate mini-temple, made of cement and painted and gilded.

In either case, these spirit houses serve as the abodes of the locality spirits. It is within their power to favour or plague the human inhabitants, so the spirit house is regularly adorned with placatory offerings of food, fresh flowers and incense sticks. If calamity or ill luck befalls the compound, it may be necessary to call in an expert to consult the unhappy spirit to determine what is wrong.

One of the most famous spirit houses in Bangkok is the Erawan Shrine, at the intersection of Ratchadamri and Ploenchit roads, adjacent the Hyatt Regency. This shrine, honouring the Hindu god Brahma, was erected by the owners during the construction of the original hotel in the 1950s, after several workers were injured in mysterious accidents. The shrine soon acquired a widespread reputation for bringing good fortune to outsiders as well.

A less well-known shrine sits in the compound of the Hilton Hotel. Its offerings consist entirely of phalluses, ranging from small to gargantuan, sculpted from wood, wax, stone or cement with full fidelity to life. They are left by women hoping to conceive a child.

To the average Thai, there is nothing inconsistent about the intermingling of such practices and beliefs with Buddhism. In the end, although deeply founded on Buddhism, Thai beliefs are both pragmatically and spiritually harmonious with the needs of the Thai people.

Protective amulets

Nearly every Thai male, and a large number of women as well, carry some sort of amulet, usually on a chain around their necks. Some wear as many as half a dozen charms to protect them from automobile accidents, gunfire, snakebite and almost any other disaster. In the provinces,

tattoos ward off evil. Astrologers are consulted regularly to learn auspicious times for weddings, important journeys, moving into a new house, and even the promulgation of a constitution or other governmental action.

Religious tolerance

A little over 90 percent of the Thai people are Buddhist, but religious tolerance is (and always has been) extended to other religions. Around 6 percent of Thais are Muslim, with the remainder Christian, Hindu and Sikh. Indeed, the national constitution declares that the king is the "upholder" of all religions.

Islam is the second largest religion in Thailand, and all over the country, but especially in the south, there are hundreds of mosques. The Thai government contributes to the repair and construction of these mosques, as well as to the Buddhist temples.

Christian missionaries have struggled for more than a century for converts in Thailand, without great success. Today, there are around 500,000 Christians in Thailand. King Mongkut suggested that Christianity had succeeded only where the indigenous religion was weak. There are pockets of Christians – notably protestants in Chiang Mai and Catholics in Chanthaburi – but few steeples amidst the chedi spires. ❐

LEFT: an extravagant and large spirit house. RIGHT: a *malai*, made of jasmine flowers; while beautiful at first, as it finally withers and decays, the malai reflects the impermanence of things and life.

IMAGES OF THE BUDDHA

From the gigantic seated Buddha at Wat Si Chum to tiny Buddhas worn as amulets, Thai artists have produced religious icons that rank among the world's greatest expressions of Buddhist art.

Images of the Buddha are devotional objects and are not considered to be works of art by their makers. When artists make an image of the Buddha, they follow specific rules – the Buddha is defined by a set of peculiar characteristics, a particular monastic garb and a series of *mudra* (attitudes, postures or gestures). The 32 bodily marks, evident at the time of the Buddha's birth, include hands that reach the knees without bending, a lion-like jaw, and wheel marks on the base of the feet. Buddhist artists have interpreted these marks according to the era in which they were working and the school of interpretation they chose to follow.

SUKHOTHAI SCHOOL

Thai Buddhist imagery was at its artistic height during the Sukhothai period (late 13th to early 15th centuries), when the smoothness and sheen of cast metals perfectly matched the graceful, elongated simplicity of the basic form. During this era, the Buddha was usually represented sitting cross-legged or with one foot forward in the "striding" position. One hand is raised in *abhayamudra* (dispelling fear). Slightly androgynous in appearance, the images also feature a flame-like *ketumula* on the crown of the head, protruding heels, flat soles and toes all the same length.

COLOSSAL CHEDI ▷
This standing Buddha in Phra Pathom Chedi, Nakhon Pathom, is said to be the world's tallest monument of its type. The relic chamber was raised to its present height of 125 metres (410 ft) in 1860.

▽ FASTING FIGURE
This statue of a fasting Buddha is in the grounds of Wat U Mong, in Chiang Mai. The wat was founded in 1371 by King Ku Na.

◁ **SPIRITUAL DETAILS**
Thai artists simplify anatomical details in their images of the Buddha to emphasise the spiritual qualities of Buddhism and to convey enigma and serenity.

SYMBOLISM OF MUDRAS

△ SUKHOTHAI SCHOOL
Buddha images at Wat Phra Sri Sanphet, Ayutthaya, are seen in the attitude of *Bhumisparcamudra* (calling the earth as witness). The images date from the 13th and 14th centuries.

▽ WHEEL OF LAW
This Chinese-style Buddha can be found in Chiang Rai, at Wat Phra Singh. The Buddha is represented in the *Vitarkamudra* (preaching mode). The gesture of the right hand symbolises the Wheel of Law.

△ RECLINING GIANT
Phra Phuttahatmongkol in Wat Hat Yai Nai is the world's third largest reclining Buddha (attaining *parinibbana* – nirvana – in death). It measures 35 metres (115 ft) from head to toe. Visitors can climb inside the Buddha's chest.

▽ SEATED IMAGE
The Temple of the Big Buddha, Ko Samui, contains a modern 12 metre (40 ft) Buddha in the attitude of *Bhumisparcamudra*.

The Buddha can be seen either sitting, standing, lying or, in Thailand, walking. Every image of the Buddha is represented in a particular *mudra* or attitude. Hand gestures in particular are key iconographical elements in representations of the Buddha:

• *Abhayamudra* is the mudra of dispelling fear or giving protection: the Buddha is usually in a standing position, the right hand raised and turned outwards to show the palm with straight fingers.

• *Bhumisparcamudra* or calling the earth as witness: this is made by a seated figure, with the right hand on the knee and the fingertips touching the ground.

• *Dharmacakramudra* means spinning the Wheel of Law: both hands are held in front of the body, with the fingertips of the left hand resting against the palm of the right hand.

• *Dhyanamudra* is the meditation mudra: the hands rest flat in the lap, one on top of the other.

• *Varamudra*, giving blessing or charity: made by the seated or standing Buddha with the right arm pointing downwards, the palm open and fingers more or less straight.

• *Vitarkamudra* is the preaching mudra: the end of the thumb and index finger of the right hand touch to form a circle, symbolising the Wheel of Law.

PERFORMING ARTS

In Thailand, performances of dance and drama are nearly one and the same.

Many performances are derived from an epic tale, Ramakien

The Thai people have combined a lively imagination, a superb aesthetic sense and a fine hand to produce some of the most detailed and arresting visual arts found in Asia. In the performing arts, Thai dance-dramas are among the world's most dazzling, with elaborate and colourful costumes, and graceful, enchanting movements.

When discussing Thai theatre, one cannot use the word "drama" without uttering the word "dance" immediately before it. The two are inseparable, the dancer's hands and body expressing the emotions that the silent lips do not. In effect, the actor is a mime, with the story line and lyrics provided by a singer and chorus to the side of the stage. An orchestra creates not only the atmosphere, but an emotive force.

It is thought that the movements of dance-drama originated in *nang yai* (shadow puppet) performances of the 16th and 17th centuries. Huge buffalo hides were cut into the shapes of characters from the *Ramakien*. Against a translucent screen, which was back-lit by torches, puppeteers manipulated these figures to tell complex tales of good and evil. As they moved the hide figures across the screen, the puppeteers danced the emotions they wanted the stiff figures to convey. It is thought that these movements evolved into an independent theatrical art.

The most popular form of dance-drama is the *khon*, performed by dancers wearing brilliantly-crafted masks. An evening's entertainment comprises several episodes from the *Ramakien*. (The entire *Ramakien* would take 720 hours to perform, slightly longer than even the most feverish theatre-goer is prepared to endure.)

The expressionless masks focus the viewer's attention on the dancers' movements, where one sees grace and control of surpassing beauty – a dismissive flick of the hand, a finger pointed in

accusation, a foot stamped in anger. The favourite character is Hanuman, in his white monkey mask, whose dance movements would tax even the strongest viewer. Only the characters of Rama, Sita and Phra Lak appear without masks, but features are kept stiff, looking very much like masks.

The most graceful of the dramatic arts is the *lakhon*. There are two forms: the *lakhon nai* ("inside" lakhon), which was once performed only inside the palace walls, and then only by women, and the *lakhon nawk* ("outside" lakhon), performed beyond the palace walls by men. Of the two, lakhon nai is the more popular entertainment.

Garbed in costumes as elaborate as their movements, the performers glide slowly about the stage, even in the most emotional moments, their faces impassive and devoid of smiles or expression. The heavily stylised movements convey the plot and are quite enchanting, though for most foreign visitors, 30 minutes is

PRECEDING PAGE: young classical dancers at the royal court. **LEFT:** a painted screen depicting *nang yai,* or shadow puppets. **RIGHT:** young dancers in traditional dance costumes.

sufficient to absorb the essentials of the play. Lakhon's rich repertoire includes the *Ramakien* and tales that have romantic story lines.

There have always been two cultures in Thailand: palace and village. The village arts are often parodies of the palace arts, but more like burlesques with pratfalls and heavy-handed humour. *Likay* is the village form of lakhon. Broad, bawdy humour is its mainstay, played out against gaudy backdrops to an audience that walks in and out of the performance at will, eating and talking and having a good time, regardless of what takes place on stage. It is possible to glimpse likay at a *wat* (temple) fair, or at Bangkok's Lak Muang, when a resident troupe is hired by a worshipper to give thanks for a wish granted. Another venue for hired performances is the Erawan Shrine, in Bangkok. A variant often seen in markets is *lakhon ling*, the monkey theatre in which the roles are played, oddly enough, by monkeys.

Bangkok's *ngiew* or Chinese opera theatres have closed their doors forever, victims of television with its unending *qong-fu* programs. Wandering in a market at night, however, one may come across a performance that has been arranged as part of the entertainment during a funeral. (Grief is experienced privately; what

INDIAN EPICS

One of the two great Indian epics informing Thai theatre and dance is the *Ramayana*. (The other is the *Mahabharata*.) From the Sanskrit meaning "romance of Rama", the *Ramayana* is the basis for many regional epic tales, including the *Ramakien* in Thailand. It's a moral tale, full of instructions and examples for leading the ethical life. In its homeland, India, the *Ramayana* has been told for 3,000 years. With the spread of Indian culture throughout Southeast Asia, the *Ramayana* has become part of the mythology of Burma, Laos, Cambodia, Indonesia, and Thailand. (See page 101 for more on the *Ramakien*.)

one shares with friends is happiness.) They may also be seen at wat fairs during the winter.

Puppet theatre has also lost most of its Bangkok audiences to television, but a few troupes remain. *Hoon krabok* puppets, similar to Punch and Judy puppets, tell the story of Phra Aphaimani. Delicately crafted, they are charming to watch. Performances are often arranged by major hotels for their guests during the year-end holiday season.

Modern Thai drama has yet to come into its own in a major way. Leading hotels produce stage plays, but they are primarily for popular entertainment – soap operas, comedies, and translations from Western plays.

Rural performances

The counterparts to the grace and beauty of classical dance are the more traditional and less structured dances performed in rural villages by farm families. Each region has a special form unique to it.

Harvest, fingernail, candle and fishing dances are performed by groups of women in village costumes. In flirtation dances, they are joined by male dancers attempting to weave romantic spells on unsmiling but appreciative partners.

MOOD MUSIC

Listen to Thai music as one would jazz, picking out one of the instruments and following it, then switching to another instrument as the mood moves one.

regard to how others are playing it. (Some say the same about Thai politics.)

Seldom does an instrument rise in uninterrupted solo; it is always being challenged, cajoled by the other instruments of the orchestra. In a sense, it is the aural counterpart to Thai classical painting, with every space filled and a number of separate strands woven together, seemingly at random but with a distinct pattern. A classical *phipat* music orchestra is made up of a single reed instrument, the oboe-like *phinai*, and a vari-

Music

Classical Thai music eludes many finely-tuned Western ears. To the uninitiated, it sounds like a mishmash of contrasting tones without any pattern. To aficionados, it has a very distinct rhythm and plan.

Thai music is set to a scale of seven full steps, but it is normally played as a pentatonic scale (the scale of *Auld Lang Syne*). The rhythm is lilting and steady, with speeds varying according to section. Each instrument plays the same melody but in its own way, seemingly without

ety of percussion instruments. The pitch favours the treble, with the result that the music sounds airy rather than stentorian. The pace is set by the *ching*, a tiny cymbal, aided by the drums beaten with the fingers. The melody is played by two types of *ranad*, a bamboo-bar xylophone and two sets of *gong wong*, tuned gongs arranged in a semicircle around the player. Another type of orchestra employs two violins, the *saw-oo* and the *saw-duang*. It is usually heard accompanying a Thai dance-drama.

The *ja-kae*, a stringed instrument similar to a Japanese *koto*, sits flush with the floor and is often played as a solo instrument in the lobbies of some of Bangkok's larger hotels and restau-

LEFT: dance-drama students learning the moves.
ABOVE: *phipat* ensemble, with oboe-like *phinai*.

rants. A separate type of orchestra performs at a Thai boxing match to spur the combatants to action. It is composed of four instruments: the ching, two double-reed oboe-like flutes, and a drum. It plays a repertoire entirely its own.

Originating in the countryside, but having found a permanent home in the city as well, are the *klawng yao* or long drums. They are thumped along with gongs and cymbals as accompaniment to group singing. Never played solemnly, they lend an exuberant note to any occasion – and for a Thai, it doesn't take much of an excuse to have an occasion. It may be a procession on the way to ordain a new monk, a

bus trip upcountry, or a *kathin* ceremony in the late autumn, when groups of Buddhists board boats to travel upriver to give robes to monks at the end of the three-month lenten season.

Literature

Thais have always placed a heavy emphasis on oral tradition, and it's a good thing, too, because most of its printed classical literature was completely destroyed by the flames of Ayutthaya's destruction in 1767.

Moreover, as tropical insects have a particular relish for the palm-leaf paper on which manuscripts were traditionally written, books are manifest examples of the Buddhist tenet that

nothing is permanent. The classical works existing today came from late-night sessions during the reigns of Rama I and II, when scholars delved into their collective memories and, on breeze-cooled palace verandas, recreated an entire literature.

At the heart of Thai literature is the *Ramakien*, the Thai version of the Indian classical tale, *Ramayana*. This enduring story has found a home in the literature of every Southeast Asian nation. In Thailand, it forms the basis of a dance-drama tradition. Understanding it allows one to comprehend a wide variety of dramatic forms, its significance for Thailand's monarchs who have adopted the name Rama as their own, and its role as model for exemplary social behaviour.

The *Ramakien* is the vividly told tale of the god-king Rama and his beautiful wife, Sita, paragon of beauty and virtue, and a model for all wives to follow.

Sita is abducted by the nasty 10-headed, 20-armed demon king Tosakan, who imprisons her in his palace on the island of Longka (Sri Lanka), importuning her at every turn to divorce Rama and marry him. With his brother Phra Lak, Rama sets off in pursuit, stymied by mammoth obstacles that test his mettle. Along the way, he is joined by the magical white monkey-god, Hanuman, a mischievous but talented general who is one of the Thais' favourite characters. Hanuman and his army of monkeys build a bridge to Longka. After a pitched battle, Tosakan is killed, Sita is rescued, and everyone lives happily ever after.

Another classical work, pure Thai in its flavour and treatment, is *Khun Chang, Khun Phaen*, a love triangle involving a beautiful young woman with two lovers – one a rich, bald widower, and the other, a poor but handsome young man. This ancient soap opera provides a useful insight into Thai customs, manners and morals of the Ayutthaya era.

Written by Sunthorn Phu, the poet laureate of the early 18th century, *Phra Aphaimani* is the story of a rebellious prince who refuses to study to be king, instead playing the flute, much to the disgust of his father. After numerous exciting adventures, this prodigal son returns home to don the crown and rule his father's realm. ❏

LEFT: traditional *nang yai* performance of *Ramakien*.
RIGHT: masked characters from *Ramakien*.

The Ramakien

If Thai literature has a long tradition and a short history, there can be no better illustration than the *Ramakien*, the Thai version of the Indian legend *Ramayana*, an epic tale that arrived in what later became Thailand some 1,000 to 2,000 years ago, with the first wave of Buddhist missionaries from Sri Lanka.

As was true for many early cultures around the world, in Southeast Asia there were few written languages, or limited literacy, and the history, myths and stories of the various peoples were passed down orally by skilled storytellers from generation to generation. In retelling the *Ramayana*, the characters and tangled plot remained, but the tale changed, becoming identifiably Thai as character names were changed and various Buddhist ceremonial elements were added to what was, originally, a Hindu text. It was not until when the Thai capital was in Ayutthaya – named for the primary city in the *Ramayana* – that the work was finally transcribed. Sadly, only fragments of that version of the epic story remained following the sack of the city in 1767 by the Burmese, who burned virtually all of the written literature. Today, it is a required part of the school curriculum, so it is an allegory of the triumph of good over evil that is familiar to virtually every Thai.

The story opens in India with a demon, who was given great physical strength by Shiva, the Hindu lord of the universe. Betraying the trust, the demon rolled up the surface of the Earth like a carpet, removing all signs of life so he could be the sole survivor. Shiva called on the powerful god Vishnu the Preserver for vengeance, who turned himself into a white boar, decapitating the demon with his tusks and restoring life to the planet.

Upon returning to his celestial home in the Cosmic Ocean, Vishnu meditated until a lotus appeared, unfolding to reveal a young man who was taken to Shiva as the future king. Shiva dispatched the god Indra to find a new city for the king, travelling on a white elephant named Erawan, leading a host of angels to Earth. A city called A-Yu-Da-Ya was founded, named for four hermits who resided there, praying for 4,000 years, a paradisiacal metropolis with a bejeweled palace, sumptuous gardens, and 56,000 maidens to cater to the king's every whim.

And this is merely the start of the story. Immodest or subtle the *Ramakien* is not, and in this lush and exuberant excess lay much of its popularity.

Battles were of such cosmic proportion that a collaboration between Steven Spielberg and Walt Disney would be required to convey them properly. Fire streamed from a god's third eye to vaporise demons caught debauching celestial maidens. A magical snake arrow was sent to coil itself around an enemy and elevate him into a fearsome thunderstorm. Hanuman was able to levitate and fly, aiding his beloved master, Phra Ram, the king of Ayutthaya (and a reincarnation of Vishnu), to defeat the dreaded King Thotsakan of Longka (Sri Lanka), the 10-headed villain who had kidnapped Phra Ram's wife. It is an imaginative and captivating tale that blends romance, high adventure, and fantasy,

three key elements that some say are essential to understanding life in Thailand today. In fact, in the earliest written Thai version, there were 60,000 verses, 25 percent more than were in the Sanskrit original transcribed in Sri Lanka. A performance of the 138 acts, or episodes, involving more than 300 characters, lasted longer than 700 hours. Today, popular episodes may be seen in briefer performances of Thai classical dance, *khon*.

Artistic representations of the plot and characters may also be seen in murals and bas-relief throughout the country, from stone carvings at Prasat Hin Phimai and other Angkor-period temples in northeastern Thailand to wall paintings at Bangkok's oldest temple, Wat Po. ∎

ARTS AND CRAFTS

With numerous cultural and aesthetic influences from around Asia, it's no wonder that Thailand's creative arts and crafts have nearly a universal appeal

As is true of its architecture, music, religion, and cuisine, the handicrafts of Thailand are the clever result of outside ingredients being stirred by skilled practitioners over centuries to form something clearly and uniquely Thai. Someone with some knowledge in the field may say, "That bit's Chinese...and

that bit's Indian...and that bit's European," yet it must also be concluded that the effect, the end-product, is entirely home-grown.

Thailand is renowned worldwide as a centre of flourishing arts and crafts – one of the reasons it's a shopper's delight – and the best-known arguably are the textiles, most notably the colourful, shimmering silk. Villagers in the northeast had woven and worn silk for centuries, but it wasn't until after World War II – when the leading silk industries in Japan, China, Italy, and France were destroyed – that Thailand emerged as a primary source. Credit is given to an American expatriate, Jim Thompson, who organised provincial weavers, introduced long-

lasting chemical dyes and improved looms, and took samples of the gleaming cloth to New York. There, the costumes were made from his silk for a new Broadway musical, *The King and I*. *Vogue* magazine followed along and within a short time, a world market had been created. Most of the raw silk is still being produced on northeastern silkworm farms and manufactured by a number of companies, in addition to the prominent Jim Thompson stores. Thailand also produces excellent cotton garments and, from the hill tribes in the north, skirts and other items with remarkable embroidery. The best are from the Lisu tribe.

Thailand is equally famous for its gold and silver jewellery and gemstones, now the country's sixth-largest export category (behind the far less glamourous computer parts, garments, integrated circuits, rubber, and sugar). It commands a part of the global jewellery market rivalled only by Sri Lanka and India. In the Ayutthaya and early Bangkok eras, gold's use in a variety of royal household items, such as cosmetic jars and tableware, as well as on thrones and ceremonial objects, brought honour to the owners and to the artisans who were commissioned by royal and other wealthy families. Today, most of the gold jewellery sold is less imaginative, taking the form of heavy chains purchased as a hedge against a fluctuating currency and as a status item.

More affordable items in great variety are fashioned from silver. Not so long ago, the silver used came from melted-down Indian, Burmese and French coins from Indochina. Nowadays, most of it is imported and then pounded into delicate and ornately crafted trays, boxes, bowls, and other containers noted for their raised designs. The finest work is done in the north and usually sold in shops in Chiang Mai and Chiang Rai.

Most of the gems sold in Thailand today are imported from neighbouring Burma and Cambodia, the bulk arriving in Thailand by sometimes questionable means. A hundred years ago, gems were set in gold and silver jewellery noted more for the artistic fittings than for the stones themselves. Precious stones also played a prominent role in the decoration of crowns and other royal implements. The Nine Gems of the Brahman faith – diamonds, rubies, emeralds, yellow sapphires, blue sapphires, garnets, moonstones, zircons, and the cat's eye – were thought to have special powers.

Contemporary Thai jewellery, some of it adapted from traditional Thai motifs, still utilises a variety of stones, but more and more, they are being purchased

CRYSTAL POWER

In the Ayutthaya period, generals rode into battle on elephants, wearing sashes encrusted with jewels the generals believed would give them protection and strength.

mainly in the north – is fashioned by highly skilled and patient artists who laboriously apply layer after layer of a resin to containers most often made from wood or woven bamboo. Some of the finest work may require several weeks or months. This art form also is used to decorate temple and palace doors, which are further illuminated by paintings depicting Buddhist legends and tales from the epic *Ramakien*.

Still another craft from China, related to lacquering, is mother-of-pearl decoration. Most of the

without settings and resold by the buyers in the west. The Khmer gem market in Trat, near the Cambodian border, and Burmese markets in Mae Hong Son offer an exciting alternative to the high-pressure Bangkok "factories", where quality is often poor and the prices are ridiculous. Unless you know gems, beware. The Tourism Authority of Thailand warns visitors not to buy gems from a source recommended by anyone they have just met.

Lacquerware is another Burmese-Chinese import, and much of that made today – again,

iridescent shell comes from the Gulf of Thailand and adorns lacquered boxes, furniture, musical instruments and statuary. One of the more stunning examples is on the soles of the feet of the huge reclining Buddha figure in Bangkok's Wat Po, but displays may also be seen in Chinese restaurant tables and chairs.

Clay pots found in the northeast have been carbon-tested back to 3600 BC. Yet even with that long history, ceramic handicrafts generally don't get the attention they deserve. Best known, perhaps, is the pale-green celadon used for everything from ash trays to dinner settings to large vases, and the enamelled terracotta ware with floral and Buddhist decorations, called

LEFT: finely woven silk is sold in countless hues and colours. **ABOVE:** lacquer hats on Royal Barge oarsmen.

bencharong, another imported Chinese art improved upon.) Realistic reproductions of those early clay pots from the Bronze Age may also be found in antique stores and at a museum shop at Ban Chiang, and replicas of old stone sculpture are offered in Ayutthaya.

A word about antique stores. Real antiques cannot be taken out of Thailand without a permit from the Department of Fine Arts. In recent years, the government has been going after museums and private collectors around the world, demanding – and getting – many old religious artifacts back. Buddha images are sold widely, but they are for local use, and unless you

can wear it around your neck, its export is strictly forbidden, even if it was manufactured last week. Also, Thai craftsmen are ingenious when it comes to copying something, from a Versace shirt to a Rolex watch. Many of the "antiques" offered are no such thing.

Another handicraft, distinctly Thai, is ornamental woodcarving. In this, the Thais have no peers, developing over time traditional motifs such as the lotus and other flowers, mythological creatures from India, serpents and dragons from China. Usually this decorative work is found on furniture and in the adornment of religious and royal buildings, royal barges and carriages, and in a modest style even in the

humblest homes. When visiting a *wat*, look up toward the eaves and don't just pass through an open door, stop to examine it; some what you see will surprise. When Thailand was covered by forest, such carving was at its peak and much of this painstaking carving has survived the wicked Thai climate. However proficient the product, it is unfortunate that most of the woodwork sold today is made from rattan and bamboo. Teak is now an endangered plant.

A category of handicrafts that never really went away and now is attracting attention are the objects of everyday rural life. Baskets whose origins were strictly utilitarian – to winnow, store, cook and carry rice to the table, to transport crops from the fields, even to tote small children – are now regarded by many as "folk art." Some of the woven containers, using thinly cut bamboo and other plants, are lightly lacquered for strength. Others are given modern handles and serve Western women as purses.

Brightly painted wooden "bells," or clappers that are hung around the necks of water buffaloes, baskets used to catch fish in the flooded rice paddies, kitchen implements made from coconut shells and carved wood, machetes used in the fields, coconut graters, large earthen water jars, even the worn wood and bamboo yokes used by villagers and street vendors to carry their heavy baskets of food to market – everything "authentic" is now in great demand. Poor northern hill-tribe villages, induced by the government and international organisations to stop growing opium, are now supplementing their meagre subsistence economy with the production of embroidered shoulder bags and native silver jewellery. There is even a market for the crossbows and old-style flintlock rifles with which the mountain tribesmen once hunted small game. Because so much is being produced quickly to satisfy the new demand, much of the quality is slipshod. A visit to the National Museum or the Jim Thompson House in Bangkok – Thompson was an avid collector blessed with impeccable taste – will reveal appropriate guidelines. The present Queen of Thailand, under her self-help organisation called SUPPORT, also sponsors a number of provincial workshops, with the product so identified and sold in many stores. ❑

LEFT: cooking items have both utility and simple elegance. **RIGHT:** silver working near Chiang Mai.

ARCHITECTURE

The temples of Thailand are top on most visitors' agendas. Beyond the temple, the traditional Thai house reflects a nearly perfect adaptation to the environment

If culture is an expression of the best of a society, architecture must occupy society's zenith, for it is defined by the designs and spaces created for home life, worship, and work. As is true in much of Thailand's artistic expression, many of the finest temples, palaces and other buildings in the kingdom show the influences of several cultures, yet all are identifiably and unquestionably Thai.

Indian, Khmer, Burmese, and Chinese architectural styles have had substantial effect through the centuries, but there is no mistaking the swooping multi-tiered roof lines, the distinctly ornamental decorations and blinding colours, the stunning interior murals and lovingly crafted and gold-adorned Buddha images, and the miles of interlocking waterways.

Sadly, many of those canals, called *khlongs*, have been replaced with traffic-jammed roadways, but thousands of the classical Thai structures may still be seen. There are approximately 30,000 temples in Thailand, and hundreds of these compounds established for the veneration of Buddha are worth visiting. So, too, the several royal residences, some blending western neoclassical features, the result of visits to Europe by early Thai kings and the European expatriate's presence in Thailand.

The temple

Any study of Thai architecture begins with the temple, or *wat*, whose traditional role was as a school, community centre, hospital, and entertainment venue, as well as the place where the lessons of Buddha were taught. Every part of a Thai wat has symbolic significance. The capitals of columns are shaped either like water lilies or lotus buds; the lotus symbolises the purity of Buddha's thoughts – it pushes through the muck to burst forth in extraordinary beauty.

Some of these compounds like Wat Po in Bangkok are vast, while others in rural villages

PRECEDING PAGE: traditional house, Nonthaburi, north of Bangkok. LEFT: from a mural at Wat Bowon Niwet, Bangkok. RIGHT: Sri Lankan-style temple stupa.

are quite modest. They generally include an assembly hall, or *bot*, where monks perform ceremonies, meditate, and sermonise. A second assembly hall, or *viharn*, is where lay people make offerings before a large Buddha figure. Dome-shaped *chedi* are where relics of the Buddha may be housed. There may also be tower-

ing, phallic spires, called *prang*, epitomised by the Wat Arun on the banks of the Chao Phraya in Bangkok, opposite the Grand Palace.

As different as the wats may be, there are similarities, or themes. Symbolism abounds in the ornate decoration. Bots are bounded by eight stones, believed to keep away evil spirits, an example of how animist beliefs coexist with Buddhism. Roof peaks are adorned with *chofa*, the curling, pointed extensions at each end that represent the *garuda*, the vehicle of Vishnu. In its claws it holds two *naga*, mythical serpents that undulate down the eaves.

The garuda is a royal symbol, imported from India. Companies bearing it on their building facades operate "by royal appointment". At the top of a chedi may be a stylised thunderbolt sign of Vishnu, ancient Hindu lord of the universe.

The various outside influences are evident in other ways. Most of the ancient remains in northeastern Thailand reveal a heritage shared by the more famous Angkor Wat in neighbouring Cambodia, as this region was once a part of the sprawling Khmer empire. In the north, many of the older chedi are Burmese in style, constructed during that country's occupation of what was then the kingdom of Lanna.

Window panels and murals in Bangkok dating to the early 18th century cross many cultural

Traditional dwellings

Homes for ordinary people share the same sensitive treatment as those for the exalted. Thai-style teak houses, with their inward-sloping walls and steep roofs, seldom fail to charm with their airiness and their marvellous adaptation to tropical climates.

Like the wat, the Thai house has gone through a centuries-old evolution. Some trace the style to southern China, origin of today's Thai population and where many ethnic Thais still live. Steep roofs, sometimes multi-layered like the wats that dominated village life, with only a few rooms or one large, divided room elevated on

---

DOMESTIC DESIGNS

The design of the traditional Thai dwelling is well suited for Thailand's tropical weather: often on stilts to rise above flooding, steep roof lines for shedding rain, materials that retain coolness, and ventilation that takes advantage of breezes.

The architectural styles of traditional homes vary depending upon region, although the characteristics noted above are common throughout. In the flat central plains north of Bangkok, an open verandah is often the focus of home life as an outside living space. To the north, where the temperatures are cooler, design of ventilation and living spaces often retains warmth. In most traditional homes, the central, innermost room is both sleeping area and home for ancestral spirits.

Outside most Thai homes and commercial buildings is the spirit house, a miniature dwelling intended for the natural spirits that are found on the land. These spirit houses can be plain and modest, or gaudy and quite large.

---

and international boundaries, and are decorated with mythological figures from the Indian *Ramayana*, Chinese dragons, Indian nagas (or serpents) and foreign merchants wearing distinctly European garb.

"They are gorgeous," summarised Somerset Maugham, the British novelist and traveller who frequently visited Southeast Asia in this century and wrote extensively about both Thailand and Southeast Asia. "They glitter with gold and whitewash, yet are not garish; against that vivid sky, in that dazzling sunlight, they hold their own, defying the brilliancy of nature and supplementing it with the ingenuity and playful boldness of man."

pilings distinguished the earliest homes. The structures were positioned to take advantage of prevailing winds, and many of the components were prefabricated, then fitted together with wooden pegs.

In time, the elevation above the ground increased to protect the home from flooding and unwanted animal visitors, while producing a space beneath the house for keeping livestock or to be used for daily work such as weaving. Such homes are common in villages throughout Thailand today, although in urban areas, nearly all homes are now more western in design and steadfastly anchored to the ground. Most of the early homes were made of native woods such as teak and bamboo, materials that are still used today, although teak is now on the nation's endangered list. The Jim Thompson House is a good example. Numerous other examples line the banks of the silvery network of canals that crisscross the Thonburi suburbs.

In Thailand's southern provinces, a different design evolved, reflecting the warmer, wetter climate. Here, the pillars were shorter, there was no exterior verandah, and windows had hinged shutters that closed from the top during torrential monsoon rains. With the arrival of Western traders and missionaries in the 18th century, and with early trips to Europe by Thai monarchy in the 19th, Western-style buildings joined the traditional Thai structures along both sides of the Chao Phraya River, the centre of Bangkok's government and commerce.

Much of this early architecture remains today, including a part of the Oriental Hotel and the original French embassy next door, both designed by European architects. Shophouse architecture in the Sino-Portuguese style uses stout walls and often ornate window and roof treatments that were the hallmark of a type of housing once preferred by Chinese shopkeepers. As in yesteryear, the downstairs serves as a place to market one's goods; the upstairs is the family home. Shophouses at Tha Chang boat landing on the Chao Phraya, to the northwest of the Grand Palace, are good examples.

The Vimarnmek, in Bangkok's Dusit district and built entirely of teak but appearing decidedly more Western than Thai, and the Italianate palace built by King Chulalongkorn at Bang Pa-In near Ayutthaya offer ample evidence of Thailand's passionate embrace of Western styles that continues to this day. (The present king and queen live in a modern palace with satellite dishes on the roof.)

Most contemporary architectural efforts show little regard for the past, as hundreds of new high-rises go up each year in the cities, while tract homes and look-alike rows of townhouses are erected for the country's growing middle class in the suburbs and small towns. During the building boom of the 1980s, many architects seemed to be trying to outdo each other. See the "robot building" on Bangkok's Sathorn Road, its sides decorated with outsized nuts and bolts,

and also the headquarters for *The Nation* newspaper in Bangkok's Bang Na district, looking like two stylised grand pianos turned on their sides. At the same time, Corinthian columns and curvilinear banisters appeared on the balconies of virtually every new townhouse, appearing not only incongruous but in many cases ridiculous.

Seeing the past

Nothing beats seeing the surviving traditional structures in their natural settings, of course, but for the traveller with limited time, a visit to the Ancient City, half an hour south of Bangkok, is a must. (See *Outside of Bangkok*, page 177.)

Here, arranged over 80 hectares (200 acres) set out in roughly the shape of Thailand itself, are more than 100 full-sized and reduced-scale replicas of the country's most important monuments, temples, and palaces, as well as a typical turn-of-the-century commercial street, a floating market, and khlong-side village. Visitors in Bangkok should also consider hiring a long-tailed boat for a tour of the Thonburi khlongs and visits to the Jim Thompson home, which was constructed from three traditional homes moved from Ayutthaya, and the Kamthieng House on the grounds of the Siam Society, a simple but elegant home transported from Chiang Mai. ❑

LEFT: ornate ceiling of a wat, or temple. RIGHT: traditional architecture depicted in a temple mural.

TEMPLE ART AND ARCHITECTURE

The wat *plays a vital role in every community, large and small. They are also home to the country's 300,000 monks. For many visitors, they are one of the most memorable sights of Thailand.*

A typical Thai *wat* (loosely translated as monastery or temple) has two enclosing walls that divide it from the secular world. The monks' quarters or dormitories are situated between the outer and inner walls. This area may also contain a bell tower (*hor rakang*). In larger temples the inner walls may be lined with Buddha images and serve as cloisters or galleries for meditation. This part of the temple is called *buddhavasa* or *phutthawat* (for the Buddha).

Inside the inner walls is the *bot* or *ubosth* (ordination hall) surrounded by eight stone tablets and set on consecrated ground. This is the most sacred part of the temple and only monks can enter it. The bot contains a Buddha image, but it is the *viharn* (assembly hall) that contains the principal Buddha images. Also in the inner courtyard are the bell-shaped *chedi* (relic chambers), which contain the relics of pious or distinguished people. *Salas* (rest pavilions) can be found all around the temple; the largest of these areas is the *sala kan parian* (study hall), used for saying afternoon prayers.

POPULAR TEMPLE ICONS

During the 10th century, the Thai Buddhist and Khmer-Hindu cultures merged, and Hindu elements were introduced into Thai iconography. Popular figures include the four-armed figure of Vishnu; the *garuda* (half man, half bird); the eight-armed Shiva; elephant-headed Ganesh; the *naga*, which appears as a snake, dragon or cobra; and the ghost-banishing giant Yak.

SINGHA HEAD ▷
Fierce-looking bronze *singha* (mythical lions) stand guard outside the ordination hall of Wat Phra Kaeo in Bangkok.

△ **WAT PHRA KAEO**
The Temple of the Emerald Buddha is one of the most impressive examples of Thai temple art, and one of the world's great religious buildings.

THE ART OF MURAL PAINTING

△ SYMBOLIC ROOF DECOR
The *bot* (ordination hall) roof of Wat Po in Bangkok is adorned with a carving of a mythical *garuda* (bird-man) grasping two *naga* (serpents) in its talons.

CHEDI ▷
Wat Po has 95 *chedi*. They contain the ashes of royalty, monks and lay people. The four large chedi are memorials to Thai kings.

◁ THE CLOISTERS
The cloisters of Wat Po are lined by 394 seated bronze Buddhas dating from the reign of Rama I.

THE LIBRARY ▷
Phra Mondop (the library), Wat Phra Kaeo. Libraries or scripture repositories *(hor trai)* are built high up above the ground in order to protect the religious scriptures from flood damage.

Thai murals are found on the interior walls of *bot* (ordination halls) and *viharn* (assembly halls). Usually painted in solid colour without the use of perspective or shading, the murals are used by monks as meditation and teaching aids. Not many murals over 150 years old remain intact in Thailand, as they were painted straight onto dry walls and therefore could not survive the ravages of the Thai climate.

The mural above comes from Wat Phumin in Nan, northern Thailand. It was painted in the mid-19th century as part of restoration carried out by Thai Lu artists. The murals depict *jataka* (Buddha's birth) tales and also illustrate aspects of northern Thai life.

Murals dating from this period commonly contain scenes from everyday life, local myths, birds, animals and plants, as well as religious themes.

Mural painting was at its height during the reign of Rama III of Thailand (1824–51), who encouraged a huge program of construction and restoration of Buddhist temples. Of special note from this period are the fine murals in Wat Thong Thammacht in Thonburi, painted in 1850.

CUISINE

You bet it can be quite hot. It can also be cool. There is nothing apathetic about Thai cuisine, which most likely explains its appeal around the world

Good food in Thailand is found in fascinating places, from seafood markets to floating restaurants to hawker stalls. Wherever one travels in the country, aromas and attractive food presentations are very appealing.

Thais take time over their meals, talking and making an entire evening of the affair. Since dishes are placed in the middle of the table and shared by all, it makes sense to take several friends so that one can order more dishes and sample more tastes.

While it's true that there are very spicy regional dishes – certain southern Thai curries are notable – not all Thai food is hot and spicy. Generally, an authentic Thai meal will include at least one very spicy dish, a few that are less hot, and some that are comparatively bland, flavoured with only garlic or herbs.

Usually, purely Siamese creations will take their place alongside adapted Chinese and Indian dishes, influences easy to spot.

Thai food is eaten with rice. Traditionally, rice has always been the most important dish in any Thai meal. In times past, Thais would eat rice with just a few condiments, or in times of hardship with nothing more than fish sauce.

Curries and sauces have become more sophisticated and more important as Thailand has become more affluent, and now it is commonplace for the central rice bowl to be accompanied by a selection of other dishes, often including chicken, pork and fish.

At the start of the meal, heap some rice onto a plate and then take a spoonful or two of curry. It is considered polite to take only one curry at a time, consuming it before ladling another curry onto the rice. Thais eat with the spoon in their right hand and fork in their left, the fork being used to push the food onto the spoon for transport to the mouth. Chopsticks are used only for Chinese noodle dishes.

PRECEDING PAGE: the cuisine of Thailand is known for both taste and aesthetics. **LEFT:** only the freshest of produce is used. **RIGHT:** grinding fresh chillies the traditional way with a mortar.

There seems to be some confusion among those who have sampled their first Thai meals abroad regarding the proper condiments to add to the food. Contrary to popular belief, peanut sauce, an "indispensable" addition to nearly every dish in Thai restaurants found in Western countries, is really of Malayan and Indonesian

origin and is used in Thailand only for *satay*. Similarly, instead of salt, Thais rely on *nam plaa,* or fish sauce, for their salt intake, often serving it with chopped chilli peppers to make a spicy dip.

Spicy and hot dishes

Kaeng means curry. The group includes the spiciest of Thai dishes and forms the core of Thai cooking.

Among the green curries is *kaeng kiaw wan kai,* a gravy filled with chunks of chicken and tiny pea-sized eggplants. A relative, *kaeng kiaw wan nua,* has slices of beef in it. *Kaeng luang,* a category of yellow curries, includes *kaeng karee*, an Indian-style curry which is made with chicken or beef. *Kaeng pet* is a red curry with beef or pork. A close relative is *penaeng nua*, a southern-style "dry" curry with a characteristic coconut flavour. *Kaeng som* is cooked in a hot-sour soup generally filled with pieces of either fish or shrimp.

Among the fiery favourites is *tom yang kung*, a lemony broth teeming with shrimp. It is served in a metal tureen that is wrapped around a mini-furnace heated by charcoal, so that it remains piping hot throughout the meal. *Po taek* (The Fisherman's Net Bursts) is a cousin of *tom yang kung*, containing squid, mussels, crab and fish.

Yam is a hot and spicy salad combining meat and vegetables. Particularly popular in northern and northeastern Thailand, it is one of the hottest dishes available.

Mild curries

Tom kha kai, a thick coconut-milk curry of chicken chunks with lemon grass, is milder than the average Thai dish and a great favourite with foreign visitors.

Plaamuk tawt kratiem phrik tai is squid fried with garlic and black pepper. When ordering, ask that the garlic (*kratiem*) be fried crispy (*krawp krawp*). The dish is also prepared with fish. *Kaeng joot* is a non-spicy curry, a clear broth filled with glass noodles, minced pork and mushrooms. *Nua pat nam man hoi* is beef fried in oyster sauce garnished with chopped shallots and green vegetables.

Muu pat priaw wan – sweet and sour pork – is probably of Portuguese origin and may have arrived in Thailand via Chinese émigrés. It is also possible to order it in most restaurants with red snapper (*plaa krapong*), beef (*nua*) and shrimp (*kung*).

Ho mok talay is a seafood casserole of fish and shellfish chunks in a coconut mousse, steamed in a banana-leaf cup.

Kaeng matsman is a southern-style curry. It consists of pieces of beef or chicken, combined with potatoes, onions and peanuts in a mildly-spiced curry sauce flavoured with coconut milk.

Of Chinese origin but having secured a place in Thai cuisine is *plaa jaramet nung kiem bueh*, steamed pomfret with Chinese plum and bits of ginger. *Pu paat pong karee* is pieces of unshelled, steamed crab smothered in a curry sauce laden with shallots.

Hoi maleng pu op moh din is a thick, savoury coconut milk gravy filled with mouth-watering mussels cooked in a clay pot.

Noodles and others

Most noon-time dishes are derived from Chinese cuisine, and noodle dishes, a Chinese invention, have been adopted by the Thais. Those served at street-side, open-front shops come in two varieties: wet and dry. When ordering either, specify the wetness by adding the word *nam* (wet) or *haeng* (dry) to the dish's name. Thus, a soupy *kuay tiaw* would be *kuay tiaw nam*.

Kuay tiaw is a lunchtime favourite, a soup of noodles with balls of fish or slices of beef. *Baa mii* is egg noodles with pieces of meat and vegetable. Some rice-based lunchtime dishes are also Chinese and include *khao man kai*, boiled rice topped with slices of chicken and chopped ginger; *khao moo daeng*, a similar dish with red pork slices; and *khao kaa moo*, stewed leg of pork with greens on rice.

Then, there are the variants using noodles. *Kuay tiaw rat naa* is broad white noodles boiled and served in a dish with morning glory. *Pat tai* is noodles fried in a wok with tofu, chopped vegetables and dried shrimp. *Pat siew* is of white noodles cooked with thin slices of beef, fresh greens and soy sauce. Served late at night and early in the morning are two soup-like dishes filled with boiled rice. The rice in *khao tom* is watery and augmented with minced pork and shallots.

A close relative is *jok,* in which the rice has been cooked until the liquid becomes viscous like a porridge. Into this mix is tossed ginger, coriander, slices of meat and generally a fresh egg.

Each of Thailand's four primary regions has its own cuisine. Northern and northeastern dishes are related to Lao cooking, which is eaten with gluti-

The sausage is roasted over a fire fuelled by coconut husks, which impart an aroma to the meat. Generally prepared hygienically, it is best to buy it only at better restaurants. Beware the *phrik kii nuu* chilies that lurk inside waiting to explode on the tongues of the unwary.

Khao soy originated in Burma. This egg noodle dish is filled with chunks of beef or chicken and is lightly curried in a gravy of coconut cream, and then sprinkled with crispy noodles and served with chopped red onions and lime.

Nam phrik ong combines

nous rice. Southern food is flavoured with the tastes of Malaysian cooking. Central cuisine corresponds closely to the food in Thai restaurants abroad.

Northern cuisine

Northern specialties are generally eaten with *khao niaw* or sticky rice, which is kneaded into a ball and dipped into various sauces and curries. *Sai oua* (also called *naam*) is an oily, spicy pork sausage that epitomises northern cooking.

LEFT: cooking giant prawns in a street market.
ABOVE: like many Asian foods, Thai meals are a balance of spicy and cool, *yin* and *yang.*

minced pork with chilies, tomatoes, garlic and shrimp paste. It is served with crisp cucumber slices, parboiled cabbage leaves, and pork rind.

Laap is a minced pork, chicken, beef or fish dish normally associated with northeastern cuisine. While northerners traditionally eat it raw, northeasterners cook it thoroughly. It is served with long beans, mint leaves and other vegetables that contrast with its pungent flavour.

Kaeng hang lay, another dish of Burmese origin, is a relatively mild northern dish which is popular with foreign visitors. Pork and tamarind flesh give this curry a sweet-and-sour flavour. The curry is especially suited to dipping with a ball of sticky rice.

Northeastern cuisine

Northeastern food is simple and spicy. Like northern food, it is eaten with sticky rice, which *Isaan* (northeastern) diners claim weighs heavily on the brain and makes one sleepy.

Kai yang, or northeastern roasted chicken, has a flavour found in no other chicken. Basted with herbs and honey, it is roasted over an open fire and chopped into small pieces. Two dips, hot and sweet, are served with it.

Nua yang is beef dried like a jerky. One can chew for hours on a piece and still extract flavour from it. *Som tam* is the dish most associated with the northeast. It is a spicy salad

made from raw shredded papaya, dried shrimp, lemon juice and chilies.

Southern cuisine

Khao yam is rice with *kapi* (a paste made of fermented shrimp). *Pat pet sataw* looks like a lima bean but has a slightly bitter yet pleasant flavour. This dish is cooked with shrimp or pork, together with a sprinkling of chilies.

Khao mok kai, essentially a Thai *biriani*, lays roasted chicken on a bed of saffron rice and mixes it with ginger, which has been fried lightly to make it crisp.

Khanom chin is found throughout Thailand but is thought to be of Mon origin. Tiny bits of minced beef are stewed in a red sauce and then served atop rice noodles. It is generally sold in markets in the early morning.

Nam phrik kung siap, or dried prawn on a stick, is grilled and served with chilies, *kapi* (fermented shrimp paste) and lime.

Kaeng tai plaa was created by bachelor fishermen who wanted a dish that would last them for days. Fish kidneys, chilies and vegetables are blended in a curry sauce and stewed for up to seven days. *Ho mok khai plaa* is made from fish roe that are stirred into a coconut mousse, wrapped in leaves and steamed.

Chinese

Most Thai Chinese are of Teochow descent, so the typical Thai Chinese restaurant serves Teochow dishes with a distinct Cantonese flavour. Teochow is famed for dishes such as thick shark's fin soup, goose doused in soy sauce, and roasted duck with fresh green vegetables. Fruits and teas are integral parts of every meal. Poultry, pork and seafood are essentials, as are a huge variety of fungi and mushrooms.

Other Chinese cuisines are well represented in Thailand. Shanghai food is typified by dishes that are fried in sesame or soy sauce for a long time, making them sweeter and oilier than the other cuisines.

Libations

The local beer is Singha, which is quite strong and, if taken to excess, can cause a fearsome hangover. Western beers such as Carlsberg, Kloster and Heineken are also widely available The local cane whiskey is called *mekhong* and packs a wallop for the unsuspecting. A bit sweet, it is drunk neat, or more popularly, mixed with club soda and lime.

Thailand has its own special coffee, made with a thick black melange of coffee, chicory and who knows what else, strong enough to set a dead person's heart beating. In the markets, Thais fill the bottom of the glass two fingers high with sweetened condensed milk and pour the coffee over it. Ask for it black (the iced version is called *oliang*) in order to gain the full flavour of this exotic mixture. Tea is usually served with a considerable amount of condensed milk, and thus is quite sweet. ❐

LEFT: cheap and ready offerings. **RIGHT:** some of Thailand's hearty sweets are of Portuguese origin.

Sweets

In Bangkok, desserts and sweets (*khanom*) come in a bewildering variety – from light concoctions through to custards, ice creams and cakes, and an entire category of confections based upon egg yolks cooked in flower-scented syrups. Bananas and coconuts grow everywhere in Thailand, and if they were to be removed from the list of ingredients available to the khanom cook, the entire edifice of Thai dessert cookery would come crashing down.

The heavier Thai confections are rarely eaten after a big meal. Desserts, served in small bowls,

Many of these sweets are made amazingly inventive, putting familiar ingredients in surprising surroundings. You may finish off a rich pudding, for example, before realising that its tantalising flavour came from crisp-fried onions.

Excellent khanom of various types can also be bought by the bag-full from roadside vendors, who prepare them fresh on portable griddles. One such sweet is the **khanom beuang**, or "roof-tile cookie", which consists in one version of an extremely thin crispy shell folded over taco-style, and filled with coconut, strands of egg yolk cooked in syrup, spiced and sweetened dried shrimp, coriander and a sugary cream.

are generally light and elegant. **Kluay buat chii**, a popular after-dinner sweet, consists of banana chunks stewed in sweetened, slightly salted and scented coconut cream, and served warm. Another favourite, **thap thim krawb**, is made from small balls of tapioca flour, dyed red and shaped around tiny pieces of water chestnut. These are served in a mixture of sweetened coconut cream and ice.

Anyone walking through a big Bangkok market is bound to come across a sweets vendor selling anything from candied fruits to million-calorie custards made from coconut cream, eggs and palm sugar. They are generally sold in the form of three-inch squares wrapped in banana leaves. Such snacks are good for a quick boost of energy.

Sangkhya maphrao awn is a magnificent custard made from thick coconut cream, palm sugar and eggs, then steamed inside a young coconut or a small pumpkin. **Khao laam** is glutinous rice mixed with coconut cream, sugar and either black beans or other goodies, and cooked in bamboo segments, then slit open and the rice eaten. **Taeng thai nam kati** consists of a Thai melon cut into small cubes and mixed with ice and sweetened, flavoured coconut cream. **Khanom maw gaeng** is a custard-like sweet, again made with coconut cream and eggs, but this time with soybean flour to thicken it. **Kluay khaek** uses bananas sliced lengthwise, dipped in coconut cream and flour, and deep fried until is crisp. Try **katit**, a rich coconut ice cream. ■

PLACES

*A detailed guide to the entire country, with principal sites
cross-referenced by number to the maps*

Diversity and contrast characterise both Thailand's people and its geography. Within an area of 514,000 square kilometres (199,000 sq mi) – roughly the size of France – are tropical rain forests, broad rice plains and forest-clad hills that lie between 5 degrees and 21 degrees north of the equator, in the centre of the geographical jigsaw puzzle of Southeast Asia.

There is an abundance of natural resources. Under the canopies of its rain forests, a wide variety of flora and fauna abound: iridescent kingfishers, parakeets, pheasants, hornbills, flying squirrels and lizards, gibbons, hundreds of species of butterflies, and nearly a thousand varieties of orchids. A cornucopia of fruit grows as well, wild in the jungles, or tended carefully on small family holdings and in larger plantations. Nearly 30 varieties of fruit are here: banana and plantain, coconut, durian, orange, lime, mango, papaya, breadfruit, jackfruit, mangosteen, rambutan, lychee and lamyai abound.

Elevations of the terrain run from sea level along the 2,600-kilometre-long (1,600 mi) coastline to a peak of 2,596 metres (8,517 ft) in the north, a region of hills clad in teak forests and valleys carpeted in rice, fruit trees and vegetables, and bordered by Burma and Laos.

The northeast is dominated by the arid Khorat Plateau, where farmers struggle to cultivate rice, tapioca, jute and other cash crops. With strong cultural affinities with neighbouring Laos and Cambodia, the region is rimmed and defined by the Mekong River.

In the central plains, monsoon rains transform the landscape into a vast hydroponic basin, which nourishes a sea of rice, the country's staple and an important export. Through this region flows the Mae Nam Chao Phraya – *mae nam* means river – carrying produce and people south to Bangkok, washing rich sediment down from the northern hills, and during the monsoons, flooding the rice fields.

The south of Thailand runs down a long, narrow arm of land leading to Malaysia. An area strongly influenced by Malay culture and Islam, this southern isthmus is peppered by rubber and palm-oil plantations that alternate with rice and fruit trees. ❏

PRECEDING PAGES: monks on a northern road; Silom area, Bangkok; dusk near Chiang Rai; limestone islands, Krabi. **LEFT:** Wat Prathat Chom Kitti, Chiang Saen.

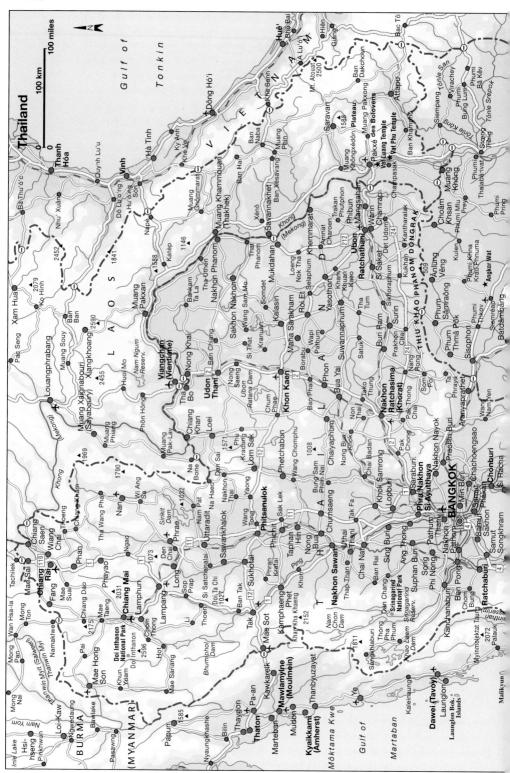

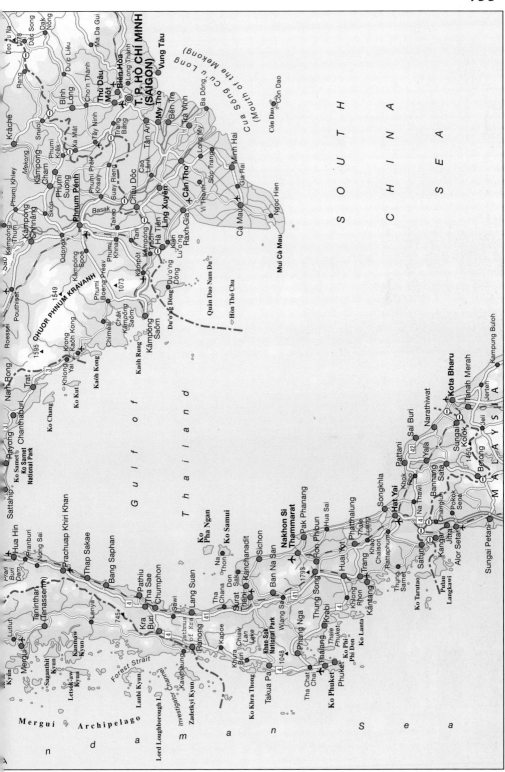

BANGKOK

A city of wild plums or angels it is not. Bangkok is rather a city of uncanny chaos anchored by the grandest of palaces

The Thai people call Bangkok, which means City of Wild Plums, Krung Thep, or the City of Angels. To be correct, however, Bangkok's full name is Krungthepmahanakhon Amonrattanakosin Mahintharayutthaya Mahadilokphop Nopphosin Ratchathaniburirom Udomrathaniwetmahasa Amonphiman Awatansathit Sakkathatiya Witsanukamprasit, or in English, City of Angels, Great City of Immortals, Magnificent City of the Nine Gems, Seat of the King, City of Royal Palaces, Home of the Gods Incarnate, Erected by Visvakarman at Indra's Behest.

Bangkok began as a city of canals and elephant paths. When motor vehicles redefined urban transportation, the old thoroughfares were simply filled in or paved over for the new wheels.

The population of Bangkok has grown nearly ten-fold since World War II. Today, about one out of every eight Thais live in Bangkok. The second-largest city in the country is just one-fortieth its size. Growth in Bangkok seems out of control, an impression most substantiated by the city's world-class traffic snarls. At first glance, the greater metropolitan area of over 15 million people appears as a bewildering melding of new and old and indeterminate, and of exotic and commonplace and indescribable, all tossed together into a gigantic urban fuss. This, in fact, is what Bangkok is. If Bangkok seems to lack order, it is because it never has had such, save for Rattanakosin, the royal core of the city where the kings built their palaces. Moving outwards from this artificial island, defined by canals and the Chao Phraya, the city becomes increasingly less and less organised.

Chaos in construction began in earnest during the late 1950s, and a large part of what assaults the eye today started then – the lofty office buildings, the air-conditioned supermarkets and shopping centres, nearly all the broad streets and international hotels, the endless blocks of shophouses following what one critic called the egg-crate principle of design. Before this boom, the now-fashionable residential streets on either side of Thanon Sukhumvit and Thanon Phaholyothin were rice paddies.

Yet despite the growth, large areas around the old Grand Palace, the Chinese district, and across the river in Thonburi (Thailand's capital before Rattanakosin and now included in the Greater Bangkok Metropolitan Area) were, for the time, hardly touched by the building fever. But the pause was momentary, of course. New construction between Chinatown and Lumpini Park, for example, is replacing the squat buildings with towering glass ones, some of them seeming to take forever to complete. ❐

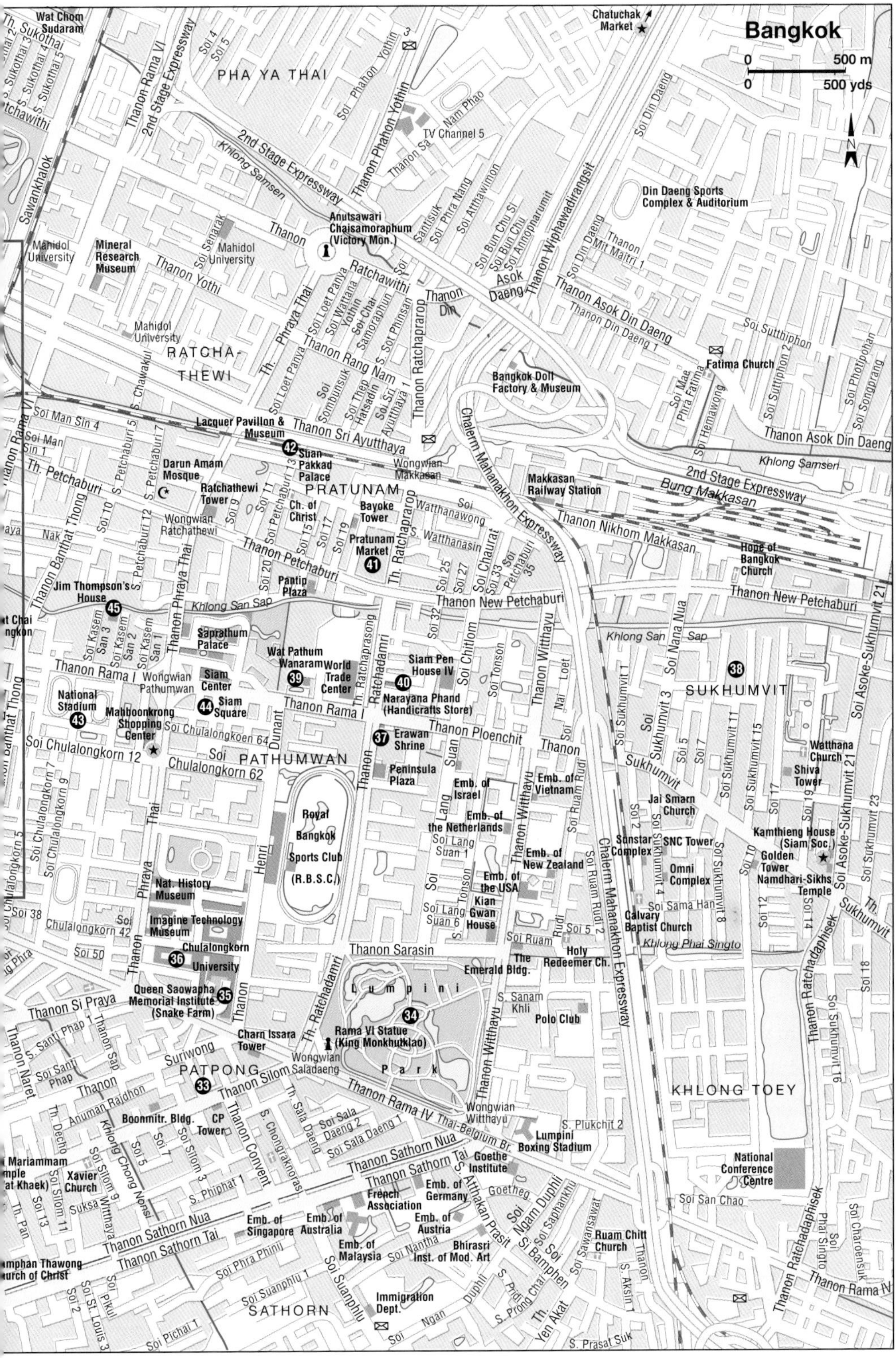
Bangkok
0 500 m
0 500 yds
N
PHA YA THAI
RATCHA-THEWI
PRATUNAM
PATHUMWAN
SUKHUMVIT
KHLONG TOEY
PATPONG
SATHORN
Chatuchak Market
Wat Chom Sudaram
TV Channel 5
Anutsawari Chaisamoraphum (Victory Mon.)
Mahidol University
Mineral Research Museum
Din Daeng Sports Complex & Auditorium
Fatima Church
Bangkok Doll Factory & Museum
Lacquer Pavilion & Museum
42 Suan Pakkad Palace
Darun Amam Mosque
Ratchathewi Tower
Ch. of Christ
Bayoke Tower
Wongwian Makkasan
Makkasan Railway Station
Hope of Bangkok Church
Pratunam Market 41
Pantip Plaza
Jim Thompson's House 45
Saprathum Palace
Wat Pathum Wanaram 39
World Trade Center
Siam Pen House IV 40
Narayana Phand (Handicrafts Store)
38
Siam Center
National Stadium 43
Mahboonkrong Shopping Center
44 Siam Square
37 Erawan Shrine
Peninsula Plaza
Watthana Church
Shiva Tower
Royal Bangkok Sports Club (R.B.S.C.)
Emb. of Israel
Emb. of the Netherlands
Emb. of Vietnam
Jai Smarn Church
Kamthieng House (Siam Soc.)
Golden Tower
Namdhari-Sikhs Temple
Emb. of New Zealand
Emb. of the USA
Kian Gwan House
Sunstar Complex
SNC Tower
Omni Complex
Calvary Baptist Church
Nat. History Museum
Imagine Technology Museum
36 Chulalongkorn University
Queen Saowapha Memorial Institute 35 (Snake Farm)
The Emerald Bldg.
Holy Redeemer Ch.
Lumpini Park
34
Rama VI Statue (King Monkhutklao)
Polo Club
Charn Issara Tower
33
Boonmitr. Bldg.
CP Tower
Lumpini Boxing Stadium
Goethe Institute
National Conference Centre
Xavier Church
French Association
Emb. of Germany
Emb. of Singapore
Emb. of Australia
Emb. of Austria
Emb. of Malaysia
Bhirasri Inst. of Mod. Art
Ruam Chitt Church
Immigration Dept.
Thanon Rama VI
2nd Stage Expressway
Khlong Samsen
Thanon Phahon Yothin
Thanon Yothi
Thanon Ratchawithi
Thanon Phraya Thai
Thanon Rang Nam
Thanon Ratchaprarop
Thanon Din Daeng
Thanon Wiphawadirangsit
Thanon Asok Din Daeng
Thanon Mit Maitri 1
Thanon Sri Ayutthaya
Thanon Petchaburi
Thanon Asok Din Daeng
Bung Makkasan
Thanon Nikhom Makkasan
Chalerm Mahanakhon Expressway
Thanon New Petchaburi
Khlong San Sap
Thanon Rama I
Thanon Ploenchit
Thanon Sukhumvit
Soi Asoke-Sukhumvit 21
Thanon Witthayu
Thanon Henri Dunant
Thanon Ratchadamri
Soi Chulalongkorn 12
Soi Chulalongkoen 64
Chulalongkorn 62
Thanon Sarasin
Khlong Phai Singto
Thanon Ratchadaphisek
Thanon Si Praya
Thanon Silom
Suriwong
Thanon Rama IV
Thai-Belgium Br.
Wongwian Saladaeng
Wongwian Witthayu
Thanon Sathorn Nua
Thanon Sathorn Tai
Soi Ngam Duphli
Soi Suanphlu
Thanon Convent
Thanon Naret
Thanon Anuman Rajdhon
Khlong Chong Nonsi
Th. Yen Akat
S. Prasat Suk
Soi San Chao
Soi Sama Han
Soi Ruam Rudi
Soi Tonson
Soi Lang Suan
Soi Chitlom
Soi Nana Nua
Soi Sukhumvit 3
Soi Phrom Chai
Soi Sala Daeng
S. Chongraknoras
Soi Kasem San 1
Th. Sukothai
Thanon Banthat Thong
Sawankhalok

THE OLD ROYAL CITY

Map, page 143

At the centre of Rattanakosin, the old royal city, is the Grand Palace and the mystical Emerald Buddha of Wat Phra Kaeo. Just outside the palace grounds are the sacred Wat Po and Lak Muang

Although it's difficult to perceive from ground level, a bird's eye view would reveal that the old royal city occupied an oval island, part natural, part artificial. The western bank of this island is formed by Bangkok's defining river, **Mae Nam Chao Phraya**, and the eastern side by an artificial canal or moat, Khlong Lot. After a brief sojourn across the river in Thonburi, in the early 1780s Rama I set out to construct a protected city on the Ayutthayan model by using the artificial canal to create an island at a bend in the river, what is called **Rattanakosin**. Until the 1932 revolution, this district housed all the royal quarters, governmental administrative offices and most royal temples.

A bird's eye view would also reveal that this inner island, Rattanakosin, is only the western half of a larger oval island. Outer Rattanakosin is bordered on the east by yet another canal, Khlong Ong Ang, which is renamed Khlong Banglampoo north of the Rathadamnoen intersection. Long settled by merchants and artisans, this outer part of Rattanakosin still holds reminders of old Bangkok.

Grand Palace

The southern side of Thanon Na Phra Lan is lined by the white crenellated walls of the **Grand Palace ①** (open daily; admission fee). The only entrance and exit to the complex is in the middle. On the right are the Royal Household offices. To the left is the ticket booth.

The first stop within the palace grounds is **Wat Phra Kaeo Ⓐ** (Temple of the Emerald Buddha), a shrine for Thai Buddhists that is comparable in religious importance to Mecca or St. Peter's. Passing though the gate, you will confront 6-metre-tall (19 ft) demon statues inspired by the *Ramakien*, the Thai version of the Indian epic *Ramayana*. You must walk the glittering length of the *bot* to reach the entrance to it. In front are scattered Chinese-style statues, which function as stand-ins for incense offerings to the **Emerald Buddha** inside. The small, clothed, 75-centimetre-tall (30 in) jadeite Emerald Buddha is perched high on an altar, shielded by a nine-tiered umbrella and enclosed in a glass case.

Non-Buddhists may be disappointed by the small size of the Emerald Buddha, but its power and importance stems from the image's mystique, which should be instantly apparent from the demeanour of the pilgrims inside the bot. (Don't wander around. Sit down promptly with toes pointed behind.) Supposedly made in Sri Lanka, the image apparently was discovered in Chiang Rai in the early 1400s. Credited with miraculous powers, over the centuries it shifted to many locations as a prize of war. While still a general, the future Rama I spirited the image away after sacking Vientiane in 1779 and placed it here in 1784. The removal is still fresh in the minds of Laotians.

OPPOSITE: Wat Phra Kaeo and the Emerald Buddha.
BELOW: the Emerald Buddha.

*The Emerald Buddha
is graced with three
costumes, which
change with the
seasons: a crown and
jewelry in summer; a
gilded robe during
the rainy season; and
a golden cloak in
winter. The change is
done in a ritual
ceremony by the king.*

Exiting the bot, note three buildings to the north aligned on a broad, raised marble terrace. On the far left is the golden **Phra Si Ratana Chedi Ⓑ**, erected by King Mongkut (Rama IV) to house a shard of the Buddha's breastbone. At the centre, tiled with green glass and topped with a crown-like tiered roof, is the **Phra Mondop Ⓒ**, a library of Buddhist scriptures. Always closed, it is surrounded by statues of white elephants. On the right is the **Prasad Phra Thep Bidom Ⓓ** (Royal Pantheon), which is open on some religious holidays. Inside are life-sized bronze and gold statues of all the Bangkok kings.

From this terrace are good views of the royal mausoleum, bell towers and eight *prang*, or Khmer-style towers. The walls of the cloister surrounding the temple courtyard are painted with vivid and detailed scenes from the *Ramakien*. The story begins in the middle panels of the northern wall and proceeds counterclockwise. Even if unfamiliar with the saga of Rama and Sita, it's enjoyable to examine the slices of ordinary life depicted, such as puppet shows, household chores, children playing ancient games, opium smokers and gamblers.

Wat Phra Kaeo's exit in the southwest wall leads to the Grand Palace's temporal sector. Although the royal family decamped to the more modern Chitralada Palace to the north in the Dusit district in 1946, most of the Grand Palace's labyrinth of structures and gardens remains closed to the public. Some official ceremonies are still held here.

What visitors can glimpse of the Grand Palace is a little of the complex's northern fringe. Directly in front is the unassuming **Amarin Vinitchai Throne Hall Ⓔ**, the northern-most of a three-building group. The three-roomed throne hall served as the bed-chamber for Rama I and as a residence for Rama II and Rama III. In the early days of Bangkok, it also served as a court of justice, where

BELOW: Dusit Maha Prasad, and throne in Chakri Maha Prasad.

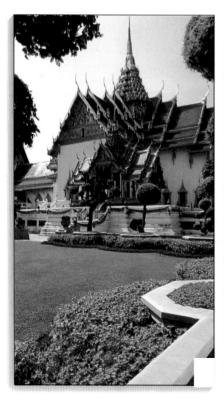

cases were judged by the king or his ministers. Each new king has spent his first crowned night here. The gold-topped red poles standing at the entrance once tethered the elephants of visiting dignitaries. Inside, a throne sits atop a boat-shaped base. In the old days, this throne and base were hidden by a screen of curtains. At the appointed time, conch shells blew and the curtain was drawn back to reveal the seated king.

To the right (or west) is the grander, perhaps incongruous **Chakri Maha Prasad ⑤**. An audience and reception hall, it was designed by an English architect on neoclassical lines on the request of King Chulalongkorn. Court elders were disturbed by this strong dose of Westernisation and persuaded the king to add the three Siamese-style towers to the roof. The top floor contains ashes of Bangkok kings.

On the left-hand side of this building is a door – always closed to the public – that leads to the Inner Palace. This was once the domain of the king's scores of concubines, and no adult male, save the king, could enter it. Nowadays, the modern king sometimes hosts receptions here for high-ranking diplomats. A cooking school for upper-class Thais also operates here.

To the far right, on the western side of the courtyard, the building with the four-tiered roof and nine-tiered spire is the **Dusit Maha Prasad ⑤**. Dating from 1789, it is a splendid example of classical Thai architecture. The balcony on the north wing contains a throne once used for outdoor receptions. Traditionally, deceased kings and queens lie here in state until their cremations on Sanam Luang. The exquisite pavilion in front of Dusit Maha Prasad was built to the height of the king's palanquin, so that he could alight from his elephant and don his ceremonial hat before proceeding to the audience hall.

Map, page 143

Dusit Maha Prasad holds Rama I's teakwood throne, adorned with inlaid mother-of-pearl.

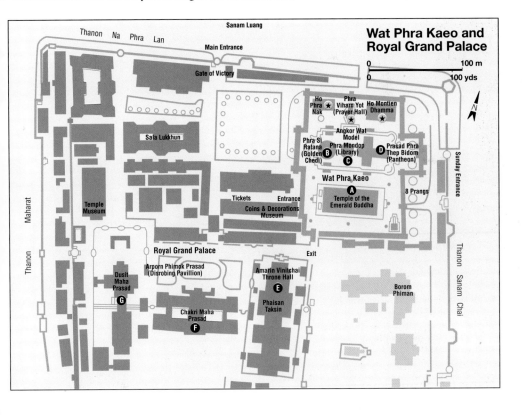

Wat Phra Kaeo and Royal Grand Palace

Detail from Wat Po.

Wat Po

Exiting from the Grand Palace, turn left on Thanon Maharat and walk south past Thanon Thai Wang (which runs into the Tha Tien river-taxi dock, after passing a fresh market surrounded by turn-of-the-century shophouses). Turn left (that is, east) onto Soi Chetuphon and head to the entrance gate of **Wat Po ❷** (open daily; admission fee), Bangkok's largest and oldest temple, predating the Chakri dynasty. Its first buildings were constructed in the 16th century. If the Grand Palace seemed a preserved museum piece, these sprawling grounds are a living, breathing organism that is still the home to several hundred monks.

Most tours only tarry at the temple housing the **Reclining Buddha** in the western courtyard. Virtually filling a chapel, the brick-and-gold-plated statue is 46 metres (150 ft) long and 15 metres (50 ft) high. It depicts the dying Buddha on his side, awaiting his escape to *nirvana*. Observe the soles of his feet, which are inlaid with intricately wrought mother-of-pearl. The 108 designs are the ancient symbols by which an enlightened one can be identified.

In the eastern courtyard, screened by cloisters, is the large beautiful bot, Wat Po's principal praying and ordination hall. Girdling its base are sandstone panels with 152 superbly carved scenes from the *Ramakien*. Nearby vendors sell rubbings of them. Yet more *Ramakien* tales are depicted in mother-of-pearl on the teak doors.

The courtyard is strewn with chedi and stone statues in strange positions. They are *rishi*, or Hindu hermits, and they were once used to instruct illiterate people on the nature of illnesses and the massage methods for treatment. Wat Po still runs an herbal medicine school. Continue to the far eastern wall to find the massage hall, where an expert, vigorous one-hour massage costs foreigners a couple

of hundred baht. Those who wish to study can take 30-hour courses, which are regularly offered in English.

Rejoining Thanon Maharat and walking south past the Ministry of Commerce and police station, you'll shortly find yourself at the very southern tip of the inner Rattanakosin oval. The landmark here is the Charoen Rat Thirty-One Bridge, built in 1910. While the reinforced concrete structure itself is nothing special, note the monkeys holding up the plaster balustrade. This was the first, but certainly not the last, bridge with *Charoen* in its name. A favourite Thai word, it means "growth" or "development". The new King Vajiravudh (Rama VI) was 31 years old the year it was built. Follow the road as it turns north and becomes Thanon Rachini. On the other side of Khlong Lot, Thanon Atsadang runs parallel. Shophouse fans may want to cross the canal at Phra Phitak Road to peer at the canal-side Atsadang structures, which were probably built late in the 19th century. Note the European style of pediments and doorway decorations. Early in this century, this was a fashionable precinct of car showrooms and boat-engine shops. As is apparent, it is still a thriving market area, but the run-down shophouses now house truck-transport companies and warehouses.

Lak Muang

If one heads on Thanon Na Phra Lan in the opposite, or easterly, direction, at the far edge of Sanam Luang is an enclosed, gilded tree trunk that is the official centre of Bangkok. Erected by Rama I in the late 1700s, this is **Lak Muang ❸**. Similar to the Shiva *lingam* that represent potency, the Lak Muang is the capital's foundation stone, where the guardian deity lives and from where the city's power emanates. (Many Thai cities have such a spiritual anchor.)

Map, page 146

Lak Muang, the foundation pillar.

BELOW: vendors at Wat Po, and exterior of Lak Muang.

Sheltered by a graceful, recently renovated shrine, Lak Muang and its attendant spirits are believed to have the power to grant fertility and other wishes. Floral offerings are piled high around the pillar, and the surrounding air is laden with incense. Devotees bow reverently before pressing a square of gold leaf to the monument. In an adjoining *sala*, classical dance and music are usually underway by a resident troupe hired by supplicants whose wishes have been granted.

Retracing your steps back to the inner island, turn northward and walk to the Ministry of Foreign Affairs, formerly the **Saranrom Palace**. This entire area was once the site of the "palaces" of members of the much extended royal family. Most were torn down during the Chulalongkorn era to make way for useful office buildings. Built in 1868, Saranrom is one of the few to survive.

Once a royal mini-zoo and crocodile garden, the front the palace today is a soothing, monument-studded public garden. The memorial at the centre honours one of Chulalongkorn's 92 concubines. On a boat journey to the summer palace in Bang Pa-In, she fell into the river and drowned before scores of peasants. They were unable to save her because commoners couldn't touch royalty.

In early May, Sanam Luang is the site of the Royal Ploughing Ceremony, which is the official start of Thailand's rice-growing season. Sanam Luang's use as a kite-flying field began when King Chulalongkorn, an avid kite-flyer, okayed using the royal field for kites.

Sanam Luang

Directly north of the Grand Palace is a disk of clipped lawn, **Sanam Luang** ➍ (Royal Field). Another by-product of the destruction of the "second king's" palace, it was established as a cremation ground for royalty. In a city so short of green spaces, it now provides desperately needed space for impromptu soccer games, jogging, kite flying and children's games. It is also the natural venue for public protests. Massacres during pro-democracy demonstrators in 1973, 1976 and 1992 took place in and around Sanam Luang.

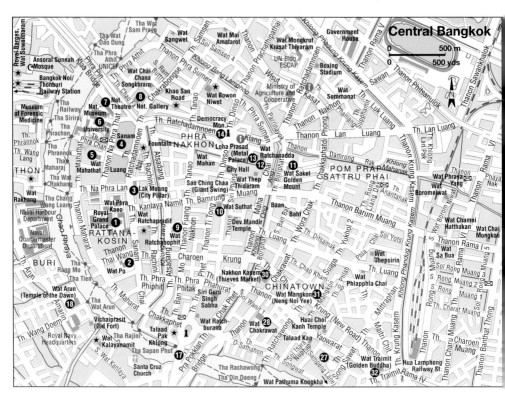

Map,
page 146

Turn right onto narrow Thanon Phra Chan (which runs into the Tha Prachan/Wat Mahathat river-taxi dock). The sidewalk becomes progressively denser with vendors of new and antique amulets, featuring Buddha, famous monks and occult objects. The amulets are guaranteed to fend off bullets, create fortunes, or induce potency or fertility. The vendors' trail eventually leads to the entry to **Wat Mahathat ❺** (open daily). The buildings here are undistinguished, but one of two universities for monks is in the wat. It is also an important meditation centre. On Buddhist holidays, it blooms with herbal medicine vendors and stalls.

Just south are former royal office buildings that belong to the government Fine Arts Department and **Silpakorn University**, Thailand's first fine-arts school. Silpakorn sometimes sponsors art exhibits of both Thai and foreign artists. But if wanting to be certain to see some contemporary art, turn right where Thanon Na Phrathat ceases at Thanon Na Phra Lan. The Na Phra Lan Cafe has art on the walls, pretty food and a handsome, artsy clientele.

Continue along Thanon Na Phra Lan to discover two groups of 19th-century shophouses. The L-shaped Tha Chang group, near the end of the road at the Tha Chang cross-river ferry jetty, is the better-preserved. A century ago, there were about 10,000 shophouses on Rattanakosin; today there are probably fewer than 1,000. Thai builders were inspired by the Sino-Portuguese models of colonial Singapore and Malaya. Bangkokians were smitten with the stucco and cement materials as much as the idea of harmonious facades. Tha Chang's 33 two-storied units have sloped roofs with pediments, pilasters and balconies at the end units. Walls and windows are adorned with Chinese Baroque touches. Like shophouses elsewhere on the island, these do not have the ground-floor open colonnades characteristic of Singapore and Malaysia.

Not coincidentally, **Thammasat University ❻** monopolises much of the western stretch of Sanam Luang. It was founded as a law university in 1932 by Pridi Panomyong, an architect of the revolution and star-crossed figure of modern Thai history. Thammasat retains a radical reputation, and its students are always at the forefront of popular protests. Foreign visitors are welcome to stroll the grounds, although they may be shocked by the dilapidated buildings and ill-supplied libraries. Bear in mind that, after Chulalongkorn University, this is the second-oldest and second-most prestigious university in the country.

A treasure house of both Thai and Southeast Asian riches is the **National Museum ❼** (open Wednesday–Sunday; tel: 224 1370; admission fee), comprising a half-dozen old and new buildings.

One of oldest is at the rear of the compound, the Wang Na, dating from 1782. The name refers to the palace of the "second king". His vast palace once extended across to Khlong Lot and up to the Grand Palace. It was occupied by the second-in-line to the throne. When his heir-apparent attempted a violent overthrow, however, King Chulalongkorn abolished the office in 1887 and tore down most of the buildings. The Wang Na today is one of the remnants; it houses *khon* masks, gold and ceramic pieces, weapons, musical instruments and an elephant riding-seat of ivory.

BELOW: Buddha image from the National Museum.

In front of the Wang Na's entrance is the similarly aged **Buddhaisawan Chapel**, once the second king's private place of worship. Today it shelters the bronze, Sukhothai-style Phra Buddha Sihing. Like the Emerald Buddha, it has a tangled history as one of the spoils of war and is reputed to have miraculous powers. On the day before the Songkran festival every year, it is paraded through the streets. Note the chapel's beautiful, well-preserved murals of Buddha's life. The two modern buildings in the rear of the complex cover an awesome chronological spectrum of Thai and Asian art. The southern building has the oldest pieces, representing the Dvaravati and Srivijaya periods, as well as examples of Khmer, Lopburi and Chaiya sculpture. Later periods are represented in the northern building. Besides ceramics and sculpture from Sukhothai and Ayutthaya, there are articles from the Lanna and Chiang Saen kingdoms.

One of the museum's most valuable possessions, familiar to every student of Thai history, is located elsewhere: a black, stone stele that is controversially accredited to King Ramkamhaeng and which is believed to bear the oldest sample of Thai script. If true, it would date from 13th-century Sukhothai. The stele's message describes or prescribes a kingdom of peace and prosperity. It's located in the same building with the ticket office, formerly an open-sided audience hall. Here can also be found some bronze tools from Ban Chiang, the archeological site in the northeast that indicates humans settled there 5,000 years ago. The museum has guided tours on several mornings a week in English and one day each week in French, German and Spanish. Check with the Tourist Authority or the museum for times.

The **National Gallery** ❽ (open Wednesday–Sunday; admission fee), on the northern tip of Sanam Luang on Thanon Chao Fa, was once the national mint.

BELOW: Buddhaisawan Chapel.

Today, the National Gallery shelters a few gems of 20th-century Thai art and the Thai film archive. It occasionally hosts shows of foreign and Thai artists. If time is limited, however, it's more rewarding to visit the National Museum immediately south.

Map, page 146

East of the Grand Palace

To the east of the Grand Palace is the first of Rattanakosin's canals. Before crossing over the canal, notice immediately to the north what, yes, appears to be a golden pig lording over a construction site. The Pig Memorial was built in 1913 as a birthday present from friends to Queen Saowapha, Chulalongkorn's favourite wife. (She was born in the Year of the Pig.) The construction site is part of an on-going archeological search for city walls built by Rama I.

Wat Ratchabophit **9** (open daily) is easily recognisable by its distinctive doors, carved in relief with jaunty soldiers wearing European uniforms. Built in 1870, the design was intended to meld Western and Thai art forms. Note the unusual layout, with a tall, gilded chedi at the centre of the courtyard and enclosed by a circular cloister. Built into the northern side of the yellow-tiled cloister is the bot, itself covered in brightly-patterned, multi-hued tiles.

Exterior detail of Wat Ratchabophit.

The bot's windows and entrance doors are works of art. Tiny pieces of mother-of-pearl have been inlaid in lacquer, in an intricate rendition of the insignias of the five royal ranks. In a recess beside one of the doors is a bas-relief of a god named Khio Kang – or Chew Hard, meaning "the one with long teeth" – who guards this sanctuary. Four chapels, connected to the central gallery by small porticoes, further enlarge this colourful temple. The doors open into a startling temple interior. Instead of murals and the customary shadowy interior of Thai temples, this has been rendered like a Gothic chapel, with all the light and delicacy of a medieval cathedral if it were infused with a Versailles salon.

BELOW: gilded stucco decor, Wat Ratchabophit.

Since the temple was begun before King Chulalongkorn's visits to Europe, he may have been inspired by his visit to the British colonial city of Singapore. The outside garden is studded with memorials, many modelled after pint-sized Christian churches. These enclose the ashes of Chulalongkorn's numerous concubines and children. The wat occupies the corner of Ratchabophit and Fuang Nakhon roads.

Continue north up Thanon Faung Nakhon and turn right at the second corner onto Soi Sukhat. Two short blocks east is **Wat Suthat ⑩** (open daily), built at the turn of the 18th century. The outdoor compound is populated by pagodas and statues, mostly brought from China as ship ballast in the early 19th century. The statues include bronze horses, Chinese scholars and homely *farang* (foreign) sailors wearing goofy hats. Wat Suthat's fame stems from the enormous dimensions of its *ubosot* and *viharn*, respectively the ceremony and main halls. Both have galleries of gilded Buddha images. Dominating the viharn is an 8-metre-tall (26 ft) meditating Buddha cast in 14th-century Sukhothai. Brought to Bangkok down the Chao Phraya on Rama I's orders, the statue is now surrounded by well-preserved 19th-century murals tracing the last 24 lives of Buddha. Note the depictions of fabulous sea monsters

and foreign ships on the columns of the viharn. The doors are one of the wonders of Thai art. Carved to a depth of five centimetres (2 in), they follow the Ayutthayan tradition of floral motifs, with tangled jungle vegetation hiding small animals. Accounts vary as to whether Rama II designed or carved the doors himself. When they were completed, he ordered the chisels thrown into the river so that the fine carving could not be duplicated.

Self-explanatory rule at all temples.

Immediately north of Wat Suthat is a giant red wooden structure. This is the 200-year-old **Giant Swing**, once the centrepiece of an annual ceremony honouring the Hindu god Shiva. A bench bearing teams of two to four standing young men was suspended from the crosspiece. When the swing was swung, the men would attempt to catch with their teeth a bag of gold suspended from on high. Accidents were so common that the ceremony was abandoned in 1933, although lately city officials have considered reviving it as a tourist attraction.

Just northwest of Giant Swing is the city's only Brahman temple. The three holy halls are about the same age as the swing and are still used. Although Thailand is a devoutly Buddhist state, Hindu Brahman rituals accompany many ancient royal ceremonies, with Brahman priests always at hand.

The stretch of road running eastward from this very busy intersection is called Bamrung Muang. It was one of the first paved roads in Bangkok. Today it is noisy, polluted, traffic-choked and frequently bereft of sidewalks. It can be hell to negotiate if not nimble-footed and quick of reflexes; the cautious may think it wise to take this route only on Sunday or holiday. Still, those who toss caution to the winds and venture a few blocks east to a cluster of alleys on the right called **Ban Bat** will note that many shops here make or sell monks' alms bowls and other religious articles for monks and laity.

BELOW: Wat Suthat and Giant Swing.

Golden Mount

Until the 1960s, the **Golden Mount ⓫** (open daily) was the highest spot in the city. Although Rama III was never able to achieve the desired height because the soft earth underneath kept sinking, King Mongkut (Rama IV), his successor, firmed matters up in the mid-19th century by placing a thousand teak logs in the boggy soil. His son, Chulalongkorn, finally completed the task.

The Golden Mount is still an excellent viewing and photographic perch. Standing 78 metres (256 ft) high, the top level is reached by a stairway that ascends around the base of the hill. The gilded chedi on top is believed to contain Buddha relics. During World War II, sirens here warned of Allied air raids.

From the Golden Mount, it is easy to spy **Wat Saket** (open daily) to the east on the same grounds. Long before the arrival of the Bangkok kings, a temple stood here during the Ayutthaya period. Rama I built Wat Saket just outside the city walls to serve as a commoners' crematorium. In the late 19th century, it became a dumping ground for the corpses of the poor felled by cholera epidemics. Dogs and vultures waited to feast on them.

Back towards the east

At the northwestern corner of the Golden Mount's grounds is the intersection of two canals holding three names: Khlong Banglamphoo, which turns into Khlong Ong Ang, and Khlong Mahanak. During daylight hours, one can catch a boat traversing eastward on the Mahanak canal and get off at Jim Thompson's House, the World Trade Centre, Soi Asoke or beyond. The much smaller motorised long-tails on Khlong Mahanak originating from Banglampoo canal veer southward to the Hua Lamphong Railway Station in less than 15 minutes.

Map, page 146

The spire atop the Golden Mount, like atop many of Thailand's sacred Buddhist structures, symbolises Mount Meru, a mythical mountain.

BELOW: the swing ceremony, and making a monk's alms bowl.

Map, page 146

Murals at Wat Bowon Niwet were painted by Krua In-khon, who had never been outside of Thailand. Look for southern America antebellum mansions, race tracks and people dressed in the fashions of 19th-century America.

OPPOSITE: Golden Mount, late 1800s.
BELOW: Golden Mount at sunset.

Just north of the Golden Mount is an intersection where six roads converge. Thanon Ratchadamnoen Klang, the broad western avenue leading to Democracy Monument, was inspired by Paris's Champs d'Elysees, and until 1941 it was lined with mahogany trees. To reach it, take the Mahathai Athit Bridge across the Mahanak canal – Thais call it the Weeping Bridge because of its bas reliefs of sobbing figures. Or else take a little detour back across Ong Ang canal via the larger Phanfalilat Bridge. This leads to **Mahakan Fort**, originally built at the turn of the 18th century, but much restored since. It is one of only two remaining watchtowers of the old city wall.

If strolling south along the busy, canal-side Thanon Mahachai, some of the other remnants of the city wall that encircled Rattanakosin in the 19th century are visible. Go through the very first archway to reach "dove's village", a calm refuge specialising in antiques, bird cages, bird accessories and birds themselves. This is where connoisseurs purchase doves for competition in singing contests. A silver-tongued dove may be worth more than US$ 10,000.

Directly behind, to the west, is **Wat Ratchanadda ⑫** (open daily), a thriving centre for amulet vendors. The best-selling amulet depicts a monkey holding a phallus in its hands. Sunthorn Phu, the greatest Thai poet, once resided in the monks' cloisters. You can't miss the large, multilayered metal pagoda: **Loha Prasad ⑬**, recently opened after 150 years of sporadic construction. Visitors can roam ground-floor corridors lined with Buddhas.

Backtrack or pick any lane northward to arrive at **Democracy Monument ⑭** – or at least a view of the 24-metre-tall (78 ft) wings in the middle of a hectic traffic circle. A major city landmark, the monument was built in 1939 to commemorate the overthrow of the absolute monarchy in June 1932. The 75 cannons around the base are symbolic of the Buddhist year 2575, equivalent to AD 1932. Plaster reliefs at the base represent the revolutionaries.

The resemblance to fascist architecture is not coincidental. The monument was designed by the Italian-born Corrado Feroci, who took the Thai name Silpa Bhirasi and is much honoured today as the founder of Silpakorn University, and as the father of the modern Thai art movement. As evident in some of this other works, Silpa was much taken by Italian fascist ideas concerning art, if not the political philosophy. Regardless, the monument is a potent symbol of democracy. The avenue between here and Sanam Luang to the west is a natural site for public demonstration. It was in this vicinity that the massacres of 1973, 1976 and 1992 took place. The monument also serves as a memorial place for making offerings to those who died in those violent years.

To the northwest is **Wat Bowon Niwet** (open daily) on the southern corner of Thanon Bowon. It was built between 1824 and 1832 by Rama III. His son, the future king Mongkut, spent many of his 27 years as a monk here, attempting to purge Thai Buddhism of superstitions and aberrant practices. Subsequent kings have served their brief monkhoods here.

The buildings are undistinguished, except for the murals inside the bot. They display a knowledge of Western perspective that is startling compared to the traditional, two-dimensional Thai mural scenes. ❑

Map,
page 146

MAE NAM CHAO PHRAYA

It was the river of kings, and is now the river of commerce. Dividing old Bangkok and Thonburi, the Chao Phraya is the most splendid part of Bangkok, lined by hotels, temples and eclectic architecture

The Mae Nam Chao Phraya, Thailand's celebrated River of Kings, snakes 365 kilometres (225 mi) south from Nakhorn Sawan in the central plains, past the ancient city of Ayutthaya, down to Bangkok and finally out at Samut Prakarn into the Gulf of Thailand. Nowadays, this historic river (*mae nam* means "river") appears at first glance as a rather murky flow of water, buzzing with industrial-looking tugs, express-boat taxis, and noisy *rua hang yao*, or long-tailed boats. Nonetheless, exploring this famous river and its intricate network of *khlong*, or canals, is one of Bangkok's more appealing highlights. Besides the towering modern apartments and the luxurious riverside hotels, there are ancient temples and the fairytale spires of the Grand Palace. And along the smaller connecting canals are rustic wooden houses, floating markets and smiling children diving unselfconsciously naked into the muddy waters – an appealing glimpse of life away from the city's pollution and congestion.

For centuries, the Chao Phraya has been the lifeblood of Thailand. It was along this river that the Thais fled from their ancient stronghold of Ayutthaya (an excellent river-cruise excursion from Bangkok) after defeat by Burmese invaders in 1767 to establish their new kingdom briefly in Thonburi, before moving to the more protected Bangkok on the opposite bank. To this day, Mae Nam Chao

BELOW: old house and spirit house on the river, and speeding along a back canal.

Phraya remains a working river, the means by which rice and a whole host of other supplies from the fertile central plains are transported to the capital.

For travel writers and other visitors, the Chao Phraya is central to the romance of Bangkok. In 1888, a little-known 30-year-old Polish seaman, Teodor Konrad Korzeniowski, wrote: "There it was, spread largely on both banks, the Oriental capital which had yet suffered no white conqueror. Here and there in the distance, above the crowded mob of low, brown roof ridges, towered great piles of masonry, king's palace, temples, gorgeous and dilapidated, crumbling under the vertical sunlight, tremendous, overpowering, almost palpable, which seemed to enter one's breast with the breath of one's nostrils and soak into one's limbs through every pore of the skin."

Oriental Hotel swimming pool and Chao Phraya.

Bangkok's venerable **Oriental Hotel** ⓕ, established in 1876, named a suite in its author's wing after this scribe, who later changed his name to Joseph Conrad. Today, the grand hotel that overlooks the banks of the Chao Phraya and operates its own luxury river cruises upstream to Ayutthaya is also where most visitors embark for their first taste of the Chao Phraya. Two minutes' walk from the hotel is the **Tha Orienten Pier**, where one can hop a 7-baht ride on an express river taxi and get off at any of the stops along the route, to as far north as Nonthaburi. Alternatively, charter a long-tail boat for a faster, private, but considerably more expensive glimpse of river life. Remember to bargain fiercely for the boat hire; expect to pay at least 300 baht an hour.

There are several pier stops south of Tha Orienten, but most of the highlights of the river are to the north, and also to the west along Khlong Mon. As the express boat noisily chugs off, filled by a mix of local commuters, tourists and saffron clad monks, take a glimpse of the old colonial buildings on the Bangkok

BELOW: Wat Arun and cross-river ferry during flooding of the Chao Phraya River.

Map,
page 146

*In the mid 1800s,
perhaps 90 percent of
the city's half-million
population lived
along the city's
khlong, or canals.*

OPPOSITE: driver of
rua hang yao, or
long-tail boat.
BELOW: river pier at
the Oriental Hotel,
with the Sheraton in
the distance.

side of the river: the **French Embassy**, the crumbling **Old Customs House** and the **General Post Office**. On the Thonburi side are the new and as yet unfinished Peninsula and Sofitel hotels. On the right side of the river is the **River City Shopping Complex** 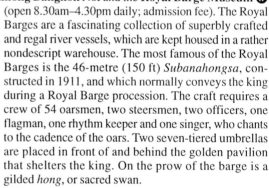, and a patch of rather tatty warehouses and shacks fronting the Chinatown area by the Tha Ratchawong pier. Just beyond a singularly tacky modern high-rise with a mock St Paul's Cathedral dome are two bridges: **Phra Pok Klao Bridge** and the **Memorial Bridge** ⓱, the first to span the Chao Phraya and opened by King Rama VII (Prajadhipok) in 1932 to commemorate the 150th anniversary of the Chakri dynasty. The bridges mark the beginning of the royal district of Rattanakosin.

On the left and directly opposite the Grand Palace is **Wat Arun** ⓲ (open daily), unmistakable and one the river's oldest and most distinctive landmarks, dating back to the Ayutthayan period before King Taksin moved the Thai capital south to Thonburi and later to Bangkok. The temple's 82-metre-high (270 ft) *prang*, which is featured on the 10-baht coin, is bedecked with millions of tiny pieces of Chinese porcelain donated by average Thai citizens during the reign of King Mongkut (Rama IV).

Named after Aruna, the Hindi god of dawn, Wat Arun is a spectacular sight from the river. The central prang, which symbolises Mount Meru, the mythical Buddhist peak, is surrounded by four minor prangs at the corners of the *wat*. In between the minor prangs are four *mondop*.

Just beyond Wat Arun, also on the Thonburi side of the river, is **Wat Rakang**, the bell wat and which has a lovely collection of bells that are rung each morning. In the library, superb murals dating from 1788 depict scenes from the *Ramakien*. Further is **Khlong Bangkok Noi** and the **Royal Barge Museum** ⓳ (open 8.30am–4.30pm daily; admission fee). The Royal Barges are a fascinating collection of superbly crafted and regal river vessels, which are kept housed in a rather nondescript warehouse. The most famous of the Royal Barges is the 46-metre (150 ft) *Subanahongsa*, constructed in 1911, and which normally conveys the king during a Royal Barge procession. The craft requires a crew of 54 oarsmen, two steersmen, two officers, one flagman, one rhythm keeper and one singer, who chants to the cadence of the oars. Two seven-tiered umbrellas are placed in front of and behind the golden pavilion that shelters the king. On the prow of the barge is a gilded *hong*, or sacred swan.

Should you have the opportunity to witness this rare event, which only happens once every few years, do not miss it. Oarsmen in traditional costumes propel the mighty vessels in a lengthy procession, chanting ancient barge songs called *bot heh reua*. Instruments play and thousands cheer. It is a sight that evokes the pomp and splendour of the early kingdom that gave the Chao Phraya its old name, River of Kings.

Further upstream on Khlong Bangkok Noi is **Wat Suwannaram**, built by Rama I on the site of an earlier temple and extensively renovated since. Within the *viharn* are well-preserved murals from the early 1800s depicting, among other events and scenes, the ten lives of Buddha. Commissioned by Rama III, they are thought by many to be Bangkok's best temple murals. ❑

Waterways

For centuries, the river and *khlong*, or canal, served as the transportation arteries of Thailand. In a land that flooded whenever the monsoon-swollen rivers overflowed their banks, it made little sense to build roads that would be washed away. Rivers and canals also provided natural defenses as moats against invaders.

In the central plains, and especially at Ayutthaya, master engineers diverted a river to turn Ayutthaya into a fortified island. Later, in Bangkok, engineers dug a canal across a neck of land between the present site of Thammasat University and Wat Arun, thereby eliminating a long roundabout route to the mouth of the Chao Phraya. Erosion eventually widened the canal, which has now become the river's main course. The original river loop became the khlong of Bangkok Noi and Bangkok Yai. When King Rama I established Bangkok, he had three concentric canals constructed, turning the royal city into an island. Other canals were dug to connect them. In the 19th century, it was estimated that more than 100,000 boats plied Bangkok's canals.

The most extensive rural canal expansion came during the reign of King Chulalongkorn. His engineers mapped the central plains, and the monarch gave farm land to those who would dig a section of canal passing through his property. In a few years, thousands of kilometres of canals crisscrossed central Thailand. The magnitude of this enormous project can only be appreciated from the air.

In the mid 20th century, Bangkok shifted from boats to cars. Canals were filled in to create roads, and houses were built on solid ground. The result is evident: congested and noisy streets in the hot season, flooded streets in the monsoon season.

Zipping along at water level in a *rua hang yao*, or long-tailed boat, is one of the coolest ways to tour the city. The rua hang yao is a particularly Thai invention, born of necessity. In engineering terms, it is simplicity itself: A car or truck engine is mounted on a pivot at the stern of a long, low and narrow boat. A long shaft, or "tail", extends from the back of the boat, the small propeller spinning furiously in the water, spitting a rooster tail and propelling the boat at quite rapid speeds. In the narrow canals, the pivot allows the boatman to turn the craft in a very tight radius.

A lovely 90-minute route zips upriver to Khlong Bangkok Noi. A short way beyond the Bangkok Noi Railway Station is the Royal Barge Museum. If asked, the driver will stop for a few minutes for a tour of the museum. Continue up the canal, turning left into Khlong Chak Phra, which soon changes its name to Bang Kounsri and eventually to Bangkok Yai.

One of the most scenic khlong in the eastern section of Bangkok is Khlong Saen Sap, dug to carry troops to Chachoengsao to fight invaders from the east, and to join the Bangpakong River for a journey into the sea. The canal begins at Pratunam, but the water is filthy and fetid there.

Better to start at the Ekamai Bridge or at Phrakanong Khlong Tan Bridge. The canal is straight and unshaded, so it's less attractive than the twisting and convoluted Thonburi canals, but nevertheless it passes through lovely rice country. In any case and on any khlong, take a look. ■

BEYOND THE ROYAL CITY

To the north of the royal city is Dusit, with the modern palace and Thailand's parliament. South is Chinatown and the old foreigners' district. West are the clutter and high-rises of a modern city

Map, page 138

T he royal district of old Bangkok – with its brightly coloured exotic temples, saffron-clad monks and the stately allure of the magnificent Grand Palace – rightly draws the first attentions of most visitors to Thailand. But it is the less picturesque, more chaotic contemporary Bangkok that gets its tenacious grip on travelers, overloading the senses with an intoxicating mixture of sunbaked petrol fumes, the hot steam of stir-fried noodles, the screech of *tuktuks* and the sing-song haggling of night-market hawkers and go-go bar touts. It's a city that doesn't so much appeal to the senses as bludgeon them with striking, vivid, noisy and contrasting images. One night in Bangkok, or even one day of wandering through the sweltering heat, is not for the fainthearted, but it is certainly a memorable experience. Still, there are quiet escapes within the city.

Dusit, north of the royal city

To the north of Rattanakosin, the old royal city, is the much more serene and dignified Dusit area. Just past the railway line on the north side of Thanon Sri Ayutthaya is a huge leafy set of grounds surrounded by a moat and high railings. Within these grounds are grazing cattle, milk churns and fishponds. It would be easy to think this was a farm, but in fact it is the **Chitralada Palace ㉕**, where the king and queen live. The current king, Bhumibol Adulyadej, has lived here throughout his reign. Chitralada Palace was built in 1913 by King Rama VI (Vajiravudh), who at the time still lived in the Grand Palace but wanted a quiet retreat from the pomp and grandeur of the court. The villa itself is a low-rise structure obscured by the greenery, but the grounds are put to good use for experimental farming projects. Chitralada Palace is not open to the public.

Just past the Chitralada compound, on the other side of Thanon Sri Ayutthaya, is **Wat Benchamabophit ㉑** (open daily), or the Marble Temple. The last major temple built in Bangkok, it was started by Rama V (Chulalongkorn) in 1900 and was finished 10 years later. Through the rear entrance of the courtyard is a huge *bodhi* tree approaching a century in age and said to be derived from a tree that came from Buddha's birthplace in India.

Just past Wat Benchamabophit is Thanon Ratchadamnoen, a pleasant, tree-lined boulevard that leads past a huge square dominated by a **statue of King Chulalongkorn ㉒** on horseback. Chulalongkorn was responsible for much of this part of Bangkok. On the anniversary of his death on 23 October, the square is crowded with students and government officials honouring him by laying wreaths at the base of his statue.

To the left of the square is **Suan Amporn ㉓**, a spacious park with fountains and trees. It is the setting for

PRECEDING PAGES: downtown looking west. **OPPOSITE:** dusk over Silom, near the Chao Phraya. **BELOW:** Bangkok's traffic.

many royal social functions and fairs. Directly behind and north of the square and statue stands **Ananta Samakom** ㉔ (Royal Throne Hall), an Italianate hall of grey marble crowned by a huge dome. It was built in 1907 by King Chulalongkorn as his throne hall, later becoming the National Assembly (Parliament) building. Special permission is required to go inside the building, decorated with huge murals depicting famous events in Thai history. In 1974, Parliament moved to new premises a short distance north.

East is **Dusit Zoo** ㉕, the city's main animal park and one of the most popular places in Bangkok for family outings. A lake with boats for rent is surrounded by an aviary and enclosures containing the exotic wildlife of Asia: gibbons, Sumatran orangutans, snakes and elephants.

Vimarnmek.

Behind the old National Assembly building is **Vimarnmek** ㉖, billed as the world's largest golden teak-wood mansion. As much a work of art as the treasures it holds within, Vimarnmek, or Cloud Mansion, was built by King Chulalongkorn as a residence for his family in what was, in 1900, the suburbs of Bangkok. The airy, 100-room home is filled with crystal, Faberge jewellery and other objets d'art brought from Europe. It demonstrates as well as any museum in the country the extent to which the royal family were influenced by European culture in the latter part of the 19th and early part of the 20th centuries.

Chinatown

South of the Dusit area, east of the old royal city and on the north side of the winding Chao Phraya, is Bangkok's Chinatown.

BELOW: studio in Vimarnmek.

Chinese merchants originally settled the area that now comprises the old royal city, but were asked to move to the present **Sampeng Lane** ㉗ (Soi Wanit 1)

when construction began on the Grand Palace in the 1780s. In 1863, King Mongkut built Charoen Krung (New Road), the first paved street in Bangkok, and Chinatown soon began to expand northwards towards it. Charoen Krung runs over 6 kilometres (4 mi) from the Grand Palace southward to where it terminates at the river, just south of the Krung Thep Bridge. Chinatown was followed at Khlong Krung Kasem by a Muslim district that, in turn, was followed by an area occupied by *farang* (foreigners) where the Oriental Hotel now stands. Later, a third road, Thanon Yaowarat, was built between Charoen Krung and Sampeng, becoming the principal road of Chinatown and the name by which this area is frequently known, **Yaowarat**.

The area has had a somewhat rowdy history. What began with mercantile pursuits soon degenerated into a lusty, earthy entertainment area. By 1900, alleys led to opium dens and houses whose entrances were marked by green lanterns (*khom khiew*). A green-light district was like a Western red-light district, and while the lanterns have disappeared, the term *khom khiew* still signifies a brothel. Eventually, Sampeng was tamed into a sleepy lane of small shops selling goods imported from China. Sampeng Lane begins on Thanon Maha Chai and is bound at either end by Indian and Muslim shops. The western end, Pahurat, has a warren of tiny lanes filled with Indians and Sikhs selling cloth. Across the canal is Sampeng proper, with shops selling inexpensive jewellery, tools, cloth, clothes, toys, shoes and novelties.

After leaving the old royal city and crossing Thanon Chakrawat, turn right a short distance to the entrance of **Wat Chakrawat** ㉘, an odd amalgam of buildings. Dating from the Ayutthaya period and thus predating Chinatown, it has a small grotto with a statue of a laughing monk. Myth says that it is the likeness of

Map, page 138

Thailand's first Chinese immigrants were merchants in the 1500s. In the centuries since, the kingdom's Chinese population has become strongly integrated in Thai society.

BELOW: shy girl in Chinatown.

Street sign for a palm-reading expert, Chinatown.

BELOW: paper images are burnt for the ancestors.

a monk who was once slim and handsome, so handsome he was constantly pestered by women. His devotion to Buddhism led him to the unusual remedy of eating until he grew so gross that the women lost interest. Near the end of Sampeng the shops bear Muslim names. The merchants here trade gems. Marking the eastern end of Sampeng is **Wat Pathuma Kongkha ㉙**, another temple from the Ayutthaya period. It was here that criminals of royal birth were executed for crimes against the state.

At places, Thanon Yaowarat looks like a somewhat dowdier version of a Hong Kong street with its forest of signs. It is best known for its gold shops, all of which seem to have been designed by a cookie cutter, so alike they look. Daily prices are scrawled on the windows of shops painted red for good luck. Mirrors and neon lights complete the decor.

Yaowarat is also an old entertainment area. Halfway down on the north side of the street is the famous "Seven Storey Mansion" that flourished well into the middle part of the 20th century. It was designed so that those interested only in dining could do so on the ground floor. As the evening progressed and one relaxed, one would ascend the stairs, floor by floor, to more Sybaritic delights. Unrepentant hedonists headed straight for the top floor. Between Yaowarat and Charoen Krung, near the western end of Chinatown, is **Nakhon Kasem ㉚** (Thieves Market). A few decades ago, it was the area a householder searched after being robbed, a likely place where one might recover stolen goods for a very reasonable price. It later became an antique dealer's area, but now handles mainly more prosaic household items.

Near the eastern end of Charoen Krung is Chinatown's biggest Buddhist temple, **Wat Mangkon ㉛**. From early in the morning it is aswirl with activity and

incense smoke reminiscent of old China. The most interesting lane nearby is Isara Nuphap, which runs south from Thanon Phlab Phla Chai. Around the entrance to Isara Nuphap are shops selling paper effigies of houses, Mercedes-Benzes, household furniture and other items. These are burnt in the Chinese *kong tek* ceremony, a ritual that, it is believed, sends the material goods to the afterlife for use by deceased relatives.

Just east of the point where Thanon Yaowarat meets Thanon Charoen Krung (not far from Hua Lamphong Railway Station, which connects Bangkok to the rest of the country by rail) is **Wat Traimit** ❷ (open daily) and the famous Golden Buddha. Found by accident in the 1950s at a riverside temple when a construction company was extending its dock, the huge stucco figure of the Buddha was too heavy for the sling. It snapped and, to the horror of all, smashed to the ground, breaking one corner. A close examination showed a glint of yellow through the crack. Further investigation revealed that the stucco was only a thin coat, and that inside was an image of solid gold weighing over five tons. Like many similar statues, it was probably made elsewhere in Thailand during the Ayutthaya period. To preserve it from Burmese invaders, it had been covered in stucco to conceal its true composition and rested undetected for centuries.

Bangkrak and Silom

Further south and just east of the Chao Phraya is **Bangkrak**, a vibrant modern district that has risen in just the past decade. This area has long been a neighbourhood of *farang*, the expat foreigners. Anchoring the western end is the grand **Oriental Hotel**, right on the bank of the Chao Phraya. From the Oriental, stroll past the gaggle of *tuk-tuk* drivers, long-tail boat touts and "copy-watch" sellers

Map, page 138

Wat Traimit's Golden Buddha may be the world's largest solid-gold Buddha at 4 metres in height. Of Sukhothai style, it may date from the 13th century.

BELOW: wholesale market, Chinatown.

Fate or Choice?

Thailand has a prostitution problem. It is of neither recent nor imported vintage. Contrary to the impression of many foreigners, prostitution has been illegal for over 30 years. Social scientists and non-governmental organisations estimate that there are between 300,000 and 2 million Thai prostitutes in Thailand and overseas in places like Japan. In Thailand, no truck stop or town with a population of 20,000 would be complete without a few ramshackle brothels.

According to a Thai newspaper editor, except for the area surrounding the Grand Palace, there is not a single neighbourhood in Bangkok where sex is not for sale, mostly to Thai men. The venues include brothels, hotels, nightclubs, massage parlours, bars, barber shops, parks, karaoke lounges and even golf courses. At the top are private-member clubs, advertised in the glossiest magazines. At the bottom are locked brothels, where the women – and young girls – are virtually enslaved. As measured by compensation and working conditions, the tawdry bars serving foreign men in Patpong are somewhere in between.

There is no single reason why Thailand has more prostitutes than many poorer countries. The traditional explanation of poverty, however, carries less and less weight. While most patrons of Thai prostitutes are Thai men, foreigners also contribute to the demand. Besides the infamous sex tours from Japan, Germany, Australia and elsewhere, there is also a sizable community of Western men, notably in Pattaya and Phuket, who live in Thailand solely because of the cheap sex, child sex or teenage wives.

Agents kidnap young girls or trick them with offers of factory jobs from remote provinces. These girls may end up in locked brothels, from which they may eventually be smuggled to other Asian countries.

It's hard for poor families to resist the blandishments. Particularly at April "harvest time", when 12- and 13-year-old girls finish the customary 6 years of schooling, agents flock to villages, where they offer parents hundreds of dollars or electric appliances in exchange for pretty daughters. A girl typically has to work off a debt that is twice her sale price, although she may have to start over if she is resold before reaching her goal.

When asked why she became or remains a prostitute, a young woman will usually talk about luck or fate. Yet true Buddhists believe in neither, and don't subscribe to predestination. Buddhism, of course, doesn't sanction prostitution at all.

Feminist NGOs don't focus their primary efforts on extricating girls and women from prostitution. They have found that regardless of how women were originally lured into prostitution, few are strongly motivated to get out. The work is easy, the money is too good, and the family pressure overwhelming. Instead, the advocates concentrate on prevention, teaching marketable skills.

Prostitution is probably the principal reason why the AIDS epidemic is so extensive in Thailand. Random blood testing indicates that just under 1 million men, women and children are now infected with AIDS in Thailand. It is neither a Thai nor a *farang* (foreigner) problem. It is a human problem. ■

to the end of the *soi* (alley or lane), turn right and you'll soon be at the less exciting end of one of Bangkok's most exciting streets, Thanon Silom. Cross over and start walking down Silom and you will quickly pick up the flavour of the city – the end-to-end gridlock of cars, the small clusters of motorcyclists with gaudy numbered vests who act as a taxi service (if you're in an adventurous mood, take one to the end of the street as they weave skillfully among the cars, buses and tuk tuks). On either side of the street are jewellery and handicraft stores, banks and restaurants, offices and shopping malls. There are some big brash eateries popular with tourists such as Silom Village, but much more appealing are the elegant restaurants for the locals tucked discreetly away in the lanes off Silom, especially Thanon Pramuan, near a Hindu temple, **Maha Uma Devi**, founded in the 1860s. In the neighbourhood is Thanying, a Thai restaurant in the style of an aristocratic Thai home, set in leafy gardens and run by a Bangkok socialite who is also closely related to the Thai royal family.

Silom really comes to life at night. The Silom night-market begins about half way down on the left side of the street, crowding the narrow pavement with a colourful array of stalls on both sides. Here you must bargain fiercely for the fake watches, jeans, T-shirts, shirts and luggage on offer. Most bargaining is done with the aid of calculators, though if you can get the hang of Thai numbers, it'll probably help bring down the price. About half way along the night-market, the stalls curve off to the left along a noisy neon-lit street. Love it or hate it, and few have any other opinion, the notorious **Patpong** ⊛ (which is actually two streets – Patpong I and Patpong II) has an electric, sinful arrogance that any visitor ought to experience at least once. It's hard to imagine a starker contrast to the serene temples and palaces and the gracious smiles and *wai* of

Map, page 138

TIP

In November, Maha Uma Devi is the centre of the Hindi festival of lights, Deepavali.

OPPOSITE: Patpong dancer. **BELOW:** transvestites in Patpong.

The tranquil airs of Lumpini Park give way to Thai boxing, or muay thai, which dates to the 1400s. Bouts are staged at Lumpini Stadium (east of the park) on Tuesdays and Fridays, and at Ratchadamnoen Stadium, south of Dusit, on Mondays, Wednesdays and Thursdays.

BELOW: morning *tai chi*, Lumpini Park.

hotel staff than the raucous touting and outrageous sex shows of Patpong. Nowadays, there seem to be as many curious middle-aged couples as die-hard sex tourists in and around the bars of Patpong, and the atmosphere is sometimes more racy fun than unrelenting sleaze. There are more bars on Thanon Suriwong, which runs parallel to Silom, and on Silom Soi 4, which runs parallel to Patpong and Patpong II. The bars in Soi 4 attract a very different kind of crowd, generally younger. Some are gay bars while others are trendy bar/cafes popular with resident expatriates. The long-running Rome Club has a decadent transvestite cabaret show every night around midnight and is well worth a visit.

At the end of Silom is a huge and busy intersection that can take a good fifteen minutes to cross. But to the northeast across the intersection lies respite from the relentless dust and petrol fumes of the city. **Suan Lumpini** ❸❹ (**Lumpini Park**), which Bangkokians call the lung of the city, is a tranquil and tropical oasis of greenery with boating lakes, open-air exercise areas, and outdoor cafes. In the morning, people jog, practice *tai chi* exercises, lift weights, even dance under the trees. Along the park's lakes, kiosks rent rowboats or paddleboats. In the afternoons, boys play *takraw* and soccer, or during the hot season, fly kites. Everything stops, momentarily, at 6pm, when the Thai national anthem is played in the park and people stand rigidly to attention in a moving and sincerely felt display of patriotism.

Directly west along Thanon Rama IV is the **Saowapha Institute** ❸❺ (open Monday–Friday 8.30am–4.30pm, Saturday and Sunday 8.30–noon; admission fee), or as it is better known in English, the **Snake Farm**. Operated by the Thai Red Cross, its primary function is not to entertain tourists (though it does) but the more serious business of producing anti-venom serum to be used on snakebite

victims, of which there are many every year throughout the country. The Snake Farm, the second oldest of its kind in the world, produces serum from seven types of snake: the king cobra, Siamese cobra, banded krait, Russell's viper, Malayan pit viper and the green and Pope's pit viper. This snake farm is professionally run, informative and well worth a visit. Adjacent is a respected clinic for sexually-transmitted diseases.

Map, page 138

Core of modern Bangkok

Coming out of Lumpini Park at the northwestern end onto Thanon Ratchadamri, head north along Ratchadamri, which eventually reaches Bangkok's prime shopping district. Along the way on the left is another section of greenery, the **Royal Bangkok Sports Club**, a private club with sports facilities, golf course, swimming pool, tennis courts and horseracing on Sundays during all but the rainiest months. The club is closed to non-members, but the racecourse is open to the public. There is no off-track betting, so you'll have to wait till other people put their baht on the line to get any idea of the winning odds. These are then displayed on a huge computerised board and the prices change dramatically as everyone places their bets at the last minute.

Access to the racetrack is from the other side along the parallel Thanon Henri Dunant. (Thais still use its old name of Sanam Ma, or Racecourse Road.) Across this road stands the temple-like buildings of **Chulalongkorn University** ㊱, the country's oldest and most prestigious institution of higher learning. Built in a mixture of Thai and Western styles, with spacious yellow-roofed pavilions, an open gallery and an assembly hall, the university was founded by King Vajiravudh, who reigned from 1911–1925 and named the university after his father.

BELOW: Lumpini Park, and downtown twilight.

Heading north along Thanon Ratchadamri towards the intersection with Thanon Rama I, one passes two of the city's most opulent hotels, The Regent and the Grand Hyatt Erawan. At the intersection, the **Erawan Shrine** ③ draws visitors and locals. To improve their fortunes or to pass exams, believers make offerings at a statue of a four-faced deity. To repay the god for wishes granted, supplicants place floral garlands or wooden elephants at the god's feet. On most days, dancers in traditional costume and paid by worshippers add to the colourful scene. Outside are little stalls where people sit all day making floral garlands that worshippers purchase as offerings. This attractive corner is, however, now somewhat marred by the ugly elevated transit rails overhead – forever under construction and dwarfing the intersection.

This intersection also marks the centre of Bangkok's prime shopping district. In the future there are plans for a series of air-conditioned walkways that will link the main shopping malls within a one-kilometre radius. East of the intersection is Thanon Ploenchit, either side of which are ritzy malls, including the international-designer showcase Gaysorn Plaza, complete with a Planet Hollywood; adjoining Thanon Chitlom has the largest branch of Thailand's Central Department Store. This was burnt down in 1995 but has now been rebuilt.

Thanon Rama I turns into Thanon Ploenchit heading east. Beyond the British Embassy, the boulevard eventually turns into Thanon Sukhumvit – an area known simply as **Sukhumvit** ③ – and stretches virtually as far as the resort town of Pattaya. Sukhumvit is a very busy commercial and residential district, with many restaurants and bars that cater to locals and expats, but relatively few tourists, as the area is not rich in cultural attractions. There are, however, the enormous **seafood market** on Soi 24, and the **Kamthieng House**, a lovely 130-

BELOW: Erawan Shrine.

year-old Thai-style house in the Siam Society compound on Sukhumvit Soi 21.

To the northwest of the Erawan Shrine – kitty-corner across the intersection – is the World Trade Centre, yet another huge shopping mall. If feeling trapped by malls and commerce, duck into **Wat Pathum Wanaram** ㊴, a quiet temple tucked in behind the World Trade Centre. The temple was built by King Mongkut in a large park that also held a palace and a lotus pond (after which the temple was named), so that he could escape the summer heat of Rattanakosin. The palace is gone, the trees have been cut and the ponds filled in to build the World Trade Centre complex. Wat Pathum Wanaram is the most popular temple in Bangkok among taxi drivers, who drive here to have their vehicles blessed against accidents. The temple also holds regular meditation classes.

Opposite the World Trade Centre is the government's handicrafts store, **Narayana Phand** ㊵. It has an excellent selection of Thai-made goods on several floors and is worth exploring, if for no other reason than to learn about the wide variety of Thai crafts. Along the way up Ratchadamri to Ratchadamri Arcade and Bangkok Bazaar are numerous small shops crammed into a small space and vendors spilling off the pavements. One can often find some good handicraft bargains at small shops in Ratchadamri Arcade. The pair serve as a link between the chic shops of Ratchaprasong and the bazaar atmosphere of the vast, sprawling **Pratunam** ㊶, a little further to the north and a favourite shopping place for many Thais and budget travellers. Pratunam means "water gate" and refers to the lock at the bridge to prevent Khlong San Sap, to the east, from being flooded by the one to the west, which leads to the Chao Phraya.

North is **Suan Pakkad** ㊷ (open Sunday–Thursday 9am–4pm) also known as the Cabbage Patch Palace, at 352 Thanon Sri Ayutthaya. The splendid resi-

Map, page 138

Two high-rise towers loom near Pratunam: a tall one and a short one. For nearly a decade, the short one was Thailand's tallest building. The taller skyscraper, 90-storey Baiyoke Tower, has been under construction for nearly an eternity.

BELOW: tourist police ready to help.

Map, page 138

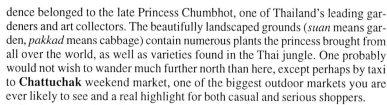

Store offerings of silk.

OPPOSITE: garden outside Jim Thompson's house. **BELOW:** looking for a bus.

dence belonged to the late Princess Chumbhot, one of Thailand's leading gardeners and art collectors. The beautifully landscaped grounds (*suan* means garden, *pakkad* means cabbage) contain numerous plants the princess brought from all over the world, as well as varieties found in the Thai jungle. One probably would not wish to wander much further north than here, except perhaps by taxi to **Chattuchak** weekend market, one of the biggest outdoor markets you are ever likely to see and a real highlight for both casual and serious shoppers.

Continue west along Thanon Rama I to yet more shopping. The intersection of Rama I and Phaya Thai roads is one of the best areas to shop, especially for those who like a little local colour and confusion. On the southwest corner next to the **National Stadium** ⓭ is the air-conditioned Mahboonkrong or MBK Centre, one of Bangkok's biggest complexes. It's more like an indoor market than a mall, with five crowded floors of cheap local clothes, stalls, supermarkets, boutiques and fast-food joints.

To the east across Phaya Thai is the Discovery Centre, a plush air-conditioned mall comprising mainly international brand names at extravagant international prices. Of more interest to visitors is the adjacent Siam Centre, a mecca for young Thai trendies looking for locally made international labels. Across the road (don't even try walking through the endless traffic – take one of the walkways across the street) is one the oldest shopping areas in Bangkok, **Siam Square** ⓮. Inside are movie theatres, bookstores and a wealth of restaurants. There is also the British Council, with its excellent library, and the Hard Rock Cafe. Chinese visitors, including movie stars from Hong Kong, frequently flock to this area for its shark's-fin and bird's-nest soup restaurants.

But there are other attractions besides shopping and eating in this area. On

Khlong Maha Nag at the north end of Soi Kasemsan II is the **Jim Thompson House** ⓯ (open daily 9am–5pm; tel: 215 0122; admission fee). This Thai-style house is, in truth, a collection of seven Thai houses acquired from central Thailand, disassembled and brought to Bangkok, and then joined together by the remarkable American. Thompson came to Thailand at the end of World War II as an intelligence agent and later revived the Thai silk industry. In 1967, while on a visit to the Cameron Highlands in Malaysia, Thompson mysteriously disappeared; despite an extensive search, no trace has ever been found of him. Some say he simply died of a heart attack, while others suggest CIA shenanigans. Nonetheless, his sumptuous traditional Thai-style home remains and is open to the public. The silk business he founded continues to flourish, and if you are looking for expensive and tasteful souvenirs to take home, Jim Thompson silks are a good value.

Inside the houses and throughout the grounds are 14 centuries' worth of Southeast Asian antiques. If looking to invest in antiques, come here first to see the best. There are, for example, a limestone torso of a Buddha image, said to be one of the oldest existing Buddha figures in Southeast Asia. Throughout the house are carved images, in wood and stone, of Burmese spirits and Buddhas. Superb paintings from the 1800s fill the master bedroom, while blue-and-white Ming-dynasty porcelain is displayed elsewhere in the house. ❐

OUTSIDE OF BANGKOK

Escaping the fuss of Bangkok is easier than might be imagined. Crocodiles, roses, immense Buddhas, World War II relics, wild tigers and elephants, waterfalls, and markets await on day-trips

Map, page 179

THAILAND
Bangkok

L ocated near enough to Bangkok for a comfortably paced day-trip, the eastern province of Nakhon Nayok offers waterfalls and a pretty park. The most scenic route to this province is Route 305, which branches off Route 1 just north of Rangsit, 30 kilometres (20 mi) north of Bangkok. A wide road runs northeast along a lovely canal, passing rice fields and small rivers to **Nakhon Nayok ❶**, about 140 kilometres (90 mi) northeast of the capital. From the town, Route 33 heads northwest and then, within a few kilometres, Route 3049 leads off to the right towards two waterfalls, including Sarika Falls. Near the parking lot are pleasant outdoor restaurants and stalls selling fruits and drinks. Sarika Falls itself is impressive around the end of the rainy season, from September to November. Wear good shoes; the stone paths are slippery.

Nearby is **Wang Takrai National Park**. Along the way is the temple of Chao Pau Khun Dan, named after one of King Naresuan's advisers whose spirit is believed to protect the area. Prince Chumbhot, who established Suan Pakkad in Bangkok, also established the 80-hectare (195 acre) Wang Takrai Park in the 1950s; a statue of him stands on the opposite bank of the small river flowing through the park. His wife, Princess Chumbhot, planted many varieties of flowers and trees, including some imported species. Cultivated gardens sit among tall trees, which line both banks of the river flowing through the park. Bungalows are available.

Khao Yai National Park ❷, the nearest highland escape to Bangkok, lies 200 kilometres (125 mi) northeast of the capital and covers 2,170 square kilometres (840 sq mi). Established in 1962, it is the oldest national park in Thailand. With its proximity to Bangkok, visitors are approaching one million in number annually. It takes about three to four hours to drive to Khao Yai from Bangkok, via one of two routes.

Several years ago, extensive accommodation was available within the park, as well as a restaurant and an 18-hole golf course. These facilities, however, have been closed in an effort to reduce the environmental damage of development. Presently, there are a campsite and some simple dormitories within the park, and camping out on one of the observation towers may be a possibility as well. (Inquire at the TAT office or the forestry department in Bangkok, or at park headquarters.) Outside of the park and on the main road from Pak Chong to Khao Yai, resort hotels and guesthouses have proliferated in recent years.

Khao Yai's highest peaks lie on the east along a land form known as the Khorat Plateau. **Khao Khieo** (Green Mountain) is 1,351 metres (4,433 ft) high and **Khao Laem** (Shadow Mountain), 1,328 metres (4,357 ft).

Khao Yai is comprised of broad-leaf evergreen forests and mixed deciduous trees, with grasslands and scrub

PRECEDING PAGES: white-handed gibbon, Khao Yai. **OPPOSITE:** school lunch. **BELOW:** Khao Yai National Park.

as secondary growth. Even on a short walk through the park, unusual palms, lush ferns and tenacious vines abound and provide a welcome respite. In the cool season, many trees and shrubs come into flower, and numerous wild orchids may be seen, including *Bulbophyllum khaoyaiense*, native only to the park.

Pig-tailed macaques and white-handed and pileated gibbons are among the most commonly seen small mammals. Larger mammals including bears, wild pigs, guars, leopards and other large cats, and various species of deer are occasionally spotted. Khao Yai is also home to about 200 elephants and perhaps 40 tigers, but these are rarely seen. In addition, over 300 species of migrant and resident birds have been identified.

The visitor's centre, adjacent to park headquarters, has somewhat disjointed but interesting displays. It is a good place to begin a tour of Khao Yai. Guides are sometimes available at the headquarters, but you'll have a better chance of getting an English-speaking one if you organise a tour of the park through one of the guesthouses in the area. A dozen or so trails, from 2 to 8 kilometres (5 mi) in length and of varying degrees of difficulty, snake through the park to waterfalls, and to grassy areas and salt licks. In several clearings there are observation towers to watch animals feed.

In the late afternoon, several guesthouses offer trips to a limestone cave at **Khao Rub Chang**, just north of the park and where, at dusk, a massive exodus of wrinkled-lipped bats darkens the sky for more than an hour.

After dark, night safaris can be arranged in which powerful halogen spotlights are used to illuminate night-feeding animals such as barking deer, sambar and civet. At night, winter temperatures may drop to below 15°C (60°F); warm clothes are handy.

TIP

At certain times of the year, the State Railways of Thailand may offer weekend day-trips to Khao Yai; however, the bus is more reliable and often faster.

BELOW: tiger cubs in Khao Yai, a rare sighting.

South of Bangkok

The **Crocodile Farm ❸** (open daily; admission fee) is located in Samut Prakarn Province, near the river-mouth town of Samut Prakam, half an hour's drive (30 kilometres/20 mi) southeast of Bangkok on the old Sukhumvit Highway (Route 3). Started in the 1960s with an initial investment of about 10,000 baht (less than US$500 back then), the owner now has three farms (two in the northeast) worth 100 million baht. At present, this farm has about 30,000 fresh- and saltwater local crocodiles, as well as some South American caimans and Nile River crocodiles. They are hatched and raised in tanks. The young are protected from mosquitoes, which can blind them by biting their eyes, with netting.

Map, page 179

The highlight of a visit to the farm is a show in which handlers enter a pond teeming with crocodiles and toss them about rather roughly. While this sounds dangerous in print, the lethargic beasts are less likely to bite because of innate viciousness than because their noon nap has been interrupted. After the crocodiles are skinned, incidentally, their meat is sold to restaurants in Samut Prakarn and Bangkok. The farm also has a zoo and amusement park with rides. The irony of all this is that the owners have succeeded in preserving the animal; nearly all the wild Asian species have been hunted to extinction.

Crocodile Farm.

Also in Samut Prakarn, a few kilometres from the Crocodile Farm, is **Muang Boran ❹** (**Ancient City**; open daily 8am–5pm; admission fee), which bills itself as the world's largest outdoor museum. The brainchild of a Bangkok millionaire with a passion for Thai art and history, it took around three years to construct. In what used to be 80 hectares (200 acres) of rice fields, designers sketched an area roughly the shape of Thailand and placed the individual attractions as close to their real sites as possible. There are replicas (some full-size,

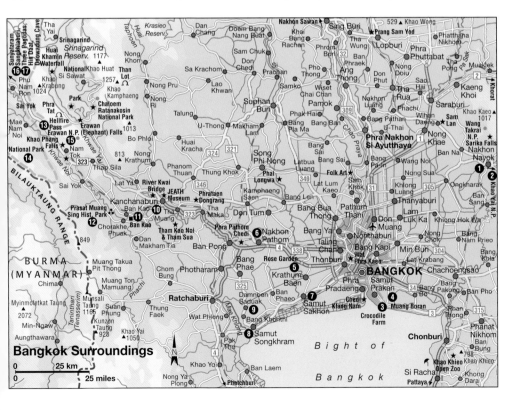

Bangkok Surroundings

most others one-third the size of the originals) of famous monuments and temples from all parts of the kingdom. Some are reconstructions of buildings that no longer exist, like the Grand Palace of Ayutthaya, and some are copies of real places, like the Phimai sanctuary northeast of Nakhon Ratchasima, and the huge temple of Khao Phra Viharn on the Thai-Cambodian border. Experts from the National Museum in Bangkok worked as consultants to ensure the historical accuracy of the reproductions. At present, there are more than 60 monuments covering 1,500 years of Thai history. The monuments are spread out over a large area; it may be most convenient to drive between them. However, the grounds are beautifully landscaped with small waterfalls, creeks, ponds, rock gardens and lush greenery; deer graze freely amongst the many interesting sculptures representing figures from Thai literature and Hindu mythology. In addition to the monuments, Ancient City also has a model Thai village, in which artisans work on handicrafts such as lacquerware, ceramics and paper umbrellas.

For those with time, Paknam is a bustling fishing town with an interesting market along its docks. Cross the river by ferry to the famous **Wat Phra Chedi Klang Nam**, which, contrary to its name ("the chedi in the middle of the river"), is now on solid land, the result of the river shifting its course. Thai kings used to stop at this temple on their way in and out of the country on state visits, praying for success in their journeys or offering thanks on their return.

West of Bangkok

Less than an hour's drive due west from Bangkok, **Suan Sam Phran ❺** (**Rose Garden**; open daily; admission fee) is the brainchild of a former lord mayor of the capital. The garden lies 30 kilometres (20 mi) west of the capital on Route 4,

BELOW: Ancient City.

en route to Nakhon Pathom. Its large area of well-landscaped gardens contains roses and orchids, and includes accommodations, restaurants, a golf course reputed to be among the 25 best in the world, paddle boats on an artificial lake, and a children's playground. Its premier attraction is a daily Thai cultural show.

In a large arena, beautifully costumed Thai actors demonstrate folk dances, Thai boxing, a wedding ceremony, cock-fighting and other rural entertainment. Outside after this show, elephants put on their own show, moving huge teak logs as they would in the forests of the north. The elephants then carry tourists around the compound for a small fee.

Just 50 kilometres (30 mi) west of Bangkok, beyond the Rose Garden on Route 4, is the town of **Nakhon Pathom** ❻, famous for **Phra Pathom Chedi**, which rises majestically over the surrounding countryside. At just over 125 metres (410 ft) in height, it is the tallest Buddhist monument in the world, a few metres taller even than the Shwedagon in Rangoon.

Nakhon Pathom is believed to be Thailand's oldest city. The name derives from the Pali for "first city." According to legend, it was the capital of Suvannab-humi, the "land of gold," and it was to here that King Ashoka (268–232 BC) sent two missionaries from India to introduce Buddhism. The first archeological records date from the 6th century when the area was populated by the Mons, Dvaravati-Buddhists who flourished in the Chao Phraya basin from the 6th to 11th centuries. The original chedi is believed to have been constructed by the Mons in the late 10th century. In the early 11th century, Nakhon Pathom and the surrounding area fell to the Khmers, who built a Brahman (Hindu) *prang* some 40 metres (130 ft) tall, which enclosed the original Buddhist structure.

In 1057, King Anawratha of Pagan besieged the city, leaving the chedi in

Map,
page 179

TIP

Southeast of the Phra Pathom Chedi is the Phra Pathom Chedi National Museum, with a nice collection of artefacts excavated from the area. Open Wednesday–Sunday. Admission fee.

BELOW: Nakhon Pathom's Phra Pathom Chedi.

ruins. Although the city regained brief importance in the 16th century as a defensive position against the invading Burmese, it wasn't until 1853 that repairs were begun in earnest to the chedi. King Mongkut, who had spent time in the area as a young monk before gaining the throne, was impressed with the age and history of the edifice, and believed it to contain a relic of the Buddha. The final structure was completed during the reign of King Chulalongkorn in the early 20th century. Set in a huge square park, the massive chedi, covered with golden-orange tiles imported from China, rests upon a circular terrace, the perimeter of which is accented with sacred trees. Walking up the enormous main staircase leads to the North Viharn and the Sukhothai-style standing Buddha, the stone head, hands and feet of which were discovered in Sawankhalok in 1900. King Vajiravudh commissioned a bronze body cast to match the stone pieces; the statue was enshrined in 1915 and is greatly revered by Thais. The king's ashes are buried at the base of the statue.

After investigating the chedi, wander around the grounds for a few moments. Have your palm read for a small fee (there's at least one fortune teller who speaks enough English to make it entertaining), enjoy a delicious iced coffee made fresh on the spot and served in a small plastic bag with a straw, and peruse the startling selection of skin magazines that are sold just at the base of the chedi.

In former times, a royal visit to Nakhon Pathom was more than a day's journey, so it is not surprising that a number of palaces and summer residences were built there. One of them, **Sanam Chand Palace**, 2 kilometres west of Phra Pathom Chedi, has a fine *sala*, a meeting pavilion now used for government offices, and a building in a most unusual Thai interpretation of English Tudor architecture, used appropriately as a setting for Shakespearean drama. In front

BELOW: riverside laundry washing.

stands a statue of Yaleh, the pet dog of King Vajiravudh, who commissioned the palace. The fierce dog, unpopular with the court, was poisoned by the king's attendants. Even as a statue, Yaleh looks insufferable. Although most of the palace buildings are closed to the public, one of them serves as a small museum and contains memorabilia of Vajiravudh.

A good way to approach the coastal port of **Samut Sakhon ❼** is by a branch railway connecting it with Thonburi, on the other side of the Chao Phraya from central Bangkok. The line, called the Mae Khlong Railway, runs at a loss, but it is subsidised because of its usefulness to the population of the three provinces west of Bangkok. The 40-minute journey first passes through the suburbs, then through vegetable gardens, groves of coconut and areca palms, and rice fields.

A busy fishing port, Samut Sakhon lies at the meeting of the Tachin River, the Mahachai Canal and the Gulf of Thailand. The main landing on the river-bank has a clock tower and a restaurant serving excellent seafood. Nearby, fish-ermen at the fish market unload fish, crabs, squid and prawns from their boats. At the fish-market pier, it's possible to hire a boat for a round-trip to Samut Sakhon's principal temple, Wat Chom Long, at the mouth of the Tachin River. Most of the buildings are modern except for an old viharn, which dates back about a century, immediately to the right of the temple's river landing. The exten-sive grounds overlooking the water are charmingly laid out with shrubs and flowering trees. There is also a statue of Chulalongkorn. His homburg hat does not in the least detract from his immense dignity.

From Samut Sakhon, cross the river to the railway station on the opposite side. Here, board a second train for another 40-minute trip to **Samut Songkhram ❽**, on the banks of the Meklong River. The journey goes through

**Map,
page 179**

BELOW: harbour at
Samut Songkhram.

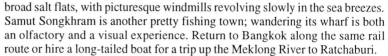

broad salt flats, with picturesque windmills revolving slowly in the sea breezes. Samut Songkhram is another pretty fishing town; wandering its wharf is both an olfactory and a visual experience. Return to Bangkok along the same rail route or hire a long-tailed boat for a trip up the Meklong River to Ratchaburi.

Eighty kilometres (50 mi) southwest of Bangkok, near Samut Songkhram, lies the town of **Damnoen Saduak ❾**, famous for its daily floating market. Beginning before dawn, women in traditional straw hats manoeuvre flat-bottomed boats laden with produce, fish and flowers into position along the canals. They hawk their wares in a colourful spectacle lasting most of the morning, but be there early (the majority of tourists arrive on buses around 9am) for the most authentic experience. Air-conditioned buses depart the southern bus terminal for Damnoen Saduak every half hour beginning at 6am.

Kanchanaburi and the River Kwai

Established in the early 1800s, thus making it a young city by Thai standards, **Kanchanaburi ❿** is about 120 kilometres (75 mi) northwest of Bangkok, past Nakhon Pathom and not far from the Thai border with Burma. It prospers from gem mining and a teak trade with Burma. The world's smallest species of bat, about the size of a bumblebee, was discovered near an odd-looking railway bridge crossing the Meklong River, also known as the Kwai Yai, a few kilometres outside of Kanchanaburi. The bridge is contoured with a series of elliptical spans, with an awkwardly rectangular centre.

This bridge is often called the "Bridge on the River Kwai". In fact, it's not. The bridge that spanned the mightier Kwai River and inspired the novel and film was farther north. Of course, the original bridge no longer exists.

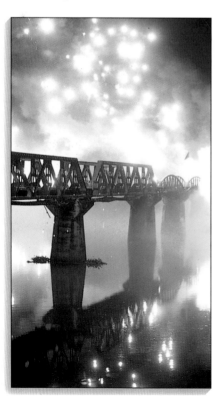

TIP

In late November and early December, Kanchanaburi has a week-long fair that features a nightly sound-and-light show celebrating the Allied attack on the bridge over the Kwai River. Make reservations well in advance – it's popular with locals.

BELOW: sound-and-light show over the Kwai Yai bridge.

Seeking to shorten supply lines between Japan and Burma in preparation for an eventual attack on British India, the Japanese began work on a railway between Thailand and Burma in 1942. For a large part of its 415 kilometres (260 mi), the railway followed the river valley. Although the logistics of doing so were often nightmarish, following the valley allowed construction of the railway simultaneously in different areas. At the end, there were nearly 15 kilometres (9 mi) of bridges completed. The Japanese forced 250,000 Asian labourers and 61,000 Allied prisoners-of-war to construct 260 kilometres (160 mi) of rail on the Thai side, to Three Pagodas Pass on the border. It is estimated that 100,000 Asian labourers and 16,000 Allied prisoners lost their lives from beatings, starvation, disease and exhaustion. In Kanchanaburi, graves mark 6,982 of those Allied soldiers. There are two cemeteries in Kanchanaburi. The larger is on the main road nearly opposite the railway station; the second, Chungkai, is across the river on the banks of the Kwai Noi. Both hold the remains of Dutch, Australian, British, Danish, New Zealander and other Allied prisoners-of-war; American dead were removed to Arlington Cemetery, outside Washington, D.C.

An appreciation of the enormous obstacles the prisoners faced is provided by the **JEATH Museum** (open daily; admission fee), near the end of Lak Muang Road. (The name derives from the first initial of those nationalities involved in the construction.) Established in 1977 by the monks of **Wat Chaichumpol** (Wat Chanasongkhram) next door, the museum was constructed like the bamboo huts in which the war prisoners lived. Utensils, paintings, writings and other objects donated by prisoners who survived share some of the horror of their hellish existence.

Don't confuse the JEATH Museum with the newer **World War II Museum** that is located beside the bridge; the signs can be misleading. The World War II Museum is a curious hodge-podge of exhibits including prehistoric village life, Thai proverbs, stamps, currency, animal skeletons, and one notable display in the rear courtyard of exceptionally poor taste.

In spite of the fact that the memorial bridge is often mistaken for the one made famous in print and film, it is worthwhile visiting from an historical point of view. It can be reached by boat or samlor from Kanchanaburi. Visit at 11am or 4.30pm if you want to see the train passing over the bridge.

The bridge has lost some of its artificial mystery with commercialisation, but walking across it is a sobering experience. (Niches between the spans provide an escape in case a train passes by.) A steam locomotive used shortly after the war is displayed beside the tiny station platform, along with an ingenious Japanese supply truck that could run on both roads and rails. Floating restaurants and hotels line the banks of the river, which is attractive and peaceful despite its grisly history.

Today, most of the old tracks have been removed, except for a section running peacefully from Kanchanaburi to the terminus at Nam Tok, a 50-kilometre (30 mi) journey taking about one-and-a-half hours across one of the shakiest bridges in the world; the wooden pillars and sleepers creak and groan as the train moves slowly across them. ❑

Map, page 179

Detail from Wat Chaichumpol.

BELOW: crossing on the modern bridge over the Kwai Yai.

Map,
page 179

THAILAND

Bangkok

BELOW: woman from near the Burmese border.

FAR TO THE WEST

Beyond the day-trip to Kanchanaburi are some of Thailand's wild lands. Keep going, and one reaches the border with Burma. Unfortunately, only Thais can continue onward beyond the frontier

To head out from Kanchanaburi towards the lush, mountainous west is to take a road to nowhere. Or so it seems. Remote Three Pagodas Pass has little to show beyond the modest markers that give it its name, a military checkpoint and a small thriving market. Nearby Sangkhlaburi is a somnolent, spacious outpost perched between lake and jungle. Beyond the peaks and clouds lies southern Burma, as inaccessible as it is close.

The highway out of Kanchanaburi winding northwest towards the Burmese frontier may be going nowhere much – no border crossings are permitted – but there is no shortage of natural and historical diversions along the way. An appropriate beginning, one which gives context to this jungled area's ancient origins, is the prehistoric burial site at the village of **Ban Kao ⓫**, on a side road about 30 kilometres (18 mi) into the 250-kilometre (150 mi) stretch from Kanchanaburi to the Burmese border. Neolithic remains discovered near the village may date as far back as 10,000 years, archaeologists believe. At a small museum near the site are pottery and human remains that date from 3,000 to 4,000 years ago.

Seven kilometres (4 mi) and a few millennia further on, the 13th-century remains of a Khmer city associated with the Angkor empire have been turned into an historical park. **Prasat Muang Singh ⓬**, situated prettily on the Kwai

Noi, covers 70 hectares (170 acres) and encompasses four groups of ruins. Sculptures of deities, laterite brick shrines, and the remains of an elaborate water system can be seen.

Jumping centuries ahead again, the tendency of jungle and time to erase the evidence of history has been energetically tackled at a World War II site 80 kilometres (50 mi) beyond Kanchanaburi on Route 323. **Hellfire Pass** ⑬ is the largest of many mountain cuttings carved out of rock in atrocious conditions by Asians and Allied prisoners-of-war forced to build the so-called Death Railway, intended by the Japanese to link Singapore and India. The pass has been turned into a memorial for the thousands who died, mainly of malaria and dysentery. The prisoners worked with hammers, picks, shovels, steel tap drills and dynamite. Close examination of the sheer walls of Hellfire Pass reveals the marks of the old drills and blast holes. Most of the railway was abandoned or dug up soon after the war ended. A portion that remains takes visitors from Kanchanaburi to Nam Tok, a small touristy market town not far from the pass.

About 20 kilometres (12 mi) further up Highway 323, and also reachable by boat from Nam Tok, **Sai Yok National Park** ⑭ evokes a light-hearted atmosphere with picnickers and swimmers – in stark contrast to the gory Russian roulette scenes filmed here for the movie *The Deerhunter*. Sai Yok is quieter than **Erawan National Park** ⑮, with one of Thailand's most popular waterfalls and about 80 kilometres (50 mi) from Kanchanaburi along a different road. Beyond Erawan to the northeast are two limestone caves, Tham Phra That and Tham Wang Badan, as well as Huay Khamin Falls, with large, deep pools.

Back on Highway 323, the **Hin Dat** hot springs make a restful stop. Just yards from the freezing and rushing river water, bathers soak quietly in calm, steam-

TIP

Within the 500 square kilometres of Sai Yok National Park, accommodations available include simple bungalows and houseboats.

BELOW: clouded leopard, and black-throated sunbird.

Map,
page 179

*Parts of Burma
beyond Three
Pagodas Pass were
taken from ethnic
groups by Burma's
army in the 1990s.
Several refugee
camps on the Thai
side, most of them
well off main roads,
hold thousands of
Mon and Karen
refugees.*

OPPOSITE: deciduous
forest north of
Sangkhlaburi.
BELOW: on the lake
near Sangkhlaburi.

ing, mineral-rich hot springs. Food stalls, shrines and pleasant walking areas add to the gently festive atmosphere. Just beyond, the Phatat waterfall is a short drive to the right from the main highway. Slightly further on, one of a number of elephant camps along this route is open to the public.

Thong Pha Thum, nestled under the mountains, is the last village before the winding, climbing ascent to Sangkhlaburi, where the combination of steep limestone mountains and a huge lake created by the Khao Laem hydroelectric dam make for dramatic views. At about the half-way mark along this stretch, high in the mountains, the **Sunyataram Forest Monastery** is a meditation retreat affiliated with the charismatic Phra Yantra Bhikku, one of Thailand's most famous and revered monks – at least until he was associated with a series of personal and financial scandals in the mid 1990s and defrocked.

The monastery, quiet now for perhaps less happy reasons than its original meditative purpose, is an attractive, slightly ramshackle collection of wooden buildings spread out over a section of old forest. Small fish pools and winding trails add to the charm. Devotees here haven't given up on the disgraced monk; the former Phra Yantra's posters still adorn some wooden walls and his sermons and books are for sale. Two other pleasant stops close by include the Dar Thongthong and Kroenkrawia waterfalls.

Sangkhlaburi 16, which may well be one of Thailand's prettiest towns, is still relatively undiscovered. Perched around the large Khao Laem reservoir, surrounded by high peaks and practically untouched by the kind of ugly concrete shophouse development that has spread throughout most of Thailand, it is a fascinating cultural meeting point. Thai, Burmese, Mon and Karen all live here, most involved in one way or another with border trade, legal and otherwise. Tourism is slowly but steadily increasing here in low-key fashion. The town has no real hotels, but a growing number of guesthouses cater to hardy travellers. The attractions include unbroken tranquillity, river rafting and hiking.

A stroll across a part of the lake, over Thailand's longest wooden bridge, leads to an attractive Mon village. Villagers, who built the bridge themselves, are experts at speedily negotiating on motorcycles the steep, bumpy lane that leads from the bridge to the main town. Just past the Mon village, the towering **Chedi Luang Phaw Utama**, which has fine vistas over the countryside, is topped by about 6 kilograms (13 lbs) of gold. The striking **Wat Wangwiwe Karam** nearby is built in an amalgamation of Thai, Indian and Burmese styles. In front of the chedi, a well-organised market sells Burmese and Mon handicrafts, textiles and other general goods.

Three Pagodas Pass 17, 16 kilometres (10 mi) beyond Sangkhlaburi at an elevation of 1,400 metres (4,600 ft), has been the main trade link between western Thailand and southern Burma for centuries. It was also the entry point into Thailand for invading Burmese troops on elephants during the Ayutthaya period. The fairly nondescript pagodas are less a draw for tourists than the busy marketing that goes on here. Beyond the checkpoints, the Burmese town of Paythonzu is generally open only to Thai day-trippers. ❑

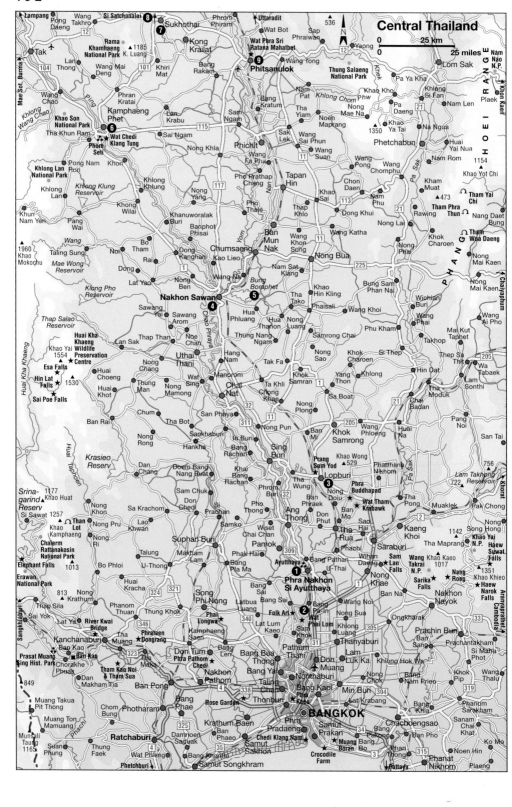

Central Thailand

0 — 25 km
0 — 25 miles

CENTRAL THAILAND

Here in the plain defined by the Mae Nam Chao Phraya,
Thailand's rice culture blossomed, as did its great empires

The traditional source of Thailand's wealth is rice. Intricately diked and irrigated rice fields have fed its people for more than 700 years. The central plains are the fertile heart of Thailand, towards which the early Thais steadily migrated from the mountains and valleys of the northern mountains.

Towards the end of the dry season, in May, the fields are alive with farmers turning the earth. A month or so later, when the rains have come, water covers the shallow paddies sprouting with young rice plants. In November, the rains fall off, and the grain turns golden. Harvest time. Afterwards, there are the festivals that coincide with the burning of the harvested fields, as the earth is prepared for another cycle of cultivation.

Several major rivers water this fertile heartland – notably the Ping, Wang, Yom and Nan, which eventually combine to form the majestic Chao Phraya, emptying into the Gulf of Thailand below Bangkok. Thai history has followed these rivers with the establishment of great empires, all found in the central plains: the Angkor-style towers of Lopburi, where the Khmers once ruled to reap the bounty of the plains, and the sprawling ruins farther south, near Bangkok, of once-great Ayutthaya. To the north, the flower of Sukhothai bloomed, perhaps the finest highlight of Thailand's past.

The wooden houses of the central plains, more than any other part of the country, reflect the classic style of Thai architecture. The paneled walls slant slightly inward to achieve an oddly graceful effect, the steep roof seeming to strain toward the sky. The faces of the people here in the central lowlands are less likely to reveal the imprint of Chinese, Lao, Burmese or Malay ancestry, as these races have intermingled with the Thai in both the cities and in the border regions.

Like the heartland of many countries, the central plains are often ignored by travelers on their way elsewhere, to Chiang Mai and the north, for example. Yet for those who stop here, perhaps more than anywhere else in Thailand, the foundations of Thai culture and society are best uncovered, and most readily understood. ❒

AYUTTHAYA AND LOPBURI

For four centuries, Thailand's capital city was at Ayutthaya, north of today's capital, Bangkok, and on the Mae Nam Chao Phraya, the great river through Thailand's central plains

Map, page 192

W ere one ignorant of the importance and history of **Ayutthaya ❶**, one would nonetheless be impressed by the beauty and grandeur of this city built by 33 monarchs over 400 years. From the ruins, it is easy to appreciate the genius of the kings who built this great city. Located 85 kilometres (55 mi) north of Bangkok, Ayutthaya was laid out at the junction of three rivers: Chao Phraya, Pa Sak, and Lopburi. Engineers had only to cut a canal across the loop of the Chao Phraya to create an island. Canals were also constructed as streets; palaces and temples were erected alongside.

To approach the city as 17th-century visitors did, travel up Mae Nam Chao Phraya from Bangkok. Several deluxe boats make a pleasant voyage of the journey. Once in Ayutthaya, a river tour around the island in a long-tail boat can be arranged on the landing stage close to Chan Kasem Palace. Not only is this an excellent introduction to the ruined city, it is also the most convenient way to reach some of the more isolated sites on the mainland side of the river. Despite the claims of some Bangkok tour operators, there is modern accommodation here, as well as several clean, inexpensive Chinese hotels.

OPPOSITE: chedi of Wat Phra Ram, Ayutthaya. **BELOW:** canal-side homes in Ayutthaya.

Foundations of Ayutthaya

Ayutthaya was founded around 1350 by a prince of U-thong. Thirty years later, the kingdom of Sukhothai passed under Ayutthayan rule, which then spread as far as Angkor in the east and Pegu, in Burma, to the west.

It was one of the richest cities in Asia by the 1600s – exporting rice, animal skins, ivory – and with a population of one million, greater than that of contemporary London. Merchants came from Europe, the Middle East and elsewhere in Asia to trade in its markets. Ayutthayan kings engaged Japanese soldiers, Indian men-at-arms and Persian ministers to serve in their retinues. Regular relations with Europe began in the early 1500s, first with the Portuguese and later with the Dutch, British, and especially the French. Europeans wrote awed accounts of the fabulous wealth of the courts and of the 2,000 temple spires clad in gilded gold.

As fast as it rose to greatness, it collapsed, suffering a destruction so complete that it was never rebuilt. Burmese armies had been battering at its gates for centuries – its strong fortifications, with ramparts 20 metres (65 ft) high and five metres (20 ft) thick, were generally effective – before occupying it for a period in the 16th century. Siamese kings then expelled the Burmese and reasserted their independence. In 1767, however, the Burmese triumphed again. In their victory, they burned and looted, destroying most of the city's monuments, and enslaving, killing, or scattering the population. Within a year, Ayutthaya had become a ghost town,

its population of over one million reduced to a few thousand. Today, the ruins stand by themselves on the western half of the island, with modern Ayutthaya a bustling commercial town concentrated in the eastern part of the island.

Start close to the junction of the Nam Pa Sak and Chao Phraya rivers, passing by the imposing **Wat Phanan Choeng Ⓐ**. Records suggest that the *wat* was established 26 years prior to Ayutthaya's foundation in 1350. The temple houses a huge seated Buddha, so tightly crowded against the roof that he appears to be holding it up. Wat Phanan Choeng was a favourite with Chinese traders, who prayed there before setting out on long voyages; it still has an unmistakably Chinese atmosphere.

Ayutthaya was at one time surrounded by stout walls, only portions of which remain. One of the best-preserved sections is at **Phom Phet**, across the river from Wat Phanan Choeng.

Upstream from Wat Phanan Choeng, the restored **Wat Buddhaisawan Ⓑ** (Phutthaisawan) stands serenely on the riverbank. Seldom visited, it is quiet, and the landing is an excellent place to enjoy the river's tranquillity in the evenings. Farther upstream, the restored **Cathedral of St Joseph** is a Catholic reminder of the large European population that lived in the city at its prime.

Where the river bends to the north is one of Ayutthaya's most romantic ruins, **Wat Chai Wattanaram Ⓒ**, erected in 1630. Perched high on a pedestal in front of the ruins, a Buddha keeps solitary watch. The stately *prang* with its surrounding *chedi* and rows of headless Buddhas make a fine contrast to the restored **Queen Suriyothai Chedi Ⓓ** on the city side of the river. Dressed as a man, the Ayutthaya queen rode into battle, her elephant beside that of her husband. When she saw him attacked by a Burmese prince, she moved between

TIP

Vendors sell ceramics they claim were dropped overboard by 17th-century sailors, only recently recovered. Given the volume of the wares and length of time they have been on sale, the sailors must have been very butterfingered.

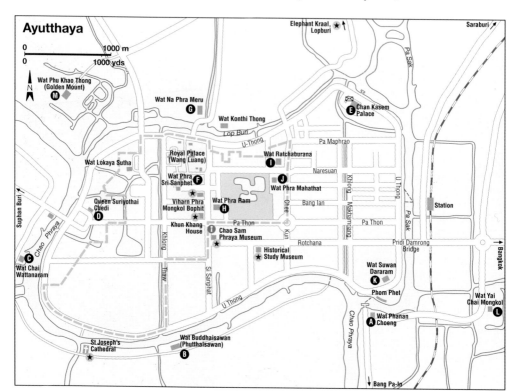

them with her elephant, receiving a lethal lance blow intended for her husband.

Chan Kasem Palace ❺, known as the Palace of the Front, was originally constructed outside the city walls, close to the junction of the rivers and the new canal. King Naresuan built it as a defensive bastion while he was engaged in wars against his northern rivals from Chiang Mai. In 1767, the Burmese destroyed the palace, but King Mongkut later resurrected it in the 19th century as a royal summer retreat for escaping Bangkok's heat. Now housing a small museum, the palace looks out on the busiest part of the modern town.

The old royal palace, **Wang Luang**, apparently was of substantial size, if the foundations for the stables of 100 elephants are any indication. It was later razed by the Burmese. The bricks were removed to Bangkok to build its defensive walls, so only remnants of the foundations survive to mark the site. Close by stands the three stately chedi of **Wat Phra Sri Sanphet** ❻, a royal temple built in 1491 that honours three 15th-century kings. The identical chedi have been restored and stand in regal contrast to the surrounding ruins.

For two centuries after Ayutthaya's fall, a huge bronze Buddha sat unsheltered near Wat Phra Sri Sanphet. Its flame of knowledge and one of his arms had been broken when the roof, set afire by the Burmese, collapsed. Based on the original, a new building, the **Viharn Phra Mongkol Bophit**, was built in 1956 around the restored statue. The resulting shrine works remarkably well, the giant black-coloured Buddha exuding a genuinely numinous feeling of power.

Across the river from the old palace stands another restored temple, **Wat Na Phra Meru** ❼. Here, a large stone Buddha is seated in the "European fashion" on a throne – a sharp contrast to the yoga position of most seated Buddhas. Found in the ruins of Wat Mahathat, the statue is believed to be one of five that

Map, page 196

An elephant-mounted Ayutthayan general prepares to lead his army against the Burmese.

BELOW: Ayutthayan jewelry, and Lopburi sculpture.

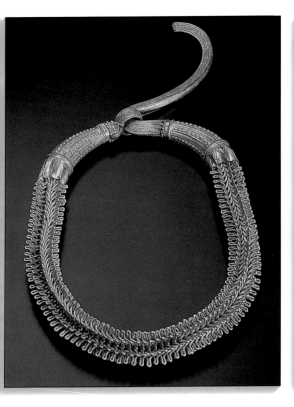

originally sat in a recently-unearthed Dvaravati-period complex in Nakhon Pathom. The bot contains an Ayutthaya-style seated Buddha on the altar. Across a bridge from Wat Na Phra Meru are the ruins of **Wat Konthi Thong**.

Back on the island and across the road from Phra Mongkol Bophit, **Wat Phra Ram** ⓗ is one of Ayutthaya's oldest temples. Founded in 1369 by the son of Ayutthaya's founder, its buildings dating from the 1400s have been completely restored twice. Elephant gates punctuate the old walls, and the central terrace is dominated by a crumbling prang to which clings a gallery of stucco *naga*, *garuda* and statues of the Buddha. The reflection of Wat Phra Ram's prang shimmers in the pool that surrounds the complex. Once a marshy swamp, the pool was dug to provide landfill for the temple's foundations.

Two of Ayutthaya's finest temples stand side by side northeast across the lake from Wat Phra Ram. Built in 1424 by the seventh king of Ayutthaya as a memorial to his brothers, the well-known **Wat Ratchaburana** ⓘ dominates its surroundings. Excavations during its restoration in 1958 revealed a crypt containing gold jewelry, Buddha images and other objects, among them a charming, intricately decorated elephant – property of the interned brothers. These treasures are kept in the **Chao Sam Phraya National Museum** (open daily; admission fee) to the south. Some of Thailand's finest ancient paintings cover crypt walls.

Across the road, **Wat Phra Mahathat** ⓙ is one of the most beautiful temple complexes in Ayutthaya, and one of its oldest, dating from the 1380s. Its glory is its huge prang, which originally stood 46 metres (150 ft) high. The prang later collapsed, but it was rebuilt four meters higher than before. Stone Buddha faces, each a metre in height, stand silently around the ruins. Together with the restored chedi that ring the prang, these combine to make this one of the most impres-

In 1957, looters removed much of the gold from Wat Ratchaburana. Only some was recovered.

BELOW: the restored Wat Phra Ram.

sive sites in Ayutthaya. Next door, the government has built a model of how the royal city may have once looked.

Wat Suwan Dararam , to the southeast and constructed near the close of the Ayutthaya period, has been beautifully restored. The foundations of the *bot* dip in the centre, in emulation of the graceful deck line of a boat. This typical Ayutthayan decoration is meant to suggest a boat that carries pious Buddhists to salvation. Delicately-carved columns support the roof, and the interior walls are decorated with brilliantly-coloured frescoes. Still used as a temple, the atmosphere of the wat is magical in the early evening when the monks chant their prayers. East is **Wat Yai Chai Mongkol** , originally established in the mid 1300s. In single-handed combat on elephant-back, King Naresuan slew the crown prince of Burma in 1592. The immense chedi, built to match the Phu Khao Thong Pagoda just north of Ayutthaya, was erected in celebration of the victory. Buddha statues line the courtyard.

Just north of Ayutthaya, the **Wat Phu Khao Thong** , better known as the **Golden Mount**, stands with its 80-metre-high (260 ft) chedi alone amidst the rice fields, its upper terraces commanding a panoramic view of the countryside. While the wat dates from 1387, the chedi was built by the Burmese after their earlier and less destructive conquest in 1569. It was later remodelled by the Siamese in their own style. In 1957, to mark 2,500 years of Buddhism, a 2,500-gram (5.5 lb) gold ball was mounted on top of the chedi.

In the opposite direction from the Golden Mount, the road runs to the only **elephant *kraal*** left in Thailand. This 16th-century kraal is a reminder of the days when elephants were not only caught and trained to work in the jungles, but were also an essential requisite for a strong army. The last elephant roundup

Map, page 196

BELOW: Wat Ratchaburana.

was in 1903. Standing at the edge of the restored stockade with its huge teak columns, one can imagine the thunder of the mighty beasts.

Bang Pa-In ❷, a charming collection of palaces and pavilions once used as a royal summer retreat, lies a short distance downriver from the ruins of Ayutthaya. The rulers of Ayutthaya used Bang Pa-In as long ago as the 17th century, but the buildings one sees today date from the late 19th- and early 20th-century reigns of Rama V and Rama VI, who used to come up from Bangkok.

Lopburi

The former summer capital of Siam, **Lopburi** ❸, lies 10 kilometres (6 mi) north of Ayutthaya. Here, the hills of the Khorat Plateau appear on the horizon, the first break in the flatness of the central plains.

Artifacts from the neolithic and bronze ages have been found in large quantity in Lopburi, testifying to the great antiquity of the city. In the Dvaravati period, from the sixth to 11th centuries, it was a major religious centre thought to have attracted savants from around the region. At the height of the Angkor empire in the 11th and 12th centuries, it was a provincial capital. Then came the Thais, who put their imprint on most of the old buildings that now survive. It was not until the mid 1600s that Ayutthaya became a bustling international city with upwards of three dozen nationalities represented. Some French architects even ventured to Lopburi, where Narai retreated in summer to escape the heat.

The grounds of **Narai Ratchaniwet**, or **Lopburi Palace** (also called King Narai's Palace), built between 1665 and 1677, are enclosed by massive walls, which still dominate the centre of the modern town. The palace grounds have three sections enclosing its governmental, ceremonial and residential buildings.

In 1688, as Narai lay mortally ill in his palace, an army officer seized the throne. The king called in a Buddhist abbot to ordain his loyal attendants as monks, to save them.

BELOW: elephant round-up at Ayutthaya's kraal, 1895.

Moving inward, the middle section once enclosed the Dusit Maha Prasat Hall, Chantra Paisan Pavilion, and Phiman Mongkut Pavilion. The inner courtyard was that of the king, where his residence, Suttha Sawan Pavilion, was nestled amidst gardens and ponds.

Of King Narai's buildings, the only one that has substantially survived is the **Dusit Maha Prasat**. This was built for the audience granted by the king in 1685 to the ambassador of Louis XIV. Near the Dusit Maha Prasat is the **Phiman Mongkut Pavilion**, a three-storey mansion in the colonial style and built in the mid-19th century by King Mongkut. The immensely thick walls and high ceilings show how the summer heat was averted most effectively before air-conditioning arrived. The mansion, small but full of character, displays a mixture of bronze statues, Chinese and Sukhothai porcelain, coins, Buddhist fans, and shadow-play puppets. Some of the pieces, particularly the Ayutthaya bronze heads and Bencharong porcelain, are superb.

King Narai had a Greek adviser, Constantine Phaulkon, who had come to Asia years earlier on a merchant ship as a cabin boy. Although not officially the foreign minister, by the mid 1680s Phaulkon was managing Siam's relations with the European powers. However, his ambition also led him to meddle in domestic matters, making him unpopular with the Buddhist clergy and with officials of Narai's government. When the king lay dying, Phra Phetracha seized power and had Phaulkon tortured, then hacked to pieces.

The remains of a grand palace in Lopburi, said to have belonged to Phaulkon, rival those of the royal palace. Located just north of Narai's residence, the buildings show strong European influence, with straight-sided walls and pedimental decorations over Western-style windows. ❏

Map, page 192

BELOW: Phaulkon's palace, Lopburi.

Map,
page 192

THE CENTRAL PLAINS

For most foreign travelers, Thailand's central plains is a fly-over or drive-through zone on the way to the north. Yet, culturally and agriculturally, it is one of Thailand's most important regions

Nakhon Sawan ❹, 250 kilometres (150 mi) north of Bangkok, has long been an important commercial centre because of its location as the hub of roads and rivers connecting north and central Thailand. The Ping and Nan rivers, already swollen by their tributaries, meet the Wang and the Yom at Nakhon Sawan, forming the Chao Phraya. Route 1 divides here, sending a branch, Route 117, due north to Sukhothai and Phitsanulok, while itself continuing northwest towards Tak. Reaching one's destination in the central plains, as in most other parts of Thailand, is generally quick and comfortable. The main cities in the centre are linked to Bangkok by road, rail and air. Of these three modes, the most common is by coach.

Under its old name of Paknampoh, Nakhon Sawan played a vital role in the teak trade. It was here that the great teak rafts, which had sometimes been travelling for two or three years from the northern forests, were broken up into smaller rafts for floating down to Bangkok on the Chao Phraya River. Teak rafts may still occasionally be seen on the river below Nakhon Sawan, but since the government's banning of logging in Thailand, they are not nearly as numerous as they were in the heyday of Thailand's teak trade. Today, there are few traces of Nakhon Sawan's historic past in the modern commercial town.

BELOW: central-plain smile, and a face at a local fair.

The most notable shrine is outside the town, across the bridge over the Chao Phraya. Here on a small hill stands **Wat Chom Kiri Nak Phrot**. On a clear day the views from the top of the hill are stunning. The main structure dates from the 14th-century Sukhothai period, but the Buddha image, seated on a throne supported by demons, is of the Ayutthaya period. Behind the main shrine is a massive, finely-adorned bronze bell about a century old, supported aloft on tall brick pillars.

A favourite outing for those living in and around Nakhon Sawan is a trip to **Bung Boraphet ❺**, a large lake a few kilometres to the east. Until they were hunted to extinction, crocodiles used to bask on its shores. This low-lying area acts as a catchment during the rainy season. At the height of the monsoon in September and October, the swollen lake covers an area of some 120 square kilometres (50 sq mi). A good time to visit is on a moonlit night, in the cool season, for a picnic on the island.

Found in the northern part of the Central Plains, this terracotta depicts Davaravati, 10th–11th century.

The "new" city of **Kamphaeng Phet ❻** lies three kilometres off Route 1, about 120 kilometres (75 mi) northwest of Nakhon Sawan and on the east bank of the Ping River. This city was built by King Li Thai (1347–1368), of the Sukhothai dynasty, to replace the older town of Chakangrao on the opposite bank. Both served as garrison towns for the Kingdom of Sukhothai.

Along the road to Kamphaeng Phet are the remains of a fort, **Phom Seti**, built to defend the former city of Chakangrao. Farther along the road is the well-restored *chedi* of **Wat Chedi Klang Tung** – the "Chedi in the Middle of the Fields" – another relic of the earlier city.

With its numerous rice and noodle houses, the modern part of town is on the other side of a bridge over the Ping River. The well-designed **Provincial**

BELOW: ruins of Kamphaeng Phet.

Map,
page 192

Museum contains one of Thailand's finest bronze statues of the Hindu god Shiva. This life-sized image was cast on the orders of the governor of Kamphaeng Phet in the first quarter of the 16th century.

Early during the reign of King Chulalongkorn, a German visitor removed the image's head and two hands. Too afraid to arrest a *farang* (Westerner), the governor quickly sent word to Bangkok that the priceless fragments were on their way by boat. Officials in Bangkok detained the German, who declared that he was going to give them to the Berlin Museum.

King Chulalongkorn, a skillful diplomat, found a way to placate the German as well as keep the cultural treasures for his country. He promised to send an exact copy of the whole Shiva image to Germany, so that the authentic fragments could remain in Thailand. And so it was done. The copy of the bronze is still in Berlin. Other exhibits in the museum include pre-Sukhothai bronzes, stucco Buddha heads from local monuments, and some ceramics.

A car or coach is necessary for a tour of the fortifications and temples, as they are some distance from the modern town. A visit to King Li Thai's fortifications reveals why the town was called Kamphaeng Phet, or Diamond Walls: the massive ramparts of earth are topped by laterite rising 6 metres (20 ft) above the outer moat, once overgrown with water hyacinths but now in the midst of an extensive restoration.

The chief monuments of Kamphaeng Phet lie northwest of the walled city. The monks who built them were of a forest-dwelling sect, strongly influenced by teachers from Sri Lanka. Their temples, constructed of laterite, are thought to show Ceylonese influence. Most of them, however, underwent major changes during restoration in the Ayutthaya period.

OPPOSITE: planting rice seedlings.
BELOW: Wat Phra Si Iriyabot.

The familiar themes of Buddhist architecture, *viharn* and chedi, are repeated in the ordination halls of two temples. These two temples are of special interest and should be seen even on a rapid tour.

The first, **Wat Phra Si Iriyabot**, derives its name from Buddha images that are depicted in four postures (*si* meaning four, and *iriyabot*, postures) on the central square *mondop* (sanctuary): walking, standing, sitting and reclining. The standing image is largely intact, with the original stucco coating on its head and lower part of the body. This is an impressive and unaltered example of Sukhothai sculpture. Unfortunately, the other images are in very poor condition. The whole temple stands on a platform that is encircled by the original laterite railing and walls. The other temple, **Wat Chang Rob**, or Shrine Surrounded by Elephants, consists of the base of a laterite chedi surrounded by elephant buttresses, a theme borrowed from Sri Lanka that claims the universe rests on the backs of these beasts.

The row of elephants on the south side is almost complete, but several are missing on the other flanks of the stupa. Unfortunately, the spire of the great monument has vanished, but the ruins of a crypt on the upper level of the stupa can still be inspected. The pillars of the former viharn also remain.

Repair work was completed in the late 1990s, restoring much of the original form without – luckily – robbing the elephants of their appeal. ❑

Culture of Rice

The Thai expression *kin khao* is translated as "to eat," but it actually means "to eat rice." Indeed, here where rice has been a staple for centuries, the two are synonymous.

The rice-planting season begins in May, when the king presides over the ancient ploughing ceremony at Sanam Luang, in Bangkok. This Brahmanic rite symbolises the attention that the spirits give to the prospects for the forthcoming rice harvest.

Cultivating rice is by necessity a cooperative effort, tightening the bonds of family and community. According to tradition, a farmer can ask fellow villagers to help with the work, and without having to pay for their labour. All that is expected from the host is a meal during the day, and perhaps some rice liquor at the end of the day's work. In the countryside, nearly everyone is a farmer as they put aside normal jobs to help with the preparation of paddy fields and the sowing of seed. Children are on holiday from school, as they will be when harvesting begins later in the year.

The social importance of this cooperation can hardly be exaggerated. It has a direct influence on individual behaviour, because if there are problems between individuals, families and communities, the work will not get done. Moreover, it is believed that quarrelling will upset the rice spirit and the crop may fail. Soon after the rice seedlings are transplanted into the paddy fields, villagers leave token packets of rice and other food in the fields as offerings to the rice spirit.

A ceremony important to the crop is the Bun Bang Fai, or skyrocket festival, which assures abundant rains. The festival that takes place as the monsoon rains begin has Buddhist origins, although it also contains elements of Brahmanism and animism. Buddhists say it began at the death of the Lord Buddha, when one of his grieving disciples, unable to touch his torch to the top of the funeral pyre, hurled it up to the top in a manner similar to the appearance of skyrockets being shot off. Villagers make their own rockets with gunpowder, launching them from a ladder-like structure, or from a very tall tree. Monks are involved, and if the rockets do not go off properly, the monks will lose prestige.

The cooperative effort given to the rice crop continues through the growing months. One of the most onerous tasks is keeping birds away from the ripening grain. By early December, rice is ripe enough for harvesting in Thailand's rice bowl, the central plains, and in the north, but the harvest comes later in the south. Harvesting schedules are fixed by common consent within each village.

Finally, when the rice is in the barns, the farmers at last relax and enjoy themselves. And it is then that they celebrate Songkran – the most joyous festival of the year, which marks the beginning of the traditional Thai new year, in April.

Big commercial farmers and agribusiness companies produce rice on a mammoth scale. Chemicals have now supplanted the powers of the rice spirit. Former farmers have left their fields altogether, and instead work on roads, drive trucks, and maintain tractors. Rice is no longer the top Thai export, but it is still a vital one – Thailand continues to remain the world's top rice exporter, earning about US$ 1.5 billion annually. ■

SUKHOTHAI

Map,
page 192

*Sukhothai, the first independent Thai kingdom, is considered to be
the golden era in Thailand's history. Some of ancient Sukhothai, at
the northern extent of the central plains, enchants today*

The route towards the ancient city of **Sukhothai ❼** (Dawn of Happiness)
passes through "new" Sukhothai, a bustling modern town of concrete shophouses. About 10 kilometres (7 mi) farther on, the road enters the limits of
old Sukhothai through the **Kamphaenghak (Broken Wall) Gate**. The authorities chose to run the road directly through the ruins, rather than around them.

The Sukhothai Kingdom began around 1240, when King Intradit asserted his
independence from the Khmers. Sukhothai, which grew to include most of modern-day Thailand and parts of the Malay Peninsula and Burma, is synonymous
with some of the finest artistic endeavours in Thai history, including perhaps
the most exquisite Buddha images. Unfortunately, the golden age was relatively
short-lived, just two centuries and nine kings long. The upstart Kingdom of
Ayutthaya absorbed Sukhothai in 1438. The most notable Sukhothai king was
Ramkamhaeng, who developed the Thai script, promoted Theravada Buddhism
and established links with China, among other accomplishments.

The remains of ancient Sukhothai's massive walls reveal that the inner city
was protected by no fewer than three rows of earthen ramparts and two moats.
The city was begun by the Khmers, who left behind three buildings and the
beginnings of a water system, similar to that of Angkor Wat. After the Angkorian
empire began to contract, the Khmers abandoned Sukhothai and the Thais
moved in, building their own structures. They eschewed the intricate Khmer
irrigation system, installing a much less complex one of their own. It is suggested that water, or the lack of it, in part contributed to the city's demise. It is
possible that the city was originally served by the Yom River, which later shifted
course and deprived Sukhothai of a dependable source of water.

Exploring the ancient city

A short distance from Kamphaenghak Gate is the **Ramkamhaeng National
Museum** (open daily, 8.30am–4pm; admission fee), a good starting point for a
tour of the enclave. The museum contains a fine collection of Sukhothai sculpture, ceramics and other artifacts, as well as exhibits from other periods. The
entrance hall is dominated by an impressive bronze image of the walking Buddha. This style of image is regarded as the finest sculptural innovation of the
Sukhothai period (1230–1440). There had been earlier essays in high and low
relief, but the Sukhothai sculptors were the first to create statues of the walking
Buddha. It also displays the elements that typify the Sukhothai style, including
fluid lines, a somewhat androgynous figure, and strict interpretation of the 32
raksana, or characteristics by which a Buddha would be recognised: wedge-
shaped heels, arms hanging to the knees, fingers and toes of equal length,
amongst other distinguishing features.

Walking in Sukhothai.

In this period, the Thais definitively embraced Theravada Buddhism and
invited monks from Sri Lanka to clarify points of scripture. While Buddhism
was blossoming, Hindu influence remained strong, indicated by the two bronze
images of Hindu gods flanking the walking Buddha in the museum. The one on
the right, with the combined attributes of Vishnu and Shiva, is especially fine.
Also worth noting is a stone torso of an *apsara,* or celestial maiden, in the Khmer
style. An important object proudly displayed on the mezzanine floor is a copy of

Opposite: Wat
Mahathat during
Loy Krathong.

the famous stone inscription of King Ramkamhaeng; the original is the most prized exhibit of the National Museum in Bangkok. It was at the **Non Prasat** (Palace Mound), now merely a slightly raised terrace of earth and brick, that the inscription was found. In 1833, the future King Mongkut, then a monk, discovered the stone, which had been inscribed in 1292. On it, King Ramkamhaeng had recorded his conquests in surrounding kingdoms, and the fact that in 1283 he devised the Siamese alphabet. However, some experts now doubt its authenticity and believe the inscription to be a much later forgery.

Once situated on the Non Prasat was the stone throne of Ramkamhaeng, and although there is little to be seen now, apart from the walled terrace, this was the numinous centre of old Siam. Alexander Griswold notes: "The political significance of the throne can scarcely be exaggerated, for the king sat on it when he discussed affairs of state… and when he received his vassals who came to do homage". The stone throne, called the Manangasila, is now in the Temple of the Emerald Buddha in Bangkok.

Over the centuries, until the 16th century, kings added to Wat Mahathat until there were 200 or so chedi.

Within the walls of Sukhothai are the ruins of some 20 temples and monuments. The greatest of them is **Wat Mahathat**, west of the museum. It is not known with certainty who founded this temple, which Griswold called "the magical and spiritual centre of the kingdom", but it is presumed to have been the first king of Sukhothai. Wat Mahathat owes its present form to a remodelling completed by King Lo Thai, around 1345.

BELOW: Wat Mahathat at sunset.

The original design, discovered a few years ago during repairs, was a quincunx of laterite towers based on a laterite platform. The four axial towers, which can still be seen, are of the Khmer style but with stucco decorations added by Lo Thai. The central tower is now hidden in the basement of Lo Thai's "lotus

bud" tower. The axial towers were linked to the central tower by laterite buttresses, which are still visible. The principal Buddha image, cast in bronze by King Lu Thai (1347–1368), is now in Bangkok, at Wat Suthat. The stucco frieze of walking monks around the base of the main tower is unusual.

Amongst the 20 other shrines within the walls, and some 70 more in the neighbourhood, many repeat familiar architectural themes. The following short-list reflects the monuments of special interest.

Wat Sri Sawai, southwest of Wat Mahathat, was originally a Hindu shrine that contained an image of Shiva. Triple towers remain, built in a modified Khmer style; the stucco decoration, added to the towers in the 15th century and showing mythical birds and divinities, is particularly fine.

Wat Chana Songkhram and **Wat Trakuan**, located immediately north of Wat Mahathat, have especially nice Sri Lankan-style chedi, of which only the lower parts still stand. Wat Trakuan has revealed many bronze images of the Chiang Saen period.

Wat Sra Sri, north on the other side of the highway and on the way to the southern gate, has a chedi of the Sri Lankan type. The ordination hall (*bot*) lies on an island to the east of the spire. The ruins of the main shrine consist of six rows of columns, which lead to a well-restored, seated Buddha image. Achille Clarac comments: "The detail, balance and harmony of the proportions and decoration of Wat Sra Sri, and the beauty of the area where it stands, bear witness to the unusual and refined aesthetic sense of the architects of the Sukhothai period".

Leaving the walled city by the northern San Luang, or the Royal Shrine gate, and travelling about a kilometre, one arrives at the important shrine of **Wat Phra Phai Luang**. It originally consisted of three laterite towers covered with stucco,

Map, page 192

BELOW: bullock cart decorated for Loy Krathong.

TIP

Perhaps the most
exquisite time of the
year to see Sukhothai
is during Loy Krathong,
during the November
full moon. This festival
celebrates the end of
the rainy season.

probably built in the late 12th century, when Sukhothai was still part of the Khmer empire. This shrine might have been the original centre of Sukhothai, since Wat Mahathat is of a later period. A fragmentary seated stone Buddha image, accurately dated to 1191 and the reign of the Khmer King Jayavarman VII, was found here and is now in the grounds of the town's Ramkamhaeng Museum. During restoration in the mid 1960s, a large stucco image of the Buddha in the central tower collapsed, disclosing numerous smaller images inside. Some date these images to the second half of the 13th century.

To the east of the main shrine lies a pyramidal brick chedi that originally contained seated stucco Buddha images dating from the late 13th century. Later, the niches were walled up with bricks, which were removed during a restoration started in 1953.

When heads of the stucco images began appearing on the antique market in Bangkok, authorities realised that the stupa was being pillaged. A team from the government was dispatched to the site, but most of the damage had already been done. Those heads – in the Chiang Saen style – that have not left the country are in private collections elsewhere in Thailand, or else in the custody of the National Museum in Bangkok.

Beyond Wat Phra Phai Luang to the west is **Wat Si Chum**, with one of the largest seated Buddha images in Thailand. The *mondop*, or enclosing shrine, was built in the second half of the 14th century, but the image itself, called Phra Achana, or The Venerable, is believed to be the one mentioned in King Ramkamhaeng's inscription. There is a stairway within the walls of the mondop that leads to the roof. The ceiling of the stairway is made up of more than 50 carved slate slabs with scenes from Buddhist folklore. Their function is to turn

BELOW: ruins of
Wat Chetupon.

the ritual climbing of the stairs into a symbolic ascent to Buddhahood. Partly because of the precarious nature of the stairway, and partially to avoid people standing above the Buddha's head, it is no longer permitted to climb the stairs.

There is a story that troops gathered here before an ancient battle were inspired by an ethereal voice that seemed to come from the Buddha itself. Some suggest a cunning ploy by a general who hid one of his men on the stairway and instructed him to speak through one of the windows concealed by the body of the image; the effect was inspiring, however, and the soldiers routed the enemy.

South of the walled city is another group of shrines and monasteries. One of the most interesting is **Wat Chetupon**, where the protecting wall of the viharn is made of slate slabs shaped in imitation of wood. The gates are also formed of huge plates of slate mined in the nearby hills. They somewhat resemble the megaliths of England's Stonehenge, but on a smaller scale. The bridges across the moat that surround the temple are also made of stone slabs. On the central tower of Wat Chetupon are Buddha images in the standing, reclining, walking and sitting postures. The walking Buddha here is regarded as one of the finest of its kind.

"To the west of the city of Sukhothai", says King Ramkamhaeng's inscription, "is a forested area where the king has made offerings. In the forest is a large, tall and beautiful viharn which contains an 18-cubit image of the standing Buddha". This is now identified as **Wat Saphan Hin**, Monastery of the Stone Bridge. It is so called because it is approached by a stairway of large stone slabs. The image is situated on the crest of a low hill and can be seen at a considerable distance. It is 12 metres (40 ft) high, with its hand raised in the attitude of giving protection, and is almost certainly the image described by King Ramkamhaeng.

Many other monuments are to be found in this western area. They were probably built by monks from Sri Lanka, who preferred to locate their monasteries in the forest. Another monument worth visiting, near the road and not far from the western gate of Sukhothai, is **Wat Pa Mamuang**, Shrine of the Mango Grove, where King Lu Thai installed a famous monk of the Theravada sect in 1361. Still standing are the shrine foundations and the ruins of the main chedi.

Outside Sukhothai

About 50 kilometres (35 mi) north of the modern town of Sukhothai, along a concrete highway, lies the venerable city of **Si Satchanalai** ❽ on the banks of the Yom River. Founded in the middle of the 13th century, as was Sukhothai, it served as the seat of the viceroys of Sukhothai and was always mentioned as the twin city of the capital. Whereas restoration, removal of trees, and the installation of lawns have removed some of the grandeur of Sukhothai, Si Satchanalai's setting gives it an aura few other ancient sites have. It is a pleasure to wander through the wooded complex, rounding a corner and being surprised by a new wat or monument.

The first and most important monument to visit in Si Satchanalai is **Wat Chang Lom**. There can be little doubt that this is the "elephant-girdled shrine" described in King Ramkamhaeng's stone inscription. The great king records that he started to build it in 1285 to house

Map, page 192

BELOW: standing Buddha at Wat Saphan Hin.

Map,
page 192

East a kilometre or so of Si Satchanalai is Chalieng, an earlier Khmer site from the late 1100s and early 1200s. It is thought to have been an outpost for travelers.

OPPOSITE: Wat Chedi Chet Thaew.
BELOW: Phra Buddha Chinaraj is venerated throughout Thailand.

some exceptionally holy relics of the Lord Buddha, and that it was finished six years later. It is the only surviving stupa that can be attributed with virtual certainty to King Ramkamhaeng. Built of laterite and stucco, it is a large bell-shaped spire in the Sri Lankan style standing on a two-storey, square basement. The upper tier contains niches for Buddha images, now mostly empty, while the lower level contains 39 elephant-shaped buttresses built of laterite blocks.

South of the Elephant Shrine are the ruins of **Wat Chedi Chet Thaew**, which include seven rows of chedi believed to contain the ashes of the viceroys of Si Satchanalai. One of the stupas has a stucco image of the Buddha sheltered by the *naga* (divine serpent), which is in unusually good repair.

Farther south still, and close to the massive walls of the city, are the remains of **Wat Nang Phya**, Temple of the Queen. This has fine stucco decoration on one of the external walls. Dating probably from the 16th century, this stucco work has some affinities with European baroque.

Other temples worth visiting include **Wat Khao Phanom Pleung** and **Wat Khao Suwan Kiri**, set on two scenic hills linked by a walkway. **Wat Phra Si Ratana Mahathat** in Chalieng, one of the most beautiful temples, lies a couple of kilometres southeast of the old city in a setting overlooking the Yom River.

Si Satchanalai is also associated with the famed Sawankhalok ceramics, which were among Thailand's first export products. The brown bowls and their distinctive double-fish design were sent to China aboard junks; remains of them have been found in the Gulf of Thailand. It is still possible to buy genuine antique Sawankhalok ceramics in the area; most, however, are copies.

Fifty kilometres (30 mi) east of Sukhothai, **Phitsanulok** ❾ now has only a few mementos of the past; a fire over three decades ago razed most of the old

town. The new city is a rather dull collection of concrete shophouses. However, nothing can detract from its superb location along the Nan River, with its quays shaded by flowering trees and its houseboats and floating restaurants moored beside the steep banks. The great fire fortunately spared **Wat Phra Sri Ratana Mahathat**, the principal shrine in Phitsanulok.

The **Phra Buddha Chinaraj**, the image in the main bot, is venerated throughout Thailand. This has given rise to a busy traffic in religious objects and souvenirs. The seated image was cast in the Sukhothai style.

The bot that enshrines the Phra Buddha Chinaraj comprises a three-tiered roof that drops steeply to head-high side walls, focusing attention on the gleaming image at the end of the nave. Flanking the image are two wooden pulpits of superb late-Ayutthaya workmanship. The large one on the left is for monks, who chant the ancient, Pali-language Buddhist texts. The smaller pulpit on the other side accommodates a single monk who translates the chants into Thai (since few of the congregation would understand Pali). Note the main doors inlaid with mother-of-pearl, dating from the late 18th century. The *prang* (spire) in the centre of the temple complex was rebuilt in the Khmer style by King Boromatrailokanat. The cloisters surrounding the prang contain Buddha images from several periods, some of them of great artistic value. A repository of art objects includes Thai and Chinese ceramics. ❏

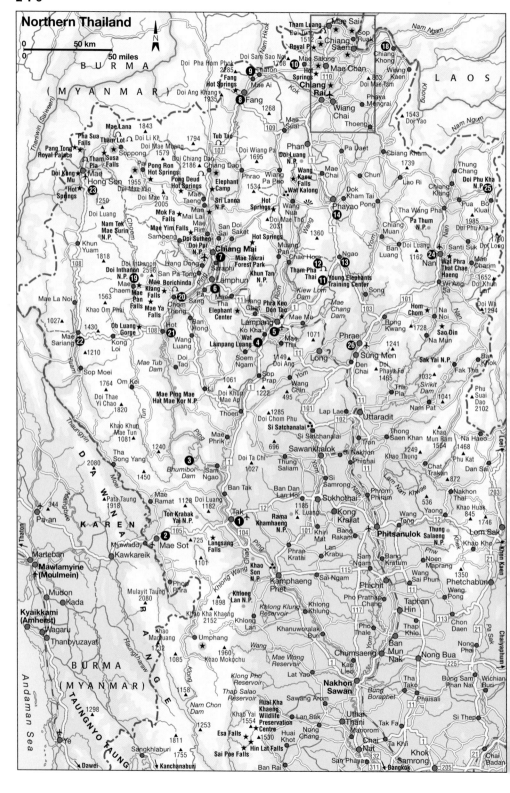

Northern Thailand

THE NORTH

*Travellers not heading for the southern beaches head for the
northern mountains, hill tribes and outdoor adventure*

The north of Thailand has been the setting for epic battles involving Burmese and Chinese invaders, and it has witnessed the magnificent rise – and collapse – of ancient kingdoms. Until the early part of the 20th century, it was accessible from Bangkok only by a complicated river trip, or by an uncomfortable journey of several weeks on elephant back.

It is not surprising, then, that the region has retained a distinct flavour all its own, one still so strong that tourists from other parts of Thailand come here almost as if to visit another country. They marvel at the profusion and beauty of the temples, with their splendid teak carvings and intricate Burmese-inspired decorations; the splendour of the wild orchids that grow so profusely in the hills; the gentle and good manners of the people (among whose hospitable habits it is to place a basin of cool water outside their gates to quench the thirst of passing strangers); and the novelty of having to bundle up in a sweater in the cool season.

The north is a region of great natural wealth and scenic beauty. Although decades of logging have reduced the hardwood forests, a logging ban has ensured the remainder will survive, whilst reforestation is already far advanced. In these jungled mountains live unusual people, now a tourist industry in their own right: Hmong people whose women wear vast, bulky turbans and clanking silver jewelry; Mien tribespeople dressed in finely-worked embroidery; and several small nomadic groups – like the Phi Thong Luang, or Spirits of the Yellow Leaves – who some thought existed only in myth. The hill tribes are still an exotic thread on the fringe of Thai life, but gradually they are being woven into the national fabric and are venturing to the larger cities of the north. Some – notably the Mien – prosper, running trendy stalls in the Chiang Mai night bazaar. Others, particularly the Akha, do less well, sitting and selling their wares on the pavement amidst the din and fumes of urban traffic.

It is hard for the authorities to adequately patrol this wild terrain, but easy for smugglers to slip back and forth across the borders with Burma and Laos in the notorious Golden Triangle. The government, however, with the active support of the king, has been increasingly successful in introducing alternatives to opium as a cash crop. Long closed on most northern frontiers, Thailand's borders are slowly opening up to foreign travellers. ❐

PRECEDING PAGES: a Lisu village brings in the traditional new year.

TOWARDS CHIANG MAI

North of Thailand's central plains, the land begins rising into highlands of the north. The approach to the north is classically transitional, whether regarding smuggling or history

Map, page 216

On the banks of the Mae Nam Ping, the quiet town of **Tak** ❶ is the gateway to the north, Thailand's most scenic region. Northwest of Kamphaeng Phet and west of Sukhothai, Tak is but a ghost of its former brawling self. Once called Raheng, it was a logger's town, and just north of Tak was the confluence of the Wang and Ping, two of the four main tributaries of the Mae Nam Chao Phraya. Logs freed from the wild rapids on the upper Ping and the Wang were floated downriver to Nakhon Sawan. The rapids have since been submerged under the reservoir of Bhumibol Dam, but the town's wild-west reputation has been sustained, to a degree, by the smuggling of gems, drugs and teak from nearby Burma.

During the 19th century, Tak was a provisions centre for journeys west into Burma and north to Chiang Mai. Until the railway was completed in the 1920s, the only way north was by boat, propelled by poles against the swift current. As the rapids were the most formidable obstacle on the river, Tak was an essential stop for rest and replenishment.

Today, Tak is a prosperous town just off Route 1. It is entered either by a direct route or by the old road that threads through tiny manicured gardens and around a pond near the provincial offices. Other than the river at sunset and the orange suspension bridge that resembles a miniature version of San Francisco's Golden Gate, Tak offers few exceptional sights. A broad esplanade separates the market from the Ping River; a dike holds back the river's waters, which once flooded during the rainy season.

OPPOSITE: officials with offerings en route to monastery, Lampang. **BELOW:** northern rice fields.

Towards Burma

Route 105 leads west through rugged hills towards the border town of Mae Sot. About 12 kilometres (8 mi) outside of Tak lies **Luang Larn National Park,** with waterfalls that are hidden behind a screen of bamboo groves. Increasingly scarce bears, deer and even leopards make the area home. If time allows, stop at the *nikhorn*, or "settlement", on Doi Musoe to view Lisu, Lahu and Hmong hill-tribe life.

Freshly brewed, locally grown coffee is on sale here to restore the passing motorist, as well as wild orchids and forest flowers. The road rises to Phawo Mountain, where truck drivers make offerings at an elaborate, *naga*-headed shrine for safe passage. Beyond the pass, the road drops through forest into a peaceful valley dotted with small farmhouses, white *chedi*, and ornate Burmese-style temples.

The streets of **Mae Sot** ❷, a somewhat boisterous frontier town, is home to a diversity of ethnic groups. Along with a vigorous smuggling trade, especially in Burmese teak since a Thai logging ban a few years ago, refugee camps on the outskirts of town have changed

much of Mae Sot's character. Shops advertise in Thai, Chinese, Burmese, and English. With its confusion of narrow streets, sidewalk stalls, bicycles, and pedestrian shoppers, it has the air of a frontier boom town.

From Mae Sot, it is a five-kilometre (3 mi) drive to the Burmese border. Worth a visit is an ornate Burmese temple with tiers of red-tiled rectangular roofs fringed with silverwork that are piled heavenward into a tower. Within the sanctuary are four Buddha images, one of which has gold jewelry distending its earlobes. Continue to the **Mae Nam Moei**, which forms the border with Burma. A new road bridge across the Moei to the Burmese town of Myawaddy has recently been completed, but has yet to open because of political disagreements.

North of Tak to Chiang Mai

Return to Tak and continue north on Route 1 and then onto Route 106, which describes an "S" and twines itself about Route 1. On the left, about 20 kilometres (15 mi) past Tak, the village of **Ban Tak** lies on the banks of the Ping River. In the days when the river offered the only passage north, Ban Tak was a village of boat builders. Today, it is quiet but picturesque, with houses on stilts that teeter on the riverbank and a rickety bamboo footbridge overlooking children swimming. Opened in 1964 and named after Thailand's current king, **Bhumibol Dam ❸** (also called Yanhee Dam), sits 30 kilometres (20 mi) north of Ban Tak, on the left of Route 1. The dam, Thailand's largest, generates enough power to light Bangkok and a large number of Thailand's rural provinces. With permission, it's possible to drive across the 154-metre-high (505 ft) cement retaining wall to view the reservoir stretching 120 kilometres (75 mi) northwest.

About 60 kilometres (40 mi) north of the Bhumibol Dam turn-off, Route 1

Bhumibol Dam.

BELOW: moving cattle on the open highway.

arrives at **Thoen**. Although Thoen can be passed through rapidly, it does enjoy a small claim to fame as the home of lucky *pohng kham* stones. Each pohng kham contains a variety of colours and encapsulated "scenes". Some of the clear pieces hold strange, crystalline formations resembling wisps of blue hair, jungle moss, or even a city skyline.

Map, page 216

From Thoen to Lampang, Route 1 undulates over teak-covered hills and a mountain pass sprinkled with spirit houses before dipping into the broad, cattle country of the Yom River Valley, dominated by the former kingdom of Lampang. Approximately 18 kilometres (12 mi) before Lampang is the junction with the road to **Ko Kha**.

Turn left past the town and cross the Wang River, bearing left for one kilometre, to reach one of the greatest treasures of the north: a revered temple, **Wat Lampang Luang ❹**. Cherished by scholars for its antiquity and delicate artwork, the temple compound is all that remains of a fortress city that flourished more than a millennium ago. It is said to have been founded by a 7th-century princess, Chama Dewi, who bore two sons; one became king of Lampang, the other, king of Lamphun. The wat, entirely rebuilt in the 16th century, played a key role in the golden period of the northern kingdoms. Nearly 200 years ago, Burmese invaders occupied the temple. According to legend, Lanna patriots sneaked into the temple through a drain, surprising and routing their enemy. Monks will point to a hole in the balustrade; it's said that the hole was caused by the cannon ball that killed a Burmese general.

The temple's museum features lacquered bookcases, jewelled Buddhas, and wooden *tong* banners that hang from poles like stiff flags. Most revered is a small Emerald Buddha believed to have been carved from the same stone as its

The main chedi at Wat Lampang Luang has taken on a bluish-green hue because of its copper covering oxidising from centuries of rain. Inside the chedi is said to be a relic of the Buddha, a strand of hair.

BELOW: teak viharn of Wat Lampang Luang.

**Map,
page 216**

Phra Keo Don Tao.

OPPOSITE: Buddha,
Wat Kukut.
BELOW: Wat Prathat
Haripunchai.

famous counterpart in Bangkok. It is displayed each November during the annual temple fair. The most important structures are the copper-plated chedi and the huge viharn with its low roofs.

About 20 kilometres (12 mi) north past Ko Kha, Route 1 enters the provincial capital of **Lampang ❺**. Half the size of Chiang Mai, it has been developed almost to the level of its northern cousin. While much of its bucolic tranquillity has disappeared, it retains one relic of the past found in no other Thai city: horse-drawn carriages. These can be hired by the journey or by the hour. There are few more romantic pursuits to be found in Asia than clip-clopping down a moon-lit back street.

Two Burmese-style temples in the town are worth visiting. Seven chapels, one for each day of the week, stand at the base of the chedi in **Wat Pha Sang**, located on the left bank of the Wang River. On the right bank, **Wat Phra Keo Don Tao** is a lovely fusion of Burmese and northern Lanna architecture. In the pavilion, columns soar to ceilings covered in a kaleidoscope of inlaid enamel, mother-of-pearl, and cut glass depicting mythical animals. North of town stand the 20 chalk-white spires of **Wat Chedi Sao Phra**, set in the rice fields.

Straddling the Ping River and once an influential centre of the Mon culture – until King Mangrai overran the city in 1281 – **Lamphun ❻** is just 25 kilometres (15 mi) south of Chiang Mai via an attractive, tree-lined highway.

Lamphun is said to date from the mid 6th century and is famed for two elegant temples, attractive and confident women, and succulent *lamyai* fruit. Located on the banks of the Mae Kuang River, the provincial town was once on the main road from Lampang to Chiang Mai. A highway now bypasses Lamphun, making for a quiet and peaceful atmosphere. The town has managed to preserve a mellow upcountry quality, appropriate to its historical dignity.

To gain the best perspective on **Wat Prathat Haripunchai**, enter it through its riverside gate, where large statues of mythical lions guard its portals. Inside the large compound, monks study in a Buddhist school set amidst monuments and buildings, which date as far back as the late 9th century, thus making the wat one of the oldest in northern Thailand. The base of the 50-metre-high (165 ft), gold-topped chedi in the centre of the courtyard is the oldest structure in the temple.

Ten centuries younger, but still respectably old, the gilt-roofed library stands to the left of a *sala* that shelters one of the world's largest bronze gongs. The somewhat disorganised temple museum contains a representative sampling of several styles of old Buddhist art.

A kilometre west of Lamphun's old moat stands **Wat Kukut**, dating from the 8th century. (It's also known as Wat Chama Devi.) The temple has a superb pair of unusual chedi. Erected in the early 1200s, the larger chedi consists of five tiers, each of which contains three niches. Each niche holds a Buddha statue, making an impressive display of 15 Buddha images on each side.

South of Lamphun, beyond the cotton-weaving town of **Pasang** – commonly believed by Thais to have the loveliest females in the country – is the hilltop pilgrimage centre of **Wat Phrabat Tak Pha**. A Buddha footprint on the hill is reached up a flight of 469 steps. ❐

CHIANG MAI

Map, page 216

Hill tribes lure travelers to the Chiang Mai area, although many hill villages and treks evoke commercialisation. Still, Chiang Mai's hospitality and the area's diverse offerings are reason enough to go

It has become commonplace in many guidebooks to bemoan the supposed demise of **Chiang Mai ❼**, Thailand's once fabulous "Rose of the North". Noisy *tuk-tuks* are said to have replaced silent *samlor* pedicabs, concrete commercial buildings to have ousted traditional wooden housing, and high-rise condominiums to have marred the serene northern skyline. Happily, this is far from being the case. Chiang Mai has grown, it is true, and the volume of traffic has certainly increased along with urbanisation.

But high-rise buildings are a thing of the past, at least in the beautiful and historically important old city, where all new construction is strictly limited to three-storey buildings. In recent years, the city streets have been attractively cobbled in red brick, concrete lamp standards replaced by ornate Parisian-style lanterns, and the city walls and moats excavated and restored.

Despite its increasingly rapid urbanisation, 700-year-old Chiang Mai remains prized as a pleasant, cool-season escape from the sticky humidity of Bangkok. Situated 300 metres (1,000 ft) above sea level in a broad valley divided by the picturesque 560-kilometre-long (350 mi) **Mae Nam Ping**, the city reigned for seven centuries as the capital of the Lanna (Million Rice Fields) Kingdom. The city's northern remoteness kept the region beyond the close control of Bangkok – 700 kilometres (400 mi) south – well into this century.

In its splendid isolation, Chiang Mai developed a culture quite removed from that of the central plains, with wooden temples of exquisite beauty and a host of unique crafts, including lacquerware, silverwork, wood carvings, ceramics and umbrella-making. Although hospitality of both the hill tribes and the northern Thais is sometimes strained by the sheer numbers of visitors, they remain more gracious than in many other cities.

OPPOSITE: northern farming.
BELOW: modern Chiang Mai.

Origins

Chiang Mai's story begins farther north, in the town of Chiang Rai. Its founder and king, Mangrai, ruled a sizable empire that ran as far north as Chiang Saen, on the Mekong River. He founded Chiang Rai in 1281. But when the Mongol ruler Kublai Khan sacked the Burmese kingdom of Pagan in 1287, Mangrai feared that his realm might be threatened and so formed an alliance with the rulers of Sukhothai, then Siam's capital. With his southern boundaries secure, Mangrai captured the old Mon kingdom at Lamphun. To centralise his rule, he established a new base in the Ping River Valley in 1296. This new capital he named Chiang Mai, or New City. The location was chosen by the auspicious sighting of white deer, and of a white mouse with a family of five, all at the same time, or so the story has it. Rather than building on the banks of the Ping, which often floods, he built his city with the help of 90,000

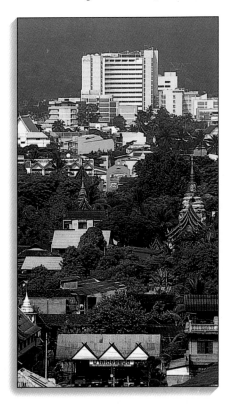

BELOW: grounds of
Wat Chiang Man.

labourers half a kilometre to the west and surrounding it with stout brick walls. Less than a century after Chiang Mai's founding, however, Ayutthaya replaced Sukhothai as the capital of Siam. This new kingdom had its own expansionist dreams and ambitions, including designs on its neighbour to the north. For the next 400 years, there was fierce competition and sometimes open warfare. In the 16th century, Ayutthaya crushed an invasion by Chiang Mai, and Chiang Mai's power waned. To compound its troubles, the region was invaded in the early 1700s by the same Burmese enemy who was laying siege to Ayutthaya.

Although the Burmese were finally defeated, the people of Chiang Mai were so exhausted and discouraged by the constant conflict that they abandoned the city. It remained deserted until 1796, when the Burmese army was finally defeated; new nobles began restoring the city to its former prominence. It continued to enjoy autonomy from Bangkok, at least until the railway brought meddling central government administrators. In 1932, following the death of the last king of Chiang Mai, the north was finally fully incorporated into the Thai nation.

Old Chiang Mai

The commercial centres of downtown are along Thanon Tapae, with numerous hotels, shops and guesthouses. Hotels have sprung up along Huai Kaeo Road, which leads out to Doi Suthep. Red *songtao* pick-ups may be hailed all over town; fares are a fixed five baht for most journeys. More expensive, but still quite cheap, tuk-tuk noisily carry passengers to any point around town. A few pedal samlor still offer a more leisurely way of travel.

The city's history began with **Wat Chiang Man Ⓐ**, which translates as "power of the city". In the northern part of the old city, it was the first temple to

be built by Mangrai, who resided there during the construction of the city in 1296. Located in the northeast part of the old walled city, it is the oldest of Chiang Mai's 300-plus temples. Two ancient, venerated Buddha images are kept in the abbot's quarters and can be seen on request. The first image, Phra Sae Tang Tamani, is a small 10-centimetre-high (4 in) crystal Buddha image taken by Mangrai to Chiang Mai from Lamphun, where it had reputedly resided for 600 years. Apart from a short sojourn in Ayutthaya, the image has remained in Chiang Mai ever since. On Songkran in April, it is paraded through the streets.

The second image, a stone Phra Sila Buddha in bas-relief, is believed to have originated in India around the 8th century. Both statues are said to possess the power to bring rain and to protect the city from fire. The only other important structure in Wat Chiang Man is Chang Lom, a 15th-century square *chedi*, buttressed by rows of stucco elephants.

Imperiously positioned at the head of the city's principal thoroughfare is **Wat Phra Singh B**, Chiang Mai's most important temple and also its largest. Founded in 1345, it dominates the quiet heart of the old, walled city, near the western gate of Suan Dok. Wat Phra Singh is noted for three monuments: a library, chedi and the Viharn Lai Kham. The magnificent Lanna-style wooden library, on the right side of the compound, is raised on a high base decorated with lovely stucco angels. Behind the main *viharn,* built in 1925, is a beautiful wooden *bot,* and behind this, a chedi built by King Pha Yu in 1345 to hold the ashes of his father. Wat Phra Singh's most beautiful building is the small Phra Viharn Lai Kham, to the left of the bot. Of all of Chiang Mai's temple buildings, it is perhaps the most outstanding. Built rather late in the Lanna period, in 1811, the wooden building's front wall is decorated in gold flowers on a red lac-

Map, page 227

Carved and gilded door, Wat Phra Singh.

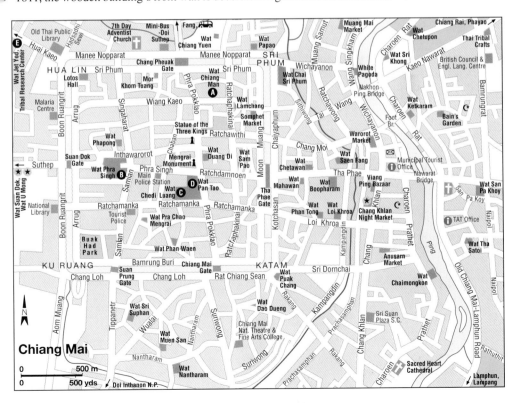

Chiang Mai

0   500 m
0   500 yds   Doi Inthanon N.P.

quer ground. Intricately carved wooden window frames accent the doors. The interior walls of the Viharn Lai Kham are decorated with murals commissioned by Chao Thammalangka, who ruled over Chiang Mai between 1813 and 1821. Although focusing on the Buddhist stories of Prince Sang Thong (north wall) and the *Tale of the Heavenly Phoenix* (south wall), they also record in fascinating detail aspects of early 19th-century Lanna society and exhibit clear indications of persisting Burmese cultural influence.

Calamity is associated with **Wat Chedi Luang ⓒ**, built in 1401 to the east of Wat Phra Singh. A century and a half later, a violent earthquake shook its then 90-metre-high (295 ft) pagoda, reducing its height to 42 metres (140 ft). It was never completely rebuilt, although recently it has been impressively restored. Even in its damaged state, the colossal monument is majestic. For 84 years the Emerald Buddha, now in Bangkok, was housed in this wat before being moved to Vientiane. King Mangrai was reportedly killed nearby by an untimely bolt of lightning. Close to the wat's entrance stands an ancient, tall gum tree. When it falls, says a legend, so will the city. As if serving as counterbalance, the *lak muang,* or city boundary stone, in which the spirit of the city is said to reside, stands near its base. The viharn of **Wat Pan Tao ⓓ**, adjacent to Wat Chedi Luang, formerly a palace, is a masterpiece of wooden construction. Its doorway is crowned by a beautiful Lanna peacock framed by *naga*, or mythical serpents.

Located one kilometre northwest of the city walls, **Wat Jet Yod ⓔ** was completed by King Trailokaraja in 1455. As its name "Seven Spires" suggests, it is a replica of the Mahabodhi Temple, in India's Bodhgaya, where Buddha gained enlightenment while spending seven weeks in its gardens. The beautiful stucco angels that decorate its walls are said to bear faces of Trailokaraja's own family.

BELOW: chedi of Wat Suan Dok hold ashes of Chiang Mai's royal family.

Although similar to a temple in Burma's then-capital of Pagan, it did not stop the Burmese from severely damaging it during the Burmese invasion of 1566.

One of the most impressive city temple complexes is **Wat Suan Dok ⑤**, one kilometre west of the wall's western gate. At its northwest corner are white-washed chedi that contain the ashes of Chiang Mai's royal family; the huge central chedi is said to hold no fewer than eight relics of Buddha. A short way out of town to the north, towards Doi Suthep, is **Wat U Mong**. With a honeycomb of underground cells used for meditation, the restored site lies amidst beautiful teak trees, and is one of the many quiet spots still left in Chiang Mai.

Map, page 231

Beyond the old city

A steep series of hairpin curves rise up the flanks of **Doi Suthep ⑥** – 15 kilometres (9 mi) northwest of the city – to Chiang Mai's best-loved temple, **Wat Doi Suthep**. The site was selected in the mid 1300s by an elephant that was turned loose with a Buddha relic strapped to its back. It climbed half-way up Doi Suthep, then stopped and would climb no more. Doi Suthep was built at the spot where it halted.

The architecture of Wat Doi Suthep is considered to be very representative of Lanna culture.

The ascending road passes the entrance to the Huai Kaeo Falls, where a minibus goes to the top. The scenery en route is spectacular, with the road winding its way to a large car park beneath Wat Doi Suthep. Seven headed naga undulate down the balustrade of a 290-step stairway that leads from the parking lot to the temple. For the weary, a funicular makes the same ascent for a few baht. From Wat Doi Suthep, Chiang Mai is spread out below at one's feet.

From the upper terrace, a few more steps lead through the courtyard of the temple itself. In the late afternoon light, there are few sights more stunning than that which greet one at the final step. Emerging from cloisters decorated with murals depicting scenes from the Buddha's life, one's eyes rise to the summit of a 24-metre-high (80 ft) gilded chedi, partially shaded by gilded bronze parasols. The chedi is surrounded by an iron fence with pickets culminating in praying *thevada,* or angels. Appearing in the east and west ends of the compound are two viharn. At dawn, the eastern one shelters chanting nuns in white robes. At sunset, the one on the west holds robed monks chanting their prayers.

BELOW: covered children.

From the parking area of Wat Doi Suthep, a road ascends 5 kilometres (3 mi) to **Phuping Palace ⑦**, the winter residence of the royal family. Constructed in 1972 and situated at 1,300 metres (4,265 ft), the palace has audience halls, guest houses, dining rooms, kitchens and official suites. It also serves as headquarters for the royal family's agricultural and medical projects, carried on among hill tribes and in nearby villages. When the royal family is absent, the public may stroll – Fridays through Sundays, and on holidays – through the well-tended gardens.

Commercialised hill tribes

From the palace entrance, the road continues through pine forests to the commercialised Hmong hill-tribe village of **Doi Pui**. The village has been on the tourist track for some time, but recent improvements have brought material benefits to its inhabitants, including a paved

street lined with souvenir stands. Once subsistence farmers, the tribespeople
have learned that visitors come bearing gifts, and a camera automatically triggers
a hand extended for a donation. Hmong are itinerant farmers here, and in Burma
and Laos. They once depended upon opium cultivation for their livelihoods.
Despite government efforts to steer them towards more socially acceptable
crops, many still cultivate patches deep in the hills.

An interesting insight into opium farming is provided by Doi Pui's Opium
Museum, which describes in detail the process of cultivation and harvest. For
those who lack the time to go deeper into the northern hills, this Hmong village
offers an example of hill-tribe life, though one doubts it retains much of its original personality.

Once an agricultural region, the **Mae Sa Valley ❶** cultivates a new money-
earner: tourism. Waterfalls, working elephant camps, butterfly farms, orchid
nurseries and a charming private museum called Mae Sa House Collection (with
prehistoric artifacts and Sukhothai ceramics, among many things) vie for the
visitor's attention. The valley also has quiet resorts along its river.

North of Chiang Mai

To reach the northern town of Fang, take Route 107 north from Chiang Mai
(beginning at Chang Puak Gate) towards Chiang Dao. The road passes through
rice fields and small villages, then begins to climb past Mae Taeng into the Mae
Ping Gorge, which forms the southern end of the Chiang Dao Valley. Ahead, on
the left as one follows the river's right bank through scenic countryside, is the
massive outline of Chiang Dao mountain.

At the 56-kilometre marker is the **Chiang Dao Elephant Camp ❶**, on the

bank of Mae Nam Ping. Twice daily, a line of elephants walk into the river to be bathed by *mahout* for the amusement of tourists, who reward the baby elephants with bananas. The elephants then move to a dusty arena to demonstrate how to make huge logs seem like toothpicks, picking them up or dragging them with great ease across the teak-shaded open space. After the show, one can take a short elephant ride, and then hire a small bamboo raft for a 45-minute trip down the Ping River.

About 60 kilometres (40 mi) from Chiang Mai on Route 107, a dirt road branches left and goes to **Doi Chiang Dao Ⓚ**, which at 2,186 metres (7,175 ft) is Thailand's third-highest peak. A jeep or a trail bike is needed to negotiate this 9-kilometre-long track, which leads up the mountain to the Hmong village of Pakkia. Entry to the sanctuary is restricted and permission must be obtained from the wildlife headquarters near Wat Pa Bong at the foot of the mountain.

The government's agricultural aid on Doi Chiang Dao is aimed at eradicating opium cultivation. From the government station here, officials trek out to assist hill tribes living on the slopes of Doi Chiang Dao and on the neighbouring mountains. At the nearby nursery, horticulturists experiment with new strains of tea that are gradually being introduced throughout the region.

Farther north, Route 107 enters the town of **Chiang Dao Ⓛ**, located 70 kilometres (45 mi) from Chiang Mai. Chiang Dao is a quiet wooden town supplying surrounding villages, but its cafes and general stores are interesting. At the far end of town, a simple road leads off west and to the left for 5 kilometres to caves. Guides with lanterns lead visitors deep into high caverns containing several Buddha statues. Further down in a deeper section of the cave is a large, reclining limestone Buddha. ❐

Map, page 231

Elephant training.

BELOW: April's Songkran festival in Chiang Mai.

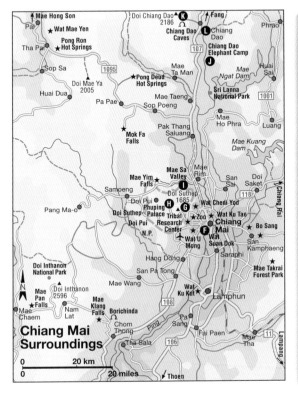

Chiang Mai Surroundings

CHIANG RAI AND THE GOLDEN TRIANGLE

Map, page 216

Just the mention of "Golden Triangle" suggests uncertain frontiers and illicit smuggling. And, indeed, both are found here. But the area north of Chiang Rai also offers escapes for the adventurous

Like other cities of the north, Chiang Rai has undergone rapid development, not only in the town itself but also in the surrounding hills where vacation homes for affluent Thais are rising. Indeed, for travellers seeking the exclusively historical, Chiang Rai has little of its rich past extant. Capital of Thailand's northernmost province, Chiang Rai lies only about 65 kilometres (40 mi) to the east of Fang. But for most visitors the trip to Chiang Rai begins in Chiang Mai, the focal point for the northern part of the country.

From Chiang Mai

Out of Chiang Mai, Route 107 heads due north past Chiang Dao to **Fang ❽**, located 150 kilometres (100 mi) from Chiang Mai. Fang is another town where development has dulled a reputation for wildness. Established by King Mangrai in the late 1260s, Fang was levelled by the Burmese in the early 1800s and remained uninhabited until the 1880s. During the 1950s, the district witnessed a "black-gold rush" following a minor discovery of crude oil. Production never matched expectations, but "nodding donkey" pumps still groan and grind in the fields to the west of the town.

OPPOSITE: ferry on the Mekong. **BELOW:** opium poppy.

Fang enjoys a reputation for opium smugglers, although nothing in its seemingly-benign appearance would suggest such. Straddling both sides of the road in a flat valley, Fang is home to remnants of Chiang Kai-shek's Guomintang (Nationalist) army; these Chinese-speaking soldiers fled China's Yunnan province after the 1949 Communist takeover, settling in Chiang Mai and Chiang Rai provinces.

Dressed in distinctively embroidered clothing, Mien hill tribes live in the mountains east of Fang. The women wear black hats decorated with red or magenta woolen balls, while babies carried on their mothers' backs sport little embroidered caps. Young girls may spend an entire year embroidering large pants for their weddings. The government has worked extensively with the Mien, promoting crops as substitutes for the more lucrative opium.

A few kilometres south of Fang, Route 109 cuts east towards Chiang Rai. North from Fang, a rough road leads 25 kilometres (15 mi) to **Thaton ❾**, on the banks of the Mae Kok. Here, rent a boat for an exciting 3-hour journey down the Kok to Chiang Rai. It is now also easy to continue north to the hill town of **Mae Salong ❿**.

The road is dusty but wide and has been paved since 1991. It swiftly climbs a ridge along the Burmese border, emerging at a small town clinging to the hillsides. At first, it seems one has taken a wrong turn and ended

Northern Akha child.

up in a Chinese village. The walls of the houses are decorated by red banners covered in gold Chinese characters; everyone speaks Chinese, while only the young speak Thai.

It quickly becomes apparent that these, too, are the descendants of Guomintang soldiers who were given refuge in Thailand. Unfortunately, many soon became involved in the opium trade and were not pacified until quite recently by the Thai army. Here, many of the inhabitants tend tea plantations and brew some rather potent wines.

Of more recent vintage is Baan Hin Taek, a few kilometres north. It was only in 1988 that the opium warlord Khun Sa was ousted from this mountain stronghold. A 13-kilometre paved road leads to the village, allowing visits by outsiders. Beyond Hin Taek lies Burma and heavily-armed soldiers man bunkers labelled with the unreassuring sign, "Tourist Security Post".

The road east drops off the ridge, eventually entering the Chiang Rai Valley just above Mae Chan.

From Lampang to Chiang Rai

The standard routes to Chiang Rai are Route 1, which continues north from Lampang, or Route 118, which leads northeast from Chiang Mai via Doi Saket, cutting travel time by half over the older route via Lampang.

Route 1 twists around and over mountains on its way to Ngao, 80 kilometres (50 mi) northeast of Lampang. At the highest point in the road, below twin rocky peaks, drivers usually stop – or if in a hurry, blow their horns – to pay respects to the *phi* (spirits) believed to inhabit the pass. Spirit houses, some simple, others as elaborate as small palaces, cluster along the side of the road.

BELOW: lush northern landscape.

Teak saplings line Route 1 between Lampang and Ngao, thanks to the Forest Industry Organisation (FIO), which also runs the **Young Elephants Training Centre ⓫** (open daily; admission fee). Here, 50 kilometres (30 mi) northeast of Lampang and a kilometre west of the highway, behind Pang-la village, visitors can watch elephant keepers put their young pachyderms through mounting, marching and log-dragging drills until around noon. If made to train beyond noon, the elephants stamp their feet in protest, until they are allowed to lumber off to their stalls for a snack of sugar cane.

About 20 kilometres (15 mi) before Ngao, a left turn leads in less than one kilometre to a small grove of teak trees and a refreshment stand that mark the entrance to **Tham Pha Thai ⓬**, probably the most interesting cave in Thailand. Climb the 283 concrete steps up the hill, then drop down into the huge arched entrance to the grotto, above which stands a gleaming white *chedi*.

Inside the main cave is a large bronze Buddha, an object of great veneration judging from the number of garlands and candles. Most striking, however, is the colossal stalagmite rising like a white explosion from a sea of limestone. Often a young novice monk will lead visitors down into the cave and point out bizarre limestone formations, which, with a little imagination, can resemble a throne, a rabbit or a turtle. Within the cave, slithering green snakes wrap themselves around electric wires or coil up in crevices. The guide explains that these snakes are protected and have never bitten anyone. The 400-metre (440 yd) walk into the cave ends at a small mound of bat guano. Light streaks down from a jagged opening in the cave roof, silhouetting flying bats onto the cavern walls.

About 10 kilometres (6 mi) before Ngao, on the left of Route 1, the Burmese-style **Wat Chong Kram** exudes charm in the face of alarming decrepitude. The

Map, page 216

Cave entrance.

BELOW: carrying a load, and entrance of Tham Pha Thai.

ceiling is gradually becoming crooked as its supporting pillars sink into the mud.

Route 1 continues through **Ngao** ⓫, another typical northern Thai town, and then 50 kilometres (30 mi) farther north to **Phayao** ⓮. Although quite small and apparently undistinguished, Phayao holds great interest for archaeologists, as the town was rebuilt in the 11th century on a more ancient site. Judging from the remains of a moat and eight city gates that enclose an area of about 2 square kilometres, scholars believe the older site may predate the Bronze Age. **Wat Li**, on the left of the road, has a fine collection of terracotta Buddha heads from Phayao's own early, distinctive and unique school, which were unearthed in the surrounding fields and land near the *wat*.

The cultivation of opium was first introduced to northern Thailand in the late 1800s by hill-tribe people from southern China.

Between the lake and the road, leaving Phayao, sits **Wat Si Khom Kham**, considered by scholars to be the area's most important temple because of its 400-year-old, 16-metre-high (55 ft) Buddha image inside a *viharn*. In a new *ubosot* on the edge of the lake, modern Thai artist Angkarn Kalayanapongsa has created a beautiful set of murals.

Chiang Rai

From Phayao, Route 1 continues north 100 kilometres (65 mi) to the provincial capital of **Chiang Rai** ⓯, located in Thailand's northernmost province at an elevation of about 580 metres (1,900 ft). King Mangrai, who also established Chiang Mai as a walled city, founded Chiang Rai in the late 1200s.

Legend claims that the king, then ruler of Chiang Saen, decided to conquer regions to the south after his favourite elephant ran away in a southerly direction. The search for the elephant led to the banks of Mae Nam Kok, where the king decided to build Chiang Rai. A much-venerated statue of King Mangrai stands in northeastern Chiang Rai, by a reconstructed stretch of the old city wall.

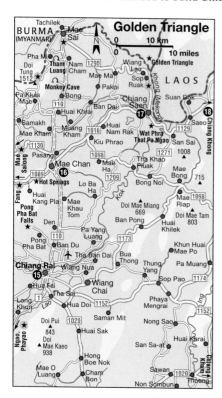

Like much of northern Thailand, lengthy wars with Burma inflicted suffering on the town and its residents; for much of the 1800s, it was almost uninhabited. In recent years, in large part due to both drug money and tourism, Chiang Rai has regained some of its prosperity, reflected in the existence of new hotels and shops.

Despite its exotic location, the city itself lacks both ambiance and historical ruins. Near the busy streets are two of the town's most important temples: Wat Phra Singh and Wat Phra Kaeo. Both share the distinction of having once sheltered famous images. The chedi and viharn at **Wat Phra Singh**, where legend holds that an important Buddha image was located, have been restored too many times to allow accurate dating, but documents suggest the 15th century or earlier.

Founded sometime in the 13th century, **Wat Phra Kaeo**, behind Wat Phra Singh, is believed to have been the original residence of the Emerald Buddha that is now in Bangkok at the royal temple of the same name. (Apparently the chedi in Chiang Rai was struck by lightning, revealing the Buddha in the 1430s.) To the west of Wat Phra Kaeo rises Ngam Muang. Atop the hill, **Wat Ngam Muang** is believed by local people to contain remains of King Mangrai.

From Chiang Rai, Route 110 continues 30 kilometres (20 mi) north to **Mae Chan** ⓰. Formerly a centre for silverwork, the tiny district town serves mostly as a trading post for hill people, especially members of the Akha and Mien tribes.

Northern border and Golden Triangle

The **Mekong River** – the name conjures up images of another time, another place, another world. It is the 12th-longest river in the world at 4,000 kilometres (2,500 mi) in length, passing through six countries on its way to the South China Sea. It is also defines much of the border between Thailand and Laos, only now a border that is significantly opening to trade and travel.

The ancient capital of **Chiang Saen** ⓱ nestles near where Burma, Laos and Thailand meet. This area, known as the Golden Triangle, has for years produced around half of the world's opium supply. Thailand's contribution has dropped to almost zero in the past 20 years, but both Laos and especially Burma continue to produce opium in major quantities.

Scholars believe Chiang Saen was founded around the end of the 13th century and strongly fortified about 100 years later by a grandson of King Mangrai. The Burmese captured it in the 16th century, but Rama I of Thailand recaptured it in the early 1800s. Fearing history would repeat itself with another Burmese invasion, however, Rama I ordered the town abandoned. It remained deserted for nearly a century. In 1957, the revived town became a district seat.

Chiang Saen's lovely setting on the Mekong River strongly enhances the charm of its old temples. Moreover, it is one of the few ancient towns in Thailand to have retained most of its lovely old trees, giving it a rare claim to tranquillity. The remains of its stout wall and moat can clearly be seen at its perimeter, and ruins of ancient monuments are scattered everywhere, popping up when one least expects them.

Map, page 236

BELOW: limestone landscape.

Just west of town stands **Wat Pa Sak**, whose name derives from the use of 300 teak, or *sak*, trunks for the original enclosure. The temple's foundation was laid in 1295 during the reign of King Mangrai. Earlier Srivijaya and Dvaravati influences, along with the then-prominent Sukhothai style, are evident in the *that* (reliquary), the clothing worn by the deities and the walking Buddhas.

Located about one kilometre west of the town gate, **Wat Prathat Chom Kitti** occupies a hill commanding a good view of Chiang Saen. Chronicles suggest that the old reliquary, with a leaning top, was first built around the 10th century and subsequently restored at least twice. Below this temple lies a ruined chedi in **Wat Chom Chang**. From here, a staircase leads farther downhill and back towards the town.

Close to the main street stand **Wat Chedi Luang** and a branch of the **National Museum**. The 60-metre-tall (200 ft), 13th-century chedi stands out in style as well as size; its bricks rise from an octagonal base to a bell-shaped top. In the grounds of the museum, one can see a good assortment of bronze Buddhas and other Chiang Saen art.

The most scenic return trip from Chiang Saen to Chiang Rai is via water in a long-tail boat down the Mekong River, as far as **Chiang Khong** ⓲, a three-hour trip after the rainy season when the river is high.

The river follows an approximately S-shaped course, first flowing southeast to the mouth of the Kok River, then curving north between beautiful hills and mountains, then finally south again for a thrilling 20 kilometres (12 mi) down deep and narrow sections, through stomach-churning rapids and swirling eddies beneath steep, jungled mountainsides.

At Chiang Khong, the river widens slightly. Set on left-bank hills, the Laotian town of **Ban Houei Sai** lies opposite the Chiang Khong district seat. Lao government officials still work in Fort Carnot built by the French. When relations between Thailand and Laos are cordial – nearly always nowadays, especially since the opening of the Friendship Bridge in the northeast at Nong Khai – a ferry boat carries visitors across the river to the customs post on the Lao side. Day visits by non-Thai nationals are not yet possible, however. A visa to enter Laos must be obtained beforehand.

Heart of the Golden Triangle

Returning to Chiang Saen and heading north for around 9 kilometres (6 mi) brings the visitor to the small town of **Sop Ruak**, which proudly promotes itself as the "Heart of the Golden Triangle". In recent years, the town has heavily cashed in on the wild mystique of the area that most Westerners hold, and now Sop Ruak is home to several high-quality resorts and hotels, which entice people to stay longer than they would have a few years ago. The main street of Sop Ruak is lined with souvenir shops that sell a variety of local textiles and plastic kitsch, as well as numerous food stalls and sit-down restaurants providing welcome refreshment to those passing through the town; the quality of culinary offerings is rather variable, however.

BELOW: black giant squirrel aloft.

In reality, the town of Sop Ruak has little to hold the traveller's attention, aside from the views of neighbouring Burma and Laos. Worth a visit, though, is the unprepossessing yet informative **House of Opium** at the southern end of town. This small museum houses displays relating to the history, cultivation and trade of the *Papaver somniferum* – the opium poppy from which heroin is extracted, and for which the area of the Golden Triangle is famous.

Several boat trips are currently available from Sop Ruak, including ferries to Chiang Saen and Chiang Khong, as well as round trips on the Mekong and Ruak rivers skirting the Burmese and Lao frontiers. Occasional trips depart for the long journey to China's province of Yunnan, but these are not yet regular.

Continuing north and east from Sop Ruak, the road finally reaches **Mae Sai**, the most northerly town in Thailand. This busy border town, with Tachilek clearly visible on the Burmese side of the small Sai River, has a real frontier feel to it. In the shops and stalls along the main streets, Burmese, Thai, Shan and hill-tribe traders sell a heady mix of gems, lacquerware and antiques – both new and old – along with imported whisky, cigarettes and medicinal herbs.

Visitors are usually allowed to cross the small bridge to Burma for up to three days, for a quick stroll around **Tachilek** – which like Sop Ruak really has little to offer except for the claim of visiting Burma – or for a longer journey as far as Kengtung, midway between Thailand and China. Frontier regulations between Thailand and Burma are prone to change, so check before crossing. And note that the bridge closes in the evening, so be sure not to be stranded on the wrong side of the river.

Map,
page 236

In the mid 1990s, the area around Tachilek was a site of the Burmese army's campaign against the Shan guerrilla movement, which was concentrated around here. As many as 3,000 refugees fled into Thailand near Mae Sai to escape the fighting. (Later, the infamous drug warlord Khun Sa, long the kingpin of the opium trade in the Golden Triangle, surrendered to the Burmese junta, only to take up residence in Rangoon.) The Shan are ethnically related to Thais and Laos, and have long had considerable autonomy from the Burmese government. Opium cultivation has financed the Shan independence movement against the Burmese government.

To the west of the main street, close to the border, there is a flight of steps ascending a small hill to **Wat Phra That Doi Wao**. This temple was purportedly constructed in memory of several thousand Burmese soldiers who died in battle against Chiang Kai-shek's Guomintang army, which was fighting against Mao Zedong's Communists for control of southern China here in 1965. The temple grounds afford splendid views over Mae Sai and Burma.

About 6 kilometres (4 mi) south of town, **Tham Luang** (Great Cave), on a turn-off to the west of Route 110 heading back to Chiang Rai, burrows for several kilometres into the hills. Gas lanterns are available for hire at the entrance. The first cavern is impressive in its size alone. Thereafter, a series of short, sometimes fairly restricting passages lead to caverns of varying magnitude, where the roof formations and crystalline deposits become more magnificent. ❏

BELOW: Lisu women in traditional attire.

Map,
page 216

MAE HONG SON

Perhaps long the most ignored part of Thailand, Mae Hong Son's isolation leaves it feeling rather unfettered by modern contrivances. Still, people have lived here for over 10,000 years

Secluded by jungle ridges and framed on the north and west by Burma, the Mae Hong Son area has benefited from years of benign neglect by the outside world. (Access was difficult until the mid 1960s, when a paved road opened up the town.) Mae Hong Son's years of human occupation, however, are rather lengthy. In a cave, an archaeologist found tools and seeds from betel nut, cucumber and black pepper, all apparently cultivated by early people. Analysis dates these between 10,000 and 6,000 BC. Later items include cutting tools from around 7,000 BC.

To reach Mae Hong Son by road, head south from Chiang Mai on Route 108. Just before the 57-kilometre marker, turn right and drive 10 kilometres (7 mi) past the entrance of **Doi Inthanon National Park** ⓳, a popular retreat named after its prime attraction, Doi Inthanon, the highest mountain in the country at 2,596 metres (8,517 ft). Girls rush out to visitors to sell bead necklaces, whilst cold beer and soft drinks are served in small shops along the river's edge, below Mae Klang Falls.

From the shops, walk up a bit to see this powerful cataract and its spectacular fusion of muddy brown water and white spray. Clearly marked footpaths branch into the rocky hills; one leads around a corner of boulders to a full view of a wider fall, Pakauna, which slides over its broad, craggy slopes for 120 metres (400 ft) like a liquid carpet.

The road continues to climb a further 25 kilometres (16 mi) to the peak of **Doi Inthanon**, whose summit is dominated by an off-limits radar station. Another spectacular waterfall, Mae Ya, is in the southern part of the park, dropping more than 250 metres (820 ft).

The limestone mass of Doi Inthanon is a comparatively modest foothill in the southern extension of the Himalayan range, which stretches southeast from Yunnan in southern China. Although less than a giant, Doi Inthanon has a majesty of its own conveyed by its steep, forest-clad slopes and mist-enshrouded summit. Karen and Hmong tribespeople still live nearby in isolated villages but are slowly being relocated, as the mountain is now a national reserve. On its summit the ashes of Chiang Mai's last king are enshrined.

By making prior arrangements with park authorities in Chiang Mai, it is possible to take a 3- to 5-day hike on foot or by pony up the mountain. Several campsites afford simple accommodation for trekkers. During the climb, one can observe rare birds and enjoy nature under a broad canopy of trees.

At the 58-kilometre marker on Route 108, one kilometre south of the park turn-off, is **Chom Thong** ⓴. The town's pride is the elegant **Wat Phra That Si Chom Thong**, where glints of subdued light accentuate a beautiful collection of bronze Buddhas. The

BELOW: Shan child.

monastery creaks with old age, as do the slumping boughs of trees scattered about its courtyard. The brilliantly gilded *chedi* dates from 1451, and the sanctuary, only 50 years later.

A large cruciform *viharn* built in 1516 – deeply incised with a profusion of floral patterns entwined with birds and *naga* serpents – dominates this temple compound. Four standing Buddhas, clothed like celestial kings, flank the viharn. Although much of the decoration in the temple reflects the Burmese penchant for elaboration, the central Buddha image, with its protective naga, seems eminently Thai and resembles the famed image at Wat Phra Singh Luang in Chiang Mai. On either side of the viharn are enshrined miniature gold and silver Buddha images, some bejeweled and metallic, others carved of crystal.

Further south on Route 108 are many northern touches: rambling, stylised elephants carved on the backs of bullock carts; *lamyai* trees and green bean-patches; giant plaited baskets, in which farmers thresh harvested rice; and shady, thatched-roof *sala* dotting the extensive rice fields.

Hot ㉑, 90 kilometres (50 mi) southwest of Chiang Mai on Route 108, once lay 15 kilometres farther south at the mouth of the Ping River, until the rising reservoir behind the Bhumibol Dam submerged it. Today, it has evolved into a fully-fledged town that seems to have been there forever. Farther south on Route 1012 lies the original site of ancient Hot. Cracked, rain-washed chedi dot the landscape – dignified relics from the time when Hot was part of the early kingdoms of the north. Excavations have unearthed gold jewelry, amulets and lively stucco carvings, which are now on display in Chiang Mai.

Route 1012 continues south to **Wang Luang**, a tiny village that earns its keep by selling dried fish caught in the catchment area created by Bhumibol Dam.

TIP

A boat can be hired at Wang Luang for an hour's voyage among the islands at the estuary of the Ping River, and out onto the expanse of water at the upper end of the reservoir. Reflections of ruined chedi and strange, eroded cliffs enliven remote mountain scenes.

BELOW: falls at Mae Klang, Doi Inthanon National Park.

Karen people have settled much of this area. Their necks hidden by a profusion of black beads and their bodices covered with thick, coloured patchwork, Karen tribeswomen walk into the tiny town to buy provisions.

From Hot, Route 108 strikes out west across the Chaem River, following its right bank toward Mae Sariang. About 20 kilometres (15 mi) from Hot, the road passes **Ob Luang Gorge**, sometimes referred to as Thailand's version of the Grand Canyon, though this requires a considerable stretch of the imagination. Stop at the sala for a look into the deep, ragged incisions in the rock.

Because northern Thailand is on a bird migratory flyway, nearly 10 percent of the world's species can be seen here at some time during the year. The Chiang Mai area alone offers around 400 species.

Hill-tribe farming

Most of the area's villages belong to the largest hill-tribe group in Thailand, the Skaw Karen, who have settled along the Thai-Burmese frontier as far south as Chumphon. In the moist valleys they plant wet rice on steep terraces. On the slopes, black tree stumps stand out like whiskers on a green background of rice sprouts; nomadic Karen burn away the forest to make clearings to plant new crops. This slash-and-burn technique has scarred the mountain sides and caused extensive erosion; today many Karen have taken to sedentary farming.

In places, the road skirts high banks of red earth. Fresh mounds of mud on the asphalt show that landslides are not uncommon – the steep banks cannot always hold back the run-off. A solution to this problem may be the pine tree. Though it is not a tree one normally associates with tropical Thailand, the pine is well suited to rebuilding the soil. Its roots form an extensive earth-holding network, and its seeds are not easily destroyed by fire.

BELOW: hill-tribe woman bottle-feeding cattle.

The drive towards Mae Sariang is more exciting than the town itself. The road runs like a roller coaster over the mountains. Not even motorbikes can reach

some of the small leaf-and-bamboo huts tucked away in these hills. Hemmed in by mountains, **Mae Sariang ㉒** itself lies 100 kilometres (65 mi) west of Hot, at the point where Route 108 bends to the north. A few Burmese-style temples, a small, white mosque and a few Karen handicraft shops distinguish this small district administrative centre and border trading post.

Route 108 continues north on a rough track from Mae Sariang, through mountain scenery that is amongst the most breathtaking in Thailand, reaching Mae Hong Son 170 kilometres (100 mi) later.

Mae Hong Son ㉓ lies in a valley between deep-green mountains, which accounts for its early morning fogs. The forest valley is buttressed by mountains that separate Thailand from Burma. Mae Hong Son has for years been a destination for seekers of old-world serenity. (Nonetheless, like most of Thailand, it is gradually being developed, including two major new hotels.) The presence of Karen, Hmong, Lawa, Shan, Lisu, and Lahu, who taken collectively easily outnumber the ethnic Thais, adds intrigue to an ill-kept secret: Mae Hong Son is smack in the middle of border smuggling routes.

A commanding view of the town of Mae Hong Son and the surrounding countryside is afforded from **Doi Kong Mu**, a hill that rises 250 metres (820 ft) above the town. At night, the two tall chedi of **Wat Phra That Doi Kong Mu** atop the hill light up like timid beacons of civilisation in this corner of Thailand. Erected in the 19th century, the wat reflects Burmese influences. A pond and a park at the centre form a core of beauty and peace that few other Thai towns possess. On the edge of the lake, across from a fitness park, are the intertwined temples of **Wat Chong Klang** and **Wat Chong Kum**. These Burmese-style temples, with their pristine, white chedi, look moving when reflected in the lake. ❒

Map, page 216

Unusual chedi of Wat Chong Kum.

BELOW: street front, Mae Hong Son.

Map, page 216

THAILAND

Bangkok

BELOW: gilded images facing the four cardinal points, Wat Phumin.

NAN VALLEY

If looking for life unjaded by tourism, along with some superb outdoor activities, seek no further than the area around Nan, once the capital of a small kingdom later to join the first Lanna empire

The Nan Valley may be Thailand's last great undiscovered tourist territory. It has lovely mountain scenery, the full complement of hill tribes, a new national park, and a friendly population not yet jaded by exposure to foreign travelers. The principal roads make for excellent mountain biking and motor-cycling, since they are sealed, hilly rather than mountainous, and not often disrupted by traffic. The drawback is that very few people speak English, many signs are not romanised, and there is barely any accommodation outside of Nan.

With its cement-block and egg-carton architecture, the town of **Nan** ㉔ initially appears to be yet another nondescript upcountry town, with a population of around 25,000. A stroll or spin beyond the downtown area, however, will soon reveal plenty of old wooden houses, which come in three upraised styles. There are exhibits of the three styles at the local branch of the **National Museum** (open Wednesday–Sunday; admission fee), which should be a first stop on any tour. Located in the former airy residence of the last two Nan princes, the museum also provides introductions to tribes, textiles, crafts and history. The 300-year-old black elephant tusk on display is reputed to have magical powers.

The first Nan dynasty emerged in the mid 1300s. By the end of the 14th century, Nan was among ten Thai-Lao states that joined to form the first Lanna

empire. The town was later conquered by the Burmese and the next few hundred years were tumultuous, but in 1788 Nan finally allied with the Rattanakosin, or Bangkok, kingdom. Because Nan's rulers fully cooperated in the drive by Bangkok's King Chulalongkorn to unite a crazy quilt of vassal states into a modern nation, the province was allowed to retain its special status as a semi-independent principality until the death of the last Nan prince in 1931.

The allegiances and influences of the past 600 years are evident in Nan temples, which display the styles of Lanna, Sukhothai, northern and southern Laos, the Thai Lu people, and combinations thereof. Styles of the Sukhothai period are prominent at **Wat Chang Kham**, which is across the street from the museum and located within the old city walls. The elephants, seven on each side, supporting the second tier of the square *chedi* are a Sukhothai motif. The standing Buddhas in the 15th century *viharn* are also Sukhothai style and very common in Laos. The *wat* library, with its high ceiling but now empty, was at one time the largest in Thailand.

Next door to the National Museum is the even older **Wat Hua Khuang** with a wooden verandah in the Luang Prabang (that is, northern Lao) style. Although it's often closed, visitors may be lucky to catch the weekend painter who for years has been restoring the murals. The town's most famous murals, however, are found a short walk south at **Wat Phumin**, which was first constructed in 1596. The building in question has a highly unusual cruciform layout that combines viharn and *bot*. If the great carved doors of the viharn wing are fully open, make sure to peek behind them to see the murals that decorate this front wall. There are rowing boats loaded with bearded foreigners, who smoke pipes and wear naval caps. Among them are even a few heavily-dressed *farang* (foreign)

From the 1960s to the 1980s, Nan Valley was a stronghold of communist insurgents, who filtered through the border with Laos. Later, Thai communists took advantage of government amnesties. Still off-limits is a small patch in the north due to "bandits".

BELOW: dragon-boat race in Nan, and mural detail, Wat Phumin.

Map, page 216

TIP

Nan's best shop for local crafts is run by the Thai Payap Development Association. This co-operative exports to North America and Europe; the quality of textiles is superior. The crafts are made by Hmong, Mien, Htin and Khmu people.

OPPOSITE: Akha tribeswoman.
BELOW: Sao Din.

women. And there's a great three-masted sailing ship. The murals depict an episode from the *Jataka* tales, the chronicle of Buddha's previous incarnations. The scenes of Asian characters engaged in war, torture and all-around mayhem on the other walls convey one hellish life. Since the murals were painted in the late 19th century, shortly after the cession to the French, it has recently been proposed that the murals may also have intended to express how Nan people regarded their long history of betrayals and abandonment.

Wat Phra That Cha Haeng is located on a hill about 3 kilometres southeast of town and across the Nan River – where the large "dragon boats" race for a week every autumn. You'll recognise the wat by the lengthy *nagas* snaking down the hill in greeting. The square gilded chedi is Lao-style. The bot, however, has many Thai Lu influences, such as the sweeping, five-layered wooden roof, the low ceilings and the dog-like dragons guarding the entry. A minority, but not a hill tribe, Thai Lu are ethnic Thai people that immigrated to the Nan Valley about 150 years ago.

On the return trip to town, turn left before crossing the river and watch how thick, rough *saa* paper is made from mulberry bark in a factory that resembles someone's backyard.

One can arrange one- to three-day hill treks in Nan, but it's also easy to visit tribal (and Thai) villages on the approximately 80-kilometre (50 mi) journey to **Doi Phu Kha National Park ㉕**. Few of the tribal villages are long standing. During the insurgency some decades ago, many people were relocated from the uplands to remove them from communist temptations. They were joined by tribal people fleeing war-torn Laos. After a decade or more in refugee camps, they have been dispersed to new villages throughout the province.

Trails meander through tribal villages. Like most of the forests that visitors will spy elsewhere in Nan, these here are the fruit of reforestation projects. The national park does have some undisturbed areas, but they are not served by trails. Park rangers or U.S. Peace Corps volunteers can direct you to some pretty spots, such as the 1,300-metre (4,300 ft) peak of Don Khao and Ton Tong waterfall. Continue for about 20 kilometres (12 mi) along Route 1256, the windy, steep road running east of park headquarters, to reach the Htin village of Ban Bor Kleua, where the salt wells still function.

On the return trip to Nan town, take the eastern branch of Route 1080, which sprouts off south of the town of Pua. About a half-dozen kilometres along the way is **Ban Pa Klang**, a veritable town of Hmong, Htin and Mien people. Mien make and sell silver jewelry here. The views of majestic mountains along this route are stunning, though it's difficult to pick out **Doi Phu Kha**, the province's highest at 1,985 metres (6,512 ft).

As for the area south of Nan, the top sights are the eerie Hom Chom and **Sao Din** rock pillars. Carved by the wind, these bare, pointed projectiles form desolate canyons. Nan, both the town and the province, are usually entered from the southwest via Route 101, a soothing ride through tobacco, cotton and rice fields and gently rolling, reforested hills.

The next substantial town south is **Phrae ㉖**, capital of the like-named province. ❑

CRAFTS AND CLOTHING OF THE HILL TRIBES

Each hill tribe of Thailand has its own customs, dress, language and spiritual beliefs that are reflected in the crafts they produce.

Textiles and silver jewelry play a very important role in the ceremonial activities of Thailand's hill-tribe communities. Hill-tribe women are defined by what they wear, and their choice of clothing and adornment can reveal not only what tribe they are from, but also their social status, age and even where their home town is located. However, the way of life of Thailand's hill-tribe people is changing as they are slowly assimilated into mainstream Thai society, abandoning many features of their traditional culture. This may be sad for visitors in search of traditional hill-tribe culture, but the process is inevitable and has distinct advantages for these ethnic minorities, since they can now benefit from educational opportunities and medical facilities.

Hill-tribe craft items started to be made commercially in the mid-1970s when small craft centres were set up in refugee camps. Authentic items are now rare and expensive, but good quality, modern crafts can be found in craft shops.

BRASS NECK RINGS ▷
Padaung women once wore brass rings around their arms, legs and necks; the tradition has, thankfully, diminished. Still, some Padaung refugees from Burma are forced by tour operators to pose for tourists.

◁ **HMONG EMBROIDERY**
Women from the Hmong hill tribe used to hand-weave cloth, but today they use ready-made fabrics for their intricately embroidered clothing. The Hmong are skilled in making indigo-dyed batik which is then embroidered with appliquéd layers of geometrically-shaped fabric to make up their skirts.

▽ **LISU TEXTILES**
Lisu women make distinctive clothing. In the past, the cloth was woven by hand but the Lisu now use machine-made material that they run up on sewing machines.

◁ AKHA COTTONS

Women of the Akha hill tribe spin cotton into thread with a hand spindle, then weave it on a foot-treadle loom. The cloth is dyed indigo and is then appliquéd and decorated with shells, seeds, silver or buttons and made into clothing for the family. The men make a variety of baskets and other items from wood, bamboo and rattan.

LISU CEREMONIAL WEAR ▷

On special occasions, Lisu men wear turbans and the women don large amounts of hand-crafted silver jewelry, chunky necklaces and colourful tunics with silver buttons. Men of the tribe are skilled blacksmiths. The sale of crafts means they no longer need to grow opium poppies to make a living.

▽ AKHA HEADDRESS

Married Akha women are famous for their head-dresses decorated with silver coins, which they wear all the time. Unmarried women from the tribe attach small gourds to their head-dresses.

HOW THE KAREN MAKE *IKAT*

The White Karen tribe (above) produce striped warp *ikat* textiles woven on back-strap looms. Ikat is a technique used to pattern cloth that involves the binding of the cloth with fibre or strips of material, so in places it becomes resistant to dyeing.

Before the cloth is dyed, the weft (yarns woven across the width of the fabric) or the warp (lengthwise yarns) is pulled tightly over a frame and then threads are bound tightly together singly or in bunches. The cloth is then dyed several times using different colours. As a result, complex and beautiful patterns are built up with soft, watery edges on the parts of the cloth not completely covered by the binding materials.

The dyeing process is complex, with the dominant colour of the ikat dyed first. Cotton yarns are the most suitable for making warp ikat, and the dyes used to produce these textiles are natural dyes that are easily absorbed by cotton. The most popular colours for warp ikat are indigo and red. Weft ikats use mainly yellow dyes (made from turmeric), diluted indigos and a deep crimson red extracted from the lac insect. Orange, green and purple are created by an overdyeing process.

Northeast Thailand

0   50 km

0   50 miles

THE NORTHEAST

To the Thais, the northeastern part of the nation is known as Isaan, a place of historical and natural importance

The northeast does not usually figure prominently on anybody's list of travel destinations in Thailand. This is a pity, for the northeast is a treasure trove of ancient monuments. Parts of the region were ruled by the Khmers, during the great period when they built Angkor Wat and colonised large areas of northeastern Thailand, building temples in key cities. Outside of Angkor itself, the northeast is certainly the best place in Asia to view the remains of the Khmer culture.

The northeast of Thailand is a high plateau upon which about one-third of the country's population lives. Many northeasterners' ancestors migrated from Laos across the great Mekong River, which forms the natural border between Laos and Thailand. Today, Thais of the northeast retain the Lao quality of sweet passivity in the face of adversity. The quality is useful, for the northeast is not always an easy place to live. The soil is often thin and infertile, there is either not enough rain, or too much, and the Mekong can be unforgiving when it floods. So many northeasterners go to Bangkok, filling unskilled jobs in the capital. Small wonder that the northeast also has a tradition of dissident politicians whose demands for social reform have been louder than those from other parts of the country.

The basic agricultural products of the northeast are poor-soil staples like cotton and tapioca. Mulberry trees, too, are grown to feed the worms that spin silk. In the late 1950s, the Friendship Highway, a joint Thai-American undertaking, opened the region. In the 1960s, large American military bases during the Vietnam War pumped money into the region and made boom-towns out of places like Nakhon Ratchasima (also called Khorat), Udon Thani and Ubon Ratchathani. In 1994, the first road bridge from Thailand into Laos, crossing the Mekong River at Nong Khai, opened.

For several years now, there has been a fairly successful effort to develop the northeast. Numerous development projects have been initiated by the royal family and the government to improve production, processing and transport for agricultural products.

Because the northeast isn't on the agenda of most foreign travelers, this reason alone, perhaps, is the major lure of the region. ❐

PRECEDING PAGES: sorting out raw silk, a product of Khorat, that has been spun.

KHORAT PLATEAU

With Cambodia to the south, it's not surprising that northeastern Thailand retains a Khmer texture to its history, whether in the architecture of ancient sanctuaries or in old tales

Map, page 252

THAILAND

Bangkok

The good roads of northeast Thailand – an area called *Isaan* by the Thais – invite travel by car, which undoubtedly is the best way to see the many out-of-the-way sights in this part of the country. The Friendship Highway, or Route 2, the main road through the northeast, begins about 100 kilometres (60 mi) from Bangkok, branching off of Route 1 just before the town of **Saraburi**. About 20 kilometres (15 mi) after the Saraburi turn-off on Route 2, a dirt road on the right leads to an experimental farm run by the Kasetsart Agricultural University of Bangkok, and then beyond to **Phra Ngam** (Beautiful Buddha Image), a cave where a Dvaravati-era image may be seen. There are numerous other caves nearby, many yet unexplored.

Another 15 kilometres (10 mi) leads to **Muaklek**. Once known for malaria, Muaklek has been transformed from an unhealthy jungle into dairy land that features a small arboretum garden, where a wonderful variety of roses bloom along a stream.

About 50 kilometres (30 mi) east of Saraburi is **Wat Teppitakpunnaram**, where a monumental white Buddha sits on a green mountain, like an alabaster relic. The countryside in this area belongs to **Khao Yai National Park ❶**, hidden 40 kilometres (25 mi) to the south. (See *Outside of Bangkok,* page 177.)

Route 2 continues northeast up the Khorat Plateau, passing the reservoir of **Lam Takhong**. Soon the blue lake disappears and scrub brush, typical of the dryer areas of the northeast, begins to dominate the scenery. About 150 kilometres (100 mi) from Saraburi is the provincial capital of **Khorat**, now officially called **Nakhon Ratchasima ❷**.

Richest and largest city in the northeast, and once an air base for American bombers during the Vietnam War, Nakhon Ratchasima now serves as a trade, communications and military centre for the entire northeast region. It is also the capital of the most densely-populated upcountry province in Thailand, with over 1.5 million residents.

Although a busy and important commercial centre, Nakhon Ratchasima has not forgotten its past. A statue of national heroine Khunying Mo (Tao Suranari) presides over the town square and the whitewashed old city wall, from around the 10th century. Khunying Mo was the wife of an assistant provincial governor in the early 19th century, when Prince Anu of Vientiane led his army to Khorat.

After taking the city, the prince threatened to enslave its residents. Khunying Mo rallied the women of Khorat, who enticed many of the Laotian soldiers to a drunken revelry and then killed them whilst they slept. Prince Anu, who meanwhile had gone to attack Saraburi, was forced to withdraw his depleted forces to

OPPOSITE: Prasat Hin Phimai. **BELOW:** young Phimai girl.

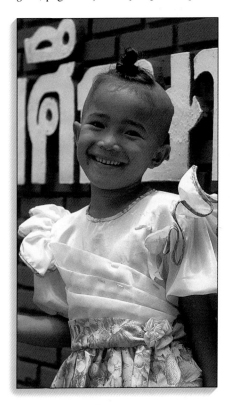

Vientiane, to the north. Outside the walls and moat is the off-beat **Wat Sala Loi**, erected in 1973 in the shape of a Chinese junk. The symbolism is clear – it will convey the faithful believer of Buddha to *nirvana*.

Silk is one of the region's most important industries. To visit a nearby silk production centre, take Route 304 south towards Kabinburi. After 30 kilometres (20 mi) is the town of **Pak Thong Chai**, where the Jim Thompson silk company has established a weaving cooperative to produce Thai silk. It is, in fact, the world's largest hand-woven-silk enterprise.

There are 300-plus Khmer ruins in Thailand, most of them in the northeast. There has been a concerted effort since the 1920s to restore many of them.

Excursions from Nakhon Ratchasima

The main attractions outside Nakhon Ratchasima are two sites created nine centuries ago by Khmer architects, both northeast of town on Route 2.

The peaceful monastery of **Prasat Phanom Wan** ❸ has heavy stone galleries, revealing the Khmer penchant for false windows with stone mullions, a method adopted to compensate for the soft stone. Elaborate zig-zag patterns cover the carved stones.

An uncommon stillness pervades this 11th-century retreat, broken only by the footsteps of resident monks. Unlike the majority of Khmer ruins, this one contains an active temple. Behind its well-preserved vaulted entrance, the original, dark sanctuary is filled with many more recent Buddha images of different styles, most of them covered with patches of gold leaf. Full-grown trees sprout from the oldest chambers. The presence of older monks in residence reminds visitors that donations are needed to help with the upkeep of the site.

BELOW: differing Buddha styles, Prasat Phanom Wan.

Farther north are the ruins of **Prasat Hin Phimai** ❹, 50 kilometres (30 mi) from Nakhon Ratchasima on the Mae Nam Mun, a tributary of the Mekong.

Renovated with the help of the same expert who restored Angkor Wat in nearby Cambodia, it has been suggested that Phimai may have been a prototype for Angkor Wat itself.

Map, page 252

The last of the great Angkor monarchs, King Jayavarman VII, who replaced Hinduism with Mahayana Buddhism as the official religion, could easily travel from his palace along a 240-kilometre (150 mi) road to Phimai, which was at the western extent of his expanding kingdom. A string of 112 rest houses was constructed along the route to shelter pilgrims and government officials making the long journey to Phimai. During the king's reign (AD 1181–1201), Phimai prospered within a walled rectangular area 1,000 metres by 560 metres, on an artificial island created by linking the Mun River and one of its tributaries via a canal. There were four entrances, with serpents, or *naga,* guarding each. The primary entrance faces south. Like the shrines at Angkor, the monuments at Phimai were never inhabited. Shops, libraries and houses were built of wood, and therefore have disintegrated centuries ago.

Detail from Prasat Hin Phimai.

However, the old city gate, most likely the main entrance to the sanctuary, still stands at the end of Phimai's present main street. Near the bridge over the Mae Nam Mun, the government maintains an open-air museum displaying some of the more beautifully carved lintels and statues found in the area.

Before leaving Phimai, visit Sai Ngam, or "Beautiful Banyan Tree", one kilometre east of the temple near an irrigation reservoir. It has an umbrella of dense leaves and roots that locals revere as a shelter for special spirits, and it is claimed to be the largest banyan tree in the world.

From Phimai, one can continue north on Route 2 to **Khon Kaen** and directly to the Mekong River town of Nong Khai. But for a better look at the rural north-

BELOW: old ruins at Phimai.

Khmer Legacy

Between the 10th and 14th centuries AD, a large part of mainland Southeast Asia, from the Mekong Delta in the east to around Phetchburi in the west, lay under the control of the Khmer Empire. Administered at the height of its power by god-kings, the empire's capital at Angkor was connected to the outlying reaches of the empire by a system of highways and religio-political strongpoints such as Khao Phra Viharn, Wat Phu, Phanom Rung, and Phimai.

By the mid-19th century, when the frontiers of present-day Indochina were effectively fixed by French colonialism, the Khmer Empire had long since disappeared, leaving Cambodia much reduced in size. It is true that the crowning glory of the Khmer past, Angkor Wat, still lay within Cambodia's confines, as did the magnificent "lofty sanctuary" of Phra Viharn, albeit only just. Yet many other symbolic relics of the Khmer past now lay outside Cambodia, most notably Wat Phu in southern Laos and

a series of magnificent sites across Thailand's Tung Kula Rong Hai, the "Weeping Plain" of the lower Northeast.

Thailand has long valued these unique historic treasures, yet only very recently have concerted efforts been made to preserve and promote them. Over the past three decades, several of the most important sites have been painstakingly and successfully restored by the government's Department of Fine Arts. Moreover, the Tourism Authority of Thailand has publicised a "Khmer Culture Trail" in lower Isaan which offers the visitor an unparalleled opportunity to explore the glories of the Khmer past.

Khorat and Buriram provinces host the major Khmer complexes: Prasat Hin Phimai, Prasat Phanom Rung and Prasat Muang Tham. All three have been carefully restored, though Phanom Rung is perhaps today the most impressive. Like Angkor Wat itself, these temples were all originally constructed as Hindu temples dedicated to Vishnu and Shiva, and as such the ruins demonstrate, particularly in their carvings, a deistic diversity and Indic sensuality not evident in more recent, Buddhist structures. It was under Jayavarman VII that Hinduism was replaced by Buddhism, and the temples were converted to *wat*. Their significance to Thai Buddhists remains strong, weakened neither by memories of foreign powers on what is now Thai soil nor by the slightly unfamiliar iconography. Phanom Rung is indeed a regular and important place of Buddhist pilgrimage.

As far away as Lopburi, Khmer influence is easily recognisable in the three ruined *prang* of Phra Prang Sam Yot, often attributed to Jayavarman VII. And in the vicinity of Phanom Rung are various Khmer *kuti*, or meditation retreats, as well as several other unrestored temple complexes languishing in the forests and undergrowth. All bear testimony to the fact that this area, far from being an outpost of the Khmer empire, was very much in its heartland. Indeed, as recently as 1976, Democratic Kampuchea's (now Cambodia) despotic regime was staking a claim to the region, promising to "liberate" lost Khmer territories in Thailand. Fortunately, whilst the the local Khmer-speakers are conscious of, and justly proud of, their cultural links with Angkor, they are also loyal Thai citizens. ∎

east, Khmer temples, and Isaan atmosphere, journey along Route 24, southeast of Khorat, running roughly parallel to the Cambodian border.

Map, page 252

Three full ponds – essential elements of Khmer monumental architecture – and pretty farmland surround **Prasat Phanom Rung ❺**. Historians believe this temple was an important station between Angkor and Phimai during the 11th and 12th centuries. Several generations must have elapsed during its construction, since several of the stone lintels resemble the early Baphuon style, while the naga date from the later Angkor Wat period. A stone inscription in Sanskrit mentions King Suryavarman II, the ruler behind the construction of Angkor Wat.

The temple includes a stolen lintel spirited out of Thailand by art thieves in the early 1960s. Later it surfaced in the United States in a museum collection. After negotiations, it was returned to Thailand in the early 1990s and put back in its original position over a temple entrance. The main *prang* of Phanom Rung, and its galleries and chapels, reflect the geometric precision of Angkor architecture; symmetrical doors and windows face the four cardinal points. The monumental staircase, relieved by landings, exudes a sense of mass and power typical of Khmer design. Look for the sandstone bas-reliefs of elephants and enthroned Hindu deities. Monks of the Dharmayuti sect maintain the temple.

Elephants are a common element not only in modern-day Surin, but also in the ornamentation of ancient Khmer ruins.

Farther east a couple of kilometres is **Prasat Muang Tham**, or Lower Temple, sitting on a mossy lawn like an art historian's daydream. Older than Prasat Phanom Rung, its cornerstones were laid in the 10th century, with the temple finished about a hundred years later. Thick jungle surrounded Muang Tham until recently, when a group of families moved there from Ubon, cleared the area and established a large village.

Opposite: example of Khmer design in Thailand's Khorat. **Below:** guardian image, Wat That Phanom.

Five prang – surrounded by galleries, protected by walls, and now shaded by trees – constitute Muang Tham, which has recently been beautifully restored. Once crazily leaning blocks of masonry and fallen lintels are now back in place, the monumental tank rebuilt and filled with lilies. The huge rectangular stone blocks that form the outer walls contain drilled circular holes, probably used for stone figures shaped like lotus buds. The outer rims of the ponds are lined with naga, whose many heads rise at the corners, marking the outer boundary of the temple.

Surin and Si Saket

Located on an old Khmer site, **Surin ❻** was known primarily for silk production until the government tourism authority began organising an annual elephant roundup each November. The people of Surin are famed for their skill at training elephants. (In the early 1900s, there were around 100,000 working elephants in Thailand; now there are but 4,000.) During the well-publicised roundup, *mahout* put their pachyderms through a variety of acts. Special buses and a train from Bangkok take tourists to the popular event.

A direct rail line connects Surin to the next main town, **Si Saket**, which borders on Cambodia. Travelling by car is less direct.

The province of Si Saket's former main attraction no longer lies in Thailand. In the early 1960s, the World Court awarded to Cambodia the splendid temple complex of **Khao Phra Viharn ❼**, southeast of Si Saket

Map, page 252

Khmer image of a garuda, the mythological creature.

about 100 kilometres (60 mi) and easily reached from the Thai side of the border. It is, however, almost inaccessible from Cambodia. Depending upon the political situation, it is sometimes possible to visit Khao Phra Viharn, which sits on a 500-metre-high (1,650 ft) perch and was opened in 1992 after being closed for decades. Nevertheless, it has sometimes closed since then because of danger from the residual Khmer Rouge insurgency in Cambodia. It can be reached from Si Saket by a 60-kilometre (40 mi) drive to Kantharalak, then into the jungle on another 40-kilometre (25 mi) leg to the border.

Its construction starting sometime in the early 11th century, Khao Phra Viharn stretches almost a kilometre in length. Its stairs alternate between hewn bedrock and imported stones placed there perhaps 100 years before the days of Angkor Wat. Each layer is marked by an increasingly large *gopura,* or gate, and ends at the topmost sanctuary that honours the god Shiva.

To the east of the first gopura, a precarious trail descends through the jungle to the Cambodian plains. Before the second gopura, a sacred pond cut in the rock was found to contain a 45-kilogram (100 lb) fish, which is now displayed in Cambodia's National Museum, in Phnom Penh.

The second gopura, shaped like a Greek cross, is superbly carved in the Khmer style of the 11th century. Its lintels show Vishnu in a scene from the Hindu myth of creation. The stairs continue in a symbolic ascent to heaven, past another purificatory basin to the first courtyard with its two palaces and gopura, finally up to the second and third courtyards and the main sanctuary. At the end of the long ridge is a breathtaking precipice, 600 metres (2,000 ft) above the Cambodian countryside, a stunning achievement of turning a natural site into a work of exquisite art.

Far to the east

Ubon Ratchathani ❽, Royal Town of the Lotus Flower, lies 700 kilometres (430 mi) east of Bangkok and about 60 kilometres (40 mi) east of Si Saket. Its size and wealth indicate the increasing prosperity of the region. In fact, much of the town's early growth coincided with the American build-up during the Vietnam War in the 1960s. Office buildings, construction sites, and some of the best-endowed temples in the northeast rise abruptly behind the banks of the Mun, which flows eastward into the Mekong, 100 kilometres (65 mi) away.

In the 1100s, the area surrounding Ubon Ratchathani was part of the Khmer kingdom, until the Ayutthayan empire supplanted the Khmers. Ubon Ratchathani itself is a rather young urban centre, founded in the late 1700s by Lao immigrants. Established by King Rama III, **Wat Thung Si Muang** is noted for its library made of teak wood. The **National Museum** (open Wednesday–Sunday; admission fee) in Ubon Ratchathani is Khorat's finest and is well worth a stop. Housed in the former country residence of King Vajiravudh, the museum displays a number of fine artefacts, including of Khmer, Lao and Hindu origins.

The highlight of Ubon's festival year is the Wax Candle Procession each July, when huge mythical animals and legendary figures are carved from beeswax and paraded through the streets.

A decent excursion out of Ubon is **Kaeng Tanna National Park ❾**, to the northeast near Laos and the Mekong River and noted for its prehistoric cave paintings and a series of rapids where the Mae Nam Mun is squeezed through a gorge before entering the Mekong.

If planning to travel north from Ubon Ratchathani, allow a full day for the trip north from Ubon to Nakhon Phanom. In the dry season the fields along Route 212 look barely arable, but after the rains they produce the rice that turns golden brown in late October. ❑

OPPOSITE: Prasat Phanom Rung.

NORTHERN KHORAT

*In the northeast, there are archeological findings that suggest not
all technological advances came south from China. But if not
interested in technology, consider the region's expansive lands*

Map,
page 252

THAILAND

Bangkok

The Thais call northeastern Thailand, *Isaan*. It is a poor part of Thailand, but its cuisine, as an off-the-wall example, dismisses any notions of a poverty in creativity or initiative. Typically overlooked by both Thai and foreign travelers, northeastern Thailand makes up for its lack of awesome scenery with a number of fine nature preserves and ancient archaelogical sites.

From just north of Bangkok, Route 2 heads northeast to **Udon Thani ⑩** via Khorat (Nakhon Ratchasima) and Khon Kaen. Udon Thani is a town that grew quickly with the arrival of American airmen during the 1960s. Today, instead of military convoys, noisy motorcycles and packed pickup trucks fill city streets that are punctuated by increasing numbers of traffic lights.

From Udon Thani, Route 2 continues north 50 kilometres (35 mi) to **Nong Khai ⑪**, on the southern bank of the Mekong River. In 1994, the 1.2-kilometre-long Friendship Bridge opened, connecting Nong Khai with the Laotian capital of Vientiane, on the other side of the Mekong River in Laos. This first bridge across the lower Mekong may mean Nong Khai's days as a quiet town are numbered. Fancy hotels are opening in anticipation of the increased tourism and business, though this has yet to materialise.

OPPOSITE: Friendship Bridge. **BELOW:** 5,000-year-old pottery unearthed at Ban Chiang.

East of Udon Thani

The people of **Ban Chiang ⑫**, long used to encountering fragments of pots, beads, and even human bones when digging around their houses or working on their farms, paid little attention to archeological finds in this area 50 kilometres east of Udon Thani. Then, in 1966, a young American anthropology student showed some of his finds to the archaeology authorities in Bangkok. His discoveries led to more comprehensive analysis of the artifacts found around Ban Chiang, leading to some surprising, if not controversial, conclusions. Not only were the finds older than believed, between 4,500 and 5,700 years old, but bronze artifacts found around Ban Chiang were dated at around 3,600 BC.

If accurate, this would put the appearance of bronze in Thailand centuries earlier than in the Middle East, until then thought to be the earliest location of such bronze manufacture. Equally intriguing is that this dating of Ban Chiang bronze would suggest that bronze manufacture may have been transmitted from Thailand to China, rather than from China to Thailand, which has long been the received wisdom. Still, many experts maintain that the dating of 3,600 BC for the appearance of bronze remains too early, suggesting that 2,000 BC, or even 2,500 BC, is more accurate. This would put the appearance of bronze in Southeast Asia later than the Middle East, but at around the same time as China. Even were the claims of antiquity not authenticated, the

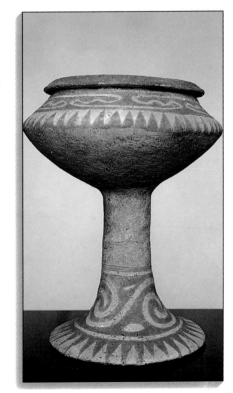

Rock inscriptions found in the northeast reflect Khmer influence over 1,000 years ago.

BELOW: traditional ceremony in the northeast.

beautiful whorl designs of the pottery and the intricacy of the bronze jewelry and implements would earn Ban Chiang culture high marks among the early peoples of the earth. Many of these artifacts can be seen in Ban Chiang's museum, established with the help of the U.S.-based Smithsonian Institution.

Farther east on Route 22 about 120 kilometres (75 mi), **Sakon Nakhon ⓭** is spread out along a low plain that borders Nong Han, Thailand's largest natural lake. (Visitors should avoid going for a swim, however, as the waters are infested with liver fluke.) Although the site was one of the Khmer's important regional centres, the ancient Khmers left monuments whose significance is so minor that only those with keen archeological interest should make a special effort to see them. In the town centre, the white *prang* of Wat Choeng Chum hides a 10th-century laterite prang; you must peer through a crack in the door to see it. West of town is Wat Narai Cheng Weng, built in the Khmer Baphuon style by a princess in the 11th century.

Farther east on Route 22 is **Nakhon Phanom ⓮**. On a fresh morning, a chain of jagged, powder-gray mountains can be seen behind the small Laotian town of Thakhek, across the wide Mekong. Over 25,000 Vietnamese refugees crossed the river during the 1950s and 1960s to settle in this province. Although security precautions long complicated their resettlement, many Vietnamese have prospered financially in the town's markets, perhaps matching the Chinese in business acumen. During the Vietnam War, American rescue and reconnaissance missions flew from the Royal Thai Air Force Base hidden behind grassy mounds west of town. The base was also a listening post filled with sophisticated radios and electronic sensors. Nowadays few signs of the base's past remain. The town is quiet, attractive and relaxed.

Fifty kilometres (30 mi) south is **That Phanom** . The route stays close to the Mekong River all the way up to the village and temple of That Phanom. The road is in good condition, straight and flat. Uncultivated brush interspersed with rice fields rushes by. Blue-shirted farmers balance produce-laden baskets from the ends of long poles.

Thousands of pilgrims from northeastern Thailand and southern Laos used to make an annual pilgrimage to Wat That Phanom to make offerings at the base of the spire, which was built around the 9th century and restored several times later. In mid 1975, the spire collapsed after four days of torrential monsoon rains. But in 1979, the temple was restored, again making it well worth a visit for those interested in history or simply seeking a beautiful setting. For a short and pleasant side trip into the countryside, north of That Phanom and inland is **Ban Renu**. Like several small weaving villages in northern Thailand, Ban Renu is famous for textiles. The people are friendly and welcome visiting bargainers.

Continuing south on Route 212 leads to the district town of **Mukdahan**, on the right bank of the wide Mekong River and opposite the Laotian town of Savannakhet. (Mukdahan is, in fact, a trading centre for Laotian timber, agricultural products and gems.) Take the road to the river, turn right, and visit Wat Sri Nongkran, a temple built by Vietnamese refugees in 1956. The gates present a curious mixture of Thai contours, Vietnamese writing and Chinese-inspired dragons. Southward on Route 212 will lead to Ubon Ratchatani.

West of Udon Thani

Route 210 runs west of Udon Thani 150 kilometres (100 mi) to the ruggedly beautiful province of **Loei**, and to the town of the same name. Midway en

Map, page 252

BELOW: Phu Kradung National Park.

Map,
page 252

TIP

The Thai government
prohibits the illegal
excavation and sale of
artifacts, but near
archaelogical sites,
villagers may
approach offering to
sell artifacts, almost
always good fakes.

OPPOSITE: typical
Isaan headscarf.
BELOW: wreathed
hornbills in flight.

route, stop at **Tham Erawan** ⓲ (Elephant Cave), about 50 kilometres (30 mi)
before Loei and a couple of kilometres off the road. Despite its isolation, the
monastery there is well organised. A life-size statue of Erawan, the triple-headed
elephant of Thai mythology, marks the steep stairway and rocky path to the
cave's entrance. The climb up is rough. Prehistoric artifacts have been found
here, but apart from its size and an occasional cobra emerging from the rocks, all
that distinguishes the cave is an elephant's skull.

An ongoing agricultural boom is slowly changing Loei's shy simplicity. The
usually placid Mae Nam Loei flows through the centre of town. Until the 1980s,
Communist insurgents hid amidst the surrounding forests. What is now the traveller's delight was once the civil servant's nightmare. In the Thai bureaucracy,
being assigned to Loei was like going to Siberia. In the old days, Loei was a
jungle outpost that meant fever, cold weather, little comfort, isolation and poor
security. Not so today – Loei has numerous hotels, restaurants, and even a street
full of karaoke bars.

Route 203 plunges west into the wilderness to **Phu Rua National Park** ⓳.
The road slices through heavy banks of red laterite, past a sawmill and fields of
kenaf and cotton, the latter being the area's primary source of income. In December, the mountains lie under thick blankets of smoke as farmers burn the forest
undergrowth. Phu Rua itself is about 1,370 metres (4,500 ft) high. A rough road
to the top affords a view of the national forest.

To reach the Mekong near where it once again becomes the border between
Thailand and Laos, drive 50 kilometres (30 mi) north from Loei to the charming
riverside town of **Chiang Khan** ⓴. A boat can be hired for the short ride downstream to the Kaeng Khut Ku rapids, worthwhile both for their beauty and for the
sheer sense of being in the deep heart of Southeast Asia.

No experience in the Loei area can match the crisp
beauty of **Phu Kradung National Park** ㉑, the most
memorable escape in northeast Thailand and just 100
kilometres (60 mi) south of Loei. Phu Kradung came to
public attention only 50 years ago during the reign of
King Rama VI. Phu Kradung, a 60-square-kilometre
(24 sq mi) plateau lying between 1,200 and 1,500
metres (5,000 ft) in elevation, beckons the naturalist-at-
heart to try some of its 50 kilometres of marked trails.

The entrance to Phu Kradung is on Route 201. About
three kilometres from the entrance is the park office,
where one can arrange for porters, storage for excess
equipment, and parking. The park provides bedding and
blankets in cabins that hold up to eleven people. It is by
no means an easy climb, but it is well worth the effort.
Ladders enable visitors to negotiate the steepest boulders; views of the valley are excellent.

Atop Phu Kradung, clear and mostly level paths criss-
cross the tableland. Rare birds, including hornbills,
woodpeckers and pheasants, may be seen. Even wild
elephants and the occasional panther make their homes
on the mountain. Most of the wildlife is quite shy, however. The park's cabins and upper offices are located 3
kilometres from a small radar station and helicopter pad.
The government closes the park in the summer months
to permit the ecology to recover. In the past forests were
cut indiscriminately, but times have changed a little. ❐

THE GULF COAST

*It was Thailand's eastern gulf coast that first lured travelers
to the country's beaches several decades ago. It still does*

The eastern coast along the Gulf of Thailand is an almost unbroken stretch of sand that runs to Trat, the narrow finger of land that abuts the neighbouring country of Cambodia. Closer to Bangkok, towns like Si Racha and Chonburi, if somewhat lacking in visual charm, are nonetheless important commercial centres, with factories for processing and canning the region's agricultural produce. Si Racha, in particular, is noted for a fiery hot chilli sauce bearing its name that is a prominent feature of Thai dinner tables.

Few areas in Asia have undergone such a precipitous rise to fame and, some say, a plummet in popularity and integrity, as the beach resort of Pattaya. This huge resort was once a beautiful and quiet beach, a graceful, 4-kilometre-long crescent of golden sand lapped by gentle waves and balmy breezes. By the 1980s, the visitors came flowing in from all directions, making it one of the great success stories in Asian tourism. By the late 1980s, there were dozens of high-rise hotels lining the beach. Pattaya's lustre had begun to dull, however, with a lack of planning that robbed the resort of the very qualities that made it so popular. Too, it gained a reputation as a seaside Patpong of pedophiles and Western men looking for cheap sex.

Nevertheless, tourism brought the Eastern Gulf new prosperity. While mainstream travelers are avoiding Pattaya, islands along the coast like Ko Samet and Ko Chang are luring visitors. Still, tourism is far from being the region's sole source of income. Older industries in the area have long played an important part in the Thai economy. Much of the seafood consumed or exported by Thailand comes from Eastern Gulf ports, and some of the largest fruit orchards are located between Rayong and Chanthaburi. The area around Chanthaburi is also noted for its gem mining, such as for sapphires.

All this industry notwithstanding, the Eastern Gulf's main lures for the average foreign visitor are its sun and sand, and its plentiful tourist facilities. Despite the naysayers, Pattaya and its sisters continue to thrive, and maybe even improve. ❏

PRECEDING PAGES: fruit stand stacked with offerings; boat on gulf harbour. **LEFT:** seller of Southeast Asia's popular durian.

SOUTH TO PATTAYA

Map, page 277

Far away and close at the same time, the coastal road southeast of Bangkok along the Gulf of Thailand offers a little of everything to travellers, whether hot beach, hot sex or hot sauce

THAILAND

Bangkok

T he main route from Bangkok to the pretty eastern Gulf Coast is the unappealing Bangna-Trad highway, lined by nondescript concrete buildings. The views pick up when Bangna joins with the older Sukhumvit highway from Bangkok – Route 3 – just outside Chonburi, and the landscape gradually starts to become green and hilly.

Chonburi ❶ is a sprawling and industrious town of about a quarter million merchants, traders and craftsmen. Filled with Bangkok-style traffic, it is also the accident capital of Thailand. Nevertheless, its attractions include **Wat Buddhabat Sam Yot**, Buddha's Footprint Mountain of Three Summits, just outside town. Built amidst green trees by an Ayutthayan king and renovated during the reign of King Chulalongkorn, this hilltop monastery was once used to conduct the water oath of allegiance, when princes and governors drank the waters of fealty, pledging loyalty to the throne.

Near the centre of Chonburi, a colossal gold-mosaic image of Buddha dominates **Wat Dhamma Nimitr**. The largest image in this region and the only one in the country depicting the Buddha in a boat, the 40-metre-high (135 ft) statue recalls the story of the Buddha's journey to the cholera-ridden town of Pai Salee. On the same hill is the local Chinese Buddhist Society, with the burial shrines of prominent members.

Those interested in the historical arts could stop near the old market at the oldest and most important *wat* in the province, **Wat Intharam**, a mix of architectural styles and one of the best examples of Ayutthayan architecture in the southeast. In the 18th century, this wat was the rallying point for soldiers recruited by King Taksin to drive the Burmese from Ayutthaya.

OPPOSITE: waiting for the show, Nong Nooch Village.
BELOW: Pattaya resort.

South of Chonburi

Seven kilometres (4 mi) south of Chonburi on a back road is the town of **Ang Sila**. Once favoured by Thai royalty as a resort, the town takes its name of Stone Basin from the chain of rocks that form an oval protrusion into the sea. The roads are lined with shops selling the sculpted wares of local craftspeople. Fishing beds line the shallow waters around the village, and the small pier is full of activity.

Farther south sits an unusual monastery on a hill, **Rua Sam Pao**. Facing seaward and recently expanded, its walls are shaped like the huge hull of a Chinese junk, which some say points to a shipwreck in which emigrants from China were lost. In fact, it represents a vessel carrying the faithful to *nirvana*. The more than 300 meditation cells arranged around the main ship are also in the shape of small boats.

Many of the residents are very old and believe that to die at Rua Sam Pao brings good fortune; many of the older Chinese women believe that, when they die, their souls will be carried on the sea back to China. Pilgrims share the hill with hundreds of monkeys, and some excellent seafood restaurants make this a popular spot with day-trippers.

On the road past Ang Sila, the long straight beach at the slightly-rundown **Bang Saen** comes alive each weekend as hordes of Thai tourists descend in buses. A profusion of beach umbrellas, inner tubes and wrinkled watermelon rinds quickly cover the sandy beach, the surf filled with bobbing people. Under the casuarina trees lining the sand, picnickers enjoy vendor food and pick up souvenirs. The south end of the beach runs into a messy, garbage-strewn fishing and factory district and is best avoided. Bang Saen's main street on Thanon Sukhumvit is lined with hundreds of stalls selling local produce.

At the Bang Saen Reservoir bird refuge, with permission it is possible to sit in a blind and observe waterfowl. Chinese graves dot the countryside outside the town – the hills and sea make this a favourite burial spot for Bangkok Chinese. Up the hill behind the bird reserve is the **Khao Khieo Open Zoo**. It presents large and small animals in relatively natural settings. A huge aviary built over a natural hill allows visitors to stroll around and relax among plants and waterfalls in the company of hundreds of species of birds. On the hill are simple, but comfortable, bungalows that can be reserved from the Dusit Zoo, in Bangkok.

Si Racha ❷, further south, descends from the hills and extends into the sea on tentacle-like piers. Its famous hot sauce can be enjoyed at waterfront restaurants, where fresh shrimp, crab, oyster, mussel or abalone are dipped into the thick, tangy red liquid. An offshore rock supports a picturesque wat with Thai and Chinese elements. A footprint of the Buddha cast in bronze graces the wat, as do pictures of the goddess of mercy, Kuan Yin, and the Monkey God.

There are many spicy if not hot sauces to be tried in Thailand. The town of Si Racha is known for a local version called nam prik si racha.

BELOW: transvestite show and beach high-rise in Pattaya.

From the longest pier at Si Racha, boats ferry passengers to a nearby island, **Ko Si Chang ❸**. On the southern end of Ko Si Chang are deserted beaches and the attractively overgrown remains of a former royal palace once used by King Chulalongkorn as a summer retreat. A few modest bungalows past the Chinese temple overlooking the main town offer good sea and cliff views. Ko Si Chang also has the Yai Phrik Vipassana Centre, a meditation retreat.

Map, page 277

Pattaya

A few kilometres south of Si Racha, the busy port of Laem Chabang has seen massive growth since the mid 1990s. Well-known is **Pattaya ❹**. Few areas in Asia have undergone such a precipitous rise to fame and, soon after, a plummet into notoriety as Pattaya.

This huge resort was once a quiet village and beach known only to a handful of foreigners and Thais from Bangkok. By the 1970s, others were starting to discover its charms. Large hotels began to rise along the seashore. By the 1980s, Europeans and American sailors flocked to its beaches, and to those of **Jomtien**, the neighbouring beach just south.

Then Pattaya's lustre begun to dull. There were disturbing signs that problems lurking beneath the surface were surfacing: polluted beaches and water, as well as crime. The town had gained a seedy reputation, a waterfront Patpong-like rest-and-recreation holdover from the Vietnam War. Visitors started going elsewhere, to Phuket and Ko Samui. Pattaya today is still primarily known as a sex resort – the go-go bars are the most noticeable feature of the main tourist areas. Paedophiles pick up boys in a large open bar fronting the street in the main tourism strip, just a few metres from a nearby police box. South Pattaya

TIP

No matter how much effort some Pattaya businesses have made to make Pattaya respectable, the place has a backdrop of sex tourism, high crime, and drug abuse. It's impossible to ignore.

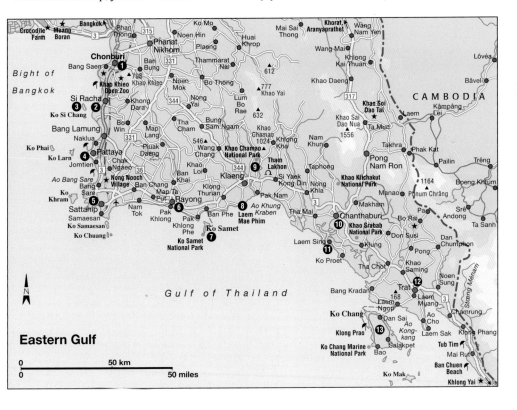

Eastern Gulf

Map, page 277

Golf swings south of urban Bangkok.

Six kilometres past Sattahip, a broad road leads to a large Thai military base, which once served the American air force as its only B-52 airstrip on the Asian mainland during the Vietnam War.

OPPOSITE: motorcycle taxi and young passenger.

is the main tourist and bar area, though bars and shops are increasingly moving into the quieter north section of town.

Hotels like the Royal Garden have attempted to publicise the resort's family attractions, with limited success. The resort is attracting a new clientele from Russia and eastern European countries. The larger hotels are well equipped with water sports and activities. New things to do include an authentic Ripley's Believe it or Not. A local English-language paper, *The Pattaya Mail*, keeps visitors and foreign residents well-informed about things to do, services and special offers and excursions. But the backdrop of sex tourism, a high crime rate and obvious drink and drug abuse is impossible to ignore in Pattaya.

The angler can test skills at landing grouper and red snapper, mackerel and bonito, sailfish and barracuda. Fishing expeditions can be arranged at Pattaya shops, and at Bang Sare farther down the coast. Off shore, **Ko Larn**, whose name translates as Bald Island, has the wide, soft-sand beaches that Pattaya lacks and it is a pleasant place to spend a leisurely day. The shore is filled with good seafood restaurants, and there are water-sports facilities for those who may be inclined to stir from their beach chairs. The island also has a golf course. Ten kilometres (7 mi) east of Pattaya is the Siam Country Club, which boasts one of the finest golf courses in the kingdom.

South of Pattaya

Excursions can be organised to visit sapphire mines, orchid farms and an elephant *kraal,* and boat trips to local islands are also easily arranged. Year by year, visitors have been exploring farther and farther south of Pattaya, discovering new resort areas with less noise and crowds. One popular resort for Thais is **Nong Nooch Village**, a complex of bungalows situated in park land around a lake and offering a variety of activities, including an elephant show, an orchid nursery and a cactus garden.

Just before Nong Nooch, a quiet resort at the end of Soi Sunset offers wonderful coastal and hill views past a quiet beach, which is almost always deserted. Beyond Nong Nooch are a number of resorts fronting waters known for deep-sea fishing, both commercial and sport. The area is one of the premier spots in the world for marlin and sailfish. The winding, busy streets of the untouristy fishing village of **Bang Sare**, cozily sheltered under a forested hill, are in great contrast to the resorts of the area. Food stalls, school children, motorbikes, dogs and cottage-industry shophouses bump up against each other in a scramble of activity and life.

Overlooking a scenic bay sprinkled with small islands, the fishing town of **Sattahip ❺**, about 20 kilometres (15 mi) south of Pattaya, blossomed overnight to become a busy deep-water port. It now acts as a headquarters for the Thai navy, which owns much of the surrounding land and many of the small islands off the coast. In the heart of town, a large and modern temple rests on turquoise pedestals, while in the commercial centre, a boisterous market teems with fish, fruit and vegetables. Sattahip is a place to decompress, offering little more to do than stroll past the shops or sit in an open-front coffee shop sipping an *oliang,* the great sweet iced coffee that originally came from French Cambodia. Enjoy a spicy curry near the market, or browse over teak elephants in the shops.

From Sattahip, the road follows the coastline eastward, but offers only occasional glimpses of the sea. The land is flat and arid, providing little scenic beauty until approaching the town of **Rayong ❻**. This area is being developed as Thailand's newest industrial region. While there are nice beaches popular with local workers at the weekends, the proximity of oil refineries and heavy industry at Maptaput make seafront alternatives further down the road more attractive. ❐

EASTERN GULF

Map, page 277

Extending down to the Cambodian border, this part of Thailand is rich in both gems and island beaches. Real gems take some knowledge to recognise, but picking the beaches is intuitive

THAILAND

Bangkok

A t the busy market town of **Rayong ⑥**, 220 kilometres (140 mi) from Bangkok, an attractive local tourism office is well-stocked with information on the east coast as far as the Cambodia border. A right turn in the centre of town leads to an old, but industrious, fishing village that occupies land between the beach and the estuary. Rayong is famed for its *nam plaa*, or fish sauce, the source of salt in Thai diets and the *sine qua non* of Thai condiments. Nam plaa is made from a small silver fish that abounds in the Gulf; it is decomposed for about seven months to produce a ruddy liquid, which is filtered and bottled on the spot.

About 20 kilometres (15 mi) past Rayong is a turn-off to **Ban Phe**, on the coast. Dressed in weathered black shirts, straw hats and sarongs, women carpet the ground with tangerine-coloured shrimp, drying them in the sun.

This busy fishing port is sheltered on the west by a rocky outcrop, and by the 6-kilometre-long island of **Ko Samet ⑦** to the south. The island is remembered by students of Thai literature as the place where Sunthorn Phu, a romantic court poet, retired to compose some of his work. Born in nearby Klaeng, Sunthorn Phu called the island Ko Kaeo Phisadan or "island with sand like crushed crystal". Ko Samet's sand is reputed to be the finest in Thailand. The island has gained popularity as a superb resort for its pristine waters and cosy coves, but not without controversy. Cheap bungalow complexes are being razed to build small hotels. Garbage and noise have increased on the larger stretches of beach. Ko Samet is, in fact, part of a national park, which means that much of the development is actually illegal and is periodically half-heartedly tackled by local authorities.

The coastal road leading east from Ban Phe passes fish mongers and barber shops before entering the kilometre-long pine forest of **Ban Pha Phrae National Park**, a refreshing change in scenery from the scrubland preceding it, and a popular picnicking spot with Thai tourists and locals.

Attractive resorts line the 10 kilometres (6 mi) from Wang Kaew to the peninsula of **Laem Mae Phim ⑧**, an underrated part of the Thai coast. Suan Wang Kaew is a landscaped garden on a hill stretching into the sea and a favourite Thai picnic spot. It has bungalows and rooms for rent on the west side. A couple of good restaurants jutting out to the sea provide views of the long stretch of sand in front.

This stretch of coast has seen little of the commercialisation that has developed at most Thai resorts. Vendors offering cheap goods and traditional massage are notable for their absence. It's not unusual for visitors to have the beaches (which could be cleaner) almost to themselves when weekend vacationers from Bangkok

OPPOSITE: popularity threatens Ko Samet. **BELOW:** coral reef off Ko Samet.

have departed. Further on from Laem Mae Phim is a popular Thai resort where excellent seafood restaurants line the top end of the beach. A few kilometres on, the charming, untouristed fishing village of **Ao Khai** is a restful place to watch the loading and unloading of all sorts of fish from old, gaily coloured wooden fishing boats.

Just offshore are a number of jagged islands. Many local resorts offer day-trips to the nearby islands, one of which has been set aside as a reserve for turtles. On the way to Chanthaburi from Laem Mae Phim, the village of Ban Krum has a small park dedicated to the poet Sunthorn Phu, with statues of the poet and some of his most famous characters.

The town of **Klaeng** is quietly busy, its streets lined with numerous and attractive old-style Thai wooden houses. The imposing Wat Saranat Thammaram is located at the market. At Klaeng, a new double-lane highway leads directly to Chonburi and Bangkok.

Khao Chamao National Park ❾, 12 kilometres (8 mi) to the north off Route 3 a few kilometres past Klaeng, has a long waterfall with eight levels. Ascent is relatively easy with the aid of special bridges and walkways. Soro brook carp cluster in the pools by the hundreds. The fish scrabble to grab green leaves that drop from trees overhead or from the hands of helpful visitors to the falls. When eaten, this carp is said to induce stomach aches or a mild "high" due to its diet of a special fruit.

Nearby are the **Khao Wong caves**, about 60 in all, many of which are occupied by Buddhist monks. One cave has been turned into a shrine with a replica of the Buddha's footprints. **Wat Khao Sukim**, a large meditation temple set high in the mountains further down the coast (turn left off Route 3), has stun-

Chanthaburi's history began as much as 6,000 years ago. But historical pages are mostly blank until the 17th century, when Ayutthaya's King Narai moved people from Chiang Mai and Laos to Chanthaburi to defend it against incursions and attacks by Khmer and Vietnamese forces.

BELOW: unloading supplies during a downpour.

ning views, tranquil shady spots and strangely life-like wax figures of Buddhist monks. There are displays of fine jade, furniture and antiques. A funicular takes visitors to the top, or else it's an energetic walk up hundreds of steps on the adjacent stairway lined with two colourfully decorated stone-and-ceramic serpents.

From Wat Khao Sukim to Chanthaburi, the mountain road has few surprises, except for an understated, official-looking sign for "Paradise", which is an invitation that may be hard to pass up. "Paradise" is a Catholic religious retreat, with a church and little bungalows clustered around a small lake and waterfalls.

Map,
page 277

Chanthaburi

The area between **Chanthaburi** ⑩ and the Cambodian border lies in a climate pattern somewhat different from the rest of Thailand, receiving the southwest monsoon that makes it wetter, but greener. The rains nurture rubber plantations, a luscious *rambutan* crop, and what are reputedly the best durians in the kingdom. (Try one, but don't bring it back to your hotel.) Gems, delicious fruits, handicrafts, beaches, an air of quiet antiquity, and relics of the past make this area a prime spot.

Chanthaburi itself sits amid rolling hills beside the winding Chanthaburi River. Its residents are a mix of Thai, Burmese, Chinese and Vietnamese faces. The lake in the town centre, built by the French, is a favourite meeting and exercise spot, and is an unusual feature in Thai towns. Motorcycles clog the town's streets. Shops along the river and elsewhere are open in the front, revealing rows and rows of grinding stones upon which artisans patiently cut facets on precious stones that are mined nearby.

Chanthaburi's recent history is contained on a hill, and in a jail. About 5 kilo-

Khmer lintel from the early 7th century found in the Chanthaburi area.

BELOW: coastal fishing trawlers.

Thailand's Gems: Crystal Power

Thais have turned a national passion for gems and jewellery into one of the country's largest export industries. Rubies, sapphires and jade are among the best bargains, while gold, silver and diamond products, finished by master craftsmen, are also popular buys.

Rubies, the name given to red, gem-quality corundum stones, vary in shade from pinkish or purplish to the brownish-red found in Thailand, depending on the stone's chromium and iron content. A really fine ruby can appear to glow like hot coal. Since prehistory, rubies have been associated with a range of spiritual and supernatural beliefs. The Burmese thought rubies conferred invulnerability, and that they could foretell danger by loss of colour or brilliance. Most of the rubies in Thailand traditionally originated from the Chanthaburi region, and from the Pailin area of

Cambodia, which together account for around two-thirds of the world's supply of rubies. A small number come from Vietnam and parts of Africa.

Thailand's ruby mines were known in early times, with the first known reference coming from a Chinese traveller, Ma Huan, in AD 1408. Now they are close to depletion. At Bo Rai, once the king of Thai ruby-mining towns, abandoned equipment litters the landscape. Where there used to be hundreds of traders, just a few remain. Supplies from the Cambodian side of the border have become more sporadic. Rubies from the remote Moguk and Mong Hsu mines in upper Burma, where primitive, back-breaking extraction methods still apply, are relatively rare and highly sought-after for the international market when they get to Thailand.

An important distinction is made between prime-quality unheated stones, most of which come from Moguk, and less valuable heat-treated samples, originating primarily in Mong Hsu. The latter tend to look like bad garnet before treatment, after which they turn into bright-red gems.

Sapphires, also composed of corundum, come in different colours, from the highly-prized rich-blue to orange, green, yellow, pink and colourless varieties. Sapphire was traditionally believed by Buddhists to produce a desire for prayer, to help ward off negative energies, and to promote calm. Thailand's sapphires now come mainly from Sri Lanka, Australia and Africa. Locally mined sapphires in Kanchanaburi and Phrae, and Cambodian stones from the Pailin area, are increasingly limited in number and quality.

In recent years, Thailand has also become a major centre for processing diamonds, catering to a large foreign as well as thriving domestic jewellery

Shopping for gems and jewellery in Thailand is easy and rewarding, so long as one sticks to reputable stores. (If in doubt, contact the local Tourism Authority of Thailand office for authorised gem and jewelry establishments.) Innumerable scams involving gullible tourists have been reported in the Thai press. They often take the form of an individual with a "special offer", backed up by a convincing story. A polite but firm refusal will deflect the scam. ■

metres south of town stands **Khai Nern Wong**, the "Camp on a Small Circular Hill." King Taksin retreated here after the fall of Ayutthaya in 1767 to regroup his forces, recruit new soldiers and construct a fleet of warships. From this staging point, he returned to Ayutthaya to rout its Burmese occupiers. On the same hill are the remains of a fortress built by King Rama III. At several points around the hill, derelict cannons point at the now-silent jungle. Several of the pieces are of great size; locals claim they protect the mouth of the Chanthaburi River, over ten kilometres away. Today, spirits are believed to keep watch in the ruins.

Across the river is the French-style **Church of the Immaculate Conception**, the largest Catholic church in Thailand. Built around 1880, its congregation is comprised of Vietnamese who migrated to Thailand over the last two centuries. The descendants of these immigrants engage in a number of businesses, foremost of which is the weaving of reed mats, handbags and purses in attractive shapes and patterns. Many items are made in homes. Some excellent products can be ordered from the nuns of the church.

Nearby is **Laem Sing ⑪**, site of a Thai confrontation with European powers. Around the turn of the century, the Thais were embroiled in a territorial dispute with the French occupiers of Cambodia. The French invaded and for 11 years stationed a garrison at Laem Sing. The Tuk Daeng (Red Building) Customs House and the Kook Khi Kai (Chicken Dung Prison) attest to their presence.

Since the 15th century, the area's prime activity has been mining for sapphires and other precious stones, especially rubies. The red soil of the rubber plantations is pitted with holes up to 12 metres (40 ft) deep, each miner staking a claim and hauling out the muck by the bucket-full. It is backbreaking work, with meagre rewards. But occasionally a giant gemstone is found.

Map, page 277

Gem dealer displays a blue-sapphire ring.

OPPOSITE: a precious sapphire find.
BELOW: tattoos protect from evil.

Map, page 277

TIP

If the political situation in Cambodia changes, then one day it may be possible to enter Cambodia from Thailand's gulf border with it. But for now, don't plan on entering Cambodia from here.

OPPOSITE: tattoos can be free-form or detailed. **BELOW:** Nam Tok Praew waterfall.

The nearest gem-mining area is at **Khao Ploi Waen** (Hill of the Sapphire Ring). To reach it, return to Khai Nern Wong, the old fort ruins. Just past it is a junction where the gemstones are traded and purchased. Another kilometre on is Khao Ploi Waen. The open pits in the hillside are up to 10 metres deep.

A side trip to the north for consideration: From **Sa Kaeo**, 200 kilometres (125 mi) to the north of Chanthaburi, drive 60 kilometres (40 mi) east on Route 33 to **Aranyaprathet**. On the border with Cambodia, until a few years ago the area held huge refugee camps. The area still sees occasional influxes of refugees, depending upon the sporadically-difficult situation in Cambodia.

Back in Chanthaburi, head down the road to its waterfalls. At the 324-kilometre marker of Route 3, directly opposite the Chanthaburi turn-off, a small road leads inland for 20 kilometres (13 mi), through orchards of rambutan, durian, oranges and lychees. **Nam Tok Krating** (Bull Waterfall) is a cascade of small falls tumbling 400 metres (1,300 ft) across a granite face.

Farther down Route 3, near the 347-kilometre marker, is another popular waterfall, **Nam Tok Praew**. Beyond makeshift stalls, where women sell sticky rice and durian jam, is an oddity: a pyramidal *chedi* overlooking the falls. The chedi commemorates a consort of King Chulalongkorn who drowned while being rowed up the Chao Phraya River. Her death was particularly tragic, since her attendants could have saved her, had they not been forbidden to touch the body of a royal person. Today, falls and pools are seldom deserted in daylight.

Trat

The road to Trat, 400 kilometres (250 mi) from Bangkok and the last major town before the Cambodian border, passes through rubber plantations, paddies and marshlands. About ten kilometres beyond Chanthaburi, the attractive Chinese temple **Wat Bang Korn** is a peaceful oasis. Further on is **Oasis Sea World**, a breeding and conservation station for dolphins. Humpbacked and Irrawaddy dolphins perform aquatic shows daily here for tourists.

A gem-trading centre, **Trat** ⑫ itself is undistinguished, but it serves as a starting point for trips to beautiful offshore islands. Head from the town clock tower to the port of **Laem Ngop**, about 20 kilometres (15 mi) southwest. There, boats leave in mornings for **Ko Chang** ⑬. Eight kilometres (5 mi) wide and 30 kilometres (20 mi) long, Thailand's third-largest island is famed for wild boar and the Mai Yom Falls. Off the northern tip of Ko Chang, some of the largest sharks in the gulf cruise near a rocky outcrop. Nearby, **Ko Mak** and **Ko Kut** offer clear lagoons and excellent diving. Lodging is of simple bungalows and a few new although modest resorts.

From Trat, drive down the scenic narrow finger of Thailand to the town of **Khlong Yai**, built over the water. From the main street, rows of houses run into the sea. Between them, parked like cars on a side street, are moored fishing trawlers that earn the inhabitants their income. The road, with unspoilt sea views, continues to **Hat Yai**, a fishing (and smuggling) village on the Cambodia border, an interesting spot from which to watch life, and trucks of whiskey and cigarettes, go by. ❑

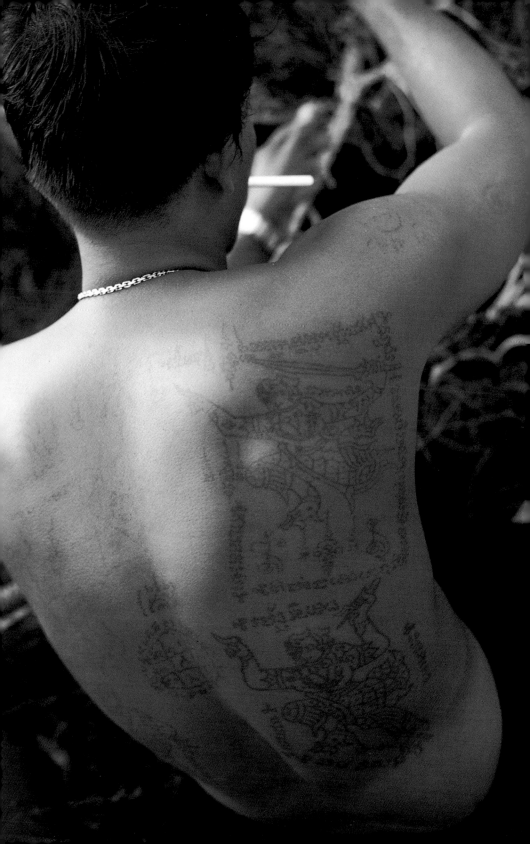

A FEAST OF FRUITS

There is a sizeable range of fruits in Thailand, many of which may be unfamiliar. As well as bananas and pineapples, there are other brilliantly coloured and strangely shaped fruits for the adventurous traveller.

Thai people love food, and during the afternoon they snack on an incredible variety of fruits. For visitors who are in need of a boost, fruit can be a great source of refreshment and energy. Traditional fruit sellers have glass-fronted carts stacked with blocks of ice and pealed pieces of seasonal fruits. Choose a selection of what you want to eat and the vendor will pop it into a bag for you along with a toothpick for spearing the slices. Some fruits, like pineapple, are eaten with a little salt and ground chilli, a twist of which is supplied separately. Don't be afraid of this combination – the natural sweetness of the pineapple is enhanced by this bitter condiment, surprisingly enough.

One of the best ways to cool down is to drink a delicious fruit juice or *naam phon-la-mai*. To order, say the Thai word for water (*naam*) in front of the name of the fruit, or just point to your selection from the fruits on display. Another favourite drink is fruit juice blended with ice – known as a *naam pon* or "smoothie". You can have syrup mixed in to sweeten your juice (*namm pan*) or salt added (as the Thais like it) to bring out the flavour of the fruit.

CONTROVERSIAL DURIAN

People either love or hate durian. Ask any visitor in Thailand to recall the first time they came across it and they will describe, in detail, its "perfume". To most *farang* (foreigners), the durian's odour is repugnant, but for the Thais the fruit commands the utmost respect.

According to devotees the rewards of eating durian far outweigh any objections to its smell. The only way to enter the great durian debate is to try it for yourself. If you can't face eating the fruit *au naturel* there is durian cake, ice-cream and chewing gum.

◁ **JACKFRUIT** *(KHANUN)*
The ripe, rich yellow sections of the jackfruit are waxy-textured and semi-sweet. When green they are used in curries, and the flowers and young shoots are eaten in salads.

RAMBUTAN *(LUUK NGOH)*▷
The hairy rambutan (*rambut* means hair in Malay) is a close relative of the lychee, and its translucent, sweet flesh has a similar taste. There is a technique to squeezing it open to avoid squirting yourself with its juices; any Thai can demonstrate this.

▽ **STAR FRUIT** *(MA DUN)*
This sweet, yellow fruit is native to India. It has a thin waxy skin with a crisp texture and sweet-tart juice. It can be found in fruit salads or can be candied and eaten as a confection. The unripe fruit is bright green and is sometimes added to dishes that require an acidic taste.

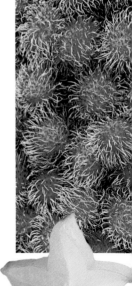

△ **CUSTARD APPLE** *(NOI-NA)*
The custard apple looks like a small, light green hand-grenade and can be pulled apart by hand. The pulp is soft, often mushy, very sweet and very tasty. It is best to eat it with a spoon.

▽ **MANGOSTEEN** *(MANGKHUT)*
Thais believe durian requires the cool, refreshing sweet taste of the mangosteen as a chaser. See if you can guess how many sections your mangosteen has before you break it open.

CROPS: A GROWING CONCERN

◁ **DURIAN** *(TURIAN)*
The most expensive of Thai fruits has mushy flesh that tastes good with sticky rice and coconut milk. Ignore the smell and you will be rewarded.

APANESE PEAR ▷
This crunchy and slightly ry. fruit is usually eaten aw. Its semi-sweet flavour an be enhanced by dipping it nto slightly salted water.

Farming and fishing have always been at the centre of Thai life. Despite rapid industrialisation, this is still the case. Thailand is self-sufficient in food, and agribusiness is an important pillar of the Thai economy, claiming nearly a quarter of GDP and making Thailand the only net food exporter in Asia. Thailand is the world's leading exporter of canned pineapple and has big overseas markets in canned logans and rambutans.

Fruit production is expected to increase as available land and labour resources dwindle and farmers switch from producing staple crops, such as rice and cassava, to cash crops like soya beans, fruits, sugar cane and rubber. Large fruit farmers are starting to process their products before they reach the consumer, and many are now applying for loans to invest in equipment to dry and freeze their produce. Although some of this produce will be sold to Thailand's neighbours, much of it will end up in the snack food departments of Japanese supermarkets – Japanese businesses have already set up factories in Thailand to process fruits, vegetables and nuts for their home market.

THE SOUTH

From carefree and warm beaches to the curries and mosques near Malaysia, surprises abound in Thailand's south

Southern Thailand, a long arm of land sometimes likened to an elephant's trunk, consists of 14 provinces and is rich in stunning scenery. Wild jungles alternate with rocky mountains and broad beaches of powdery sand. While a few select areas are increasingly world-class destinations, other parts of the region are still being discovered by the outside world.

Countless islands, large and small, are scattered down this narrow strip of land that leads to Malaysia. The eastern coast of the Isthmus of Kra faces the Gulf of Thailand, while the other shore lies on the Andaman Sea and Indian Ocean. Other than the larger islands like Ko Samui (*ko* means island in Thai) and Phuket, which have been developed for tourism, few of the many other islands are visited.

In many ways, the south of Thailand is a world far removed from the rest of the country, especially in the deep south. A different climate, religion and type of farming make it unique among Thailand's regions. Groves of rubber trees are more common than fields of rice. The gilded dome of a Muslim mosque becomes a more familiar sight than the sloping orange roof of a Buddhist temple. In the provinces near the border, the people speak Malay as well as Thai, and throughout the region, there is a distinctive southern dialect, as well as a cuisine resembling that of Malaysia.

From time to time there is talk – as there has been since 1793 – of building a 100-kilometre-long (60 mi) canal, like the Panama and Suez canals, across the Kra Isthmus, from outside Songkhla to north of Satun. Alternative "land bridge" proposals include from Songkhla to Penang, in Malaysia, and from near Surat Thani to Krabi. Any of these routes would minimise the need to use Singapore as a shipping transit point, but the environmental concerns are monumental.

Rich in natural resources, the south is Thailand's most prosperous region after Bangkok. (And like the north, only in the present century has the south become fully integrated into the Thai kingdom.) Rubber, the country's second-largest agricultural export product after rice, thrives so well that Thailand is one of the world's largest exporters, as with tin, which is mined in southern provinces. And until the government banned logging, so too with teak. Tourism is a fairly new industry in the south, but already it has become a major foreign exchange earner.

For many years, access to the south's secluded areas was a major undertaking. Only the really adventurous attempted it. While getting around the southern areas is easy these days, there is still a sense of adventure and remoteness to one's travels here. ❐

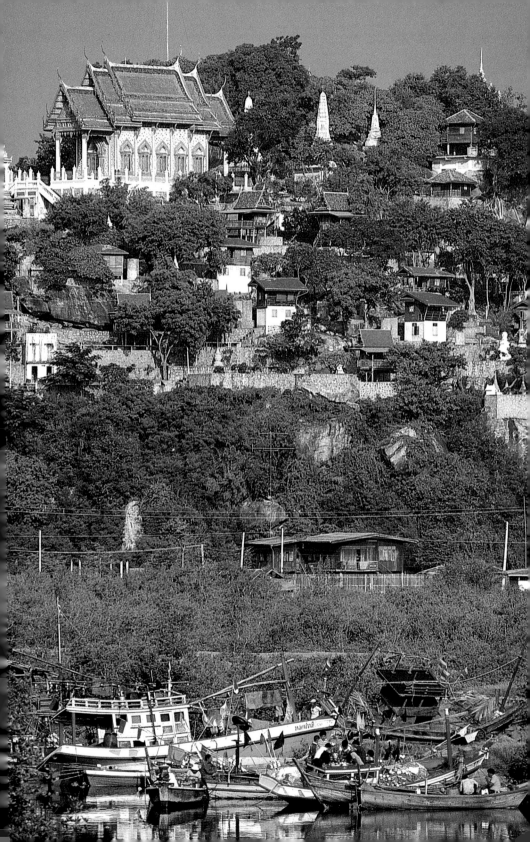

NORTHERN ISTHMUS

Looking like the trunk of an elephant, the Isthmus of Kra is Thailand's overland link to the Malaysian peninsula. Both sides of this narrow isthmus offer some of the world's finest beaches

Map, page 297

THAILAND

Bangkok

There is little to distinguish **Ratchaburi ❶**, but in recent years it has become a ceramics centre, manufacturing everything from large brown rainwater storage jars decorated with dragons and known as *ong*, to exquisite *benjarong* wares, small porcelain vessels with intricate, five-coloured designs. One can spend a day wandering from shop to shop in Ratchaburi, contentedly browsing among a wide variety of styles and types. Prices are generally very reasonable, and outlets will be only too pleased to arrange shipping.

Phetchburi ❷, 160 kilometres (100 mi) south of Bangkok, has far more to offer. Approaching the town on Route 4, take the left fork and continue past a rocky hill on the right. Cross the railroad tracks and stop under the shady trees for a visit to the cave at **Khao Luang**. Around midday, huge stalactites and dozens of Buddha images are bathed in a soft light that pours through the cave roof.

Entering Phetchburi, *naga*-topped walls frame the pathway to **Khao Wang**, a palace built by King Mongkut in the 1860s. Ascend by foot or miniature railway the fragrant frangipani-fringed path, past the royal stables, to the restored palace at the summit. The gleaming – sometimes blindingly – white palace is dominated by an observatory, which the king constructed to pursue his favourite pastime of astronomy. The view from the parapet is superb; one can survey the entire city, its river, the rice fields and the mountains along the Burmese border to the west.

Four temples are worthy of a visit. **Wat Yai Suwannaram** is east of the river, and **Wat Kamphaeng Laeng** is just southeast of it. Wat Yai Suwannaram, built in the 17th century, has murals that are among the oldest in the country. Wat Kamphaeng Laeng, a Khmer temple, is thought to delineate the most western frontier of the Angkorian empire. **Wat Ko Keo Sutharam** contains fading, but beautiful, Ayutthaya-period murals dating from 1734. **Wat Mahathat**, in the middle of town, is marked by a huge *prang* that towers over it. Much of the decor is new, but it nevertheless acts as a magnet for Buddhists, and visitors will find that festivals are often in progress there.

About 20 kilometres (15 mi) southeast of Phetchburi is **Kaeng Krachan Dam** (or Ubol Ratana Dam, after the current king's daughter). Visitors may stay at bungalows overlooking the scenic reservoir and take boats up the reservoir to the river.

Forty kilometres (25 mi) south is **Cha-am**, the first of several beach resorts along the peninsula. Better known is the sister resort of **Hua Hin ❸** further south, Thailand's oldest major beach resort. It was put on the map in 1910 by the brother of King Rama VI, Prince Chakrabongse, who led a party of European and Thai royalty down the peninsula to hunt game. King Prajadhipok (1925–1935) built a palace here called **Klai**

OPPOSITE: wat and dwellings, Hua Hin.
BELOW: Khao Luang.

A 1932 guide called Hua Hin "the most popular with travellers... longing for a game of golf". In those days, sand traps were assisted by roaming tigers on the links. Today, Hua Hin's well-tended and world-famous 18-hole courses are considerably tamer.

Klangwan, meaning "far from worries". Ironically, he was vacationing here in 1932 when a bloodless coup toppled him, replacing 700 years of absolute monarchy with a constitutional one. Unfortunately, the palace is not open to the public. Remnants of the 1920s and 1930s linger at the **Hotel Sofitel Central**, better known by its former name, the **Hua Hin Railway Hotel**. Renovated, it retains its air of gentility with ceiling fans and gardens filled with a menagerie of animal topiary. The tea room is, in fact, a museum collection of domestic Thai artifacts from the 1920s and 1930s. Because of its old-world atmosphere, this hotel stood in for the French Embassy in Phnom Penh in the film *The Killing Fields*.

A bit further south, the Royal Garden Hotel offers modern amenities amidst luxury accommodations. **Hua Hin Beach** itself is wide, flat, and shelves very slowly. Its regency character lingers in the availability of horses, which can be rented for a gallop, or a trot, along the sand. As a booming weekend resort for Bangkok residents, Hua Hin's modern development generally lacks the charm lingering in the old Railway Hotel. The town nevertheless has a thriving night market with a range of food stalls, international restaurants, and shops that are open late to satisfy the appetite of visitors.

For some lively local colour, stroll down to the pier in the morning, or else in the evening, to watch fishermen unload their catches while women examine and bargain for a wide variety of fresh seafood, including an occasional catch of shark or stingray.

South of Hua Hin

BELOW: white-sand beach, and Hua Hin's train station.

Leave Hua Hin by heading south again on Route 4. About 20 kilometres (15 mi) from the town, the highway crosses a river, then enters **Pranburi**. Children play

under stilt-houses while fishermen hang their nets to dry on wooden racks.

Further south, the jagged outline of the **Khao Sam Roi Yot National Park ❹** comes into view. The gorges and caves here once sheltered bandits who robbed unwary travellers; their haunts were cleared out long ago. Now, deer, monkeys and numerous species of birds roam the park, the coastal areas of which have been badly denuded by prawn farms.

The sky above Khao Sam Roi Yot (300 Peaks Range) is remembered in the annals of the Chakri dynasty. In 1868, King Mongkut, an astute mathematician and astronomer, brought the governor of Singapore and the Bangkok court here to view a total eclipse of the sun, which he had foretold. The king's prediction, to the astonishment of local astrologers, was only four minutes off. News of this event helped to discredit the superstition that an eclipse occurred when a giant swallowed the sun and disgorged it only when impelled by gongs and general noise-making. (Unfortunately, King Mongkut contracted a fever and died a week after his return to Bangkok.)

About 90 kilometres (55 mi) south of Hua Hin, **Prachuap Khiri Khan ❺** faces a scenic little harbour enclosed by knob-like hills. A natural arch at Khao Chong Krachok frames the sky. Steps – 404 in all – lead up the hill to a small monastery surrounded by frangipani trees. Within the *chedi* are special Buddha relics bequeathed to the state by Rama I and Rama IV and used in the coronation of Chakri kings.

From Prachuap, continue to **Huai Yang**. The waterfall here cascades over 120 metres (400 ft) of boulders in a forest setting not far from the Burmese border. Beyond lies **Bang Saphan ❻**, divided in two by the tracks of the south-bound railway. A wide bay is rimmed by a pretty, 6-kilometre-long beach. A green hill, Khao Mae Pamphung, is to the north; Ko Thalu is to the south. Here, seafood and drinks are served on the beach.

South of Bang Saphan, the countryside eventually becomes lush and mountainous. Rubber plantations spread beneath

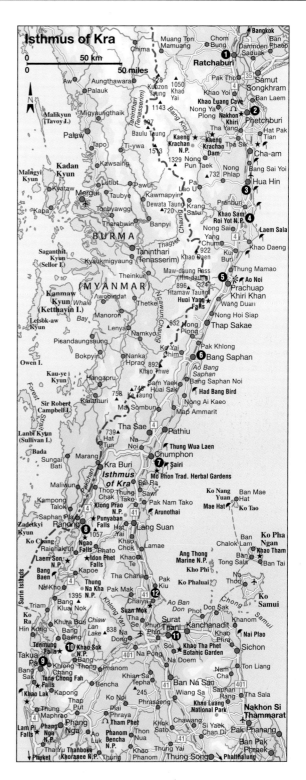

TIP

BELOW: southern street market.

limestone cliffs that erupt from the Kra Isthmus and further south down the Malay Peninsula.

Around 500 kilometres (300 mi) south of Bangkok, Route 4 comes to an important junction, where it branches right and heads west to the Andaman Sea, on the west coast. The left branch leads to Chumphon, Lang Suan and the east coast towns of Surat Thani, Nakhon Si Thammarat and Songkhla. Turn left at this junction to reach **Chumphon ➐**, noted for its inexpensive bird's nest soup. East of it lies **Paknam Chumphon**. Situated at the mouth of the Mae Nam Chumphon, this fishing port rents boats by the hour for trips to nearby islands, where swallows build their nests. The island of **Lanka Chio** is especially famous. The island-dotted coastal waters make for exciting sailing, too, for those so inclined.

To the west coast

South on Route 41 is Surat Thani. A longer way, and more scenic, is Route 4, which strikes west across the narrowest point on the Kra Isthmus, then veers south, following the Pakchan River through **Kraburi** on the way to Ranong.

About 12 kilometres (8 mi) beyond Kraburi, turn left just before the 504-kilo-metre marker to reach **Tham Prakayang**, a temple in a cavern. If you lack a flashlight, the monks may lend one for the dark ascent into the image-filled cave. One completely black Buddha gazes upon visitors through mother-of-pearl eyes. A limestone-and-wooden staircase leads up and out of the cave to well-worn paths, trodden by monks who meditate amid the solitude atop the outcrop.

South of Tham Prakayang, the highway winds through jungled hills and crosses a wide river. Punyaban Falls appears next to the road. Truck drivers stop,

don sarongs, and take a quick dip in the cool water. This is a popular spot for Thai tourists, who stop for snacks at the teahouse near the falls. Climb a path to the left of the falls for a good view of the Pakchan estuary, nearby islands, and the contours of mountains on the southern tip of Burma.

Further down the road, turn right near the Thara Hotel to enter **Ranong ❽**. The hotel itself holds one of Ranong's main attractions: hot mineral water piped from nearby thermal springs. A well encloses the main outlet, which pours forth 500 litres (130 gal) per minute of sparkling mineral water at 70°C (160°F). Cross a suspension bridge to a little park, or climb the hill behind the shrine to a small wat enclosed in a secluded grove.

The road past the hot springs leads to the village of **Hat Supin**. This is tin-mining country; stark landscapes of white silt, bamboo scaffolding, deep and dark pits, and gouged-out cliff faces are everywhere. In open-cast mining, water from high-pressure hoses carves holes in the earth. The mineral-laden water is filtered through a sieve, which separates the tin ore from the mud and sand. One of Thailand's major exports, tin is mined all along the Indian Ocean coast of the isthmus. Much of the ore comes from private holdings, like those around Hat Supin. A small sign with fish painted on it points the way to **Wat Hat Supin**, where children rush up to sell sweet popcorn, which is fed to hundreds of carp that swarm in a pool located by the side of the temple.

Drive back to Ranong, then take the three-kilometre road to **Saphan Pla**, on the sea where boats unload fish at a modern wharf and trucks dump tons of crushed ice on emptied decks. From this port, some boats sail the Indian Ocean as far as Bangladesh in search of fish. Directly opposite Saphan Pla is **Ko Pak Nam**, with its stilt houses and fishing boats. Boats can be rented for trips to the

Map, page 297

Spirit house.

BELOW: across the Kra Isthmus.

island. Continuing south past Kapoe and Khuraburi for 160 kilometres (100 mi), the road meets the junction of Route 401, near the town of Takua Pa. From here, the highway heads east towards Surat Thani.

The indifferent appearance of **Takua Pa ❾** belies its rich past. In the third century BC, Emperor Ashoka of India sent troops to conquer Klingkarach, in the southeast of his country. Natives of that region fled overseas and resettled in Takua Pa and Takua Tung. Later, the area became a significant port for Indian traders, who settled along the Malayan coast when the region was called Suvannabhumi, Land of Gold, over 1,500 years ago. Three statues of Brahma, Shiva, and Vishnu – all four-armed and larger than human size – found in nearby hills, and two 7th-century Dvaravati statues, discovered on an island in the mouth of the yellowish Mae Nam Takua Pa, add to the archeological evidence. By the 16th century, Portuguese merchants were buying and selling goods on this coast, especially at Phuket and Malacca.

Today, Takua Pa has little to claim except as the district centre of a rich tin-mining area. South of Takua Pa, a road branching off Route 4 leads to **Bang Sak**, a beach that rims a scenic, wide bay. It is typical of sparsely-touristed bays along the Andaman Sea coast in Phang Nga. Out at sea, barges engage in small-scale tin mining.

Forty kilometres (25 mi) south of Takua Pa, at **Khao Lak**, about 30 families live most of the year in the natural shelter of this cove. The men do not fish, but rather dive for tin, with the aid of air pumps and goggles. Like nautical prospectors, they stay underwater one or two hours at a time, loading tin-bearing sand into buckets. Workers hoist the full buckets onto bamboo rafts and sieve their contents. Every June, the powerful monsoons churn up the ocean and halt the

Some scholars think Indian traders sought shortcuts across Thailand to the South China Sea. Unearthed statues have traced caravan routes across the Kra Isthmus to Surat Thani. Takua Pa is thought to have been a major centre for the spice trade.

BELOW: coconut-hunting patrol.

tin diving. The mining families abandon their huts to the destructive lashing of wind and sea until the monsoon relents.

If continuing south from here, one will reach the island of Phuket and the Phang Nga Bay area.

Return to the eastern seaboard

Back at Takua Pa, Route 401 cuts east across the isthmus, a great drive full of ups, downs and challengingly-sharp corners, zig-zagging over and around the cloud-cloaked limestone pinnacles of the Kra Isthmus. First the road enters the hills, plunging through a remarkable series of streaked limestone precipices and splintered rocks. Then it traverses the wide valley of the Takua Pa River, passing tin mining camps flanked by mountains. For a midway rest, stop at **Wat Thamwaran**, just to the left of a small river. The wat provides a simple shelter for monks who often meditate near a cave.

Nature-oriented travellers have the pleasure of stopping at the well-marked **Khao Sok National Park** ❿. The park, in combination with Klongsang Wildlife Sanctuary and the Ratchaprapha Dam (sometimes called Chiaw Lan), covers 123,600 hectares (300,000 acres) of mostly virgin rain forest, with surrounding peaks rising to over 1,000 metres (3,300 ft). Although poaching is rife, the sheer size of the forest has helped protect sizeable populations of elephant, bison, langur, bear, Asiatic wild dogs, and even brilliant-beaked hornbills, as well as tiger, leopard and other jungle cats. The world's largest flower, the 80-centimetre-wide (2.6 ft) *Rafflesia* (known in Thai as *bua phut*), was recently found in the park, one of the few places in the world where it occurs. A number of Spartan, but clean, bungalow resorts along the Khlong Sok River act as a base

Map,
page 297

The Rafflesia is a real stinker, with the intent of attracting pollinating insects. Parasitic and lacking leaves, it grows in roots of host trees. Once a year, it surfaces and blooms, smelling foul and hoping for a passing insect. Days later, the flower withers.

BELOW: the banteng, a wild cattle species found in the south of Thailand.

Map, page 297

for guided treks and canoeing excursions, and for trips to floating villages on the lake. The road leaves the hills and enters dense rubber plantations before entering the town of **Surat Thani** ⓫. This busy shipbuilding, fishing and mining centre lies on the bank of the Tapi River. Surat itself has little worth seeing, but it is a point of departure for several interesting side trips, not to mention a primary departure port for ferries to Ko Samui and beyond.

Ancient empire

Twenty kilometres (12 mi) north of Surat Thani is **Chaiya** ⓬, a small and sleepy town of unpainted wooden buildings, like any small town of south Thailand. But the area is the subject of a debate about whether or not it was the capital of a once-great empire.

Ancient votive tablet from the Srivijaya empire.

Some historians now believe that the capital of the Srivijaya empire – described by the wandering Chinese monk, I Ching, in AD 671 – was not Palembang, in Sumatra, but rather Chaiya. In fact, they claim, the date previously accepted as the founding of the empire in Palembang was actually the date it was conquered by Chaiya. The name Chaiya may be a contraction of Srivijaya.

In any case, only a few traces remain of this mighty empire, which once stretched from Java through Malaysia and into Thailand. Less than two kilometres out of town stands **Wat Mahathat**, one of the most revered temples in Thailand. Its central chedi is thought to be over 1,300 years old, a direct visual link between Chaiya and the Srivijaya period. A small museum adjoining the wat displays some interesting relics found in the vicinity.

OPPOSITE: Wat Mahathat, in Chaiya. **BELOW:** Suan Mok art.

Closer to town is **Wat Wieng**, where an inscription from AD 755 is ascribed to a King Vishnu. It was the erroneous attribution of this inscription, 50 years ago, to a different location that led to the hypothesis that Nakhon Si Thammarat was an important local Srivijayan centre.

Two other wats, Wat Long and Wat Kaeo, equidistantly spaced from Wat Wieng, mark the sites of Srivijaya edifices. Today, only Wat Kaeo holds a dim reminder of a forgotten past in the crumbling wall of a once-great chedi. All that's known is that it commemorates a victory in battle.

A few kilometres west of these historic remains, a small hillock rises from the flat countryside. Here stands a Buddhist retreat named **Suan Mok**, as new as Chaiya's past is old. The walls and columns inside the central building are covered with an eclectic series of paintings, which run the gamut from the history of Buddhism in Asia to Aesop's fables from Europe.

Suan Mok owes a surrealistic touch to a wandering Zen Buddhist, Emanuel Sherman, whose search for enlightenment led him from the United States to Japan and Thailand, eventually ending on the island of Pha Ngan, off the Thai coast.

After his death, local artists covered one wall with illustrations to portray Sherman's epigrams. Bas-reliefs telling the story of the Buddha decorate the outer walls. They were modelled locally from photos of the Indian originals. Suan Mok's quirky touch continues into its adjoining structures. The *bot* is a large concrete ship that serenely sails the sea of suffering to eventual *nirvana*. ❐

KO SAMUI AND KO PHA NGAN

Map, page 309

Savvy travelers need little introduction to the appeal of Ko Samui, once a backpacker's retreat but now an international resort. A few of the other islands nearby, however, are not as well-known

THAILAND

Bangkok

Sometime during your stay in Thailand you will probably meet a few entrenched expatriates or aging tourists who will be unable to resist waxing nostalgically about the Ko Samui they discovered a generation ago. They camped under the stars on powdery Chaweng Beach. They explored coral reefs from fishermen's boats. And they shared the simple meals of coconut farmers by the light of flickering kerosene lamps. That island is long gone.

Nowadays, about 3 million tourists descend upon Ko Samui every year. There are luxury hotels, fancy restaurants, a modern airport, easy transport, and the full panoply of water sports and other diversions. Despite that, the island's 250 square kilometres (100 sq mi) retain much natural beauty. The interior is still the preserve of coconut farmers and forested hills. Unlike high-rise Phuket, buildings are prohibited from surpassing the height of palm trees on Samui. Hire a motorbike or hop on a circulating *songtao* – pick-up trucks with benches in back—and follow the paved, well-fringed rolling road that rings the island.

The choice of beach or diving spots, nonetheless, should take into consideration the monsoonal wind factor. From May to October, the southeast monsoon blows on the western and northern coasts. From October to January, unleashing the heaviest rains in November, the northeastern monsoon can disrupt the eastern coast. Usually you can still swim during these periods, if not lounge and read on the beach.

In addition to all the outlets for water sports, in the island's interior are several waterfalls descending from the heights of **Khao Phlu**, the island's highest point at 635 metres (2,080 ft).

Aside from attendance at the Catholic Church or immigration office, there's no reason to linger among the drab cement blocks of Samui's biggest town, the western port of **Na Thon ❶**. Ferries to Ko Pha Ngan and Ang Thong National Marine Park depart from Na Thon, however.

The original beachcombers and today's tasteful hotels were drawn to Ko Samui by a 6-kilometre-long swathe of soft, silky sand at **Chaweng ❷**. The sand at its half-sized southern neighbour, **Lamai ❸**, is slightly lower grade. Behind each beach runs a treacherous road—pitted, potted and often swamped—that barely supports a sprawl of all the traveler's necessities: post office, e-mail, banks, money exchanges, travel agencies, clothing shops, tailors, gyms and body piercers. Not to mention all manner of restaurants, bars and music clubs, with old rock and reggae prevailing over techno. Samui never approaches the sleazy excesses of Pattaya and Phuket, but Lamai has a conspicuous share of open-air hostess bars, go-go girls and transvestite shows.

South of Lamai, the small beaches of **Ban Hua Thanon ❹** and **Ban Bangkao ❺** are nothing to write

PRECEDING PAGES: island silhouette. **OPPOSITE:** a boring Ko Samui beach. **BELOW:** waterfall at Na Muang.

home about, but the coral reef is healthy near the former, and the latter is a charming, wooden Muslim village. From either, make a day trip inland and swim at the two-tiered waterfall at **Na Muang ❻**.

Coming up the western side of the island, **Ban Taling Ngam ❼** offers a couple of rather deluxe resort retreats. Further north, just before the road juts east along the northern coast, is Na Thon.

For panorama, head along the north shore to **Maenam ❽**. The sand is coarser than that of the east, but the 4-kilometre stretch is little developed. East of Maenam, **Bo Phut ❾** is much narrower, but relatively protected, whichever way the wind blows. Popular with French and Italian families, it's a short walk from the cute little fishing village of Ban Bo Phut. As for **Bangrak ❿** (better known as **Big Buddha Beach**), it's a mystery why anyone stays here unless they enjoy the din from the adjacent road or the airplanes roaring overhead. Or perhaps it's the view of the indisputably large Buddha statue and its complement of especially garish souvenir shops. Quieter **Choeng Mon ⓫**, on the island's north-eastern spur, has decent sand and is within quick access of Chaweng's facilities.

Sprinkled elsewhere around the island are a go-kart track, snake farm, butterfly aviary and lots of snooker parlours. With 10 stadiums and counting, water-buffalo fights are Samui's newest entertainment. The bulls don't draw blood, but the high-stakes betting is fast and raucous. The numerous signs for "monkey shows" are actually opportunities to see pig-tailed macaques engaged in their usual jobs on coconut farms. They twist coconuts from the tree tops, then retrieve and deposit them in burlap bags. Copra, the dried coconut flesh, will eventually be pressed to produce coconut oil.

Last but not least are the attractions of 41 brilliant isles comprising **Ko Ang**

The gold-gilded Buddha near Big Buddha Beach is actually on a small island, Ko Faan. The Buddha statue is 12 metres (40 ft) high.

BELOW: Bo Phut, on Ko Samui.

Thong National Marine Park 12. Day-long package trips voyage to Ko Wua Talab, park headquarters, and Ko Mae Ko. But these tours allow little time to investigate any more than a viewpoint and a cave on Wua Talab and the clear, pea-green saltwater lake on Mae Ko. On both, the designated swimming spots have negligible coral and fish. It's better to take the standard tour out, but stay a few days on Wua Talab. Visitors can rent park bungalows or tents, or set up their own. The island is teeming with macaques, langurs, otters, birds and other wildlife. Hire one of the fishermen to take you to a smaller isle with virgin coral.

Ko Pha Ngan

If Ko Samui is the land of package tours and brief vacations, its neighbour 15 kilometres (9 mi) to the north, **Ko Pha Ngan**, is a refuge for backpackers on leisurely world tours and Europeans whiling away winter-long holidays. Smaller, rustic and rugged, and with horrible roads, Pha Ngan lacks Samui's spectacular beaches, but has plenty of secluded, craggy bays sheltering small sandy jewels adorned with coral. As of last count, over a dozen of these host a bungalow resort or two (or 40, in the case of Hat Rin), where US$ 5 will get you a sturdy roof, a cold-water bath and electricity at least until midnight.

Ah, yes, about the roads... From the cacophonous southern port town of **Thong Sala 13**, a ferry port for Ko Samui and Ko Tao (except for e-mail and mountain bike rentals, there's little call to hang around Thong Sala), there is a newly-paved 10-kilometre stretch that runs due north to the village of **Cha Loak Lam 14**, a favourite stopover on the north coast for trawlers. This route is plied by *songtao* "taxis," which can drop you off for the short walk to Pang waterfall, followed by a challenging 400-metre (1,300 ft) climb to the island's stellar view-

Map, page 309

TIP

Many people prefer Chaweng and Lamai in a stiff wind – usually in winter between November and February – because it forces jet-skiing and water-skiing, and the incessant droning of motors, to a halt.

BELOW: statue of Buddha, near Big Buddha Beach.

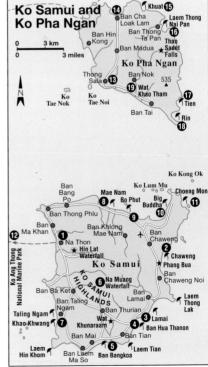

Another sunset on Ko Pha Ngan.

ing point. The dirt trails branching off to the western coast lead to about a half-dozen beaches and are navigable by motorbike if it hasn't rained recently. These are not Pha Ngan's premier beaches, although there's fine snorkelling coral at Hat Yao (West) and Mae Hat to the north. The rutted trails meandering around the eastern quadrant, however, are always hazardous and should not be attempted by novice cyclists, whether on motorbike or mountain bike.

East of Cha Loak Lam, the justly prized beach of the moment is **Hat Khuat** ⓰ (Bottle Beach), which can only be reached by sea. The quickest approach is from Ban Cha Loak. Continuing eastward and down the coast, one could enjoyably argue the merits of **Hat Sadet** (with a waterfall and jumbo rocks bearing the graffiti of Thai royalty) or **Thong Nai Pan** ⓰, with its wonderful cliff viewpoints, a double-barrelled bay and a coral reef. Eventually you will reach the pretty southern cove of **Hat Tien** ⓱, which offers an additional choice of beaches on either side. One of the two bungalow resorts here is The Sanctuary, with an arresting central building constructed amidst enormous boulders and outcroppings. From September through May, it sponsors alternative health and New Age courses. Hat Tien forswears videos, noise and mind-altering drugs.

Not coincidentally, the next sign of habitation, a mere 10 minutes away by long-tail boat, is **Hat Rin** ⓲, better known internationally than Pha Ngan itself. The fame, or notoriety, stems from the monthly all-night "full-moon" party. The biggest bashes of the year take place in December and January, when leading British deejays fly in with cutting-edge sounds and hordes of young clubbers. Together with the island's semi-permanent foreign residents and the charters from Samui, the numbers can swell to 10,000. Even in the slowest months, when the ambience is more akin to a frat party, 3,000 people may dance into the next

BELOW: manta rays in formation.

day. Poopers gripe that the party has become detached from its pagan roots; others say that undercover policemen have put a damper on the chemical enhancements. Of the two beaches that comprise Hat Rin, the eastern side of the headland, known as Sunrise Beach, is far superior with a wide bay of sand, good swimming and a bit of coral. West of the headland, Sunset is scraggy and usually strewn with flotsam, but it's so quiet that you can fall asleep to the waves. Besides, it's only a 10-minute walk to Sunrise. In between, there's a grid of dirt lanes lined with clothing, jewelry and dive shops, as well as two banks, a clinic, post office, pharmacies, tattooists and overseas telephones. Besides the usual video cafes and unusual MSG-free zones, there are genuine Italian restaurants.

There's even a thrice-daily boat connection between Hat Rin and Samui. Nonetheless, the roller-coaster road joining Hat Rin and Thong Sala is now cemented and has further opened up the intervening villages and so-so beaches of Ban Tai and Ban Khai.

An easy stroll up a hill from Ban Tai brings you to **Wat Khao Tham** ⑲. During most months of the year, Australian and American teachers run well-recommended 10- to 20-day Buddhist meditation courses at this temple.

Ko Tao

Alone in the middle of the ocean, flung a good 40 kilometres (25 mi) northwest of Ko Pha Ngan, tiny **Ko Tao** is the third principal island of the 80-strong Samui archipelago. The home of fewer than 800 fisher folk, it was colonised in the past decade by backpackers ever on a tireless search for "somewhere quiet." Ko Tao is quiet. The brief strip of paved road supports only one or two trucks. There's no place to race motorcycles. There are no bars, nightclubs, banks or jet skis. No go-karts. You can fall asleep listening to the waves.

Arriving by boat from either Chumphon or Ko Pha Ngan at **Ban Mae Hat**, the only proper village, you will be greeted by long-tail-boat touts proclaiming the virtues of their often isolated bungalow resorts. Be wary. Those located on the northern and eastern coasts probably do provide fine snorkelling sights surrounding cottage-sized boulders, but there is no beach or sand.

To the left (north) of Ban Mae Hat, the long beach of **Sai Ree** is deceptive, since the water is too shallow for anything more vigorous than the breast stroke. Likewise with Coral Beach on the right. Better to heed the touts from the southern coast. Or walk the few kilometres to **Ao Cha Loak** and **Hai Sai Daeng**.

Once settled, nature lovers can happily explore the island's 21-square kilometres (8 sq mi) on foot. Rough trails criss-cross the uninhabited, thickly forested interior. Although you may never glimpse the gibbons, you will probably hear their distinctive *whoop-whoop* signaling their presence in nearby tree tops.

For a cooling drink and a swim, follow the obvious signs for those boulder-strewn bungalows dotted around the coast. Ko Tao's strongest attraction, though, is its proximity to about 25 excellent scuba diving sites. In fact, these are where many diving trips originating in Ko Samui or Ko Pha Ngan head each day. At Ban Mae Hat, at least a dozen foreign-managed dive shops fiercely compete. Certified instruction is available. ❑

Map, page 309

TIP

Diving services operate year-round, but January through May offers the best visibility, reaching up to 30 metres. Visibility drops markedly from June to September, as well as in November, when the monsoonal winds shift.

BELOW: macaques are often heard, not seen, aloft.

PHUKET

Long before Ko Samui hit the limelight, Phuket was the prime beach destination in Thailand. It still is, and unlike Pattaya, which has sunk into sleaziness, Phuket retains its tropical charms

Map, page 313

Phuket's physical beauty is even greater than its exquisite beaches. This beauty stems from its picturesque villages, coconut groves, and rubber plantations, as much as from its patchwork of wild flowers presented against a backdrop of forested hills. Seaward from the beaches, coral reefs teem with marine life. It can be a dangerous beauty. During the monsoon season, May to October, rough surf and high winds can make swimming unsafe. The eastern shore is comprised primarily of rocky shoals, mud flats and mangroves. Nearly all of Phuket's decent beaches are located on the western side of the island. Landward, Phuket people exude the confidence of islanders who have prospered from an island rich in natural resources.

For centuries Phuket was a backwater. The long road south from Bangkok to reach it, the lack of a bridge across to the mainland, bad roads on the island itself, and a seeming lack of interest in developing it for recreation meant that it languished in relative isolation for decades despite natural resources of tin, rubber and coconut. Indeed, Phuket airport was only upgraded to international status in the 1970s to let tin and rubber merchants travel easily to Penang, Kuala Lumpur and Singapore. No one thought about tourism back in those days.

In the late 1970s, Phuket began appearing on the maps of budget backpackers. They stayed in fishermen's bungalows or camped out on the beach at Patong. Word spread, and developers descended on the island. The airport was expanded to handle long-haul jets from Europe. Dirt roads were paved. As tourist dollars flowed towards the beaches, the island grew to become the richest province in Thailand, second only to Bangkok.

The lion's share of Phuket's wealth now comes from tourism. The boom has had a social knock-on. Although there are only 10,000 native Phuket inhabitants, an estimated 240,000 migrant Thais, drawn from all 76 provinces in the kingdom, now live and work on the island, mostly in tourism-related activities.

Urban Phuket

The road from Phang Nga crosses the 600-metre (2,000 ft) Thaothep Kasaetri Bridge to Phuket, an island about the same size as Singapore. The sojourn to Phuket town, 30 kilometres (19 mi) to the south, soon reaches the emotional heart of the island. The intersection at **Ban Tha Rua ❶**, leading to Surin Beach and Khao Phra Taeo National Park, is dominated by a bronze statue of two women warriors, swords in hands. The pair are sisters: Chan and Muk. In 1785 they led an army of villagers against Burmese invaders.

Unlike many provincial centres, **Phuket ❷**, a town on the island's southeast coast, has a rich identity of its own. The style is set by the beautiful colonial-style

OPPOSITE: yet another typical Phuket sunset.

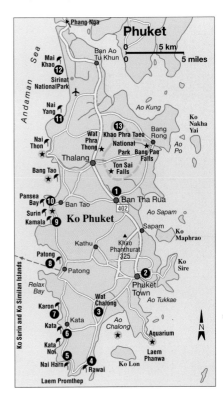

Phuket

houses built by tin and rubber barons at the end of the 19th century. The construction followed a disastrous fire that destroyed the downtown area. Thanon Thalang, Thanon Phang Nga, and some of the smaller surrounding streets are still lined with Sino-Portuguese-style shophouses. Three storeys high, the rowhouses were built by middle-income Chinese to house their extended families. The ground floor normally serves as a shop and reception hall; the upper floors are the living quarters. Huge signs with large Chinese characters etched in gold are hung over, or alongside, the doors to identify the family residing within. The Chartered Bank building, Thai Airways office and others, with their arched loggias, resemble buildings of colonial Singapore and Penang.

The charm of Phuket's old buildings is complemented by the many Chinese shrines that accent the town with bright splashes of colour. Of note is the brightly painted temple of **Jui Tui** and its smaller companion Put Jaw next door, which sit just past the market on Thanon Ranong. Like many similar Chinese shrines elsewhere in Asia, their central altars are dedicated to Quanyin (Kuan Yin), the goddess of mercy. Jui Tui is the starting point for the five days of colourful and bizarre parades that mark the annual Phuket Vegetarian Festival each October.

Outside of town, the only building worthy of note is **Wat Chalong ❸**. It sits 6 kilometres further south on the Phuket Bypass, a ring road of sorts that runs west of Phuket. The opulently decorated temple is famed for the gilded statue of Luang Pho Chaem, the wat's abbot who gained fame as a lay physician.

Southern Phuket

South along the coast from the town of Phuket is **Rawai ❹**, whose foreshore is a mass of rocks that lie exposed during low tide, when clam hunters venture out,

In 1786, Capt. Light of the East India Company sought to secure Phuket for England. Thai claims and England's desire for a more strategic island to guard the Straits of Malacca led Light to drop the plan. So he founded Penang, which became the chief British colony on the Malay peninsula until the 1819 founding of Singapore.

BELOW: offering at a Chinese temple, town of Phuket.

turning over the stones in search of dinner. Rawai offers many tasty seafood snacks sold along the beach. Rawai also holds one of the island's handful of *chao lay* (sea gypsy) villages. The sea gypsies were once nomadic fishing families, roaming from island to island. They are skilled fishermen both above and below the water. From a young age, they learn to dive to great depths in search of lobsters, prawns, and crabs, staying below for up to three minutes. However, diminishing stocks and environmental and tourism concerns have robbed the sea gypsies of traditional fishing grounds.

Because the sea gypsies are not allowed to own the land they live on, they cannot install permanent facilities, such as brick houses or even septic tanks. Their villages are effectively shanty towns, impermanent shacks reflecting their lack of spiritual attachment to terra firma. The gypsies are not materialistic. Even as fish stocks dwindle, they are reluctant to take up waged employment. They fear complicated involvement with government officers or business people. Proposals have been made to enhance the sea gypsies' standards of living, but lacking strong collective will, the placid gypsies are losing their identity. The youngsters speak Thai instead of Urak Lawoi, their indigenous tongue.

From Rawai the coastal road continues over the north-south ridge of hills, offering great views of Ko Phi Phi, 45 kilometres (30 mi) away. Continuing south around the point at **Laem Prom Thep**, you come to one of the island's prettiest beaches. Nestled between two hills, fronted by a calm sea and backed by a lagoon, **Nai Harn** ❺ is a serene setting. The surrounding headlands are lashed by a salty breezes that allow only sturdy grasses to grow.

The picturesque bays of **Kata** ❻ and **Kata Noi** have a more intimate feel due to their smaller size. There is fine snorkelling at the southern end of Kata Noi

Map,
page 313

TIP

Prom Thep Cape is a well-visited vantage point for viewing the sunset. The gold-and-green promontory plunges into the hissing sea.

BELOW: Kata Noi.

beach. Relax Bay, with its single hotel, Le Meridien Phuket, offers some snorkelling along its northwestern rocks. **Karon Beach** ➐ is a long and quiet strip of sand backed by hotels and restaurants at its top, middle and bottom, with empty plots of former rice paddy in between. Both Karon and Kata are much less frenetic than Patong, but with a growing choice of hotel, dining and water-sport facilities.

The most developed beach is **Patong** ➑, due west of the town of Phuket and north of Karon. In the early 1970s, Patong was little more than a huge banana plantation wedged between the mountains and a wide crescent of sand. The plantation is now a tourist city-by-the-sea, with multi-storey condominiums and hotels rising above night markets, seafood emporiums, beer bars, discos, and tour shops. The beach itself is dotted with colourful parasols.

In the calm weather from November to May, the bay is peppered with visiting yachts. Unlike most other Phuket beaches, Patong has a wide range of water-sports facilities, including scuba diving, windsurfing, waterskiing, parasailing, jetskis, sailing and boogie boards. Dive shops offer trips Racha and Phi Phi islands, or 80 kilometres (50 mi) northwest to the Similan Islands Marine National Park, considered one of the best diving areas in Asia. Patong also has the most developed land-sports facilities on the island. Most large hotels have pools and many have tennis courts. There are four 18-hole golf courses in Phuket, and one 9-hole.

BELOW: Le Meridian Phuket, one of several world-class resorts on Phuket.

Patong is a gourmet's delight. Seafood is a specialty. The legendary Phuket lobster, however, each weighing up to 3 kilograms (6 lb), is now caught in Burmese or Indonesian waters. Patong is also a great place to eat Western, Indian, Mexican, Italian, Japanese and Korean cuisines.

After dark, Patong has many open-air bars along Soi Bangla in the middle of the resort. These barbeers, as they are called, lure customers with a heady mix of female company, rock music, and an ocean of booze. Within a few steps you can eat great seafood, barter your price for a silk shirt, go bungy jumping, join some Thai boxing, or buy real estate. Patong is all things to all people. At any major beach you can rent cars, jeeps or motorcycles to explore the island. A valid driver's license is all that is necessary. The town itself is reputed to have had the first paved road in the kingdom. Phuket also has the highest road fatality statistics in Thailand. Usually only vehicles rented by the large international firms carry insurance, despite signs and verbal promises to the contrary.

Travelling cheaply means relying on the blue-and-white *songtao* – two-row, wooden buses that leave the Phuket town market for every point on the island. Alternatively, small and cramped red vehicles called *tuk-tuk* function as taxis. Barter for the fare before starting off.

Northern Phuket

Some 3 kilometres (2 mi) north of Patong, quiet **Kamala Bay** ➒ retains charm around its Islamic hamlets, with their well-kept gardens against a backdrop of forested hills rising to over 500 metres. The tranquillity won't last. At the northern end of Kamala, a giant Disney-like theme park is being built.

The attractive coastal road north to **Surin Beach** passes mouthwateringly compact Singh Beach, its sandy cape hedged by verdant headlands. Larger Surin Beach with its seafood shacks soon gives way to idyllic **Pansea Bay** ➓, dominated by two proprietary resorts, the Chedi and the Amanpuri. The long beach at **Bang Tao** is dominated by the immense Laguna Phuket Resort, housing five hotel complexes. Much of the land around here used to be a tin mining wasteland. In 1785, the Burmese invaded here, seeking to takeover the island.

Nai Yang ⓫ beach, just south of the airport, is now under the jurisdiction of **Sirinat National Park**. It is a pleasant hangout where local people and tourists come to eat seafood and spicy papaya salad under the casuarina trees. An offshore reef allows year-round swimming in the shallow bay. There are a few Spartan bungalows for rent in the national park. With a good map, it is possible to drive along Phuket's scenic west coast all the way from Nai Yang to the island's southern tip, Laem Prom Thep.

North of Nai Yang is Phuket's longest beach, **Mai Khao** ⓬. The 9-kilometre-long (6 mi) beach is undeveloped, a haven for beachcombers and the giant sea turtles that come ashore December through February to lay their eggs.

The last main outpost of the island's monsoon evergreen forest can be inspected on an organised hike through **Khao Phra Taeo National Park** ⓭. Wild bears and cats still live within the small park, and all of the wildlife is rather keen to avoid all human contact. The park is fringed by two pretty waterfalls: Ton Sai on the west, and Bang Bae on the east.

The sheltered waters off the northeast coast around **Ao Po** contain numerous pearl farms. Organised tours to the farms are informative. ❑

Map, page 313

BELOW: pearls.

Map, page 319

PHANG NGA AND KRABI

The traveller couldn't ask for a more exquisite, seductive, and resplendent retreat than the islands and bays of Phang Nga. Increasingly popular – and threatened – is Ko Phi Phi

THAILAND

Bangkok

I n the waters east of the island of Phuket, the spectacle of towering limestone massifs reaches its zenith with 300-metre (1,000 ft) peaks crowding together in close proximity. The same unlikely topography imposes itself throughout Phang Nga Province, making it the most spectacular and visually opulent province in Thailand. The appeal isn't just physical. The ingenious ways people have adapted to such surroundings makes Phang Nga and its bay one of the wonders of the world.

On the mainland north of the island of Phuket, the town of **Phang Nga ❶** is revealed as a lovely, docile township left behind in Thailand's development surge. The main source of employment seems to be in sleepy government offices. Several small hotels provide simple accommodation.

The main objective of any first-time trip, however, should be to the geological wonderland of **Phang Nga Bay**. A long-tail boat trip from near the Phang Nga Bay Resort Hotel reveals Andaman mangrove culture at its best, with mussel farms, floating fish traps, and Brahminy kites circling overhead looking for scraps. The mangroves are fertile breeding, spawning, and feeding grounds for mud skippers, crabs, prawns, and an assortment of fish such as sea bass. Hungry dolphins penetrate the upper reaches of the channels at high tide. Mangrove

BELOW: one of Phang Nga Bay's many caves.

wood also feeds the long-established charcoal-making industry, a feature of the Andaman coast from Ranong to Malaysia.

Just before the mouth of the Mae Nam Phang Nga, an excursion boat approaches the base of the mountain of **Khao Kien**, where a cavern contains primitive paintings depicting human and animal forms. Such cave daubings are quite common in the limestone caves in the area, and were painted by primitive people around 2,000 years ago. The strange forms depicting sea creatures, six-fingered hands, and semi-human shapes are thought to have played a religious-shamanistic role for the cave dwellers. Prior to hunting expeditions or battles, primitive people would make sacrifices to placate spirits in front of the paintings. The floors of many caves in Phang Nga and Krabi are still scattered with the discarded sea shells of prehistoric people. Tide fluctuations have compromised archeological evidence. Forty thousand years ago it was possible to walk to Phi Phi. Five thousand years ago sea levels were higher than at present.

On what seems a collision course with a huge limestone outcrop, the boat then slips into the barely discernible, overgrown cave entrance of **Tham Lod**. For more than 50 metres, the boat slides under giant stalactites. Rocks protruding from the water appear to have been sliced by a sword-wielding god. In **Tham Nak**, a twisted stalagmite at the cave's entrance resembles a *naga* serpent, giving this cave its name. Green stalactites burst from the ceiling like a frozen waterfall. The whole mountain-island drips with streaked limestone.

Ko Talu receives its name from *talu,* meaning to pass from one side to the other – in this case, not over the mountain, but under it as the boat squeezes through a cave filled with stalactites. **Ko Khao Ping Gun** is perhaps the most spectacular of Phang Nga's islands. Behind the beach, the mountain seems to

Ancient cave paintings of the Phang Nga Bay region.

BELOW: limestone, or karst, pillar.

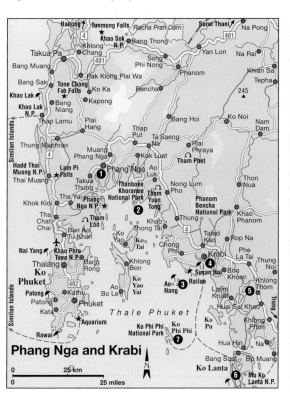

Phang Nga and Krabi

have split in two, the halves leaning against each other. Locals say they are two lovers. This area was the setting of part of the James Bond movie *The Man with the Golden Gun*. A small beach overlooks another island, **Ko Tapoo**, or Nail Island, which looks like a thorny spike driven into the sea.

Further south in Phang Nga Bay, the towering islands hold natural treasures hidden from passing boats. Far from being impregnable, a few of the sheer islands allow cave access by canoe when the tide is right. By squeezing in through minute gaps at the correct tidal window, canoeists paddle into a lost world, an open-top sea chamber, its sheer walls covered with vines and ferns. It's like entering the hole in the middle of a donut through a side door. These are ecological time capsules where eagles, macaques, and other mangrove species have dwelled for millennia unfettered by people. The chambers are caused by acidic rain water percolating into the limestone peaks. The soluble limestone island becomes addled with hidden chasms, causing the roof to cave in.

To the south

South of Phang Nga, the journey southward on the mainland coast takes the traveller further into the heart of limestone country. At times, the horizon resembles the graph line of a seismic tremor, with huge jutting rocks thrusting out of the plantations and forests.

About 50 kilometres (30 mi) southeast of Phang Nga, **Tanboke Koranee National Park ❷** is one of the most beautiful in Thailand. Like a scene from *Lost Horizon*, the park is dominated by lofty cliffs. In one spot, an underground stream rises amid lush vegetation at the base of a mountain. Foot paths wind beneath cliff faces covered in green vines, punctuated with brilliant hibiscus.

TIP

A small number of sea canoe companies in Phuket arrange superlative day trips into the hidden *hong* of Phang Nga Bay. Of the operators, the pioneering SeaCanoe Thailand has the best safety, service, and environmental track record.

BELOW: rocky retreat near Krabi.

At **Ao Nang Bay ❸**, near Krabi and 3 kilometres eastwards along the coast road, comfortable resorts act as a base for exploring nearby islands and hidden coves. The Ao Nang area, with its low-key bungalow developments, seafood restaurants, scuba diving and sea canoeing and mountain bike options, makes a refreshing alternative to brassier beach resorts on Phuket.

The town of **Krabi ❹** is a small but bustling service centre built opposite mangrove swamps along the Krabi River. From here, long-tail boats sail out to Railae Beach; larger ones leave for Ko Phi Phi daily, and for Ko Lanta, November to May. From town, the Krabi River mangroves can be explored by renting a long-tail boat, first stopping off to visit the huge cavern inside the Kanab Nam twin peaks, which flank the river. Traditionally, the leaves, bark, fruit and mosses of the surrounding mangroves provided folk cures for the alleviation of lumbago, thrush, kidney stones and menstrual pains. The trees also provided a source of weak alcohol and leaves for wrapping tobacco. Two rare bird species inhabit the mangroves: the mangrove pitta and the brown-winged kingfisher.

Southeast from Krabi the land gradually flattens. Dike-enclosed rice fields appear on both sides of the road. Seemingly-abandoned suitcases and boxes on the roadside designate bus stops; passengers wait under banana trees nearby.

Forty kilometres (25 mi) south of Krabi, a hot spring and nature trail make **Klong Thom ❺** a rewarding stop. The small museum at Wat Klong Thom displays artefacts such as beads, pots and religious icons, purportedly from the 5th to 7th centuries AD, when the area was a port for traders, monks and diplomats crossing the peninsula. A bumpy laterite trail eastwards from the main intersection leads to a hot spring suitable for bathing. Farther on, the Tung Tieo nature trail starts and finishes at an inviting emerald pool. Southwest of Klong Tom,

Map, page 319

BELOW: busy beach on Ko Phi Phi.

Map,
page 319

and also accessible by boat from Krabi, quiet **Ko Lanta ❻** offers some rustic bungalow accommodation along its 19 powdery beaches. At low tide there is as much chance of finding monkey or lizard tracks as human, although one might prefer the former.

Ko Phi Phi

Turquoise waves caress a beach so dazzlingly white it is almost painful to the eye. The water is so crystalline that colourful fishing boats seem suspended in mid-air. With palm-fringed beaches and lofty limestone mountains as a backdrop, **Ko Phi Phi ❼** arguably surpasses Phuket as one of the most beautiful islands in Asia. Where Phuket is undulating, physically sociable and with a sizeable population, Phi Phi, like the karst islands of Phang Nga, is geologically dramatic, its population confined to low-lying sand bars below towering rocks.

Phi Phi lies equidistant, about 45 kilometres, from both Phuket and Krabi. The island is in fact two islands: the smaller **Phi Phi Ley**, a craggy limestone monolith similar to the other shrub-covered peaks of Phang Nga Bay, and **Phi Phi Don**, a national park with an epicentre of anarchic tourism development. Ironically, it is the unprotected Phi Phi Ley which remains environmentally pristine. By contrast, the tiny village of Phi Phi Don is now a riot of Kodak signs, T-shirt shops, mini-marts, dive centres, burger joints, tour counters, and hair-braiding shacks – a cheap and cheerful tourist ghetto surrounded by resorts charging from US$5 to $200 a night. Like Thailand itself, Phi Phi is full of contradictions. Infuriating one moment, a joy the next. Until 1994, it was the only marine national park in the world with a transvestite cabaret.

If you move out of the village, the grandeur of the island reasserts itself. A 30-minute hike up to a flower-covered viewpoint reveals Phi Phi Don's layout: barbell-like rock massifs connected by a spit of sand covered in coconut trees.

From the village, an easy 40-minute coastal walk leads to **Had Yaow** (Long Beach), with some of the whitest sands and clearest water imaginable. Swimming and snorkelling here takes place with a majestic view of Phi Phi Ley's vertical north face in the distance.

To enjoy the best of Phi Phi, take a long-tail boat ride around both islands. The boat stops at the so-called Viking Cave on Phi Phi Ley first. The cave is renowned as a site for swallows that build their nests on the ceilings of rocky caverns. A web of bamboo scaffolding reaches up, disappearing into the gloomy upper recesses of the cave. Sinewy young men climb up these precarious ladders to collect the swallow nests, which are sold as delicacies to Chinese restaurants. However, there is no demonstration of nest gathering in any cave that still hosts swallows. The nests are more valuable, ounce by ounce, than pure gold, so no concessionaire is going to publicise the location of a productive site.

Viking Cave is named after its wall painting of long boats with sails. How old these pictures actually are, and who painted them, remains in dispute. What is certain, of course, is that before the 19th century, no Norsemen ever visited the Andaman Sea. It is likely the cave painting here is of later origin than others in Phang Nga and Krabi.

At **Maya Bay**, the long-tail boat stops for snorkelling in a horseshoe bay of corals surrounded by steep cliffs and a deserted white beach. After circumnavigating much of both Phi Phi islands, the boat stops at Bamboo Island for more snorkelling. The reefs at Bamboo are bigger, with more branch and seafan forms. Fish life is more diverse, including groupers lurking in the nooks and crannies. Should the diving bug bite, Phi Phi has dive shops where visitors can earn their open-water diving card. The deeper waters of Ko Bida and Hin Muang, with their barracudas, manta rays, and whale sharks, can then be explored. ❑

The underwater grinding you hear while snorkelling is the sound of hungry parrot fish munching their way through the 12 kilos of coral reef they consume each year. The coral is digested and excreted as fine sand.

Tropical fish find sanctuary in the coral reefs of Ko Phi Phi.

OPPOSITE: Ko Phi Phi.

THE DEEP SOUTH

South of the resort islands of Samui and Phuket, the peninsular character of Thailand takes on subtle changes as it approaches Malaysia. Mosques replace wats, and coconut joins curry

Map, page 327

THAILAND

Bangkok

Lower peninsular Thailand is where Thai-speaking Buddhism meets Malay-speaking Islam. It's a land of verdant jungle and limestone peaks, azure seas and rich, coconut-flavoured cuisine. Southern peninsular Thailand is criss-crossed by a network of excellent roads that connect the Andaman Sea with the Gulf of Thailand. Once troubled by insurgent guerrillas of the People's Liberation Army of Thailand in the north, and by guerrillas of the Communist Party of Malaysia in the south, the region is now completely safe for the traveller. True, a handful of Muslim separatists still hide in the jungled hills that straddle the Thai-Malay frontier, but these regions are well off the beaten track, and the problem is rapidly disappearing. The deep south is an area of pristine beaches, friendly, predominantly rural communities, and markets overflowing with exotic fruits and other native produce. Amongst Thais elsewhere in Thailand, the people of the deep south have a reputation for quickness of thought and swiftness to anger – though this is far from apparent to the foreign visitor. It's a land where travellers can revel in the sun or explore ancient Srivijayan sites.

OPPOSITE: painted prow of Muslim *korlae*, or fishing boat. **BELOW:** southern woman.

Trang ❶ is an industrial town inhabited primarily by the descendants of Teochew-speaking Chinese immigrants, who originally sought work here panning tin but wound up running the region's rubber trade. Trang's Chinese heritage is reflected in monuments at the northern approach to the city. At **Ban Bangrok**, 3 kilometres north on Route 4, a shrine honours Kwan Tee Hun, a red-faced, bearded god believed to have the power to prevent or start war. Farther south, a dragon gate guards the city from intruders. From Trang, there are a number of interesting side trips. The beach at **Pak Meng** lies on the Indian Ocean, a long and rough trip from Trang, but the scenery and sunsets are memorable. **Surin**, which lies a short distance west, has a large and beautiful pond surrounded by well-kept gardens.

The port of Pak Bara, on the opposite coast of the isthmus in Satun Province, around 150 kilometres (90 mi) southwest of Hat Yai, serves as the port for remote **Ko Tarutao Marine National Park ❷**. The 51-island archipelago, with a mixed Thai and sea gypsy population, is known for its extensive corals, unpopulated sandy beaches, and simple beach huts. After the monsoon abates, small tour and supply boats link the islands between November and May each year.

Nakhon Si Thammarat

Continuing northeast from Trang through Huai Yot, a beautiful and winding valley threads its way to **Nakhon Si Thammarat ❸**. Nakhon may well have been the capital of the illusive kingdom Tambralinga, mentioned in Chinese annals. A large hoard of silver coins of a type sometimes attributed to Funan, dating from the fifth or

sixth century AD, was discovered near Moklan village. Nakhon later became a regional centre of the Sumatra-based Srivijaya empire, at least until the 10th century. Trade and ecclesiastical links between Nakhon and southern India and Ceylon flourished. Around this time, the city's name evolved to the Sanskrit Nagara Sri Dhammaraja, or City of the Glorious Dharma-Observing King, and numerous Indian migrants settled in an area known as Hat Sai Kaeo, or Beach of Crystal Sand, where the city's most sacred site, Wat Phra Mahathat, still stands. Later, the city became an important regional centre whose governors ruled the entire south. From the 16th century it was known to Europeans by the Malay name of Ligor.

The human legacy of Nakhon's rich history is evident in the surviving traditions of the *nang thalung* shadow-puppet play, and also in exquisite classical dance-dramas called *lakhon* and *manohra* performed to acclaim by the city's fine-arts school. At **Suchart House**, on Si Thammasok Soi 3, it is possible to watch puppets for shadow-puppet plays being made from leather, and perhaps enjoy an impromptu performance by a master puppeteer.

While Wat Phra Mahathat may be up to 10 centuries old, the chedi dates from the 1400s.

BELOW: interior and exterior, Wat Phra Mahathat.

The physical aspects of Nakhon's history are extensively displayed in the **National Museum** (open Wednesday–Sunday; admission fee), at the southern end of Thanon Ratchadamnoen and housing one of the most important collections in Thailand outside of Bangkok. **Wat Phra Mahathat** is Nakhon's most revered temple, and one of the country's oldest. The *wat*'s prime attraction is a 77-metre-high (250 ft) *chedi*, the top of which is covered by an estimated 270 kilograms (600 lbs) of gold. To the right of the chedi, a temple museum houses an assortment of delicate gold and silver offerings. South of the chedi, the Viharn Luang, with its inward-leaning columns, is a fine example of Ayutthayan design.

In the city centre, the outdoor **Boworn Bazaar** near the Thai Hotel presents a pleasant environment for Thai dining and drinking, especially at the Ban Lakhon wooden restaurant, built round a mature *takian* tree. Nakhon comes alive, literally, during the Festival of the 10th Lunar Month, usually in October, when spirits of ancestors return in response to donations of food at temples by devotees.

The road north leads to the gulf-coast town of **Sichon**, which offers scenic views and southern-style handicrafts. Nearby, it is also possible to visit the cave that some believe sheltered King Taksin after he was deposed by Rama I. (More orthodox histories hold that Taksin was tied up in a velvet sack and beaten to death with a sandalwood club in the manner reserved for royalty.) Take the road across the railroad tracks to the village of Lan Saka, then right at the first fork and go 9 kilometres (6 mi) to the cave, with a magnificent view of the countryside.

Map,
page 327

Heading south

The mostly coastal Route 408 links Nakhon to Songkhla, running south through extensive shrimp farms, lime orchards, dusty training arenas for fighting bulls, and the village of Sathing Phra, where many ancient artifacts have been found.

An alternative to the coast road are the inland routes 403 and 41 leading to **Phatthalung ➍**, which offers rather basic hotels, though one may wish to continue without stopping. If so, head back to Route 4 and turn south for Hat Yai.

In Khuan Khanun district, just north of Phatthalung, Route 4048 leads to **Thale Noi**, the largest waterfowl reserve in Thailand. Around 150 species of birds make up a population of about 100,000 during the peak migratory period, from December to April. The average depth of the lake is just 1.5 metres (16 ft).

Westwards from the main Phatthalung intersection along Route 4, motorists

Phatthalung may be where nang thalung – *shadow-puppet plays of local folklore – was first performed in Thailand.*

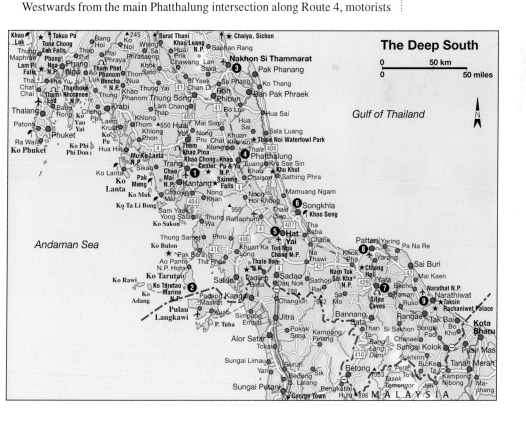

were sometimes relieved of their cash and valuables in the past by highway robbers, but this is no longer the case. You will likely only see Thai soldiers camped in tents between rows of rubber trees.

About 35 kilometres (20 mi) west of Phatthalung, the **Khao Chong Centre of Wildlife and Nature Study** encompasses jungle, a rocky creek, and a number of waterfalls. Drive into the reserve, but do not panic if you encounter soldiers brandishing weapons; the reserve hosts a military camp.

Khao Chong represents part of Thailand's developing conservation and ecology movement. Students at its Nature Education Centre study local flora and fauna in their natural rain-forest environment. The small zoo houses local wildlife such as the *binturong*, Prevost squirrel, Brahminy kite, hog badger and several endangered species, including the white-handed gibbon, which poachers usually capture at a young age by killing the mother.

The hog badger has a curious connection with southern Thai bullfighting, which draws gamblers from far and wide. The long-clawed mammal is occasionally hunted for the fat of its nose. It's claimed that a bull with this wild-smelling fat rubbed on its horns can intimidate and defeat any opponent. The use of this fat is regarded, understandably, as cheating.

From Khao Chong, the return drive to Phatthalung zigzags under towering trees, past pink rocky outcrops, and up and down the mountainous watershed along the spine of the isthmus. About 3 kilometres before Phatthalung, the highway branches south to Hat Yai.

Continue straight, past the provincial administrative offices, and then bear left on a road to Khuan Khanun (Jackfruit Hill) and **Wat Ku Ha Sawan**. This antiquated temple was recently renovated, but behind its yellow buildings, a staircase climbs up to a large grotto lighted by a natural arch. A delightfully obese and laughing Buddha marks the entrance. Around a copper-leafed *bodhi* tree are dozens of Buddha images. Light from the arch glints off the statues' gold leaf.

BELOW: Muslim women at prayer.

To the right of Wat Ku Ha Sawan lies another cave, formerly inhabited by a hermit monk. His personal collection of Buddha images is kept there.

To visit another temple and the northern end of the Thale Luang inland sea, take the road leading east from here. **Wat Wang** (Palace Temple) is 8 kilometres (5 mi) from the city. An attractive chedi graces the temple courtyard. Inside the temple proper are unrestored frescoes dating back about two centuries.

Down the road is Ban Lampam, where the waters of the inland sea, 70 kilometres (40 mi) from its entrance to the Gulf of Thailand, are fresh.

A short boat trip from Phatthalung leads to **Tham Malai**, a cave lying between the province's two famous peaks: Broken-Hearted Mountain and Broken-Headed Mountain. Legend says these represent two women turned to stone as punishment for jealousy, perhaps sharing a common and lasting interest in the same man. To reach the cave, best is to catch the boat behind the Phatthalung train station for the 15-minute ride to Tham Malai. A monk caretaker will turn on a generator to light up the stalactites, a useful idea if one has not brought a torch along for the journey.

Hat Yai

The commercial capital of south Thailand, **Hat Yai** ❺ is a boom town. Rubber and tin have been its traditional income earners, but they are rapidly being over-shadowed by an entertainment and commercial centre geared towards thousands of sybaritic Malaysians, who pour over the border each month to enjoy illicit pleasures denied at home. Nightclubs with singers, massage parlors and broth-els are the magnets for some single men, whilst women and families come for the wide range of shopping and reasonably-priced restaurants.

Map, page 327

Hat Yai has several cultural points of interest, nonetheless. **Wat Hat Yai Nai**, in the middle of town, has the third-largest reclining Buddha in the world. One can do more than just admire the exterior of this giant atop its 3-metre-high (10 ft) base. Ascend the pedestal and enter the Buddha's innards, where lungs and shrines are displayed side by side.

Sunday is usually the day for bullfights. The TAT office will confirm dates and fight locations, which rotate around the city's handful of arenas. Do not envisage a *corrida* with matadors and picadors; Thai-style bull fighting is a contest that pits one bull against another. Two animals are brought face to face. They lower their heads, clash horns and paw the ground, each pushing against the other like sumo wrestlers. The fight may last minutes or a couple of hours. It ends when one bull "bulldozes" the other to the edge of the ring, or when one simply turns and takes flight.

Tapping the latex from a rubber tree.

For those with more gastronomic interests, the shark's fin soup at Hat Yai's restaurants draws people all the way from the reaches of Bangkok and Kuala Lumpur. Other specialties are poached duck and fried pigeon. Several large open-air restaurants serve superb seafood to the accompaniment of live music.

BELOW: Songkhla harbour.

From Hat Yai, there are two rail and three road routes to Malaysia. The more frequently used railway line runs southwest, crossing the border to Alor Setar and But-terworth, the connection port for Penang island.

The second heads southeast through Yala and ends at the border town of Sungai Kolok. From there, it is a short walk and taxi ride to Kota Bharu on Malaysia's east coast.

The **Rubber Research Centre** on the outskirts of Hat Yai, en route to Songkhla, serves all of Thailand. It experiments with new grafting and tapping methods, and with how to induce the rubber trees to be more bountiful in their production of latex. Small-holding farmers study at the centre, where there is a rubber pro-cessing laboratory. Next to the research centre is the **Songkhla Nakharin University**, a splendid complex set on a 120-hectare (300 acres) campus. A pumpkin-shaped building containing the auditorium and labora-tories is surrounded by a moat. Arched windows in the pumpkin-shaped building catch breezes from all direc-tions and funnel them through the building to provide natural air-conditioning. An exhaust pump in the cen-tre sucks the warm air out.

Songkhla

If Hat Yai is brash, then **Songkhla** ❻ is discreet, a well-kept secret from the pleasure-seekers who visit Hat Yai. Trains, buses and taxis cover the 25 kilometres (15 mi) between the two towns. Located at the tip of a quiet peninsula, Songkhla is an old city showing clear signs of Chinese influence. Only the seaward (eastern) shore is suitable for sunbathing and swimming. The north portion of the beach is backed with lush casaurina trees, and here one finds monks in saffron robes walking past humpbacked bulls being prepared for the bullfights. The focal point of the beach is a bronze statue of a little mermaid, perched on a rock and looking wistfully seaward.

Immediately northwest of the mermaid, a score of seafood restaurants occupy the sandy strand. Select your ingredients from fresh seafood displayed on ice, including 35-centimetre-long (15 in) tiger prawns.

Across the road from the mermaid is **Khao Noi**, a topiary garden with realistic fighting bulls, birds in flight and an elephant sculpted out of living yew. Around the corner, on Thanon Sukhum, a group of monkeys gathers in the late afternoon to scratch, screech and scowl. They sit, hands on knees, looking like crotchety members of a debating society.

Songkhla boasts two museums. The dusty museum in **Wat Matchimawat** is in marked contrast to the spic-and-span **Songkhla National Museum** (open Wednesday–Sunday; admission fee), set in a beautifully-proportioned Chinese mansion built in 1878. The latter contains an excellent collection of ceramics and documented relics, recovered by scuba divers from an ancient wreck in the Gulf of Thailand. The Wat Matchimawat museum collection ranges from early Thai *bencharong* (five-colour) pottery and 200-year-old shell boxes, to oddities like a gas-powered fan.

The 200-year-old marble Buddha gracing the altar inside the *viharn* is minus its gold lotus crown, which is now preserved in a vault to protect it from thieves.

Image from Wat Matchimawat.

BELOW: fishermen near Songkhla.

Stone lions, a gift of a rich 19th-century Chinese merchant, guard the doorway that opens onto a set of interesting murals. Some show scenes of Songkhla's history, while others depict European sailors and a steamboat.

Map, page 327

Lift your eyes as you walk along Thanon Nakhon Nawk and Thanon Nakhon Nai; old Chinese families living in these lovely Sino-Portuguese shophouses are reputed to be extremely rich and conservative.

Continue towards the lake to Thanon Vichianchom. A steep path leads, 20 minutes later, to the summit of **Tangkuan** and the ruins of an ancient chedi. The panorama is superb, and the bustle at the wharves along the lake bear witness to Songkhla's status as a busy fishing port.

A pleasant excursion can be made to **Ko Yor**, situated in **Thale Sap** or Songkhla Lake, one of the largest lakes in Southeast Asia. The lake is, in fact, a deep ocean inlet, and its waters are rather brackish. En route to Ko Yor, stop at the fisheries station, where enormous white *plaa kapong* (white snappers) are bred. Ko Yor is renowned for its locally-woven cotton, ancient Buddhist monuments and its simple tranquillity.

The lake is also home to tens of thousands of water birds, which migrate here to settle among the rushes. With special permission, it is possible to take a boat onto the lake to observe their habits. The water, even in the middle of the lake, is no more than one metre deep, making the grassy bottom with its darting fish easy to see.

Another excursion by boat is to the offshore islands of Maew and Nuu (Cat and Mouse). Nuu is the larger of the two and has some pleasant picnic spots and swimming beaches.

Three kilometres south of the town is a small, extremely active fishing village, inhabited mainly by Muslims. It is the fishing boats, rather than the people, however, that are the most colourful. It would be difficult to beat these brightly-painted *korlae* for imaginative themes and execution.

Beyond the fishing village lies the rocky beach of **Khao Seng**, whose fame rests on an apparently precariously poised giant boulder called Nai Bang's Head. Legend says that if you succeed in pushing it over, you will uncover the millionaire's treasure buried beneath it. Inland from the beach is the Banloa Coconut Plantation, where you can watch monkeys trained to climb trees and toss down selected coconuts.

Wat Kho Tham is built among enormous boulders on a nearby hilltop. The cave contains the inevitable Buddha's footprint, and a reclining Buddha sheltered by an overhanging rock. Around the corner is **Wat Mae Chi**, a charmingly sandy spot inhabited by Buddhist nuns. The shaven-headed nuns, often quite young, dress in white robes, grow flowers and, like monks, rise at 4am to meditate before setting out to collect alms.

South of Songkhla

Down the east coast from Songkhla are the provincial capitals of Yala, Pattani and Narathiwat. Many of the residents of **Yala ❼** are ethnic Chinese, whilst Pattani and Narathiwat are fascinating centres of southernmost Thailand's Malay Muslim culture. **Pattani ❽** is home to a large fishing fleet and the 400-year-old Kreuse

BELOW: mosque.

Map, page 327

Mosque, built in 1578 by a Chinese settler, To Khieng, who converted to Islam. In fact, construction seems never to have been fully completed. According to legend, this is because To Khieng's sister, Lim Ko Niaw, sailed from China and begged her brother to renounce Islam and return to their ancestral home. When he refused, she cursed the mosque, saying it would never be completed, then hanged herself from a nearby cashew-nut tree.

Today, the mosque is maintained by the faithful in its original state. No attempt is made to complete it, because local Muslims believe lightning will strike anyone who makes the attempt. Meanwhile, Lim Ko Niaw has acquired a certain religious status herself – her shrine at San Jao Leng Ju Kieng is always packed, and in February it is the site of an important ceremony featuring fire walking and a vegetarian food festival.

Of interest near Yala are the Silpa caves. The large cave of Tham Koo Hu Pimuk contains a 25-metre-high (80 ft) Buddha, considered a holy pilgrimage site by southern Thai Buddhists.

Towards Malaysia

Narathiwat ❾ is markedly distinguished by its rural charm, prized songbirds and succulent mangoes. Next stop further south is Malaysia, accessible by ferry from the small town of Tak Bai. Yet before moving on, the traveller should linger a while in Narathiwat, which offers fine swimming at the beach at Narathat, a delightful and pleasant stretch of all-but-deserted white sand shaded by tall casuarina trees.

Wat Narathiwat is reached by walking north along Thanon Pichitbamrung, the town's main street, and towards the green dome of the provincial mosque.

OPPOSITE: climbing for the boss. **BELOW:** Diard's trogon.

Here a bridge leads right across a branch of the Mae Nam Bang Nara to the beach. A fascinating and informative glimpse of the life of southern Thai Muslim villagers can be gleaned at this point by walking through the fishing village at the mouth of the Bang Nara. Brightly painted fishing vessels jostle for space in the clear waters, and everywhere fish of all sizes and species are laid out on racks to dry in the sun. While the people are welcoming to visitors, the people here are conservative and Islamic, and female travellers should take care that their dress does not offend local sensibilities with halter tops or shorts.

Satun is an overwhelmingly rural province with the largest Muslim population – over 80 percent – in Thailand. A tiny, riverside town, it's a pleasant place to overnight if en route to Malaysia by sea. Boats to the Malaysian province of Perlis, just south of Thailand, cost around US$2, departing either from Khlong Bambang, which is directly in the centre of Satun, or at Tammalang Pier, in the estuary just south of the town.

Boats also leave Tammalang three times daily for Malaysia's fabled Langkawi Island, costing around US$5 each way. Travellers exiting Thailand for Malaysia via Satun should remember to get their passport stamped at the immigration office in town; if you forget, there is a distinct possibility of bureaucratic delays and perhaps even a bureaucratic nightmare on arrival in Malaysia. ❑

INSIGHT GUIDES
TRAVEL TIPS

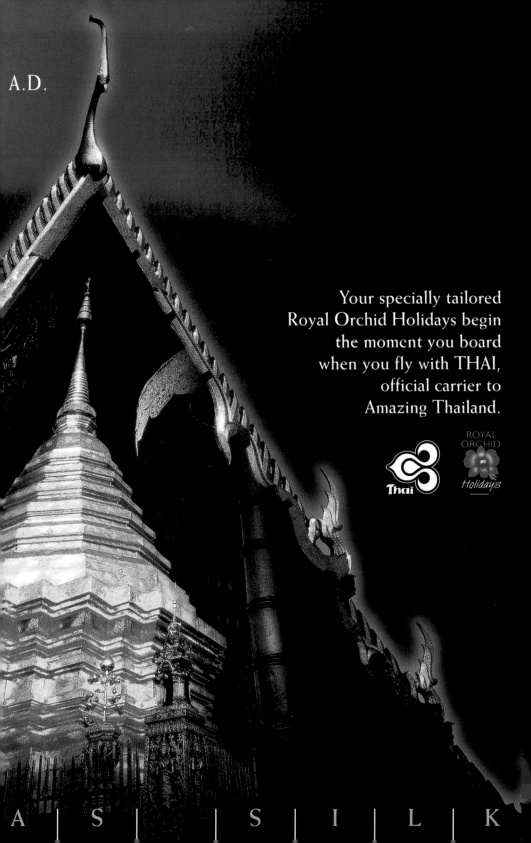

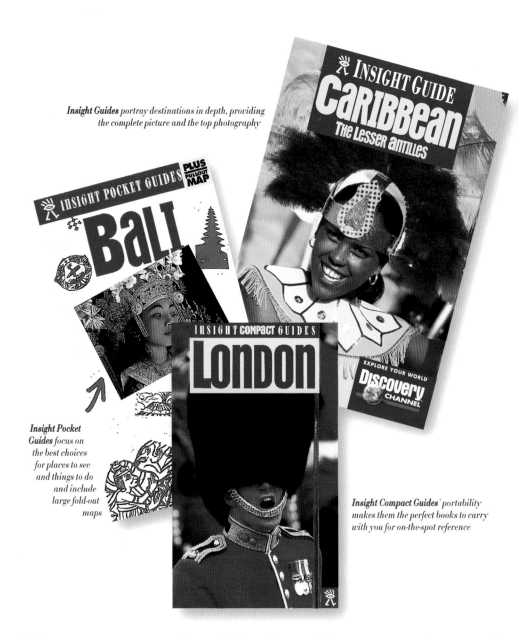

Insight Guides portray destinations in depth, providing the complete picture and the top photography

Insight Pocket Guides focus on the best choices for places to see and things to do and include large fold-out maps

Insight Compact Guides' portability makes them the perfect books to carry with you for on-the-spot reference

Three types of guide for all types of travel

INSIGHT GUIDES Different people need different kinds of information. Some want *background information* to help them prepare for the trip. Others seek *personal recommendations* from someone who knows the destination well. And others look for *compactly presented data* for on-the-spot reference. With three carefully designed series, Insight Guides offer readers the perfect choice. Insight Guides will turn your visit into an experience.

The world's largest collection of visual travel guides

CONTENTS

Getting Acquainted

The Place

Lying between 7 degrees and 21 degrees latitude, Thailand has a total land area of 514,000 sq km (198,000 sq mi), nearly the size of France or twice as large as England. The country is said to resemble an elephant's head with its trunk forming the southern peninsula. Bangkok, its capital, is sited at its geographic center, approximately at the elephant's mouth. The country is bordered by Malaysia on the south, Burma on the west, Laos across the Mekong River to the northeast and Cambodia to the east.

The north is marked by low hills and contains the country's tallest peak, Doi Inthanon, standing 2,590 meters (8,500 ft) tall. A range of hills divides Thailand from Burma and forms the western boundary of the broad alluvial central plains, the country's principal rice-growing area. To the east, the plains rise to the Khorat Plateau, which covers much of the Northeast. The spine of the southern peninsula is the same range of hills that separates Thailand from Burma, sloping down to the Andaman Sea on the west and the Gulf of Thailand on the east. Thailand has a total of 2,600 km (1,600 mi) of coastline.

Bangkok is situated at 14 degrees north latitude. Bangkok is a city divided into halves by a river, the Chao Phraya, which separates central Bangkok and Thonburi. The city covers a total area of 1,565 sq km (605 sq mi) of delta land, of which no natural area is more than 2 meters (7 ft) above any other.

Chiang Mai lies 700 km (435 mi) north of Bangkok. It sits 300 meters (1,000 ft) above sea level, and is crowned by Doi Suthep, which rises to a height of 1,675 meters (5,495 ft). The city is home to over 150,000 people.

Phuket, an island in the Andaman Sea, lies 890 km (550 mi) or a 70-minute flight south of Bangkok. Measuring 50 km (30 mi) long by 20 km (13 mi) wide, it is approximately the size of the city-state of Singapore.

Time Zones

Thailand Standard Time is 7 hours ahead of Universal Time (Greenwich Mean Time).

Climate

There are three seasons in Thailand: hot, rainy and cool. But to the tourist winging in from anywhere north or south of the 30th parallel, Thailand has only one temperature: hot. To make things worse, the temperature drops only a few degrees during the night and is accompanied 24 hours by humidity above 70 percent. Only air-conditioning makes Bangkok and other major towns tolerable during the hot season. The countryside is somewhat cooler, but, surprisingly, the northern regions can be hotter in March and April than Bangkok.

Hot season (March to mid-June), 27˚–35˚C (80˚–95˚F).
Rainy season (June to October), 24˚–32˚C (75˚–90˚F).
Cool season (November to February), 18˚–32˚C (65˚–90˚F), but with less humidity.

Adding together the yearly daytime highs and the nighttime lows for major world cities, the World Meteorological Organization has declared Bangkok to be the world's hottest city. When the monsoon rains fall, most of the country swelters.

Chiang Mai enjoys a cooler climate. In the cool season, temperatures range between 13˚ and 28˚C (55˚ and 82˚F) and are lower in the hills. Like Bangkok, the heaviest rain falls in September, and some of the city streets are often flooded.

In Phuket, the monsoon begins in early May, but generally ends late in October. Temperatures range from 34˚C (93˚F) in the hot season to nighttime temperatures of 21˚C (70˚F) in the cool season. The water temperature never drops below 20˚C (67˚F).

Economy

Nearly 70 percent of Thailand's 60 million people are farmers who till alluvial land so rich that Thailand is a world leader in the export of tapioca (No. 1), rice (No. 2), rubber (No. 2), canned pineapple (No. 3), and is a top-ranked exporter of sugar, maize and tin. Increasingly, Thailand is turning to manufacturing, especially in clothing, machinery, and electronics.

Government

Thailand is a constitutional monarchy headed by His Majesty, King Bhumibol. The royalty's power has been reduced considerably from the period before the 1932 revolution. However, the present king can, by the force of his personality and moral authority, influence the direction of important decisions merely by a word or two.

Although he no longer rules as did the absolute monarchs of previous centuries, he is still regarded as one of the three pillars of the society – monarchy, religion and the nation. This concept is represented in the five-banded national flag of Thailand: the outer red bands symbolizing the nation; the inner white bands the purity of the Buddhist religion; and the thick blue band at the centre representing the monarchy.

His dedication over many years in working with farmers to improve their lands and yields has influenced others to follow his example in serving the people. Her Majesty Queen Sirikit and other members of the royal family have also been active in promoting the interests of Thais in the lower economic strata. Thus, the photographs of the king and queen hang in nearly every home, shop and office, placed there, not out of blind devotion, but out of genuine respect for the royal family.

The structure of the government is defined by the constitution and its enabling ordinances. A new constitution, designed to reform the political system, was passed in 1997. Despite its frequent revisions, the constitution has remained true to the spirit of the original aim of placing power in the hands of the people; the exercising of it, however, has often favored certain groups over others, especially the military, which has sometimes abused its power.

Modeled loosely on the British system, the Thai government consists of three branches: legislative, executive and judiciary, each acting independently of the others in a system of checks and balances. The legislative branch is composed of a senate and a house of representatives. The senate consists of 262 leading members of society, including business people, educators and a heavy preponderance of high-ranking military officers. They must be over 35 years of age and must not be members of political parties. Members are selected by the prime minister and approved by the king. The house of representatives comprises 391 members elected by popular vote from each of the 76 provinces of Thailand.

The executive branch is represented by a prime minister, who must be an elected member of parliament. He is selected by a single party or coalition of parties and rules through a cabinet of ministers, the exact number dependent on his own needs. They, in turn, implement their programs through the very powerful civil service. The judiciary consists of a supreme court, an appellate court, and a pyramid of provincial and lower courts. It acts independently to interpret points of law and counsels the other two branches on the appropriateness of actions.

Planning the Trip

What to Bring

Bangkok, Chiang Mai, Pattaya, and Phuket are modern destinations with most of the modern amenities found in similar places in Europe or North America.

Lip balm and moisturizers are needed in the north during the cool season. Sunglasses and hats are useful items to protect eyes and sensitive skin from tropical glare.

Electricity

Electrical outlets are rated at 220 volts, 50 cycles, and accept either flat-pronged or round-pronged plugs.

What to Wear

Clothes should be light and loose; natural blends that breathe are preferable to synthetics. Open shoes (sandals during the height of the rainy season, when some Bangkok streets get flooded) and sleeveless dresses for women or short-sleeved shirts for men are appropriate. Suits are worn for business and in many large hotels but, in general, Thailand lacks the formal dress code of Hong Kong or Tokyo. Casual but neat and clean clothes are suitable for most occasions. Some formality is needed for business appointments.

The cool season in the north can be chilly. A sweater or sweatshirt will be welcome, especially when traveling in the hills.

One exception is the clothing code for Buddhist temples and Muslim mosques. Shorts are taboo for both women and men wanting to enter some of the important temples. Those wearing sleeveless

dresses may also be barred from certain temples. Improperly dressed and unkempt visitors will be turned away from large temples like the Wat Phra Kaeo (Temple of the Emerald Buddha) and from the Grand Palace. Dress properly in deference to the religion and to Thai sensitivities.

Entry Regulations

VISAS AND PASSPORTS

Travelers should check visa regulations at a Thai embassy or consulate before starting their journey. All foreign nationals entering Thailand must have valid passports. At the airport, nationals from most countries will be granted a free transit visa valid up to 15 days, provided that they have a fully-paid ticket out of Thailand.

Tourist visas allow for a 60-day stay from the date of entry into the kingdom. A 30-day transit visa may also be issued to some visitors. People who are waiting for a work permit to be issued can apply for a non-immigrant visa which is good for 90 days. A letter of guarantee is needed from the Thai company you intend to work for, and this visa can be obtained from a Thai embassy or consulate at home.

Visas can be extended before they expire by applying at the **Immigration Bureau** on Soi Suan Plu, Sathorn Tai Road, tel: 286 4231, 287 3101, ext. 2271. (8.30am–4pm, Monday–Friday.) Visitors wishing to leave Thailand and return before their visas have expired can apply for a re-entry permit prior to their departure at immigration offices in Bangkok, Chiang Mai, Pattaya, Phuket and Hat Yai. An exit visa is not required.

VISA EXTENSIONS

If planning a longer stay, a transit visa valid for 30 days or a tourist visa valid for 60 days must be obtained from a Thai embassy or consulate abroad by filing an application, supplying three passport-sized photographs and paying a fee. Visas can be extended by applying at the **Immigration**

Bureau on Soi Suan Plu (8.30am–4pm, Monday–Friday) before the visa's expiration date. There is a fee.

CUSTOMS

The Thai government prohibits the import of drugs, dangerous chemicals, pornography, firearms and ammunition. Attempting to smuggle heroin or other hard drugs may be punishable by death. Scores of foreigners are serving long prison terms in Thai jails for drug-related offenses.

Foreign tourists may freely bring in foreign banknotes or other types of foreign exchange. For travelers leaving Thailand, the maximum amount permitted to be taken out in Thai currency without prior authorization is 50,000 baht.

Foreign guests are allowed to import, without tax, one camera with five rolls of film, 200 cigarettes, and one liter of wine or alcoholic spirits.

Health

Visitors entering the kingdom are no longer required to show evidence of vaccination for smallpox or cholera, but immunization against cholera is still a good idea. Before you leave home, check that tetanus boosters are up to date. Malaria and dengue fever persist in the rural areas. When in the hills – especially in the monsoon season – tuck pants legs into socks to deter leeches, and apply mosquito repellent on exposed skin when the sun begins to set.

Most first-time visitors experience a degree of heat exhaustion and dehydration that can be avoided by drinking lots of bottled water and slightly increasing the amount of salt in the diet. Sunblock is essential.

AIDS is not confined to "high risk" sections of the population in Thailand, and visitors are at risk from casual sex if they do not use condoms. It is estimated that almost the entire population of prostitutes in the country are HIV positive.

HYGIENE

Thais place high value on personal hygiene and are aware of the dangers of germs and infections. They do not, however, place such a high priority on keeping the environment clean. Establishments catering to foreigners are generally careful with food and drink preparation and sanitation.

Bangkok water is clean when it leaves the modern filtration plant; the pipes that carry it into the city are somewhat less than new, however, and visitors are advised to drink bottled water or soft drinks. Both are produced under strict supervision, as is the ice used in large hotels and restaurants. Most streetside restaurants are clean; a quick glance should tell you which are and which are not.

PRECAUTIONS

With its thriving nightlife and transient population, Bangkok is a magnet for sexual diseases. The women (and men) in these service industries are aware of the consequences of carelessness and of not insisting that their partners take precautions, but economic necessity, coupled with a Thai reluctance to offend anyone, means that there is a great risk of taking home a souvenir one would rather not share with friends and loved ones. Assume that there is a good chance of picking something up and take appropriate measures. Some massage parlors, mindful of the dangers, now bar foreign patrons and cater only to Thais in the belief that they reduce their risks.

Malaria is still highly dangerous in some regions of Thailand. The best protection is to avoid being bitten. Mosquitoes are most active at night, between the hours of sundown and sunrise. After dark you should wear long trousers, long-sleeved shirts, shoes and socks or stockings. Hands and neck should be protected with an insect repellent, and you should sleep in rooms with adequate mosquito screens on the windows and under a mosquito net. If you decide to

protect yourself with anti-malarial tablets, remember that mosquitoes in many areas are resistant to many of the proprietary brands of medication. Seek advice from a tropical institute before your departure. Should you nonetheless contract malaria, there is a network of malaria centers and hospitals throughout Thailand. It is important to remember that the most dangerous form of malaria often appears disguised as a heavy cold. If you contract what appears to be influenza, you should consult a doctor immediately. This also applies during the weeks after your return from the tropics.

Currency

The *baht* is the principal Thai monetary unit. It is divided into 100 units called *satang*. Banknote denominations include 1,000 (gray), 500 (purple), 100 (red), 50 (blue), 20 (green) and 10 (brown) baht.

While the banknotes are easy to decipher, the coinage is a confusing matter with a variety of sizes and types for each denomination. There are 10-baht coins (brass centre with a silver rim), two different 5-baht coins (silver pieces with copper rims), three varieties of 1-baht coin (silver; usually only the small-size will fit in a public telephone), and two small coins of 50 and 25 satang (both are brass-coloured).

EXCHANGE RATES

The once-stable Thai currency was devalued in mid-1997. Since then, the exchange rate, which for years had hovered at 25 baht to the US dollar, has risen to an average of around 35 to 45 baht to the dollar. There is no currency black market.

BANKING SYSTEM

Thailand has a sophisticated banking system with representation by the major banks of most foreign countries. Money can be imported in cash or traveler's checks and converted into baht. It is also possible to arrange telex bank drafts from one's hometown bank. There is no minimum requirement on the amount of money that must be converted. Both cash and traveler's checks can be changed in hundreds of bank branches throughout the city; rates are more favorable for traveler's checks than for cash. Banking hours are 10am–4pm, Monday–Friday, although some banks near major tourist areas maintain longer operating hours for foreign exchange. Hotels generally give poor exchange rates in comparison with banks.

ATM/DEBIT CARDS

Most banks now have ATM machines, usually outside the bank proper and accessible around the clock. Currency is dispensed in baht only. Note, however, that many banks only accept ATM cards linked directly to Thai bank accounts; for those with ATM cards on the Plus or Cirrus networks who wish to withdraw funds directly from their home bank accounts, Hongkong and Bangkok banks are good bets.

Occasionally, an ATM card may not work at one machine for some unspecified reason; try another branch of the same bank and results may be different. Alternatively, MasterCard and Visa debit cards (as distinct from credit cards; with debit cards, the money is withdrawn immediately from an associated bank account) are also accepted at many ATM machines. Most banks have signs with an array of symbols indicating which cards are accepted at the machine. Periodically, cards are accepted at machines in spite of the fact that no related sign appears out front. When in doubt, give it a try, but be prepared to be flexible.

CREDIT CARDS

American Express, Diners Club, MasterCard and Visa are widely accepted throughout Bangkok. In provincial destinations, it is better to check that plastic is accepted, and not to count on using cards.

Credit Card Warning: Credit card fraud is a major problem in Thailand. Do not leave credit cards in safe deposit boxes. Notification

of loss of credit cards can be made at the following offices:

Bangkok
American Express, 388 Phaholyothin Road. Tel: 273 0033 (customer service), 273 0022 (24-hour emergency), fax: 273 0464. Open 8.30am–5pm Monday–Friday. **Diners Club**, Silom Complex, 12th Floor, 191 Silom Road. Tel: 238 3660, fax: 231 3550. Open 8.30am–5pm, Monday–Friday. **Visa Centre**, Bldg. One, 11th Floor, 99/38 Witthayu Road. Tel: 256 7324/9, fax: 256 7151. **MasterCard International**, Sermmitr Tower, 11th Floor, Soi 21 (Soi Asoke), Sukhumvit Road. Tel: 260 8572/3, fax: 260 8574.

Chiang Mai
American Express, Bangkok Bank, 2/3 Prachasampan Road. Tel: 276 816. **Visa and MasterCard**, Thai Farmers Bank, Ta Pae Road. Tel: 270 151. Hours: 8.30am–3.30pm Monday–Friday.

Phuket
American Express, 95/4 Phuket Road. Tel: 218 887. **Visa and MasterCard**, contact any branch of Thai Farmers Bank or Bangkok Bank.

Public Holidays

The following dates are observed as official public holidays:
New Year's Day January 1
Magha Puja February (full moon)
Chakri Day April 6
Songkran (Thai New Year) April 13–15
Labor Day May 1
Coronation Day May 5
Ploughing Ceremony May (variable)
Visakha Puja May (full moon)
Asalaha Puja July (full moon)
Khao Phansa July
Queen's Birthday August 12
Chulalongkorn Day October 23
King's Birthday December 5
Constitution Day December 10
New Year's Eve December 31
Chinese New Year in February is not an official public holiday, but

many businesses are closed for several days.

Getting There

BY AIR
Bangkok is a gateway between east and west and a transportation hub for Southeast Asia served by most of the major airlines. In addition to Bangkok, Thailand has three other international airports: Chiang Mai, Phuket and Hat Yai.

Thai Airways International flies to more than 50 cities on four continents. The flying time from the UK is about 12 hours, from the west coast of America, about 21 hours. Flights from Australia and New Zealand take about 9 hours.

BY SEA
The days when travelers sailed up the Chao Phraya River to view the golden spires of Bangkok are long gone. Luxury liners now call at Pattaya and Phuket but have ceased serving Bangkok. Check with a travel agent or shipping company to find those which depart from your city.

A regular cruise ship, *Andaman Princess*, operates between Bangkok and Singapore. Details from Siam Cruise Co., Bangkok. Tel: 255 8950, fax: 255 8961.

BY RAIL
Trains operated by the State Railways of Thailand are clean, cheap and reliable, albeit a little slow. There are only two railroad entry points into Thailand, both from Malaysia on the southern Thai border. The trip north to Bangkok serves as a scenic introduction to southern Thailand.

The *Malay Mail* leaves Kuala Lumpur every day at 7.30am, 8.15am, 3pm, 8.30pm and 10pm, arriving 7 to 9 hours later at Butterworth, the port opposite Malaysia's Penang Island, at 1.35pm, 5.50pm, 9.10pm, 5.30am and 6.40am respectively. A daily train leaves Butterworth at 1.40pm, crossing the border into Thailand and arriving in Bangkok at 9.30 the next morning. There are second-class cars with seats which are made into upper and lower sleeping berths at night. There are also air-conditioned first-class sleepers and dining cars serving Thai food. Prices from Butterworth to Bangkok are US$50 or less, depending upon class of service.

Trains leave Bangkok's Hua Lampong Station daily at 3.15pm for the return journey to Malaysia. A second, somewhat less convenient but more entertaining, train travels from Kuala Lumpur up Malaysia's east coast to the northeastern town of Kota Bahru. Take a taxi across the border to catch the SRT train from the southern Thai town of Sungai Kolok. Trains leave Sungai Kolok at noon and 3pm, arriving in Bangkok at 8.35am and 10.35am the following day.

If you like to travel in style and prefer not to fly, the Eastern & Oriental Express (Tel: 251 4862) is Asia's most exclusive travel experience. Traveling several times a month between Singapore, Kuala Lumpur and Bangkok, the 22-carriage train with its distinctive green-and-cream livery passes through spectacular scenery. It's very expensive, but classically elegant and high-brow.

BY ROAD

Malaysia provides the main road access into Thailand, with crossings near Betong and Sungai Kolok. It is possible to cross to and from Laos from Nong Khai by using the Friendship Bridge across the Mekong River. Visitors need visas. Drivers will find that most Thai roads are modern, paved and usually well maintained.

Special Facilities

LEFT LUGGAGE

There are two left luggage facilities at Don Muang International Airport. One is on the 1st floor on the northern end of the arrival hall after passing through customs. The second is in the departure hall on the 3rd floor near the currency exchange counter. The fee is 20 baht (US$0.60) per bag per day.

RESERVATIONS

Hotel reservations can be made in the airport arrival lounge once you have passed through customs. It is recommended that you book a room in advance during the Christmas-New Year and Chinese New Year holidays and, for destinations outside of Bangkok, during Songkran in mid-April.

CHILDREN

Children may enjoy the unusual animals of **Dusit Zoo** (Ratchawithi Road, off Rama V Road), or paddling boats in the lake at the zoo, or in **Lumpini** or **Chatuchak Parks**. Miniature golf is available at **Yama's Golf Course**, Si Nakharin Road, tel: 721 8888, daily 10am–9pm. **Safari World**, Thailand's only drive-through wildlife park, is at 99 Ramindra Road, Minburi (40 km (25 mi) east of Bangkok). Tel: 518 1000/19. Daily 9am–7pm. In addition to elephants, lions, giraffes and other mammals, look for dolphin and sea lion shows at **Marine Park** and white pandas at the **Panda House**. An exciting day out for the whole family. Alternatively, an afternoon at one of Bangkok's many amusement parks is guaranteed fun.

Adventureland, Seacon Square, 904 Si Nakharin Road. Tel: 721 8888/96. Weekdays: 11am–9pm, weekends: 10am–10pm. Upside-down roller coaster, go-karts, roller blade rink.

Dream World, Nakhon Nayok Road, Rangsit (north of Don Muang Airport). Tel: 533 1152. Weekdays: 10am–5pm, weekends: 10am–7pm. Four different themes, largest water log slide in Asia.

Magic Land, 72 Phaholyothin Road (near Central Plaza). Tel: 513 1731. Weekdays: 10am–5.30pm, weekends: 10am–7pm. Ghost house, roller coasters, ferris wheels.

Siam Park, 101 Sukhapiban 2 Road, Minburi (east of Bangkok). Tel: 517 0075. Weekdays: 10am–4pm, weekends: 9am–9pm. Amusement park and water park, also a small zoo. Note: The park

prohibits the wearing of T-shirts in the swimming areas, so take plenty of suntan oil for tender young skins.

In Pattaya children may enjoy a day at **Water World** at the Pattaya Park Beach Resort or a visit to **Ripley's Believe It or Not** museum at the Royal Garden Plaza. In Phuket head for the **Crocodile Farm and Elephant Land** on Chana Charoen Road. Shows are held at 11am and 3.30pm daily.

GAYS

Gays quickly discover that Thailand is one of the most tolerant countries in the world. In Bangkok, most of the gay bars are on Soi Patpong 3 or the upper end of Silom Road. Transvestites and transvestite shows are common in Bangkok, and also in both Pattaya and Phuket.

DISABLED

To say that facilities for the handicapped in Thailand, even in Bangkok, are underdeveloped is something of an understatement. Sidewalks are uneven, riddled with potholes and studded with obstructions; ramps are non-existent. (It's no accident that on many street corners sit cobblers repairing damaged shoes.) Crossing major streets in Bangkok without making use of the pedestrian bridges (steep flights of stairs on either side of the street linked by an overhead walkway) is to court disaster, even for the non-disabled. Few buildings in Bangkok have ramps, although the various hotels throughout Thailand in the Holiday Inn, Hyatt International, Novotel and Sheraton chains are wheelchair-accessible. While there is no taxi service specifically geared towards the disabled, and ordinary taxis often do not have enough storage room for a wheelchair, some of the newer taxis are modified station wagons with ample room in the back. Hiring a private car, however, may be the most reliable alternative.

In spite of this disheartening picture, disabled travelers can visit and enjoy the wonders of Thailand. Forethought and flexibility are key.

Some organizations to contact for further information include:

Association of the Physically Handicapped of Thailand, 73/7-8 Soi 8, Tivanon Road, Talaat Kawan, Nonthaburi 11000. Tel: (2) 951 0569.

Mobility International, Post Office Box 10767, Eugene, OR 97440. Tel: (541) 343 1284.

Society for the Advancement of Travel for the Handicapped, 26 Court Street, Brooklyn, NY 11242. Tel: (718) 858 5483.

Useful Addresses

DOING BUSINESS

Most hotels have business centers with communications and secretarial services in several languages. Elsewhere in Bangkok, it is possible to lease small offices with clerical staff.

Chambers of Commerce

American, Kian Gwan House, 140 Witthayu Road. Tel: 251 1605, 251 9266, fax: 651 4474. Open 7.30am– noon, 1.30–3.30pm Monday–Friday.

British, 54 Soi 21 (Soi Asoke), Sukhumvit Road. Tel: 260 7288/9, fax: 260 7287. Open 8am–noon, 1–4.30pm, Monday–Friday.

Franco-Thai, Richmond Tower, 10th Floor, Soi 26, Sukhumvit Road. Tel: 261 8276, fax: 261 8278. Open 9am–noon, 1–6pm, Monday–Friday.

German-Thai, Klongboonma Bldg., 4th Floor, 699 Silom Road. Tel: 266 4924/5, fax: 236 4711. Open 8am–4pm, Monday–Friday.

Thai-Canadian, CP Tower, 19th Floor, 313 Silom Road. Tel: 231 0981/2, fax: 231 0893. Hours: 8am–4pm.

SPECIAL CLUBS

Alliance Francaise, 29 Sathorn Tai Road. Tel: 213 2122/3, fax: 213 2064. Open 8am–6.30pm, Monday–Friday; 8.30am–1.30pm, Saturday. Library, bookshop and cafeteria; open to all. In Chiang Mai: 138 Charoen Prathet Road. Tel: 275 277.

American University Alumni (AUA), 179 Ratchadamri Road. Tel: 252

8170/3. Library open to non-members. American films, monthly newsletter, cafeteria. In Chiang Mai: 24 Ratchadamnern Road. Tel: 211 973, 278 407.

Bangkok Cosmopolitan Lions Club, 10 Soi Soonvijai, New Phetburi Road. Tel: 318 1518. Meetings on the last Thursday of the month. Foreign members welcome.

British Council, 254 Chulalongkorn Soi 64, Siam Square, Rama I Road. Tel: 252 6136, 252 6111. Open 8.30am–4pm, Monday–Friday. Library open to members only. British films, monthly newsletter. In Chiang Mai: 198 Bamrungrat Road. Tel: 242 103.

Foreign Correspondents Club of Thailand, Maneeya Centre, 518/5 Ploenchit Road (next to Amarin Plaza). Tel: 652 0580. Non-members may browse in the small library with the purchase of something at the bar or restaurant.

Goethe Institut, 18/1 Soi Ngam Duphli, Rama IV Road. Tel: 287 0942/4. Open 8am–5pm, Monday–Friday; and from 8am–12.30pm on Saturday. German films, restaurant, monthly newsletter. Open to all.

Rotary Club, Bangkok Rotary, Grand Hyatt Erawan Hotel. Tel: 254 1234. Foreign members welcome; English is the medium.

TOURIST OFFICES

Planning a trip to Thailand can be made easier if you contact a travel agent or an office of the **Tourism Authority of Thailand** (**TAT**), the Thai government's official tourism promotion organization. These offices offer promotional brochures, maps and videotapes of the country's many attractions. The head office at 372 Bamrung Muang Road (Tel: 226 0060, 226 0085, fax: 226 0072) will provide you with essential tourist information; for a more complete service, the information office, at 4 Ratchadamnern Nok Avenue (Tel: 282 9775/6), has a wealth of brochures on various attractions and personnel to answer questions.

TAT has its own travel information site on the Internet: www.cs.ait.ac.th/tat/. The TAT's e-

mail address for sending inquiries is tat@cs.ait.ac.th.

Below are some of the offices of the Tourism Authority of Thailand.

Asia and the Pacific

Australia: Royal Exchange Bldg., 7th Floor, 56 Pitt St, Sydney 2000. Tel: (02) 247 7549, fax: (02) 251 2465.

Hong Kong: Room 401, Fairmont House, 8 Cotton Tree Drive, Central. Tel: (852) 868 0732, 868 0854, fax: (852) 868 4585.

Japan: Hibiya Mitsui Bldg., 1-2, Yurakucho 1-chome, Chiyoda-ku, Tokyo 100, tel: (03) 358 06776/7, fax: (03) 358 07808; Hirano-machi Yachiyo Bldg., 5th Floor, 1-8-13 Hiranomachi Chuo-ku, Osaka 541, tel: (06) 231 4434, fax: (06) 231 4337; Hakata Pal Bldg., 2nd Floor, 2-63 Gokushu-machi, Hakata-ku, Fukuoka 812, tel: (092) 262 3031, fax: (092) 262 3032.

Malaysia: c/o Royal Thai Embassy, 206 Jalan Ampang, Kuala Lumpur. Tel: (093) 248 0958, 248 6529, fax: (093) 241 3002.

Singapore: c/o Royal Thai Embassy, 370 Orchard Road, Singapore 0923. Tel: (65) 235 7694, 235 7901, 733 6723, fax: 733 5653.

South Korea: Room 2003, 20th Floor, Coryo Daeyungak Centre Bldg., 25-5, 1-ka. Chungmu-ro, Chung-ku, Seoul. Tel: (02) 779 5417, fax: (02) 779 5419.

Taiwan: Thailand Trade and Economic Office, 2B Central Commercial Bldg., 16-18 Nanking East Road, Section 4, Taipei. Tel: (02) 579 6111, fax: (02) 577 9914.

Europe

France: 90 Avenue des Champs-Elysees, 75008 Paris. Tel: (01) 4562 8656, 4562 8748, fax: (01) 4563 7888.

Italy: Ente Nazionale per il Tourismo-Thailandese, Via Barberini 50 00187, Rome. Tel: (06) 487 3479, 481 8927, fax: 487 3500.

England: 49 Albemarle St, London WIX 3FE. Tel: (171) 499 7670/9, fax: (171) 629 5519.

Germany: Bethmannstr, 58/IV., D-6000, Frankfurt/M.I. Tel: (069) 295 704, 295 804, fax: (69) 281 468.

USA
Chicago: 303 East Wacker Drive, Suite 400, Chicago, IL 60601. Tel: (312) 819 3990/5, fax: (312) 565 0359.
New York: 5 World Trade Centre, Suite 2449, New York, NY 10048. Tel: (212) 432 0433, 432 0435, fax: (212) 912 0920.
Los Angeles: 3440 Wilshire Blvd, Suite 1101, Los Angeles, CA 90010. Tel: (213) 382 2353/5, fax: (213) 389 7544.

Thailand
Bangkok: 372 Bamrung Muang Road. Tel: 226 0060, 226 0085, fax: 226 0072.
Ayutthaya: Si Sanphet Road. Tel: (035) 246 076/7, fax: 246 078.
Cha-am: 500/51 Phetkasem Road. Tel: (032) 471 005/6, fax: (032) 471 502.
Chiang Mai: 105/1 Chiang Mai-Lamphun Road. Tel: (053) 248 604, 248 607, fax: (053) 248 605.
Chiang Rai: 448/16 Singhakhlai Road. Tel: (053) 717 433, fax: (053) 717 434.
Hat Yai: 1/1 Soi 2 Niphat Uthit 3 Road. Tel: (074) 243 747, 238 518, 231 055, fax: (074) 245 986.
Kanchanaburi: Saeng Chuto Road. Tel: (034) 511 200, fax: 511 200.
Khon Kaen: 15/5 Prachasamosorn Road. Tel: (043) 244 498/9, fax: (043) 244 497.
Krabi: Uttarikit Road, opp. Thai Farmers Bank. Tel: (075) 612 740.
Lopburi: H.M. The Queen's Celebration Building, c/o Lopburi Provincial Hall, Narai Mahart Road. Tel: (036) 422 768, fax: 422 769.
Nakhon Nayok: 084/23 Suwannason Road. Tel: (037) 312 282, 312 284, fax: (037) 312 286.
Nakhon Phanom: 184/1 Sunthornvichit Road. Tel: (042) 513 490/1, fax: (042) 513 492.
Nakhon Ratchasima: 2102-2104 Mittraphap Road. Tel: (044) 213 666, fax: (044) 213 667.
Nakhon Si Thammarat: Sanam Na Muang, Ratchadamnern Road. Tel: (075) 346 515/6, fax: 346 517.
Pattaya: 246/1 Moo 9, Beach Road, Pattaya. Tel: (038) 428 750, 427 667, fax: (038) 429 113.
Phitsanulok: 209/7-8 Surasi Trade Centre, Boromtrailokanat Road. Tel: (055) 252 743, fax: 252 742.
Phuket: 73-75 Phuket Road. Tel: (076) 212 213, 211 036, fax: (076) 213 582.
Rayong: 153/4 Sukhumvit Road. Tel: (038) 655 420/1, fax: (038) 655 422.
Surat Thani: 5 Talat Mai Road, Ban Don. Tel: (077) 281 828, fax: (077) 282 828.
Trat: 100 Moo 1, Trat, Laem Ngop Road, Laem Ngop District, Trat (opp. pier at Laem Ngop). Tel: (039) 597 255, 597 259/60, fax: (039) 597 255.
Ubon Ratchathani: 264/1 Khuan Thani Road. Tel: (045) 243 770, fax: (045) 243 771.
Udon Thani: 16/5 Mukkhamontri Road. Tel: (042) 325 406/7, fax: (042) 325 408.

WEB SITES
www.tat.or.th: Tourism Authority of Thailand.
www.thnic.net: Thailand Network Information Centre provides a list of Thailand's major web servers.
www.asiaaccess.net.th/citymap: an interactive map library.
www.bkk.post.co.th: *Bangkok Post*.
www.bkkmetro.com: *Bangkok Metro* magazine.
www.khonkaen.com: Everything you need to know about Khon Kaen, including accommodation, entertainment, events, maps, weather forecast. Excellent links to other parts of the country.
www.kohphangan.com: Sponsored by the merchants and resort operators on Ko Pha Ngan.
www.mahidol.ac.th: Mahidol University.
www.samart.co.th/hps: Although based in Thailand, this site is a directory of New Age information and alternative health care on offer throughout Southeast Asia.
utopia-asia.com: Regional information relevant to gays and lesbians, many hits, voted a "cool site" by Yahoo.

AIRLINE OFFICES
Bangkok
Air France, Vorawat Bldg., 20th Floor, 849 Silom Road. Tel: 635 1199 (reservations & ticketing), fax: 635 1204; airport: 523 7302, 535 2112/3.
Air India, c/o S.S. Travel Service, SS Bldg., 10/12-13 Convent Road. Tel: 235 0557, 236 7188 (reservations & ticketing), fax: 631 0340; airport: 535 2121.
Air Lanka, Charn Issara Tower, 6th Floor, 942/34-35 Rama IV Road. Tel: 236 0159, 236 9292/3 (reservations & ticketing), fax: 236 7617; airport: 535 2331/2.
Air New Zealand, 1053 Charoen Krung (New) Road. Tel: 237 1560 (reservations & ticketing), fax: 267 0300; airport: 535 3981/2.
Alitalia, Boonmitr Bldg., 8th Floor, 138 Silom Road. Tel: 233 4000 (reservations & ticketing), fax: 237 6454; airport: 535 2602.
All Nippon Airways, C.P. Towers, 2nd Floor, 313 Silom Road. Tel: 238 5121 (reservations), 238 5141 (ticketing), fax: 238 5137; airport: 531 8899, 535 2037.
Bangkok Airways, Queen Sirikit National Convention Centre, New Ratchadapisek Road. Tel: 229 3456 (reservations), 229 3434 (ticketing), fax: 229 3454; airport: 535 2497/8; email: bkkair@loxinfo.co.th.
British Airways, Abdulrahim Place, 14th Floor, 990 Rama IV Road. Tel: 636 1747 (reservations), 636 1770 (ticketing), fax: 636 1749 (reservations), 636 1748 (ticketing); airport: 535 2220.
Canadian Airlines International, Maneeya Bldg., 6th Floor, 518/5 Ploenchit Road. Tel: 251 4521 (reservations), 255 5862 (ticketing), fax: 254 8376; airport: 535 2227/9.
Cathay Pacific, Ploenchit Tower, 11th Floor, 898 Ploenchit Road. Tel: 263 0606 (reservations), 263 0616 (ticketing), fax: 263 0622 (reservations), 263 0631 (ticketing); airport: 535 2155/6.
China Airlines, Peninsula Plaza, 4th Floor, 153 Ratchadamri Road. Tel: 253 4242 (reservations), 253

5733 (ticketing), fax: 253 4791;
airport: 535 2366, 535 2466.
Dragonair, 37/52 Montri Road,
Phuket. Tel: (76) 215 734, 217
300/1, fax: 217 299.
Garuda Indonesia, Lumpini Tower,
27th Floor, Rama IV Road (opp.
Lumpini Boxing Stadium). Tel: 285
6470/3, 679 7371/2 (reservations
& ticketing), fax: 285 6474; airport:
535 2171.
Japan Airlines, JAL Bldg., 254/1
Ratchadapisek Road. Tel: 692
5151 (reservations), 692 5185
(ticketing), fax: 274 1410
(reservations), 274 1460
(ticketing); airport: 535 2135/6.
KLM, Thai Wah Tower II, 19th Floor,
Sathorn Tai Road. Tel: 679 1100
(reservations & ticketing), fax: 679
1415; airport: 535 2191.
Korean Air, Klongboonma Bldg.,
699 Silom Road. Tel: 635 0465/72
(reservations & ticketing), fax: 267
0992; airport: 523 7320.
Lao Aviation, Silom Plaza, Ground
Floor, 491/17 Silom Road. Tel: 236
9822/3, 237 7139 (reservations &
ticketing), fax: 236 9821; airport:
535 3786.
Lufthansa, Q House Bldg., 18th
Floor, Soi 21, Sukhumvit Road. Tel:
264 2400 (reservations), 264
2401 (ticketing), fax: 264 2399;
airport: 535 2211.
Malaysia Airlines, Ploenchit Tower,
20th Floor, 898 Ploenchit Road. Tel:
263 0565/71 (reservations), 263
0520/9 (ticketing), fax: 263 0577
(reservations), 263 0576
(ticketing); airport: 535 3781, 535
3679.
Myanmar Airways, Jewelry Trade
Centre, 23rd Floor, Unit H1,
919/298 Silom Road. Tel: 630
0334/8 (reservations & ticketing),
fax: 630 0339; airport: 523 7420,
535 2484.
Northwest Airlines, Peninsula
Plaza, 4th Floor, 153 Ratchadamri
Road. Tel: 254 0789 (reservations),
254 0771 (ticketing), fax: 254
0741; airport: 535 2413.
Orient Thai Airlines (domestic),
Jewelry Centre, 17th Floor, 138/70
Nares Road. Tel: 267 3210/4
(reservations & ticketing), fax: 267
3216; airport: 535 2021.

Pakistan International,
Chongkolnee Bldg., 2nd Floor, 56
Suriwongse Road. Tel: 234 2961/5
(reservations & ticketing), fax: 234
2357; airport: 535 2127/9.
Philippine Airlines, Chongkolnee
Bldg., 1st Floor, 56 Suriwongse
Road. Tel: 233 2350/2
(reservations & ticketing), fax: 234
8455; airport: 531 1021.
Qantas, Abdulrahim Place, 14th
Floor, 990 Rama IV Road. Tel: 636
1747 (reservations), 636 1770
(ticketing), fax: 636 1749
(reservations), 636 1748
(ticketing); airport: 535 2220.
Royal Brunei, Charn Issara Tower,
20th Floor, 942/135 Rama IV
Road. Tel: 233 0056, 233 0293
(reservations & ticketing), fax: 267
5036; airport: 535 2627.
Royal Air Cambodge (Cambodia),
Two Pacific Place Bldg., 17th Floor,
Room 1706, 142 Sukhumvit Road.
Tel: 653 2261/6 (reservations &
ticketing), fax: 653 2267; airport:
535 3781.
SAS, Glas Haus Bldg., 8th Floor,
Soi 25, Sukhumvit Road. Tel: 260
0444 (reservations & ticketing),
fax: 260 6269; airport: 535 2716.
Singapore Airlines, Silom Centre
Bldg., 12th Floor, 2 Silom Road. Tel:
236 0440 (reservations &
ticketing), fax: 236 5294; airport:
535 2260.
Swiss Air, Abdulrahim Place, 21st
Floor, 990 Rama IV Road. Tel: 636
2160/5 (reservations & ticketing),
fax: 636 2168; airport: 535
2371/2.
Thai Airways, head office: 89
Vibhavadi Rangsit Road, tel: 513
0121 (general), 545 1175/6, 280
0060 (reservations), 545 3691
(ticketing), fax: 628 0111
(reservations), 691 5007
(ticketing); Larnluang branch office:
6 Larnluang Road, tel: 280 0100,
280 0119 (general), 628 2000
(reservations), 280 0119, ext.
1766 (ticketing); fax: 628 2486,
628 0111 (reservations), 280
1748 (ticketing); Silom branch
office: 485 Silom Road, tel: 234
3100/19 (general), 628 2000
(reservations), 266 8307
(ticketing), fax: 628 0111
(reservations), 237 4114

(ticketing); airport: 535 4646/8
(domestic), 535 2836/7
(international).
United Airlines, Regent House,
19th Floor, 183 Ratchadamri Road.
Tel: 253 0558 (reservations), 253
0559 (ticketing), fax: 251 4406;
airport: 535 2231/2.
Vietnam Airlines, Ploenchit Centre
Bldg., Soi 2, Sukhumvit Road. Tel:
656 9056/8 (reservations &
ticketing), fax: 656 9101; airport:
535 2671, 535 5327.

Chiang Mai
Thai Airways, 240 Phra Poklao
Road. Tel: (53) 211 541, 210 042.

Phuket
Bangkok Airways, 158/2-3
Yaowarat Road. Tel: 225 033/5,
212 341.
China Airlines, 59/29 Bangkok
Road. Tel: 223 939/40.
Dragonair, 37/52 Montri Road. Tel:
217 300/1.
Malaysian Airlines, 1/8-9 Tungka
Road. Tel: 216 675, 213 749.
Silk Air, 183/10 Phangnga Road.
Tel: 213 891, 213 895.
Thai Airways, 78 Ranong Road. Tel:
212 946, 216 755, 216 678.

EMBASSIES

Australia, 37 Sathorn Tai Road. Tel:
287 2680. Visas: 8am–12.30pm.
Austria, 14 Soi Nantha, Sathorn Tai
Road. Tel: 287 3970/2. Visas:
9am–noon.
Belgium, 44 Soi Pipat, off Silom
Road. Tel: 236 0150. Visas:
8am–noon.
Brunei, 154 Soi 14, Soi 63 (Soi
Ekamai), Sukhumvit Road. Tel: 381
5914/6, fax: 381 5921. Visas:
8.30–11.30am.
Burma, 132 Sathorn Nua Road. Tel:
233 2237, 234 4698. Visas:
8.30am–noon.
Canada, Boonmitr Bldg., 11th Floor,
138 Silom Road. Tel: 237 4126.
Visas: 8–11am.
China, 57 Ratchadapisek Road. Tel:
245 7032, 245 7044, 247 7554,
fax: 246 8247. Visas: 9am–noon.
Denmark, 10 Soi 1 (Soi Atthakan
Prasit), Sathorn Tai Road. Tel: 213
2021/5. Visas: 9am–1pm (Friday:
9am–noon).

France, 35 Soi 36 (Soi Rong Phasi Kao), Charoen Krung (New) Road. Tel: 266 8250. Visas: 8.30am–noon, issued by Consular Section, 29 Sathorn Tai Road. Tel: 287 2585/7.

Germany, 9 Sathorn Tai Road. Tel: 287 9000, fax: 287 1776. Visas: 8–11am.

Indonesia, 600 Phetburi Road. Tel: 252 3135/40. Visas: 8am–4pm.

Israel, Ocean Tower II, 25th Floor, 75 Soi 19, Sukhumvit Road. Tel: 260 4854/9, fax: 260 4860. Visas: 8am–noon.

Italy, 399 Nang Linchi Road. Tel: 285 4090, fax: 285 4793. Visas: 8.30–11.30am.

Korea (South), 23 Thiam Ruam Mit Road, off Ratchadapisek Road (near Thai Cultural Centre). Tel: 247 7537/9. Visas: 8.30am–noon and 1.30–4.30pm.

Laos, 520 and 502/1-3 Soi 39, Ramkhamhaeng Road. Tel: 539 6667, fax: 539 6678. Visas: 9am–4pm.

Malaysia, Regent House, 183 Ratchadamri Road. Tel: 254 1706; fax: 253 8970. Visas: 8.30–11.30am.

Netherlands, 106 Witthayu Road. Tel: 254 7701/5. Visas: 9am–noon.

New Zealand, 93 Witthayu Road. Tel: 254 2530. Visas: 8am–noon.

Pakistan, 31 Soi 3 (Soi Nana Nua), Sukhumvit Road. Tel: 253 0288/90. Visas: 9am–noon.

Philippines, 760 Sukhumvit Road (opposite Soi 47). Tel: 259 0139/40. Visas: 9am–4pm.

Singapore, 129 Sathorn Tai Road. Tel: 286 2111, 286 1434. Visas: 9am–noon.

Sri Lanka, Ocean Tower II, 13th Floor, Soi 19, Sukhumvit Road. Tel: 261 1934/8. Visas: 8.30am–noon.

Switzerland, 35 Witthayu Road. Tel: 253 0156/60. Visas: 9am–noon.

United Kingdom, 1031 Witthayu Road. Tel: 253 0191/9. Visas: 8–11am, (Friday: 8am–noon).

United States, 120/122 Witthayu Road. Tel 205 4000. Visas: 7am–3pm.

Vietnam, 83/1 Witthayu Road. Tel: 251 5836, 251 5838, fax: 251 7203, 254 4730. Visas: 8.30–11am and 1.30–4pm.

BANKS

Bangkok

Banks in Bangkok include Thai institutions as well as branches of foreign banks. Most are equipped to handle telegraph and telex money transfers and a wide range of money services. In the provinces, the services are much more restricted. If you have overseas business to conduct with a bank, it is better to do it in Bangkok.

Thai Banks

Bank of Asia, 191 Sathorn Tai Road. Tel: 287 2211/3, fax: 287 2973/4.

Bank of Ayutthaya, 550 Ploenchit Road. Tel: 255 0022, 255 0033.

Bangkok Bank, 333 Silom Road. Tel: 231 4333.

First Bangkok City Bank, 20 Yukon Road. Tel: 223 0501, fax: 255 3036.

Krung Thai Bank, 35 Sukhumvit Road. Tel: 255 2222, fax: 255 9391.

Siam City Bank, 1101 New Phetburi Road. Tel: 253 0200/9, fax: 208 5489.

Siam Commercial Bank, 9 Ratchadapisek Road. Tel: 256 1234.

Thai Farmers Bank, 400 Phaholyothin Road. Tel: 470 1122.

Thai Military Bank, 3000 Phaholyothin Road. Tel: 299 1111, fax: 273 7121/4.

Overseas Banks

Bank of America, 2/2 Witthayu Road. Tel: 251 6333, fax: 253 1905.

Bank of Tokyo, Harindhorn Tower, 2nd Floor, 54 Sathorn Nua Road. Tel: 266 3011, fax: 266 3055.

Banque Indosuez, 152 Witthayu Road. Tel: 651 4590/2, fax: 651 4574.

Banque Nationale de Paris, Dusit Thani Bldg., 5th Floor, 946 Rama IV Road. Tel: 651 5678/84.

Chase Manhattan Bank, Bubhajit Bldg., 2nd Floor, 20 Sathorn Nua Road. Tel: 234 5992/5, 238 1720/4, fax: 234 8386.

Citibank, 82 Sathorn Nua Road. Tel: 232 2484, fax: 639 2560.

Deutsche Bank, 208 Witthayu Rd. Tel: 651 5000, fax: 651 5151.

Hongkong Bank, Hongkong Bank Bldg., 64 Silom Road. Tel: 233 5995, fax: 236 7687.

Sakura Bank, Boonmitr Bldg., 1st Floor, 138 Silom Road. Tel: 234 3841/8, fax: 236 8920, 634 2383.

Standard Chartered Bank, 990 Rama IV Road. Tel: 636 1000, fax: 636 1198.

Chiang Mai

Bangkok Bank, 53-59 Ta Pae Road. Tel: 272 938. Kiosk open 8.30am–8.30pm.

Bank of Asia, 149/1-3 Chang Klan Road. Tel: 270 029/30. Kiosk open 8.30am–8pm.

Bank of Ayutthaya, 222-6 Ta Pae Road. Tel: 252 446, 252 441. Kiosk open 8.30am–8pm.

Krung Thai Bank, 298/1 Ta Pae Road. Tel: 214 696, 225 738. Kiosk open 8.30am–4.30pm.

Siam Commercial Bank, 17 Ta Pae Road. Tel: 273 171, 274 520. Kiosk open 8.30am–7pm.

Thai Farmers Bank, 194, Chotana Road. Tel: 222 897. Kiosk open 8.30am–6pm.

Thai Military Bank, 207 Chang Moi Road. Tel: 251 058/9. Kiosk open 8.30am–6pm.

Phuket

Bangkok Bank, 22 Phangnga Road. Tel: 211 292/5.

Bank of Ayutthaya, 64 Rasda Road. Tel: 211 577.

Siam City Bank, 33/124 Patak Road, Karon. Tel: 396 095.

Siam Commercial Bank, 66 Rasda Road. Tel: 212 254/5.

Siam Commercial Bank, 89/2-4 Beach Road, Patong. Tel: 321 467.

Thai Military Bank, 76/3 Ranong Road. Tel: 212 123, 212 978.

RELIGIOUS SERVICES

Bangkok

Christian

Assumption Cathedral, 23 Oriental Lane, Charoen Krung Road. Tel: 234 8556. Sunday Mass: 10am.

Calvary Baptist Church, 88 Soi 2, Sukhumvit Road. Tel: 251 8278. Service: 10.45am.

Holy Redeemer Catholic Church,

123/19 Soi Ruam Rudi, Witthayu Road. Tel: 256 6305, 256 6578. Sunday Mass: 8.30am, 9.45am, 11am and 5.30pm.
International Christian Assembly, 196 Soi Ekamai, Sukhumvit Road. Tel: 391 4387. Services: 10.30am.
International Church of Bangkok, Student Christian Centre, 328 Phaya Thai Road (near Asia Hotel). Tel: 258 5821. Service: 9.30am.
St. Louis Church, 215/2 Sathorn Tai Road. Tel: 211 0220. Sunday Mass: 6am, 8am, 10am, 11.15am and 5.30pm.

Hindu
Thamsapha Association, 50 Soi Wat Prok, Charoen Krung (New) Road. Tel: 211 3840. Services: 7am–10pm.

Jewish
Jewish Association of Thailand (Ashkenazi), Jewish Community Centre, 121 Soi 2, Soi 22 (Soi Sai Nam Thip), Sukhumvit Road. Tel: 258 2195, fax: 663 0245. Services: Friday evenings and holidays.
Even Chen Synagogue (Sephardic), The Bossotel Inn, 55/12-14 Charoen Krung (New) Road (near Oriental Hotel). Tel: 630 6120, fax: 237 3225. Services: daily at 8am, Friday at sundown, Saturday at 9am. Shabbat meals at synagogue by advance reservation.

Muslim
Sha-Roh-Tal Islam Mosque, 133 Soi I Sukhapiban Road. Tel: 328 8950.

Sikh
Wat Sirikurusing Saha, 565 Chakraphet Road. Tel: 221 1011. Services: 6am and 5pm.

Practical Tips

Emergencies

SECURITY AND CRIME
If you run into trouble in Bangkok, the **police emergency number is 191**. There are also Tourist Police assigned specially to assist travelers, and who are more likely to speak English.

When in Thailand, avoid:
• Touts posing as Boy Scouts soliciting donations on Bangkok's sidewalks. The real Boy Scouts obtain funds from other sources.
• Touts on Patpong offering upstairs live-sex shows. Once inside, one is handed an exorbitant bill and threatened with mayhem if he or she protests. Pay, take the receipt, and go immediately to the Tourist Police to gain restitution, which may or may not be forthcoming. (If you do venture into one of these establishments, keep track of the number of drinks you order and check your bill carefully.)
• Persons offering free or very cheap boat rides into the canals. Once you are well into the canal, you are given the choice of paying a high fee or being stranded.
• Persons offering to take you to a gem factory for a "special deal." The gems are usually flawed and there's no way to get a refund.
• Persons on buses or trains offering sweets, fruits or soft drinks. The items may be drugged and the passenger is robbed while unconscious. This is unfortunate because Thais are generous people and it is normal for them to offer food to strangers. Use discretion.

The **Tourist Police headquarters**

is at 29/1 Soi Lang Suan, Ploenchit Road, tel: 255 2964; another office is at the Tourist Assistance Centre at the Tourism Authority of Thailand headquarters at 372 Bamrung Muang Road, tel: 282 8129; or they can be reached by simply dialling 1699. Tourist police booths can also be found in many tourist areas including Lumpini Park (near the intersection of Rama IV and Silom Roads) and Patpong (at the Silom Road intersection). Most members of the force speak English. Their offices can be found in Chiang Mai, Pattaya and Phuket as well. In Chiang Mai, they are located below the Tourist Authority of Thailand office at 105/1 Chiang Mai-Lamphun Road. Tel: 248 604/5, 248 607. In Pattaya, their office is on Second Road, near Soi 6. Tel: 429 371 or 1699. In Phuket, go to the TAT office at 73-75 Phuket Road. Tel: 212 213, 211 036.

Medical Services

HOSPITALS
First-class hotels in Bangkok, Chiang Mai and Phuket have doctors on call for medical emergencies. The hospitals in these three destinations are the equivalent of those in any major Western city. Intensive-care units are fully equipped and staffed by doctors to handle emergencies quickly and competently. Nursing care is generally superb, because there is a higher staff-to-patient ratio. Many doctors have been trained in Western hospitals, and even those who have not speak good English.
  Most small towns have clinics which treat minor ailments and accidents. In the unlikely event that you suffer a criminal attack in Bangkok, you must go to a police hospital, normally the one at the Ratchaprasong intersection.

Bangkok
BNH Hospital, 9 Convent Road. Tel: 632 0560, 632 0582/6. All major specialties, several Western doctors, convenient to the Silom Road area.

Samitivej Hospital, 133 Soi 49, Sukhumvit Road. Tel: 392 0010/9, 655 1024/5. Popular with expatriates living in the area.
Thai Nakharin Hospital, 345 Bang Na Trat Road. Tel: 361 2712/61. All major specialties represented by mostly US-trained doctors, excellent ambulance service.

Chiang Mai
Lanna Hospital, off the super highway on the north side of town. Tel: 211 037.
McCormick Hospital, on Kaeo Nawarat Road, on the northeastern edge of town. Tel: 241 311/2.
Suan Dok Hospital, on the corner of Boonruangrit and Suthep roads, across from Wat Suan Dok. Tel: 221 122.

Pattaya
Pattaya International Hospital, Soi 4, Second Road. Tel: 428 374/5.
Phyathai Siracha General, 90 Si Racha Nakorn Road, Si Racha, Chonburi. Tel: 770 200/8.
Pattaya Memorial, 328/1 Pattaya/Klaeng Road. Tel: 429 422/4.

Phuket
Bangkok-Phuket Hospital, 2/1 Hongyok Utit Road, Phuket town. Tel: 254 421/9. Emergency, ext. 1060.
Patong-Kathu Hospital, Sawatdirak Road, Patong Beach. Tel: 340 444.
Phuket International Hospital, Chalermprakiat Road, Phuket. Tel: 249 400. Emergencies: 210 935.

MEDICAL CLINICS

For minor problems, there are numerous clinics in all the major towns and cities. The **British Dispensary**, located at 109 Sukhumvit Road (between Soi 3 and 5), tel: 252 9179, has British doctors on its staff. In Chiang Mai, go to Loi Kroh Clinic on Loi Kroh Road, tel: 271 571. Most international hotels also have an on-premises clinic or doctor on call.

DENTAL CLINICS

Dental clinics are almost as numerous as medical clinics.

In Bangkok, one clinic with a long-standing reputation is the **Dental Polyclinic**, at 2111/2113 New Phetburi Road, tel: 314 5070. The **Dental Hospital**, Soi 49, Sukhumvit Road, tel: 260 5000/15, looks more like a hotel than a dental hospital and has the latest imported dental equipment.

In Chiang Mai, there is The **Dental Hospital**, 1/42 Mu 3, Chiang Mai-Lampang Superhighway. Tel: 411 150.

In Phuket town, the **Dental Care Clinic** is located at 62/5 Rasda Centre. Tel: 215 025.

STD CLINICS

Clinics along Ploenchit Road perform tests for sexually transmitted diseases; there are several similar clinics in Patpong. **Bangkok General Hospital**, Soi Soonvijai, New Phetburi Road, tel: 318 0066, is reputed to offer the most reliable tests for the presence of HIV, and **BNH Hospital** on Convent Road is a good source for HIV/AIDS information.

PHARMACIES

Pharmaceuticals are produced to the highest standards, and pharmacies must have a registered pharmacist on the premises. Most pharmacy personnel in the shopping and business areas speak English. Many prescription drugs in other countries can be bought, legally, over the counter in Thailand.

Pharmacies, or chemists, are everywhere in Bangkok; look for a green cross. Some of the more common ones are **Siam Drugs**, **People's Health & Beauty Care**, and **Boots**, an English chain which opened in Bangkok in late 1997.

In addition, many of the larger grocery stores have pharmacy counters with helpful personnel who generally speak passable English. Try branches of **Foodland**, **Central** or **Robinson**.

SNAKE BITES

There is little chance of being bitten by a poisonous snake in Bangkok or its environs, but should it occur, most clinics have anti-venom serum on hand. If they cannot acquire any, travel to the **Saowapha Institute** (Snake Farm) on Rama IV Road. They maintain sera against the bites of six types of cobras and vipers. Provincial clinics maintain a constant supply of anti-venom serum supplied by the Institute.

OTHER SERVICES

Counseling: Community Services of Bangkok, 15/1 Soi 33, Sukhumvit Road, tel: 258 4998, 258 5652, fax: 260 3563. **CSB** is a volunteer organization made up of foreigners to provide information and assistance to families living in Bangkok. They offer a counseling service, a telephone hotline (662 0979) and are always willing to help travelers with problems who have nowhere else to turn. In addition they offer interesting courses on a variety of subjects.

Group Meetings: Alcoholics Anonymous (AA) meets daily, and Al-Anon meetings are held on Saturdays, at Holy Redeemer Catholic Church, 123/19 Soi Ruam Rudi, Witthayu Road, tel: 256 6305, 256 6157; for information on Overeaters Anonymous (OA) and Narcotics Anonymous (NA) meetings, contact Community Services of Bangkok, tel: 258 4998, 258 5652.

Weights and Measures

Thailand uses the metric system of meters, grams and liters.

Business Hours

Government offices are open from 8.30am–4.30pm on Monday–Friday. Business hours are from 8am or 8.30am–5.30pm on Monday–Friday. Some businesses are open half days from 8.30am–noon on Saturdays. Banks are generally open from 10am–4pm, five days a week, but many operate money-changing kiosks throughout the city, which are open until 8pm, seven days a week.

The **General Post Office** in Bangkok is located on Charoen Krung (New) Road between Suriwongse and Si Phraya roads. It is open from 8am–8pm Monday–Friday, and from 8am–1pm on weekends and holidays.

Branch post offices are located throughout the city, and many of these usually stay open until 6pm. Kiosks along some of the city's busier streets sell stamps and aerograms and ship small parcels. Hotel reception counters will send letters for their guests at no charge. Most department stores are open 10am–9pm seven days a week.

Ordinary shops open at 8.30am or 9am and close between 6pm and 8pm, depending on the location and type of business. Some pharmacies in the major cities remain open all night. Small open-air coffee shops and restaurants open at 7am and close at 8.30pm though some stay open past midnight. Large restaurants generally close at 10pm. Most coffee shops close at midnight; some stay open 24 hours.

Tipping

Tipping is not a custom in Thailand, although it is becoming more prevalent. A service charge of 10 percent is generally included in restaurant bills and is divided among the staff. A bit extra for the waitress would not go unappreciated.

Do not tip non-metered taxi or *tuk-tuk* drivers unless the traffic has been particularly bad and he has been especially patient; 10 baht would suffice for a long journey over 60 baht. Hotel bellmen and room porters are becoming used to being tipped in urban centres but will not hover with hand extended.

Media

PRESS

The English language morning newspapers are one of the foreigner's lifelines to the outside world. There are two national English-language dailies – *Bangkok Post* and *The Nation*. The *Asian Wall Street Journal* is printed in Bangkok. The *International Herald Tribune* is available at most bookstalls after 4pm. Newsstands

in major hotel gift shops carry air-freighted, and therefore expensive, editions of British, French, American, German and Italian newspapers. Newsagents on Soi 3 (Soi Nana Nua), Sukhumvit Road also offer Arabic newspapers.

In addition, check out *Bangkok Metro*, a lush, well-put-together monthly magazine which features interesting writing; book, film & restaurant reviews; shopping information; and a calendar of Bangkok events, including sports and health pursuits, as well as activities for children. Several pages are devoted to happenings in Phuket and Samui.

In Pattaya, the weekly *Pattaya Mail* contains local news and features, as well as information on events, special offers and new facilities and services in the area.

RADIO

AM radio is devoted entirely to Thai-language programs. FM frequencies include Radio Thailand (92.5 FM) with a variety of English-language programs including a travel show in the late afternoon, and Chulalongkorn University (101.5) which plays jazz from 5pm–6pm and classical music from 8pm–10pm. Other popular stations can be found at 89 FM (Thai rock); 95.5 FM (English-speaking DJs playing hits from the 70s, 80s and 90s); 105 FM (easy listening with hourly international, local and traffic news); 107 FM (hits from the 50s through the 90s with hourly CNN broadcasts).

In addition, Voice of America, BBC World Service, Radio Canada, Radio Australia, Radio New Zealand, Radio France Internationale, Deutsche Welle, Singapore Broadcasting Company and Radio Japan all offer shortwave radio broadcasts in English and Thai throughout the day. Check newspapers for current frequencies and program schedules.

TELEVISION

Bangkok has five Thai language television channels, in addition to a variety of satellite and cable

television services: Satellite Television Asian Region (STAR), International Broadcasting Corporation (IBC), Thai Sky and UTV. BBC World, Australia TV, CNN, HBO, Discovery, TNT and ESPN, as well as other news, sports, music and entertainment programs, are widely available on these networks.

Postal Services

Thailand has a comprehensive and reliable postal service. Major towns offer regular air mail service, as well as express courier service that speeds a package to nearly every point on the globe.

Main post offices in Bangkok, Chiang Mai and Phuket have special facilities where stamp collectors can browse and buy from a wide selection of beautiful Thai stamps. In Bangkok, the General Post Office (GPO), on Charoen Krung (New) Road between Suriwongse and Si Phraya roads, tel: 233 1050/9, 235 2834, is open from 8am–8pm during the week, and from 8am–1pm on weekends and holidays. (Note that it will be easier to conduct business at the GPO in person, rather than relying on telephone service.) At the right side of the lobby is a packing service with boxes in various sizes; charges are nominal and depend on the size of the parcel. A separate building to the right of the main GPO provides telecommunications services (telephone, telegram, fax and telex) around the clock.

Branch post offices are located throughout the country. Hours vary but they generally close at 4.30pm, although some stay open as late as 6pm. Post office kiosks along some of the city's busier streets sell stamps, aerograms and ship small parcels. Hotel reception desks will also send letters and postcards for no extra charge.

Courier Service

A number of international courier agencies have offices in Bangkok: **DHL Worldwide**, Grand Amarin Tower, 22nd Floor, 1550 New

Phetburi Road. Tel: 207 0600, fax: 207 0630.
Federal Express, Green Tower, 8th Floor, Rama IV Road. Tel: 367 3222, fax: 367 3221.
TNT Express Worldwide, 599 Chong Non Si Road, Khlong Toey. Tel: 249 0242/6, 249 5702/6, 671 9300/13, fax: 249 1264.
United Parcel Service, 16/1 Soi 44, Sukhumvit Road. Tel: 712 3090, 254 5066 (cargo only); fax: 712 1818.

Telecommunications

Thailand has a sophisticated communications system, not that it always works; the lines have a way of getting jammed, like the traffic, especially after a heavy rain. Most hotels have telephone, telegram, e-mail, and fax facilities.

TELEPHONE
Most international telephone calls can be dialled direct from Bangkok. International telephone calls can be placed at the General Post Office (GPO) 24 hours a day. Most provincial capitals have telephone offices at the GPO; hours are generally 7am–11pm.

Area Codes
Thailand country code: 66
Bangkok: 02
Chiang Mai: 053
Chiang Rai: 053
Chiang Saen: 053
Chumphon: 077
Hat Yai: 074
Hua Hin: 032
Kanchanaburi: 034
Ko Samui: 077
Krabi/Ao Nang: 075
Mae Hong Son: 053
Mae Salong: 053
Nakhon Ratchasima (Khorat): 044
Pattaya/Jomtien: 038
Phang Nga: 076
Phi Phi: 075
Phuket: 076
Songkhla: 074
Sukhothai: 055
Surat Thani: 077

Note that any telephone number beginning with 01 indicates a cellular telephone, and the zero must be dialled. Note, also, that telephone calls to Malaysia do not require a country code; simply prefix the number, including the area code, with 09.

Operator Assistance
For directory assistance in Bangkok, dial 13; for assistance in the provinces, dial 183. There is a serious shortage of telephone lines in Bangkok, which is being addressed by the installation of an additional two million lines. The modernization has meant that some existing telephone numbers have changed, often with little advance notice. For information regarding changed telephone numbers, dial 233 1199 or 13.

For operator assistance with a **domestic call** (including those to Malaysia), dial 101; for assistance with an **international call** (including collect/reverse charges calls), dial 100. Note that calls to Laos must be operator-assisted; dial 101 for help. Operators at these numbers speak English.

International Telephone Calls
The international prefix from Thailand is 001. Home Direct is a service whereby one can reach an international operator in a number of countries worldwide. Home Direct is accessible from most private telephones, the GPO in Bangkok, many post office telephone offices in the provinces, and at the airports in Bangkok, Chiang Mai and Phuket. It is not, unfortunately, widely available from hotel telephones. To access Home Direct, dial 001 999, and then the following: Australia, 61 1000; Canada, 15 1000; Germany, 49 1000; Italy, 39 1000; New Zealand, 64 1066; United Kingdom, 44 1066; USA, 1111 (AT&T), 12001 (MCI), 13877 (Sprint).

TELEGRAM, E-MAIL AND FAX SERVICES
Main post offices in nearly every city offer telegram, telex and fax services to all parts of the world. Many small shops throughout the country also offer a variety of telephone and fax services, although the prices may be a little steep, particularly for faxes.

On-Line Access
Some of the larger hotels now offer Internet access and/or e-mail services; if this is a requirement for your stay in Bangkok, check in advance to make certain such facilities are available at the hotel of your choice. An option might be one of the Internet cafés and coffee houses which are becoming popular in Bangkok:
Byte in a Cup, Siam Discovery Centre, 4th Floor, Room 401, 989 Rama I Road. Tel: 658 0433/5, fax: 658 0436, website: www.byte-in-a-cup.com. Daily 10am–7pm. Elegant coffee house, convenient location, but busy.
Cyber Café, Ploenchit Centre, 2nd Floor, Sukhumvit Road (between expressway and Soi 2). Tel: 656 8472/3, email: cybercafe @chomanan.co.th; website: www.cybercafe.co.th. Daily 10am–10pm. Spacious, but a little out of the way. Over 20 terminals, non-smoking bar. Several other locations, including one at Don Muang International Airport, Terminal 2 (opposite John Bull Pub). Tel: 535 5671. Daily 24 hours. Note that foreigners are charged more than Thais.
Cyber Pub, Dusit Thani Hotel, 946 Rama IV Road. Tel: 236 0450, ext. 2971. Ten terminals with charges of 5 baht per minute; food and beverages available.
Cyberia, 654/8 Sukhumvit Road (corner Soi 24). Tel: 259 3356/7, fax: 259 3358, email: svars@cyberia.co.th, website: www.cyberia.co.th. Daily 10.30am–11pm. Bangkok's most popular Internet café. Beer, wine, Italian menu.
HelloPub, Hello Guest House, 1st Floor, 63-65 Khao San Road. Tel: 281 8579, email: hellopub@loxinfo.co.th. Daily 10am–10pm. Three terminals, coffee, snacks. Convenient to many inexpensive guesthouses.

Getting Around

BANGKOK AIRPORT

From Bangkok's Don Muang International Airport, the journey along the expressway into the city can take from 30 minutes to one hour or more, depending on traffic conditions. Larger hotels will often send a limousine to meet their guests, if arranged before arrival.

Mini-bus/Limousine Service: Thai Airways runs both a mini-bus (100 baht) and limousine service (350 baht) from the airport to the major hotels. The limousines, while more expensive than any other mode of transport, may be the most convenient way into Bangkok, particularly during rush hour. Because they have to fight traffic to deliver their passengers to various hotels around the city, the mini-buses can take considerable time to get you to your hotel.

Airport Bus: In 1996, a special express bus service began operations from the airport to three areas of Bangkok: **route A1** goes to the Silom Road area; **route A2** goes to central Bangkok, including Chinatown, and **route A3** runs along Sukhumvit Road. Detailed maps of the routes are available at the bus counter (to the left of the taxi counter); the fare is 70 baht.

Taxis: You can book an air-conditioned public taxi at the taxi counter at the left-hand side of the arrivals hall. The fare is determined according to your destination, and should be around 200 baht for most points in the city. The clerk will write down your destination and the price. Give this ticket to the taxi driver, and pay him the price noted

on it when you arrive at your destination. Occasionally, someone may approach you in the arrivals hall in an attempt to sell you a similar ticket for a vastly inflated price. Needless to say, he should be ignored.

It's also theoretically possible to get a metered taxi into town from the airport; in practice, however, the drivers often refuse to turn on the meter in favour of seeing how much you're willing to pay for the trip. Note that if you do find a metered taxi willing to take you into Bangkok, you will be liable for the additional 30-baht expressway fee. On the other hand, if you arrange your taxi through the taxi counter for a set fee, the expressway surcharge, if any, should be included in the price.

Public Buses: For economy-minded travelers, air-conditioned buses – Nos. 4, 13, and 29 – stop in front of the airport. The trip into town costs 16 baht. The last buses leave about 8pm.

For the **return trip to the airport**, the Thai Airways limousine service has in-town offices at Montien Hotel, tel: 233 7060, and Asia Hotel, tel: 215 0780. Most major hotels have airconditioned limousines, often available to non-guests if you book in advance. Non-metered taxis make the trip for 150–250 baht depending on traffic conditions. Metered taxis will be less expensive if there are no traffic jams on the way.

International and domestic transfer: The 500-m trip between Bangkok's international and domestic airports is by way of a free shuttle bus at 15-minute intervals from 6am–11pm.

CHIANG MAI AIRPORT

Chiang Mai's airport is a 10-minute drive from the city centre. There is frequent bus service, but it runs a circuitous route, and visitors with a lot of luggage might prefer the following modes of transportation:

Limousines: Major hotels have limousines to ferry guests with reservations (one can make a reservation at the airport) to their

premises. They charge about 100 baht per person.

Mini-bus: Thai Airways operates a mini-bus between the airport and its town office on Phra Poklao Road. The cost each way is 20 baht per passenger. You must find your way from the office to the hotel.

PHUKET AIRPORT

Limousines: Thai Airways offers air-conditioned limousines to each beach. The price is computed per vehicle, and each vehicle holds up to four persons.

Mini-bus: Major hotels maintain mini-buses to ferry guests with reservations (it is possible to make a reservation at the airport) to and from the airport. The Thai Airways mini-bus runs hourly between the airport and its Phuket town office on Ranong Road. You must then find your own way from the office to the hotel.

BY AIR

The domestic arm of Thai Airways operates a network of daily flights to 21 of Thailand's major towns aboard a fleet of 737s and Airbuses. From Bangkok, there are daily flights to Nakhon Si Thammarat, Narathiwat, Trang, Nan, Phrae, Nakhon Phanom and Sakon Nakhon; two flights daily to Surat Thani, Lampang, Nakhon Ratchasima and Ubon Ratchathani; three flights daily to Udon Thani; four flights daily to Chiang Rai and Khon Kaen; five flights daily to Phitsanulok; six flights daily to Hat Yai; eight to ten daily flights to Chiang Mai; a dozen daily flights to Phuket; and five flights a week to Buri Ram. Connections to Mae Hong Son and Mae Sot are made via Chiang Mai (four flights daily) and Phitsanulok (four flights a week) respectively. Thai Airways offers a "Discover Thailand" visitor's pass, allowing four domestic flights, for about US$250. Certain conditions apply, notably that this pass must be purchased outside Thailand. Contact a Tourism Authority of Thailand (TAT) office for further details. In addition, Bangkok Airways, Thailand's first privately owned domestic airline, flies from Bangkok to Ko Samui more than a dozen times daily; to Sukhothai and Chiang Mai twice daily; and to Ranong at least once daily.

Note that if you are planning a trip to the tropical island of Ko Samui from Bangkok, you will save much traveling time if you go by air, a journey of less than two hours; the same trip by road and boat may take as long as 14 hours.

BY RAIL

The State Railways of Thailand operates three principal routes from Hua Lampong Station. The northern route passes through Ayutthaya, Phitsanulok, Lampang and terminates at Chiang Mai. The northeastern route passes through Ayutthaya, Saraburi, Nakhon Ratchasima, Khon Kaen, Udon Thani and terminates at Nong Khai. The southern route crosses the Rama VI bridge and calls at Nakhon Pathom, Phetchaburi, Hua Hin and Chumphon. It branches at Hat Yai, one branch running southwest through Betong and on down the western coast of Malaysia to Singapore. The southeastern branch goes via Pattani and Yala to the Thai border opposite the Malaysian town of Kota Bharu.

In addition, there is a line from Makkasan to Aranya Prathet on the Cambodian border.

Another line leaves Bangkok Noi station, in Thonburi, on the western bank of the Chao Phraya River, for Kanchanaburi and other destinations in western Thailand. There is also a short route leaving Bangkok Noi that travels west along the rim of the Gulf of Thailand to Samut Sakhon and then on to Samut Songkram.

Express and rapid services on the main lines offer first-class, air-conditioned or second-class, fan-cooled cars with sleeping cabins or berths and dining cars. There are also special air-conditioned express day coaches that travel to key towns along the main lines. 20-day rail passes are available.

Reservations can be made at the station or with any travel agent within 30 days prior to departure.

In Bangkok, details from: **Hua Lampong Station**: Rama IV Road. Tel: 233 7010, 233 7020 (information), 223 3762, 224 7788, 225 6964 (reservations), fax: 225 6068. **Bangkok Noi (Thonburi) Station**, Arun Amarin Road (near Siriraj Hospital). Tel: 411 3102.

Note that it is often difficult to get through to the train station by telephone; it may prove nearly impossible to get through to anyone who speaks English. A better alternative may be to book your train trip through your hotel or a local travel agency. There will likely be a small additional service charge, but it will save heartburn and headaches.

Also, make certain that you know from which station your train leaves, particularly if you are travelling west to Kanchanaburi.

BY ROAD

Bus service is reliable, frequent and very affordable to most destinations in Thailand. Rest stops are regular, and in some cases limited refreshments are available on the bus.

Fan-cooled buses, painted orange, are the slowest since they makes stops in every village along the way. For short distances, they can be an entertaining means of travel, particularly in the cool season when the fan and the open windows make the trip reasonably comfortable.

Blue air-conditioned buses, however, are generally a faster, more reliably comfortable way to get to your destination. VIP buses are available on some of the longer routes; these usually have larger seats, more leg room and toilets.

Bus Stations

For bus and coach journeys to destinations outside of Bangkok, the major terminals are:

Eastern, Sukhumvit Road, opposite Soi 63 (Soi Ekamai). Tel: 391

2504, 391 9829, 392 2520/1. Departures for Pattaya, Rayong, Chanthaburi.
Northern and Northeastern, Moh Chit, Phaholyothin Road. Tel: 271 0101/5, 279 4484/7, 271 2961. Departures for Ayutthaya, Lopburi, Nakhon Ratchasima, Chiang Mai.
Southern, Boromrat Chonnani Road (western bank of Chao Phraya). Tel: 435 1199/1200, 391 9829, 435 0511, 434 5557/8. Departures for Nakhon Pathom, Kanchanaburi, Phuket, Surat Thani.

To reach a small town from a large one, or to get around on some of the islands, *song taos* (meaning two benches), pick-up trucks with benches along either side of the bed, function as taxis.

Public Transport

BANGKOK

Taxis, Tuk-Tuks & Motorcycles
There are two types of taxi available in Bangkok, metered and non-metered. Both are air-conditioned and reliable, but the drivers' command of English is usually minimal. This might present a problem, not only in conveying your destination, but with non-metered taxis, in bargaining the price.

Do not step into a non-metered taxi without having first agreed on a price, which can fluctuate depending on the hour of the day and the amount of traffic, rain, and the number of one-way streets he must negotiate. The base fare for all journeys is 30 baht. Taxi drivers do not charge you an extra fee for baggage stowage or extra passengers, and there is no tipping. Check at hotels for typical fares.

The metered taxis are a much better choice if you do not know the precise distance to your intended destination. If you know Bangkok well, you might be able to negotiate a price below that which you would pay for a metered taxi. However, taxi drivers are experts at outwitting their less knowledgeable passengers, so if you are just a casual tourist, stick to the metered taxis. The minimum basic fare is 35 baht, and it rises in two-baht increments depending on the length of time and distance involved in the trip. Make sure the driver of the metered taxi does, in fact, turn his meter on after you get in.

Occasionally a driver will try to negotiate a flat fare from you instead of turning on his meter; this practice is particularly common in the area of the World Trade Centre and the Erawan Shrine. Sometimes the fare quoted amounts to thievery; you will nearly always get a better rate from a metered taxi. Note that any trips made along the expressway ("highway" to some drivers) will involve an additional toll of 30 baht, which you will be expected to pay. Also, most taxi drivers do not maintain a ready supply of small change; it's best not to offer anything larger than a 100-baht note in payment of fare.

If the English fluency of taxi drivers is limited, that of *tuk-tuk* (also called *samlor*, meaning three wheels) drivers is even less. *Tuk-tuks* are the brightly coloured three-wheeled taxis whose nickname comes from the noise their two-cycle engines make. They are fun for short trips, but choose a taxi for longer journeys, particularly during the heat of the day. A tuk-tuk driver on an open stretch of road can seldom resist racing, and the resultant journey can be a hair-raising experience. For very short trips, the fare is 20 baht.

As the traffic situation continues to worsen in Bangkok, motorcycle taxis have proliferated; their drivers wear single-colour vests. Passengers are required to wear helmets on the major roads, but the drivers do not always supply them. Be aware that in the case of an accident, not a rare occurrence, the driver will likely not hold any insurance. In spite of the risks, this means of travel is worthy of consideration when the streets are hopelessly deadlocked.

Note that Wireless Road, location of many embassies, a large hotel and several banks, is more commonly known by its Thai name, Thanon Witthayu. Similarly, Sathorn Road, a main thoroughfare divided into north and south which runs between Lumpini Park and the river, is often referred to as Sathorn Nua (north) and Sathorn Tai (south). A certain amount of confusion can be avoided if you have your destination written in Thai to hand to the driver.

Buses and Mini-buses

Bangkok buses come in four varieties: executive, air-conditioned, ordinary, and the green mini-buses. They operate every two or three minutes along more than 100 routes and are an excellent way to see the outer areas of the city. Bus maps give the routes for all types of city buses.

Buses are especially useful during rush hours when traveling up one-way streets, like parts of Sukhumvit Road, because they can speed along specially marked bus lanes going against on-coming traffic. Conductors prowl through the aisles collecting fares and issuing tickets. Unfortunately, destinations are only noted in Thai so a bus map is needed. Most routes cease operating around midnight, though some run all through the night.

Red executive micro-buses hold 20 seated passengers in air-conditioned comfort; they charge a fare of 30 baht regardless of the destination, but serve fewer routes. Ordinary buses come in two varieties: red and white (more expensive) and blue and white. Aside from the price, there is no difference in service routes. Both can be very crowded. (It is a sight to see one listing heavily to one side while students cling to the open doors.) Their drivers are the cowboys of the road and usually drive in very colourful fashion. Some drivers deck out their buses with stereo sets; others even have television sets, though on bumpy roads the reception is less than perfect. Note that pocket-picking and bag-slashing is not an uncommon occurrence on Bangkok buses. Keep your wallet in a front pocket and your bag in front of you at all times.

Mass Transit Projects

Several mass transit projects are in various stages of planning or construction in Bangkok. Bangkok Metropolitan Authority has plans for a subway and elevated rail system (Hua Lampong-Khlong Toey-Lard Prao) as well as the addition of several more elevated expressways.

Unfortunately, the economic crisis of the late 1990s put many of these projects on hold. When they will be completed is anyone's guess, but visitors will see the half-completed work everywhere in downtown Bangkok

Skytrain, an ambitious elevated rail system, will link Phra Khanong-Bang Seu and Sathorn-Lard Prao initially; other lines will follow. Although this project was first proposed in 1986, construction did not begin until 1994. The **Bangkok Elevated Road and Train System (BERTS)**, a US$3.2 billion project, envisions 60 kilometers (35 mi) of elevated rail lines and nearly 50 kilometers (30 mi) of additional expressways around Bangkok, much of it stacked one on top of the other. Although a certain amount of preliminary construction has been undertaken for this project, serious problems arose with the Hong Kong-based contractor. It is possible that Bangkok's Metropolitan Rapid Transit Authority (MRTA) may assume control of this endeavour. Finally, MRTA has its own plans for a 21-kilometer (13-mi) subway system, encompassing 18 stations and running from Hua Lampong to Bang Seu via Huay Khwang. Other proposals have involved construction of a monorail "beltway" around Bangkok and introduction of a tram system in the heavily congested area of the Grand Palace, Wat Phra Kaeo and the National Museum.

Sadly, each of these projects has suffered from interdepartmental bickering and a lack of central administration. The absence of cohesive oversight resulted in frequent route changes, land expropriation problems and no real solution to Bangkok's traffic.

Boats

Chao Phraya River express boats (white with red trim) run regular routes at 15- to 20-minute intervals up and down the Chao Phraya River, going all the way to Nonthaburi, 10 km (6 mi) north of the city. The service begins at 6am and ceases at 6pm. Fares are 5–10 baht depending on the distance, and are collected on board.

Ferries, often red, cross the river at dozens of points and cost just a couple of baht per journey. They begin operating at 6am and stop at midnight. It is also possible to catch a long-tail taxi to many points along the Chao Phraya or the canals; it helps to be fairly familiar with the waterways before doing so. Fares begin at 5 baht.

CHIANG MAI

Buses: Chiang Mai has red mini-buses known locally as *song tao*. They are prepared to carry passengers almost anywhere within the town.

Tuk-tuk: They charge according to distance, starting at 10 baht. You must bargain for the price before you get in.

Samlor: These pedal trishaws charge 5 baht for short distances. Bargain before you board.

PHUKET

Buses: Picturesque wooden buses ply regular routes from the market to the beaches. They depart every 30 minutes between 8am and 6pm between Phuket town market and all beaches except Rawai and Nai Harn. Buses to Rawai and Nai Harn leave from the traffic circle on Bangkok Road. They prowl the beach roads in search of passengers. Flag one down, 15–20 baht per person.

Tuk-tuk: The small cramped *tuk-tuks* function as taxis. They'll go anywhere. Barter your fare before getting on. For example, Patong to Karon, 120 baht, Patong to airport, 300 baht. Within town is 10–20 baht if shared.

Motorcycle taxis: 10–20 baht per ride. A convenient if dangerous way to get around.

Private Transport

LIMOUSINES

Most major hotels operate air-conditioned limousine services. Although the prices are at least twice those of ordinary taxis, they offer the comfort and convenience of English-speaking drivers and door-to-door service.

RENTAL CARS

Thailand has a good road system with over 50,000 km (31,000 mi) of paved highways, and more are being built every year. Road signs are in both Thai and English, and you should have no difficulty following a map. An international driver's license is required.

Driving on a narrow but busy road can be a terrifying experience; right of way is generally determined by size. It is not unusual for a bus to overtake a truck despite the fact that the oncoming lane is filled with vehicles. It is little wonder that, when collisions occur, several dozen lives are lost. In addition, many of the long-distance drivers consume pep pills and have the throttle to the floor because they are getting paid for beating schedules. One is strongly advised to avoid driving at night for this reason. When dusk comes, pull in at a hotel and get an early start the next morning.

Avis, Hertz and numerous local agencies offer late-model cars with and without drivers, and with insurance coverage for Bangkok and upcountry trips. A deposit is usually required except with credit cards.

In the provinces, agencies can be found in major towns like Chiang Mai, Pattaya and Phuket. These also rent four-wheel-drive jeeps and mini-buses. When renting a jeep, read the fine print carefully and be aware that you are liable for all damages to the vehicle. Ask for first class insurance, which covers both you and the other vehicle involved in a collision.

Bangkok

Although Avis has a desk at the international terminal at Don Muang Airport, and Hertz one at the domestic terminal, the general practice is for car rental agencies to deliver the car to your hotel; you fill out the rental agreement there. Check the brakes and air conditioning, and make certain to read the fine print for insurance terms before accepting the car.

Avis, 2/12 Witthayu Road. Tel: 255 5300/4; airport: 535 4031/2.
Hertz, 1526/40 Patanakarn Road. Tel: 722 6151/61; airport: 535 3004.
Grand Car Rent, 233-5 Asoke-Dindaeng Road (near Rama IX intersection). Tel: 248 2991/2.
Khlong Toey Car Rent, 1921 Rama IV Road. Tel: 251 9856.
Sathorn Car Rent, 6/8-9 Sathorn Nua Road. Tel: 633 8888.
SMT Rent-a-Car, 931/11 Rama I Road, (opposite National Stadium). Tel: 216 4436, 216 8020.

Chiang Mai

Avis, 14/14 Huay Kaeo Road. Tel: 222 013, 221 316.
Hertz, 90 Sri Dornchai Road. Tel: 279 474. Branch at Suriwongse Hotel, tel: 270 051.
Car Rent, 49 Chang Klan Road (opposite the Night Bazaar). Tel: 249 197.

Pattaya

Budget, 333/1 Moo 6, Sukhumvit Road, Naklua, Banglamung. Tel: 726 185, 422 149/50.
Via, 215/15-18 Second Road, South Pattaya. Tel: 426 242.

Phuket

Budget, opposite airport. Tel: 205 396/7. Good for Suzuki Caribians. Free delivery.
Pure Car Rent, 75 Rasda Road, Phuket town. Tel: 211 002.
Via, 70/85 Rata Utit Road, Patong. Tel: 341 660.

MOTORCYCLE RENTAL

Motorcycles can be rented in Chiang Mai, Pattaya and Phuket (just about everywhere, in fact) for economical rates. Remember that when you rent a motorcycle, you must surrender your passport for the duration of the rental period.

Motorcycles range in size from small 90cc models to giant 750cc behemoths. The majority are 125cc trailbikes. Rental outlets can be found along beach roads and main roads in each town.

It is not uncommon for rental motorcycles to be stolen; lock them up when not in use, and only park them in areas with supervision.

On Foot/Hitchhiking

There are not many places one can walk in Thailand, other than national parks like Khao Yai and Phu Kradung. It is possible to hitch a ride on ten-wheel trucks but it is not advisable; if female, you are asking for trouble. It is strongly recommended that you do not travel at night on trucks, as the drivers are often tanked up on amphetamines and cause some of Thailand's horrendous accidents.

Khao Yai Nat'l Park

GETTING THERE

It takes about three to four hours to drive to Khao Yai from Bangkok, via one of two routes. The northern entrance to the park may be reached by following Route 1. Go through Saraburi and Muak Lek, and turn right onto Route 2090 five kilometres (3 mi) before Pak Chong.

The route to the southern entrance of Khao Yai requires driving to Nakhon Nayok. About 25 kilometres (15 mi) beyond the town, turn left onto Route 3077. The park headquarters is approximately 40 kilometres (25 mi) from either of the entrances.

There are frequent buses from Bangkok's northern bus terminal to Pak Chong, a pleasant ride of about three hours, which costs around 70 baht. (Look for the enormous white Buddha on the right hand side of the road on the way out.) In Pak Chong, you can catch a *song tao* in front of the 7-11 market across the street from the small bus station. Alternatively, most of the hotels and guest houses in the area will arrange to pick you up if you plan to

stay with them. At certain times of the year, the State Railways of Thailand may offer weekend day-trips to Khao Yai; however, the bus service is more reliable and, surprisingly, faster.

GETTING AROUND

Most of the guesthouses around Khao Yai conduct tours of the park.

Ko Samui/Pha Ngan

KO SAMUI

Getting There

Air: 14 flights daily from Bangkok, 2 flights daily from Phuket, 1 flight daily from U-Tapao, 4 flights weekly from Singapore. Additional international flights are being considered.

Bus/train/boat: Two overnight and one daytime train run daily from Bangkok to the mainland town of Surat Thani. Train-bus-boat or bus-boat packages (the latter start from Khao San Road in Bangkok) deposit travelers in the early morning hours at Tha Thong pier, 5 km (3 mi) east of Surat Thani. From here, two express boats (sometimes three) take less than three hours to reach Na Thon, Samui's main port. Directly from Surat Thani, at Ban Don pier, a slower boat, with stuffy berths, departs at 11pm daily and arrives at Na Thon six hours later.

Getting Around

Song taos circulate around the island's principal ring road throughout the day and well into the evening. Motorbikes are very popular and can be rented on every beach and at just about every bungalow, starting at about $6 per day. Rental mountain bikes can be found at Chaweng and Lamai beaches. Jeeps and cars can be rented at the biggest hotels and the airport, as well as at shops in Chaweng, Lamai and Na Thon.

KO PHA NGAN

Getting There

Air: Ko Pha Ngan has no airport. See Ko Samui details.

Boat: Two boats per day (three in peak season) travel from Samui's

Na Thon port to Pha Ngan's Thong Sala, a journey of about 45 minutes. Three boats per day take one hour to travel between Bangrak (also known as "Big Buddha Beach" pier) and Ko Pha Ngan's Hat Rin Beach. The 7.30am and 1.30pm express boats departing from Tha Thong near Surat Thani, on the mainland, proceed to Thong Sala after taking on and discharging passengers on Ko Samui. The strangely named "Speed Ferry" is a vehicle ferry that takes between five and six hours to travel directly between Surat's Tha Thong and Thong Sala. It leaves Tha Thong daily at 4pm. All boat schedules may be disrupted by weather conditions, especially between late August and early December.

Getting Around

Song taos regularly ply the cement roads between Thong Sala and Cha Loak Lam, and between Thong Sala and Hat Rin. When sufficient numbers pile on, they depart; they will pick up or discharge passengers anywhere along the way. Arriving by boat at Thong Sala or Hat Rin, passengers will be greeted by touts in long-boats sent from the various resorts. Especially in the rainy season, this is probably the best mode. At other times, long-boat travel to other coastal points will require haggling. If there is a semblance of a trail, motorbikes can be rented from bungalows and small shops, as well as in Thong Sala. Mountain bikes can be rented in Thong Sala.

KO TAO

Getting There

Air: Ko Tao has no airport. See Ko Samui details.

Boat: From Ko Samui and Ko Pha Ngan, one boat per day (sometimes two) travels from Thong Sala on Ko Pha Ngan to Ko Tao's only port, Ban Mae Hat. It departs at 12.30pm for the one-hour journey. The 8am boat from Surat Thani on the mainland, which continues directly on from Ko Samui to Ko Pha Ngan each day, arrives at

Ko Pha Ngan's Thong Sala port at noon. So there is just enough time to transfer to the Ko Tao-bound boat. Day trips to Ko Tao are also common packages vended on the two bigger islands.

From Chumphon: Two daily boats travel directly to Ko Tao from this fishing port 450 km (280 mi) south of Bangkok. The express boat, departing at 8am, takes less than two hours. The much slower boat leaves at midnight and arrives at 6am. This boat is a small converted fishing vessel and does not have berths.

Because of Ko Tao's distant and exposed location, between June and November boats to and from the island are often canceled due to inclement weather. Ko Tao boats are canceled more often than boats between Ko Samui and the mainland, or between Ko Samui and Ko Pha Ngan.

Getting Around

Long-boats transport new arrivals to various beaches. But once settled in, one can walk anywhere.

Where to Stay

Hotel accommodation in all the major tourist destinations in Thailand is equal to the very best anywhere in the world. The facilities in the first-class hotels may have as many as 10 or more different restaurants serving Western and Asian cuisine, coffee shops, swimming pools, exercise rooms, business centers, banqueting halls, shopping arcades, and cable & satellite television. The service is second to none. Indeed, most of the moderately priced hotels rival what in Europe would be considered first-class hotels. Even the budget and inexpensive hotels will invariably have a swimming pool and more than one food outlet.

Because of the financial and tourism slumps that plagued Southeast Asia in 1997 and 1998, hotel rates can range widely, even amongst the top-end hotels. Depending upon season and the situation at the moment, discounts can exceed 50 percent or more of the published rack rate. It pays to shop around and try bargaining – even at the best hotels.

Following the Bangkok listing is a selection of regional hotels from among the many available. They have been chosen to show a range of facilities and prices and, in a few cases, because they are different.

Note that a resort hotel does not always have the same connotation in Thailand that it might in the West; often it means nothing more than that the hotel is located in the countryside. One might be surprised by excellent service and luxurious accommodations at a resort hotel, but to expect it, particularly in the smaller areas, is to court disappointment in many cases. Hotels also charge a value added tax (VAT) of 10 percent and often, service charges of 10 percent or more.

During peak holiday periods (holidays, Christmas, New Year, etc.), accommodation is at a premium rate, as it is during high season, from November through April. But the rest of the year, it is always worth asking for a discount.

ABOUT ROOM RATES

Rather than using absolute dollar or baht values for room rates, we have chosen to use relative categories of very expensive, expensive, moderate, inexpensive, and budget.

First, rates are highly elastic right now, especially with the economic problems in Thailand. In Bangkok there is a glut of rooms, and rates can often be highly discounted. Moreover, in Bangkok especially, some luxury hotels quote prices in baht, while others, such as the Oriental, quote only in dollars. Even if a room rate is quoted in dollars, it may be billed on the credit card in baht, and so can vary depending upon exchange rates.

Bangkok

EXPENSIVE

Amari Airport, 333 Choet Wutthakat Road. Tel: 566 1020/1, 566 2060/9, fax: 566 1941. Closest hotel to international airport and therefore popular with travelers arriving late and departing early. Connected to airport with footbridge and shuttle bus.
Amari Boulevard, 2 Soi 5, Sukhumvit Road. Tel: 255 2930, 255 2940, fax: 255 2950. Small but luxurious. An oasis in a raucous tourist area filled with street markets, noodle shops and bars.
Amari Watergate, 847 Phetburi Road. Tel: 653 9000/19, fax: 653 9044, 653 9048. Contemporary high-rise hotel in old market area. The roaring expressway in front of it can be a problem for guests.
Arnoma Swissotel, 99 Ratchadamri Road. Tel: 255 3410, fax: 255 3456/7. Good location, and good restaurants and service.
Asia, 296 Phaya Thai Road. Tel:

215 0808, fax: 215 4360. Offers many extra facilities possibly to offset the noisy, non-stop traffic at its doors.

Beaufort Sukhothai, 13/3 Sathorn Tai Road. Tel: 287 0222, fax: 287 4980. Quiet, luxurious, a cool, green hotel favored by diplomats. Near the city's centre on a busy thoroughfare but set well back amid tropical gardens.

Bel-Aire Princess, 16 Soi 5, Sukhumvit Road. Tel: 253 4300/30, fax: 255 8850. One of the small "boutique" hotels offering personalized service. Close to many big business organizations.

Central Plaza, 1695 Phaholyothin Road. Tel: 541 1234, fax: 541 1087. Midway between the airport and city, but a long way from anywhere except the popular weekend market at Chatuchak Park.

Dusit Thani, 946 Rama IV Road. Tel: 236 0450/9, fax: 236 6400. Bangkok's first high-rise hotel. Adjacent to major banks and business headquarters on Silom Road. Close to nightlife on Patpong.

Emerald, 99/1 Ratchadapisek Road. Tel: 276 4567, fax: 276 4555/6. A large establishment in a growing business, shopping and recreation quarter, but a long journey from the centre at peak traffic periods.

Evergreen Laurel, 88 Sathorn Nua Road (intersection with Soi Pipat). Tel: 266 7223, fax: 266 7222. Smallish but elegant, European atmosphere. On a busy thoroughfare but close to big business and foreign embassies.

Grand Hyatt Erawan, 494 Ratchadamri Road. Tel: 254 1234, fax: 254 6308. On a major intersection and home to the famous Erawan Shrine, one of the best known religious symbols in Bangkok. Adjacent to shopping and horse-racing and golf courses.

Hilton International, 2 Witthayu Road. Tel: 253 0123, fax: 253 6509. Set in beautiful garden with pool. Close to embassies. Good access to and from the airport.

Holiday Inn Crowne Plaza, 981 Silom Road. Tel: 238 4300, fax: 238 5289. Between business

centre and river. A choice location with small shops nearby.

Imperial Queen's Park, 199 Soi 22, Sukhumvit Road. Tel: 261 9000, fax: 261 9530/4. With 1,400 rooms, it is Bangkok's biggest hotel. A cavernous place where guests must walk long distances. Interesting shops, bars and restaurants in the vicinity.

Indra Regent, 120-126 Ratchaprarop Road. Tel: 208 0033, fax: 208 0388. Surrounded by old markets and eating places which are gradually making way for Thailand's largest wholesale centre for garments.

JW Marriott, 4 Soi 2, Sukhumvit Road. Tel: 656 7700, fax 656 7711. Opened in 1997. 446 rooms in an excellent location, close to major shopping and business areas, and with direct freeway access.

Landmark, 138 Sukhumvit Road. Tel: 254 0404, fax: 253 4259. Central location, and near airport road. Well-equipped for business travelers. Good shopping in and outside the hotel.

Le Méridien President, 971 Ploenchit Road. Tel: 253 0444, fax: 253 7565. Central location. The hotel has a French flavour and the best hotel coffee shop in town. Elegant shops and restaurants nearby.

Marriott Royal Garden Riverside, 257/1-3 Charoen Nakhon Road. Tel: 476 0021/2, fax: 476 1120. A resort hotel with the conveniences of nearby downtown. On the western side of the river, a bit to the south, but there are fine views of the riverside life from the hotel terraces. Free river shuttle to Oriental Pier.

Monarch Lee Gardens, 188 Silom Road. Tel: 238 1991, fax: 238 1999. In the heart of the banking and insurance district, but conveniently placed for good shops and restaurants. Nightlife is close.

Montien, 54 Suriwongse Road. Tel: 234 8060, fax: 236 5219. Across the street from Patpong and convenient to the business district along Silom Road. Two pleasant restaurants, a coffee shop, and the

only in-house fortune teller in a Bangkok hotel.

Novotel Bangkok, 392/44 Soi 6, Siam Square, Rama I Road. Tel: 255 6888, fax: 255 1824/7. French management. This is a busy quarter of small shops, movie theaters, eating places and traffic chaos.

Oriental, 48 Oriental Ave. Tel: 236 0400/20, fax: 236 1937/9. A visit is a must, even if it is only to have a drink on the river terrace. The Oriental is part of the history of East meeting West. Repeatedly voted one of the world's best hotels because of its riverside location and its superb service.

Regent Bangkok, 155 Ratchadamri Road. Tel: 251 6127, fax: 253 9195. High luxury in the heart of the city. With music and tea in the lobby lounge, there are echoes of the old Orient. The best hotel swimming pool in Bangkok.

Royal Orchid Sheraton, 2 Captain Bush Lane, Si Phraya Road. Tel: 237 0022, 266 0123, fax: 236 8320. One of the big three riverside hotels with high levels of services and exceptional facilities. All have road access difficulties at peak traffic times but guests may travel by river and see little-known areas of Bangkok.

Shangri-La, 89 Soi Wat Suan Plu, Charoen Krung (New) Road. Tel: 236 7777, fax: 236 8579. Every room has a river view. The evening buffet on the riverside terrace is famous. The biggest hotel on the river.

Sheraton Grande, 250 Sukhumvit Road. Tel: 653 0334/8; fax: 653 0400. Opened in late 1996. 445 rooms in a prime location along the Sukhumvit corridor. Four restaurants, including Italian and Chinese. Expect excellent service in elegant surroundings.

Siam City, 477 Sri Ayutthaya Road. Tel: 247 0120, 247 0130, fax: 247 0178. Good facilities near government offices and army headquarters. A prime spot to hobnob and people-watch.

Siam Intercontinental, 967 Rama I Road. Tel: 253 0355, fax: 253 2275. With 10 acres of gardens, tennis courts, jogging paths, swimming pools, golf greens and driving ranges, this is a cool retreat from the roar of the city. Big and small shops, movie houses and restaurants are just beyond the front gates.

Westin Banyan Tree, Thai Wah II Tower, 21/100 Sathorn Tai Road. Tel: 679 1200, fax: 679 1199. Occupying the lower two and top 28 floors of the tallest building in Thailand. The well-equipped and spacious suites are ideal for the business traveler.

MODERATE

Ambassador, 171 Soi 11-13, Sukhumvit Road. Tel: 254 0444, fax: 253 4123. Large complex with over 1,000 rooms, good food court, several fine restaurants and nightclubs. Close to shopping and restaurants.

Maruay Garden, 1 Soi 40, Phaholyothin Road. Tel: 561 0510, fax: 561 0549. Located 20 miles north of the heart of Bangkok, but close to the expressway and well-served by metered taxis. Over 300 rooms, daily dim sum lunch buffet.

Mercure Hotel, 1091/336 New Phetburi Road. Tel: 253 0510, fax: 253 0556, email: mercureb@ksc15.th.com. 650 rooms centrally located, close to expressway and shopping areas, excellent executive services.

Plaza, 178 Suriwongse Road. Tel: 235 1760/79, fax: 237 0746. Part of the Mandarin Group, close to business district, shopping and sights on Silom and Patpong, rooftop tropical garden.

Somerset, 10 Soi 15, Sukhumvit Road. Tel: 254 8500/24, fax: 254 8534. Small, elegant hotel, conveniently close to a variety of restaurants and shops.

Tai-Pan, 25 Soi 23 (Soi Prasanmit), Sukhumvit Road. Tel: 260 9888, 260 9898, fax: 259 7908, website: www.taipanhotel.co.th. 150 rooms situated close to the business, shopping and entertainment areas along the Sukhumvit corridor.

Tartawan Place, 119/510 Suriwongse Road. Tel: 238 2620, fax: 238 3228. Located in a quiet

soi off Suriwongse, in the heart of the business district. Also very convenient to shopping and entertainment. Excellent service. Major European languages spoken in addition to Thai and English.

Windsor Palace, 8-10 Soi 20, Sukhumvit Road. Tel: 262 1221, 262 1234, fax: 262 1212, website: asiatravel.com/embassysuites. This 34-storey Embassy Suites property offers 463 suites, with three non-smoking floors.

INEXPENSIVE

Bangkok Centre, 328 Rama IV Road. Tel: 238 4848/57, fax: 236 1862. Central location; convenient to railway station. Over 200 rooms.

Euro Inn, 249 Soi 31, Sukhumvit Road. Tel: 259 9480/7, fax: 259 9490. Convenient to shopping and entertainment areas.

Golden Dragon, 20/21 Ngam Wong Wan Road. Tel: 589 0130/41, fax: 589 8305. 114 rooms. Close to airport; 20 minutes from centre of Bangkok. Swimming pool. Good service.

Grand Inn, 2/78 Soi 3 (Soi Nana Nua), Sukhumvit Road. Tel: 254 9021/7, fax: 254 9020. 24 rooms. At the lower end of the Sukhumvit corridor.

Jim's Lodge, 125/7 Soi Ruam Rudi, Ploenchit Road. Tel: 255 3100, 255 0190/9, fax: 253 8492. 75 rooms. Convenient to many embassies. Pleasant restaurant. Good service.

New Trocadero, 343 Suriwongse Road. Tel: 234 8920/9, fax: 236 5526. 130 rooms. Popular with Westerners. Coffee shop. Good travel services.

Park, 6 Soi 7, Sukhumvit Road. Tel: 255 4300/8, fax: 255 4309. 140 rooms, most bright and cheerful. Restaurant, coffee shop and bar. Small pool set in peaceful garden.

President Inn, 155/1416 Soi 11, Sukhumvit Road. Tel: 255 4230/4, fax: 255 4235. Conveniently located.

Rajah, 18 Soi 4, Sukhumvit Road. Tel: 255 0040/83, fax: 255 7160. 450 rooms. Near good shopping and restaurants.

Silom Street Inn, 284/1113 Silom Road. Tel: 238 4680, fax: 238

4689. Pleasant restaurants and shopping in the vicinity.

Thai, 78 Prachatipatai Road. Tel: 282 2831/3, fax: 280 1299. Pleasant surroundings, convenient to TAT office, Banglampoo Market and other attractions.

Tower Inn, 533 Silom Road. Tel: 234 4051, 234 4053, fax: 234 4051. 140 rooms. Midway between Patpong and the river. Good shopping in the area.

Viangtai, 42 Rambutri Road, Banglampoo. Tel: 280 5392/9, fax: 281 8153. In central Banglampoo, on the edge of the Khao San Road area. Convenient to the National Museum and Sanam Luang.

BUDGET

A-One Inn, 25/12-15 Soi Kasem San 1, Rama I Road. Tel: 215 3029, fax: 216 4771. Located beside Siam Square and close to World Trade Centre and Chulalongkorn University. Spacious rooms, friendly service.

Atlanta, 78 Soi 2, Sukhumvit Road. Tel: 252 6069, 252 1650, fax: 255 2151, 656 8123. 50 rooms, some without air conditioning, no TV. Excellent restaurant with tea-time classical music and jazz most evenings. Pool. Well regarded by return visitors. Great value.

Bangkok Christian Guest House, 123 Soi Sala Daeng 2, Silom Road. Tel: 233 2206, 253 3353, fax: 237 1742. Despite its name, more expensive than most guesthouses, with pleasant rooms starting at 650 baht, breakfast included. Convenient to nightlife.

Burapha, 160/14 Charoen Krung (New) Road. Tel: 221 3545/9, fax: 226 1723. On the edge of Chinatown and therefore a little noisy. Reasonable service.

Comfort Inn, 153/11-14 Soi 11, Sukhumvit Road. Tel: 251 9250, 254 3559/60, fax: 254 3562. 60 rooms. Convenient location close to shopping and restaurants.

Florida, 43 Phaya Thai Road. Tel: 247 0990, fax: 247 7419. Interesting, rather old building, near the Victory Monument.

Opera, 16 Soi Somprasong 1, Phetburi Road. Tel: 252 4031, fax:

253 5360. Convenient to Pratunam Market and Siam Square. Pool. Coffee shop.

YMCA, 27 Sathorn Tai Road, and **YWCA**, 13 Sathorn Tai Road. Tel: 286 1936, fax: 287 1996. 50 rooms, some cottages, sports facilities, European, Chinese and Thai restaurant. Quiet.

Outside of Bangkok

KANCHANABURI (034)
Moderate

Duen Shine Resort, Kanchanaburi. Tel: 513 611. Bungalows by the river near the bridge.

Felix River Kwai Resort, Kanchanaburi. Tel: 511 184, fax: 511 259. Comfortable hotel in a pretty garden setting near the bridge.

KHAO YAI PARK (044)
A campsite and some simple dormitories are available within the park, and camping out on one of the observation towers may be a possibility as well. Policy changes are not uncommon; inquire at the TAT office or the Royal Forestry Department in Bangkok, or at park headquarters for further details.

Moderate to Expensive

Juldis Khao Yai Resort, 54 Moo 4, Thanarat Road (km 17), Pak Chong. Tel: 297 297, fax: 297 291. In Bangkok, tel: (02) 613 7273/77, fax: (02) 613 7272. A beautifully situated hotel favored by corporate groups and well-heeled Thais. Adequate food; surprisingly inadequate service. No regularly scheduled tours of the park, although arrangements can be made with other tour operators.

Moderate

Khao Yai Garden Lodge, Thanon Thanarat, Kilometer 7, Pak Chong. Tel: 313 567, fax: 312 143. A cozy atmosphere and excellent food are offered by this German-Thai couple. 35 rooms ranging from 100 baht (fan-cooled, shared toilet) to 1,400 baht (air-conditioned, traditional Thai decor, private bath). Spacious grounds include a bird garden, a 40-year old tortoise, and many

botanical wonders; herbal sauna and swimming pool with waterfall available from 1998. Offers a range of tours, not only of Khao Yai, but throughout the Northeast as well. Will pick up from Bangkok with prior arrangement.

Budget

Jungle Adventure Guest House, Kongwaksin Road, Soi 3, Pak Chong. Tel: 313 836. Dormitory accommodation and basic rooms ranging from 70–200 baht per night. One-and-a-half-day tours of Khao Yai at 950 baht per person.

Wildlife Safari, 39 Subsanun Road, Pak Chong. Tel/fax: 312 922. Simple, clean accommodation ranging from 100–400 baht. Note that lodging is limited to those taking the one-and-a-half-day tours of Khao Yai at around 750 baht.

Central Plains

SUKHOTHAI (055)
Moderate

Wang Neua, Singhawat Road. Tel: 611 193, fax: 612 038. A modern provincial hotel with swimming pool.

Inexpensive

River View Hotel, Nikhornkasem Road. Tel: 611 656. As the name implies, with a river view but not much else.

North and Northeast

CHIANG MAI (053)
Expensive

Amari Rincome, 1 Nimmanhemin Road. Tel: 221 044, fax: 221 915. One of the best hotels in Chiang Mai. Elegant, but situated on the edge of town.

Pornping, Charoen Prathet Road. Tel: 270 099, fax: 270 119. Centrally situated tower housing the famous Bubbles disco.

Royal Princess, Chang Klan Road. Tel: 281 033, fax: 281 044. Managed by the Dusit group, this first-class hotel is well known for its service. Located next door to the night market.

Moderate

Chiang Inn, Chang Klan Road. Tel: 270 070, fax: 274 299. Located near the night market, with a pool

and one of the city's most popular discos, The Wall Club.

Galare Guest House, Charoen Prathet Road. Tel: 273 885, fax: 279 088. Attractive and inexpensive location by the river.

Inexpensive

Top North Guest House, Moon Muang Road, Soi 2. Tel: 278 900, fax: 278 485. Quiet, central, cheap and with pool; one of the most attractive offers in town.

CHIANG RAI (053)
Moderate

Dusit Island Resort, Kraisorasit Road. Tel: 715 777, fax: 715 801. The best hotel in town lies on an island in the Kok river.

Wiang Inn, Phaholyothin Road. Tel: 711 533, fax: 711 877. No pool, but a disco and a central location.

CHIANG SAEN (053)
Moderate

Le Méridien Baan Boran. Tel: 784 084, fax: 784 090. Attractive luxury resort directly at the Golden Triangle, with elephant stables on the premises.

MAE HONG SON (053)
Moderate

Holiday Inn. Tel: 612 234/9, fax: 611 524. Ultra-modern and with all amenities. On the edge of town.

Inexpensive

Baiyoke Chalet. Tel: 611 486, fax: 611 533. Friendly little hotel, near lake.

MAE SAI (053)
Moderate

Wang Thong. Tel: 733 388, fax: 733 399. Luxury hotel with Chinese decor and a view of the bridge marking the border.

Inexpensive

Mae Sai Hotel. Tel: 731 462. Directly next to the ruby market.

MAE SALONG (053)
Moderate

Khum Naiphol Resort. Tel: 765 014. Built by General Tuan's family and still run by them.

NAN VALLEY (054)

Inexpensive

City Park Hotel, 99 Moo 4, Yontakakit Koson Road, Tambon Tuu Tai. Tel: 710 376. Air-conditioning, pool, satellite TV. Inconvenient location about 10 km (6 mi) southwest of town.

Dhevaraj Hotel, 466 Sumonthewaraj Road, Amphur Muang. Tel: 710 078, 710 212, 710 803; fax: 771 365. Standard plastic and tile provincial hotel, circa 1980. Air-conditioning, TV, elevator. Central location.

Nan Fa Hotel, 440 Sumonthewaraj Road, Amphur Muang. Tel: 772 640, 771 697. Central location. Air-conditioning, TV, dubious plumbing. Clean, well-maintained old wooden building. For sheer atmosphere, this is it. On ground floor, craft store and Thai restaurant, which features live folk music in early evening.

Papua Bhuka Hotel, 141 Pua-Namyao Street, Moo 4, Tambon Xilalang, Amphur Pua. Tel: 791 156, 791 166; fax: 791 166. About a half dozen kilometers (4 mi) south of the town of Pua on Route 1080, this is the only option outside of Nan town. Air-conditioning, satellite TV, small restaurant. Beautiful views of misted mountains, convenient for jaunts to tribal villages and Silaphet waterfall.

Doi Phu Kha National Park. Budget accommodation (100–200 baht) in bungalows on edge of park. Visitors can set up tents. Small restaurant. Advisable to bring extra supplies.

N. RATCHASIMA (KHORAT) (044)

Moderate

Sima Thani, Mittraphap Road. Tel: 213 100, fax: 213 122. Best hotel in Nakhon Ratchasima with a beautiful lobby dotted with Khmer-style figures.

Royal Princess, 1137 Suranari Road. Tel: 256 629/35, fax: 256 601. On the edge of town. Decorated in northeastern Thai style.

CHANTHABURI (039)

Moderate

Maneechan Resort, 110 Moo 11, Plubpla, Chanthaburi. Tel: 343 777/8, fax: 344 123. A complex with private homes and a resort with excellent sports facilities.

PATTAYA/JOMTIEN (038)

Expensive

Dusit Resort, 240 Beach Road. Tel: 425 611, fax: 428 239. Top-class service and all the requisite amenities plus a good range of water sports.

Royal Cliff, 353 Moo 12, Cliff Road. Tel: 250 421/40, fax: 250 511/513. One of Pattaya's top addresses, ostentatiously built into a cliff with a good private beach.

Royal Garden Resort Pattaya, Beach Road. Tel: 412 120/6, fax: 429 926. Operated by the group that owns the Marriott Royal Garden Riverside, in Bangkok, the Royal Garden had led the drive to make Pattaya a family destination. First-class facilities.

Moderate

Amari Orchid Resort, Beach Road, North Pattaya. Tel: 428 161, fax: 428 195. A welcoming beach hotel with a luxuriant garden.

Inexpensive

Cosy Beach Hotel, 400 Moo 12, Pratmnak Road, Pattaya. Tel: 250 800, fax: 250 799. Lush gardens, good facilities, quiet beach.

Diana Inn, 216/6-9 Pattaya 2 Road, Pattaya Beach, Chonburi. Tel: 429 675, fax: 428 239. A pleasant hotel with an attractive pool and friendly service.

HUA HIN (032)

Expensive

Melia Hua Hin, 33 Naresdamri Road. Tel: 511 612, fax: 511 135. An elegant resort hotel on the beach at Hua Hin. Features over-sized ocean-view rooms and a spectacular pool.

Royal Garden Resort, Phetkasem Beach Road. Tel: 511 881, fax: 512 422. A low-rise resort on Hua Hin's

long, snow-white beach. Operated by the same group that owns the Marriott Royal Garden Riverside, in Bangkok. Uncrowded retreat with full services. Nearby is the sister hotel Royal Garden Village.

Sofitel Central Hua Hin. Tel: 512 021, fax: 511 014. The former Railway Hotel, this establishment is full of Old World splendour.

CHUMPHON (077)

Moderate

Cabana Resort. Tel: 501 990. A bungalow complex with a famous diving school. Guests will be met in Chumphon on request.

Inexpensive

Jansom Chumphon, Sala Daeng Road. Tel: 502 502, fax: 502 503. Large central business hotel with popular coffee shop and disco.

Sai Ree Lodge, Sai Ree Beach, Pak Nam. Tel: 521 212, fax: 502 479. Pleasant, clean thatched cottages beside the beach linked by elevated wooden walkways. Good sea view.

SURAT THANI (077)

Moderate

Saowaluk Thani, 99/44-46 Surat-Kranchanadit Road. Tel: 283 295/6, fax: 273 977. The best hotel in Surat, located in eastern end of the city and run by the Dusit group from Bangkok.

Wang Tai Hotel, Talad Mai Road. Tel: 283 020, fax: 281 007. On the edge of town, but with a pool. Excellent coffee shop with good food to match the live (Thai) music.

KO SAMUI (077)

Expensive

Baan Taling Ngam, 295 Moo 3, Ban Taling. Tel: 423 019/22; fax: 423 220. Part of the Oriental Hotel chain. The beach on this secluded western coast is mediocre with coarse sand, but the views are stunning from the rooms perched on a hillside. Pools at beachside and hilltop. Ideal when the northwest monsoon is blowing.

Moderate to Expensive

Imperial Boat House, Choengmon Beach. Tel: 425 041; email:

imperial@ksc.net.th. North of Chaweng and a quieter alternative. Luxury rooms in two-storey converted rice barges.

Laem Set Inn, 110 Moo 2, Hua Thanon. Tel: 424 393, 233 299, fax: 424 394, 233 301. Chinese-style hardwood houses have been transplanted and restored to form this boutique hotel. This southeast beach is unremarkable, but good snorkeling. Excellent for children.

Moderate

Chaweng Regent Resort, 155-4 Central Chaweng Beach. Tel: 422 389, 422 008. Three swimming pools, meeting facilities. Smack in the middle of Chaweng Beach, backs onto the nightlife scene.

Poppies Samui, PO Box 1, Chaweng Noi. Tel: 422 419. Twenty-four cottages hidden among greenery, Balinese style. Near the southern end of the beach. Reputed for its restaurant.

The Princess Village, Central Chaweng. Tel: 422 382. South-central location. Pretend you're back in Ayutthaya in these period-style bungalows with traditional furnishings and all mod-cons.

Samui Euphoria Resort, 101/3 Bo Phut Bay. Tel: 425 100/6, fax: 425 107. Tennis, billiards, badminton, putting green, petanque, fitness club, pool. Popular with French and Italian families.

Inexpensive

Spa Resort, North Lamai Beach. Tel: 230 855, fax: 424 126. A hotel and New Age health centre. Fasting regimes, herbal saunas, colonic irrigation as well as traditional Thai massage, hikes and mountain-biking trips. Services also offered to non-guests.

Samui Palm Beach Resort, Bo Phut Bay. Tel: 425 494. Well-appointed cottages. Top of the line for around Bo Phut.

KO PHA NGAN (077)

Inexpensive

Panviman Resort, Thong Nai Pan Beach. Tel/fax: 377 048; Bangkok reservations: 587 8491; fax: 587 8493; email: panviman@ kohphangan.com. The island's most upscale resort straddles a steep headland that overlooks two fine, secluded northeastern beaches. Excellent snorkeling, fishing, views. Some air-conditioned cottages and hotel-style rooms.

The Sanctuary, PO Box 3, Hat Tien Beach. A low-budget, attractively designed bungalow resort. Four km (2 mi) from Hat Rin Beach. Between September and May, hosts a series of New Age courses ranging from massage and tai chi to past-life regression and "cranial sacral."

KO TAO (077)

Inexpensive

Koh Tao Cottage, Ao Chalok Ban Kao Beach. Tel: (01) 725 0751; fax: (01) 725 0662. The island's poshest resort. Twenty-four bungalows with fan, fridge and window screens. No air-conditioning.

Nang Yuan Resort, Ko Nang Yuan. Tel: (01) 726 0085. These simple bungalows may seem overpriced for these parts, but you're paying for the beaches, coral and exclusivity on this sandbar off Ko Tao.

Phuket

PHUKET TOWN (076)

Moderate

Metropole, Montri Road. Tel: 215 050, fax: 215 099. Modern and elegant high-rise hotel. Staff wear Thai traditional garb. Popular with business travelers as well as tourists. Very good food and beverage outlets, particularly the coffee shop's buffet lunch. This is a four-star hotel at three-star prices.

Inexpensive

Thavorn, Rasda Road. Tel: 211 333/5. One of the first hotels in Phuket. Lobby displays historical pictures of local culture. Rooms fronting Rasda Road are noisy but otherwise comfortable. Central location.

BEACHES (076)

Very Expensive

Banyan Tree, The, 33 Moo 4, Srisoonthorn Road, Choeng Talay District. Bang Thao/Laguna. Tel: 324 374, fax: 324 375. Individual bungalows encircling a larger lagoon; some are garden bungalows, the more expensive ones come with private outdoor pool. Full range of spa facilities. Low key, discreet, quite romantic and luxurious. The perfect quiet and private getaway.

The Chedi, Choeng Talay. Pansea. Tel: 324 017/20, fax: 324 252. High-class Asian-inspired resort bungalows linked by elevated walkways. Strangely, no tubs, only showers in rooms. Most balconies overlook an immaculate beach. A romantic setting with first-rate cuisine, but isolated setting.

Le Méridien, 8/5 Moo 1 Karon Beach. Relax Bay. Tel: 340 480/5, fax: 340 479. Huge 470-room 5-star hotel filled with activities year-round, including a glitzy variety show every night. Mega- sized swimming pools. Guests have access to what is effectively the hotel's own private beach, in a small bay midway between Patong and Karon.

Phuket Yacht Club, 23/3 Viset Road. Nai Harn. Tel: 381 156/63, fax: 381 164. Deluxe hotel, operated by the Le Méridien group. A beautiful luxury hotel hugging one end of isolated but spectacular Nai Harn beach. Elegant rooms with equally large private sun decks, with classic views of the spectacular Nai Harn Bay and Promthep Cape.

Sheraton Grande Laguna, Choeng Talay District. Bang Thao/Laguna. Tel: 324 101/7, fax: 324 108. A 341-room deluxe hotel built around fresh water lagoons reclaimed from an old tin mining site. Numerous dining outlets. The star attraction is the unique winding swimming pool with piped-in music underwater.

Expensive

Amari Coral Beach, 104 Moo 4, South Patong. Tel: 340 106/10. Well-run remote hotel on its own site, about 10 minutes' walk from the southern tip of Patong Beach. Uninspiring beach front. Trips to nearby Paradise Beach are popular with guests. First-rate Kinaree Thai restaurant.

Boathouse, The, 2/2 Patak Road. Kata. Tel: 330 015/7, fax: 330

561. Situated on the quiet end of Kata, this small and elegant beach-front "boutique" hotel prides itself on attentive and personalized service. Main building built in the Ayutthaya style with steep sloping roofs. Famous for its sophisticated Boathouse Wine & Grill restaurant, and for its wine list.

Club Andaman Beach Resort, 77/1 Thaviwong Road, Patong. Tel: 340 530, fax: 321 527. Large hotel in expansive, manicured gardens close to but not on the beach. Cottage accommodation in addition to hotel wing. Tennis courts, gym, pool. Well-appointed rooms with in-house video, fridge and safe deposit box.

Club Med Phuket, 7/3 Patak Road. Kata. Tel: 330 455, fax: 330 461. Large resort in front of central Kata Beach. Caters to the young-at-heart with lots of organized activities. Excellent French and international cuisine.

Dusit Laguna, Choeng Talay District. Bang Thao/Laguna. Tel: 324 320/32, fax: 324 174. Part of the Dusit chain of deluxe hotels in Thailand, this five-star resort reflects its Thai heritage, apparent in the decor, staff costumes and the acclaimed Ruen Thai restaurant. Broad, sweeping Bang Thao Bay is exposed and unsafe to swim in the monsoon season.

Holiday Inn, Thaviwong Road. Patong. Tel: 340 608/9, fax: 340 435. Right beside the beachfront action. Very popular and large resort hotel that attracts families on long vacations. Swimming pool and the Pirate's Cove minigolf for the children. Superlative steaks at Sam's Chicago Steak House.

Karon Beach Resort, 5/2 Moo 2, Patak Road. Karon. Tel: 330 006, fax: 381 529. Small family-run bungalow resort located at quiet end of Karon beach. There are a restaurant, snack bar, swimming pool and tour counter on site with the facilities of both Kata and Karon beaches a short walk away.

Marina Cottage, South Karon Bay. Karon. Tel: 330 625, fax: 330 516. Thai-style cottages exquisitely landscaped into a hilly coconut plantation. Dino Park crazy golf appeals to adults as well as kids. Two excellent restaurants: Sala Thai (central Thai cuisine) and On the Rock (seafood mostly).

Inexpensive
Jungle Beach Resort, 11/3 Viset Road. Nai Harn. Tel: 288 264. Fan-cooled and air-conditioned rooms in a tourist-class bungalow resort tastefully melded into its surroundings. Good place for nature-oriented relaxation on the remote southern tip of Phuket.

Krabi/Phang Nga
KRABI (075)
Very Expensive
Dusit Rayavadee Resort, Phra Nang Headland. Tel: 620 740/2. Sumptuous deluxe resort discreetly landscaped alongside Phra Nang and Railae beaches. Water sports, tennis courts, sauna, gym. Two restaurants: Thai/seafood and international.

Moderate
Meritime Hotel, 4 Pipatkul Road. Tel: 620 028, 620 046, fax: 612 992. Krabi town's most luxurious hotel 2 km (1 mile) from the town centre. Each room has a balcony overlooking limestone karsts, mangrove forests and the township. Satellite TV, coffee shop, pool.

Phra Nang Inn, Ao Nang Beach Road. Tel: 637 129. Conveniently located hotel fronting Ao Nang beach. The old wing is more sociable than the new. Owners organize nature and culture tours. Has its own sea canoe facility for guests. Beachside restaurant and sunset bar.

Inexpensive
City Hotel, 15/2 3 Sukon Road. Tel: 611 961. Clean and friendly family-run hotel, with nice touches like fruit basket and TV in each room. Both fan and air-conditioned rooms available.

Gift's Bungalows, Ao Nang Beach Road. Tel: 637 193. Simple but clean jungle huts in a verdant tropical garden. Atmospheric restaurant serves tasty food and homemade breads. Surprisingly good for the price range.

Viengthong Hotel, 155/7 Uttarakit Road. Tel: 611 188, fax: 612 525. Centrally located hotel overlooking the river. Fan and air-conditioned rooms and a popular coffee shop open late.

PHANG NGA (076)
Moderate
Phangnga Bay Resort Hotel, 20 Tha Dan Road. Pansea. Tel: 412 067/70, fax: 412 057. Long-established hotel built right on the mangrove waterside in majestic Phang Nga Bay. Excellent location beside the river, ideal as a base for the exploration of nearby islands. Quality of service and dining fails to match the setting.

PHI PHI (075)
Expensive
Palm Beach Travelodge Resort, Laemthong Beach. Phi Phi. Tel: (076) 214 654 (Phuket town office); (01) 723 0922 (resort). Designer award-winning bungalows on isolated beach facing Bamboo and Mosquito islands. Desert island setting. Varied water sport facilities, including scuba diving. Internationally run.

Moderate
Phi Phi Princess Resort, Loh Dalam Bay. Phi Phi. Tel: 612 188. Comfortable newly built beach-front bungalows with satellite TV and minibar. Faces Phi Phi's most attractive beach. Convenient to village.

Inexpensive
Charlie Beach Resort, Loh Dalam Bay. Phi Phi. Tel: 620 615. Centrally located, quiet set of bungalows with immaculate beach setting. Good room choice. 24-hour security. Restaurant is only good for drinks and satellite TV.

Deep South
HAT YAI (074)
Moderate
Central Sukhotha, 3 Sanehanusorn Road. Tel: 352 222, fax: 352 223. The most upmarket hotel in town, plumb in the centre of city.

The Regency, Prachathipat Road. Tel: 234 101. Modern tower in the middle of the market with a view.

Inexpensive
Laemthong Hotel, Thamamoonviti Road. Tel: 352 301. Large, simple and clean Chinese hotel in a central location.

SONGKHLA (074)
Moderate
Haad Kaeo Princess Resort, Kilometer 5, Tambon Chingkoh, Songkhla. Tel: 331 059/67, fax: 331 058. The only beach resort in Songkhla. Suitable for families. Located 30 minutes' drive from town on the road to Sathing Phra.
Samila Hotel, 1/11 Ratdamnern Road. Tel: 322 448. Ideally situated at the crossing between the two beaches. With garden and pool.
Inexpensive
Lake Inn, 301 Nakhon Nawk Road. Tel: 314 823, fax: 314 843. High-rise with lake views.
Pavilion, 17 Platha Road. Tel: 311 355, fax: 323 716. Good-value hotel with large pool and modern, well-appointed rooms.

Guesthouses

If you are on a limited budget, there are numerous guesthouses offering clean, economical accommodation. Once of primary interest only to backpackers because of their sparse facilities, many have now been upgraded to include fans, air-conditioning and bathrooms in the rooms rather than down the hall. As such, they afford a viable alternative to the frugal traveler. Prices range from 80 to 400 baht.

Generally possessing no more than a dozen rooms, they are more like pensions than hotels, and appeal to travelers who like personalized service, friendly staff and a more relaxed pace.

Their numbers are legion, and to list them would fill several books. In Bangkok guesthouses are found in Banglampoo, particularly along Khao San Road, and in the Soi Ngam Duphli area off Rama IV Road. In Chiang Mai, check along the river and in the area of Chaiyaphum Road. In Pattaya and Phuket, guesthouses are much less common.

In other towns, guesthouses are generally family-run establishments and so are scattered around town. But look in the vicinity of bus and railway stations, and along main streets. The smaller the town, the more likely they are to be found on the main street.

BANGKOK
Apple Guest House, 10 Phra Athit Road. Tel: 281 6838. 70–100 baht. Restaurant.
Bangkok International Youth Hostel, 25/2 Phitsanulok Road. Tel: 282 0950, 281 0361, fax: 281 6834. A range of accommodations from dorm rooms to rooms with bath, choice of fan or air-conditioning. 70–300 baht. Cafeteria. Hostel members only; temporary membership may be purchased.
Chart Guest House, 61 Khao San Road. Tel: 280 3785. 60–100 baht. Some air-conditioned rooms available for 400+ baht.
Lee 4 Guest House, off Soi Si Bamphen, Soi Ngam Duphli, Rama IV Road. 120–180 baht. Said to be the best of the three Lee guesthouses in the vicinity. Clean, large rooms.
P. Guest House, 151-157 Trok Sa-Ke, Tanao Road. Tel: 224 1967. 80–120 baht. Helpful staff.
Peachy Guest House, 10 Phra Athit Road. Tel: 281 6471, 281 6659. 85–150 baht, extra for air-conditioning. Garden restaurant.
Shanti Lodge, 37 Sri Ayutthaya Road. Tel: 281 2497. 50–150 baht. Clean rooms, friendly service, coffee shop.
Tavee Guest House, 83 Sri Ayutthaya Road. Tel: 280 1447, 282 5983. 50–150 baht. Clean. Reasonably quiet.

Eating Out

What to Eat

The dramatic rise in the number of Thai restaurants around the world says something about the popularity of one of the world's supreme cuisines. It is no surprise that when gourmets arrive on these shores fresh from Thai dining experiences at home, they fall into a feeding frenzy that lasts their entire stay.

The base for most Thai dishes Is coconut milk. Ginger, garlic, lemon grass and fiery chilies give Thai dishes a piquancy that can set tender palates aflame. While many of the chilies are mild, their potency is in obverse proportion to their size; the smallest, the *prik kii no* or "rat dropping chilies," are guaranteed to dissolve your sinuses and cloud your vision with tears.

For those averse to spicy food, chefs can tone down the curries or serve one of the dozens of non-spicy curries.

Where to Eat
BANGKOK
In Europe, the very best restaurants are not usually to be found in hotels. In Thailand, the reverse is true. There are, of course, exceptions to both these generalities. All the following restaurants contribute to making Thailand a gourmet's paradise.

Thai Dinner and Cultural Shows
Baan Thai, 7 Soi 32, Sukhumvit Road. Tel: 258 5403, 258 9517. Pleasant atmosphere in a group of old Thai houses in a tropical garden. Popular with group tours. Thai dancing begins around 9pm.
Maneeya Lotus Room, 518/4 Ploenchit Road. Tel: 251 0382, 252

6312. Open daily. Lunch 10am–2pm. Nightly 7pm with Thai classical dance performance at 8.15pm.

Sala Rim Nam, Charoen Nakhon Road. Tel: 437 9417, 437 3080, 437 2918. Located in a beautiful, temple-like building across the river from the Oriental – particularly good Thai dancing. Free boat service from Oriental Hotel landing. Book in advance.

Sala Thai, Indra Regent Hotel, 120-126 Ratchaprarop Road. Tel: 208 0033. Attractive reproduction of a classic building on an upper floor of the hotel.

Silom Village Trade Centre, 286 Silom Road. Tel: 234 4448, 233 9447. Open-air and indoor restaurants, traditional food stalls, Thai cultural show presented every Saturday and Sunday from 12.45am and Thai classical dance shows daily at 8pm. Informal atmosphere.

Hotel Buffets

Many hotels in Bangkok vie with each other to prove that their lunch and dinner buffets surpass that of their competitors, both in quality and value for money. The result is an overwhelming choice of prices. You will not be disappointed wherever you choose to go, and even the least-expensive buffets still offer a bewildering variety of dishes. All are highly recommended. In addition, many hotels offer lavish Sunday brunches, with clowns, magicians, games, videos and other diversions to keep children amused.

Thai Cuisine

All Gaengs, 173/8-9 Suriwongse Road. Tel: 233 3301. Elegant, modern decor and delicious Thai cuisine. $$

Baan Kanitha, 36/1 Soi 23 (Soi Prasanmit), Sukhumvit Road. Tel: 258 4181. A good introduction to Thai cuisine with tasteful decor and attentive service. $$

Benjarong, Dusit Thani Hotel, 946 Rama IV Road. Tel: 236 0450/9. Superlative Royal Thai cuisine served on exquisite bencharong ware. $$$

Bon Vivant, Tawana Ramada Hotel, 80 Suriwongse Road. Tel: 236 0361/98. Splendid cuisine with a host of Thai dishes, beautifully prepared and presented. $$

Bussaracum, 35 Soi Pipat 2, Convent Road. Tel: 235 8915. Extremely popular with local connoisseurs of classical Thai cuisine; pleasant, informal atmosphere. $$

Cabbages and Condoms, 8-10 Soi 12, Sukhumvit Road. Tel: 252 7349, 251 5552. Value for money and first-class cuisine. If you are not familiar with Thai food, this should be among your first choices. The profits support various family planning and HIV awareness programs and other charitable projects. Entertaining gift shop adjacent. $

Celadon, Beaufort Sukhothai, 13/3 Sathorn Tai Road. Tel: 287 0222. Exceptional cuisine in the setting of an exotic water garden. $$$

Chilli House, Soi 4, Silom Road (near the Rome Club). Tel: 266 9564. You can enter either via Silom Road or through the Patpong Car Park on Soi Patpong 2. Everything expertly prepared and presented by a top Thai chef, especially the seafood dishes. $

D'Jit Pochana, 62 Soi 20, Sukhumvit Road. Tel: 258 1578. Branches at 1082 Phaholyothin Road (near Chatuchak Park), tel: 279 5000/2, and at Ploenchit Centre, 3rd Floor, tel: 656 8454. A long-established Thai restaurant, diverse menu. Try the wild boar curry. $

Hemlock, 56 Phra Athit Road (opposite River Express Boat entrance). Tel: 282 7507. Excellent food, impressive wine list, many foreign beers. $

Krua Langsuan, 93/12 Soi 5, Soi Lang Suan. Tel: 252 1945. Picturesque venue. Dine on pleasant Thai and Chinese cuisine while listening to Thai folk music. $

Laicram, 120/12 Soi 23 (Soi Prasanmit), Sukhumvit Road. Tel: 258 9616, 238 2337. Branches at 11/1 Soi 49/4, Sukhumvit Road, tel: 392 5864; Thaniya Bldg., Thaniya Road, tel: 231 2117.

Excellent variety of Thai dishes. $–$$

Lemongrass, 5/21 Soi 24, Sukhumvit Road. Tel: 258 8637. Known for its excellent cuisine. $$

Nipa Thai, Landmark Hotel, 138 Sukhumvit Road. Tel: 254 0404. As with all the many restaurants in this hotel, its Thai restaurant is of the highest standard. $$$

Pan Kitchen, Tai-Pan Hotel, 25 Soi 23 (Soi Prasanmit), Sukhumvit Road. Tel: 260 9888. Tasty Thai cuisine. Worth going out of your way to try the inexpensive buffet set lunch which also includes some European dishes. $–$$

Salathip, Shangri-La Hotel, 89 Soi Wat Suan Plu. Tel: 236 7777. Superb Thai dining on the river's edge. $$$

Sidewalk, 855/2 Silom Road. Tel: 236 4496. The owner is French-born Pierre Chaslin, the author of the best selling "Discover Thai Cooking." Superb cuisine, ordinary decor. $

Sorn Daeng (at the Democracy Monument), 78/2 Ratchadamnern Road. Tel: 224 3088. One of the oldest restaurants in town, known for good Thai food. $

Spice Market, The Regent Hotel, 155 Ratchadamri Road. Tel: 251 6127. Beautifully decorated restaurant, with dishes that the chef can adapt to suit Western palates. $$

Thai Pavilion, Holiday Inn Crowne Plaza, 981 Silom Road. Tel: 238 4300. Traditional Thai cuisine in a traditional setting. $$

Thai Room, 37/20-5 Soi Patpong 2. Tel: 233 7920. Serving Thai, Mexican, Chinese and European food. One of the oldest restaurants in the city. $

Thanying, 10 Pramuan Road, Silom Road. Tel: 236 4361. Excellent Thai food in very pleasant surroundings. $$

The Glass, 22/3-5 Soi 11, Sukhumvit Road. Tel: 254 3566. As well known for its food as its live music in the evenings. $$

Isaan/Lao and Northern Thai

Ban Chiang, 14 Soi Srivieng, Surasak Road (off Silom Road). Tel:

236 7045, 266 6994. Pleasant surroundings, comprehensive selection of central Thai and Isaan dishes, good wines. $

Bua Luang, 116 Soi Rambutri, Banglampoo. Tel: 282 2635. A long-standing restaurant with good Northern dishes. $

Khing Klao, Soi 22, Sukhumvit Road (just beyond Washington Square). Tel: 259 5623. Interesting decor, great Chiang Mai sausage dishes. $

Mai Klang Krung, 114/3 Sethasiri Road, Phaya Thai. Tel: 279 2866. Peaceful garden setting serving traditional Northern fare. Chicken wrapped in banana leaves a specialty. $

Panjimhut Isaan Restaurant, Sukhumvit Road, between Soi 51 and 53. Tel: (none). Excellent Isaan food, but not for those with delicate palates. $$

Sara Jane's Larb Lang Suan, 36/2 Soi Lang Suan. Tel: 252 6572. Traditional, spicy Northeastern dishes. $$

Som Tam, Si Nakharin Road, opposite Seri Centre. Tel: 393 5884, 748 0794. Delicious Isaan cuisine, very popular. Will tone down spices if asked. $

Seafood

Dusit Rimtarn Seafood Restaurant, Supakarn Shopping Centre, Sathorn Bridge. Tel: 437 9671. A view of the river. Seafood and other Thai and Chinese cuisine superbly prepared under the supervision of the Dusit Thani Hotel. $$–$$$

For Hor Gor Dor, 15 Soi 4, Soi 63 (Soi Ekamai), Sukhumvit Road. Tel: 391 1326. Quiet location, beautiful decor, generous portions. $$

Lord Jim's, Oriental Hotel, 48 Oriental Avenue. Tel: 236 0400. Top-quality restaurant noted for its good atmosphere, excellent food and service. $$$

Sammuk Seafood, 2140-4 Soi 90, Lard Prao Road. Tel: 539 2466/9. One of many inexpensive Thai seafood restaurants in Bangkok. This particular one has won many accolades for the quality of food. $

Sea Food Market, 89 Soi 24, Sukhumvit Road. (Look for the large neon lobster sign.) Tel: 261 2071/4. Novel grocery store layout; pick out the seafood of your choice from a vast variety on ice and have it cooked to suit your taste; informal. Great selection of wines. Can be expensive if you succumb to the temptation of ordering too much. $$–$$$

Talay Thong, Siam Inter-Continental Hotel, 967 Rama I Road. Tel: 253 0355. High quality dining, decor and service. $$

Wit's Oyster Bar, 21/10 Soi Ruam Rudi, Ploenchit Road. Tel: 252 1820, 251 9455. A plush English-style oyster bar. $$

Outdoor Thai Restaurants

When giving instructions to the taxi driver, tell him "Suan Aahaan" (garden restaurant) before giving him the name of one of the restaurants below.

Baan Buang, 32/10 Mu 2, Ratchadapisek Road (opposite Nikko Hotel). Tel: 277 8609, 277 7563. $–$$

Buatong, 30 Ratchadapisek Road. Tel: 245 5545. $–$$

Tum Nak Thai, 131 Ratchadapisek Road. Tel: 276 7810. This restaurant has merited an entry in the Guinness Book of Records as the largest in the world. Waiters on roller skates serve food from all regions of Thailand; very popular with tourists. $–$$

Riverside Restaurants

Baan Khun Luang, 131/4 Khao Road (off Ratchawithi Road). Tel: 241 0928, 241 0521, 241 2282. Thai, Chinese and Japanese cuisine in a riverside setting. $

Kaloang Home Kitchen, on the river, behind the National Library (at the end of Sri Ayutthaya, cross Samsen, turn right, then left to the river). Tel: 281 9228, 282 7581. Very popular, generous portions. $$

Rim Naam Terrace, Montien Riverside Hotel, Rama III Road. Tel: 292 2800. Lovely setting with Thai and Vietnamese specialties. $$

Savoy Seafood Restaurant, River City Complex, 23 Yotha Road. Tel: 435 0611. Excellent Thai and Chinese seafood dishes. $$

Chinese

Canton Palace, Evergreen Laurel Hotel, 88 Sathorn Nua Road. Tel: 266 7223. An elegant restaurant with excellent Cantonese cuisine. $$

Chinatown, Dusit Thani Hotel, 946 Rama IV Road. Tel: 236 0450. Less expensive than the Mayflower also within the hotel, but just as delicious. $$

Chiu Chau, Ambassador Hotel, 171 Soi 11-13, Sukhumvit Road. Tel: 254 0444. Delicacies from the Southern Chinese province of Chiu Chau (Guangchao). $$

Coca Noodles, 8 Soi Tartawan, Suriwongse Road. Tel: 236 9323. Branches at Siam Square, 416/3-8 Henri Dunant Road, tel: 251 6337; The Mall 4, 1911 Ramkhamhaeng Road, tel: 318 0997; 1/1 Soi 39, Sukhumvit Road, tel: 259 8188. Cantonese hot pot, sukiyaki and noodle dishes. $$

Dynasty, Central Plaza Hotel, 1695 Phaholyothin Road. Tel: 541 1234. Traditional cuisine with Peking duck, shark's fin and abalone all featured in the extensive menu. $$

Great Wall, Asia Hotel, 296 Phaya Thai Road. Tel: 215 0808. The heart of any good hotel is in the kitchen; at the Asia Hotel there are several different kinds of restaurants, this being one of the best. $$$

Hoi Tien Lao, 762 Laadya Road, (Thonburi bank of river, opp. Royal Orchid Sheraton Hotel). Tel: 437 1121. Cantonese food; one of Bangkok's oldest and most popular Chinese restaurants. $$

Hong Teh, Ambassador Hotel, 171 Soi 11-13, Sukhumvit Road. Tel: 254 0444. A favorite with local gourmets for banquets. $$

Jade Garden, Montien Hotel, 54 Suriwongse Road. Tel: 234 8060. Southern Chinese dishes prepared by Hong Kong chefs in an elegant setting. $$

Lin-Fa, Siam City Hotel, 477 Sri Ayutthaya Road. Tel: 247 0120, 247 0130. An elegant Chinese restaurant in one of Bangkok's most stylish hotels. $$$

Lok Wah Hin, Novotel, 392/44 Soi 6, Siam Square, Rama I Road. Tel:

255 6888. Cantonese and Szechuan cuisine at its best. $$
Mayflower, Dusit Thani Hotel, 946 Rama IV Road. Tel: 236 0450. One of Thailand's best hotel Chinese restaurants. $$$
Ming Palace, Indra Regent Hotel, 120-126 Ratchaprarop Road. Tel: 208 0033. Southern Chinese dishes. $$
New Great Shanghai, 648-652 Sukhumvit Road (near Soi 24). Tel: 258 7042. Popular with local Chinese, especially for Sunday lunch. Tremendous variety of duck, marvelous rice bread. $$
Noble House, Hilton International Hotel, 2 Witthayu Road. Tel: 253 0123. Cantonese cuisine, profuse all-you-can-eat dinner buffet with over 75 items to choose from, tasteful decor. $$–$$$
Nguan Lee, 101/25-26 Soi Lang Suan, Ploenchit Road. Tel: 251 8366, 252 3614. Covered market; real atmosphere. One of the few restaurants where you can eat the famous Mekong giant catfish. $$
Rice Mill, Marriott Royal Garden Riverside, 257/1-3 Charoen Nakhon Road. Tel: 476 0021/2. Built on the site of an old rice mill, this luxury riverside hotel has a splendid Chinese restaurant. $$$
Royal Kitchen, 146 Soi 55 (Soi Thong Lo), Sukhumvit Road. Tel: 391 0252, 391 9634. Excellent food in an elegant setting. $$–$$$
Scala Restaurant, 218/1 Soi 1, Siam Square, Rama I Road (near Scala Theatre). Tel: 254 2891. One of the house specialties is Peking Duck. The adjoining restaurant specializes in shark's fin. $$
Shang Palace, Shangri-La Hotel, 89 Soi Wat Suan Plu. Tel: 236 7777, ext. 1350 & 1358. Superb Cantonese and Szechuan specialties. The lunchtime dim sum is a real treat. $$–$$$
Shangrila, 58/4-9 Thaniya Road. Tel: 234 0861. Branches at 154/4-5 Silom Road, tel: 234 9147/9; 306 Yawarat, tel: 224 5933. Cantonese cuisine. $$
Silom Restaurant, 793 Silom Road. Tel: 236 4442. One of the oldest Chinese restaurants in town; northern Chinese dishes. $$

Silver Palace Restaurant, 5 Soi Pipat, Silom Road. Tel: 235 5118/9. Well known for the variety of its delicious dim sum menu. Cantonese cuisine in opulent surroundings. $$$
Sui Sian, Landmark Hotel, 138 Sukhumvit Road. Tel: 254 0404. Cantonese and regional delicacies to the highest standards. $$$
The Chinese Restaurant, Grand Hyatt Erawan, 494 Ratchadamri Road. Tel: 254 1234. Sophisticated Cantonese specialties prepared by Hong Kong chefs. $$$
The Empress, Royal Princess Hotel, 269 Lan Luang Road. Tel: 281 3088. Delicious lunchtime dim sum. $$
Ti Jing, Monarch Lee Gardens Hotel, 188 Silom Road. Tel: 238 1999. A dazzling array of dim sum and other Cantonese delicacies. $$
Tien Tien Restaurant, 105 Soi Patpong. Tel: 234 8717, 234 6006. Located in the middle of busy, bustling Patpong. The decor takes second place to the food. $

Indian/Arabic/Muslim

Akbar Restaurant, 1/4 Soi 3 (Soi Nana Nua), Sukhumvit Road. Tel: 255 6935, 655 5097. Tasty northern Indian food. Try the prawn korma. $$
Bangkok Brindawan, 44/1 Soi 19, Silom Road. Tel: 233 4791. Simple decor and some excellent vegetarian dishes. Daily buffet lunch. $
Bukhara, Royal Orchid Sheraton Hotel, 2 Captain Bush Lane. Tel: 237 0022, 266 0123. Superb Indian cuisine with impeccable service. $$$
Cedar, 4/1 Soi 49/1, Sukhumvit Road. Tel: 391 4482. Excellent Lebanese and Greek cuisine. $$
Himali Cha Cha, 1229/11 Charoen Krung (New) Road. Tel: 235 1569. Northern cuisine created by a master chef. $$
Maharajah's, 19/1 Soi 8, Sukhumvit Road. Tel: 254 8876. Some tasty tandoori dishes. $
Moghul Room, 1/16 Soi 11, Sukhumvit Road. Tel: 253 4465. Popular, but more expensive than some. $$

Mrs. Balbir's, 155/18 Soi 11, Sukhumvit Road. Tel: 253 2281. Good north Indian cuisine, a favorite with Bangkok expats. $$
Rang Mahal, Rembrandt Hotel, 19 Soi 18, Sukhumvit Road. Tel: 261 7100. First-class cuisine and impeccable service in this rooftop restaurant. Excellent samosas. $$
Tandoor, Holiday Inn Crowne Plaza, 981 Silom Road. Tel: 238 4300. North Indian cuisine of exceptional quality. $$

Indonesian

Bali, 15/3 Soi Ruam Rudi, Ploenchit Road. Tel: 250 0711, 254 3581. The best of Javanese cuisine in a peaceful atmosphere. $

Japanese

Benihana, Marriott Royal Garden Riverside, 257/1-3 Charoen Nakhon Road. Tel: 476 0021/2. The preparation of the dishes is a combination of knife-wielding and juggling. The end result is always a superb meal. $$$
Benkay, Royal Orchid Sheraton Hotel, 2 Captain Bush Lane. Tel: 237 0022, 266 0123. The restaurant is noted for its exquisite Japanese cuisine served in an ambience of quiet elegance; a place for refined tastes. $$$
Endogin, Shangri-La Hotel, 89 Soi Wat Suan Plu. Tel: 236 7777. All that you would expect from one of Bangkok's top hotels. $$
Genji, Hilton International Hotel, 2 Witthayu Road. Tel: 253 0123, ext. 8141. Expensive. $$$
Hagi, Central Plaza Hotel, 1695 Phaholyothin Road. Tel: 541 1234. Popular, with reasonable prices. $$
Hanaya, 683 Si Phraya Road. Tel: 234 8095. Clean and unpretentious. $
Kagetsu, Asia Hotel, 296 Phaya Thai Road. Tel: 215 0808. Traditional cuisine and setting. Very popular. $$
Kiku-No-Hana, The Landmark Hotel, 138 Sukhumvit Rd. Tel: 254 0404. First-class Japanese cuisine. $$
Kobe Steak House, 460 Soi 7, Siam Square, Rama I Road. Tel: 251 1336. Excellent beef, good service. $

Mizu's, 32 Soi Patpong. Tel: 233 6447. One of the oldest Japanese restaurants in the city. The house specialty is sizzling steak. $

Nishimura, Siam City Hotel, 477 Sri Ayutthaya Road. Tel: 247 0120, 247 0130. First-class dining in style. $$$

Shogun, Dusit Thani Hotel, 946 Rama IV Road. Tel: 236 0450. Sashimi and other Japanese delicacies; elegant decor. $$$

Teio, Monarch Lee Gardens Hotel, 188 Silom Road. Tel: 238 1999. Sophisticated Japanese dining. Special family buffet lunches on Saturday and Sunday. $$

Tokugawa, Ambassador Hotel, 171 Soi 11-13, Sukhumvit Road. Tel: 254 0444, ext. 1569. The teppanyaki is delicious and fun to watch the chef preparing. $$

Kosher

Ohr Menachem Chabad House, 108/1 Rambutri Road, Khao San Road, Banglampoo. Tel: 282 6388, fax: 629 1153. Close to many guesthouses on Khao San Road, popular with young Jewish travelers. Open 12–9pm daily. $

Pacific

L'Orangery, 48/11 Soi Ruam Rudi, Witthayu Road. Tel: 253 6941. Interesting menu with Californian and Asian influences. $$–$$$

Trader Vic's, Marriott Royal Garden Riverside, 257/1-3 Charoen Nakhon Road. Tel: 476 0021/2. The unique style of oven gives a different flavour to the dishes. A delightfully different dining experience. $$$

Vegetarian

Ambassador Kitchen, Ambassador Hotel, Forum Bldg., 171 Soi 11-13, Sukhumvit Road. Tel: 254 0444. Excellent Chinese vegetarian cuisine. $$

May Kaidee, 117/1 Tanao Road, Banglampoo. Tel: (none). Near the Regal Fashion shop on a small soi opposite the eastern end of Khao San Road. Good service. Try the tofu curry. $

Veg House, 1/6 Soi 3 (Soi Nana Nua), Sukhumvit Road. Tel: 254

7357. Great selection of Indian and Thai dishes, emphasis on fresh ingredients. $

You Sue Vegetarian, 241 Rama IV Road, opposite Bangkok Centre Hotel. (Look for small sign in window which reads "health food.") Tel: 214 2801. Traditional Chinese menu, popular with locals. $

Whole Earth Café, 93/3 Soi Lang Suan. Tel: 252 5574. Branch at 71 Soi 26, Sukhumvit Road. Tel: 258 4900. Bangkok's best-known Thai vegetarian restaurant; comfortable and friendly. There is also a tasty menu of non-vegetarian fare with excellent Indian dishes. $$

Vietnamese/Burmese

Cherie Kitchen, 593/13 Soi 33/1, Sukhumvit Road. Tel: 258 5058. $

Le Dalat, 47/1 Soi 23 (Soi Prasanmit), Sukhumvit Road. Tel: 258 4192 and Patpong Bldg., 2nd Floor, Suriwongse Road. Tel: 234 0290. Two of the best in town in the moderate price range. $$

Le Danang, Central Plaza Hotel, 1695 Phaholyothin Road. Tel: 541 1234. A long-established Vietnamese restaurant renowned for its authentic cuisine. $$

Mandalay, 23/7 Soi Ruam Rudi, Witthayu Road. Tel: 255 2893. One of the only Burmese restaurants in Bangkok. Good food. $$

Saigon, Asia Hotel, 296 Phaya Thai Road. Tel: 215 0808. Luxury in an elegant setting under supervision of a Vietnamese chef. $$$

Saigon-Rimsai, 413/9 Soi 55 (Soi Thong Lo), Sukhumvit Road. Tel: 381 1797. Small, beautifully decorated and the Vietnamese chef produces a variety of dishes. $$

Vietnam, 82-4 Silom Road, (opp. Convent Road). Tel: 234 6174. Southern-style Viet cuisine. $

CHIANG MAI

Thai

Antique House, 71 Charoen Prathet Road, across from the Pornping Hotel, is situated in a wonderful old wooden house. $$

The Gallery, on Charoenrat Road, tel: 248 601, combines an art gallery with a Chinese garden and riverside terrace. $$

Kafe, 127-9 Mun Muang Road. Tel: 212 717. An old wooden building next to the moat. A fine selection of Thai and Western food. $

Krua Khun Phan, 80/1 Intrawarorot Road (near Suan Dok Gate), displays a variety of ready-made Thai dishes. $

Nang Nual, 27/2-5 Koh Klang Road. Tel: 281 961. A riverside restaurant, down river a few hundred meters off the Chiang Mai-Lamphun Road. $$$

Phuket Laikhram, 1/10 Suthep Road, an excellent southern Thai restaurant serving various curries and tom yam-style noodles. $

The Riverside Bar and Restaurant, 9/11 Charoenrat Road. Tel: 242 239. Excellent meals on the banks of the Ping River. Live music. $$

Tha Nam, 43/3 Mu 2, Chang Klan Road. Tel: 404 371. A large wooden building with a pleasant riverside terrace. $$

Whole Earth, 88 Sri Dornchai Road, tel: 232 463, serves vegetarian and non-vegetarian Thai dishes in a garden setting. $$

There are also Lanna *kantoke* dinners, where you can dine on northern Thai kantoke cuisine and then sit back to enjoy a program of northern dances and music. **The Diamond Hotel** on Charoen Prathet Road serves a nightly Lanna Kantoke dinner with classical Lanna and hill-tribe dancing. Tel: 234 155 for reservations. **Old Chiang Mai Cultural Centre** also presents a Kantoke dinner with a program of Northern and hill-tribe dances. Offered nightly from 7–10pm in a beautiful Northern Thai style house at 185/3 Wua Lai Road. Tel: 275 097 for reservations. Modest fee, begins at 7pm. Reserve ahead.

Asian

Akamon (Japanese), Chiang Mai Hills Hotel, 18 Huay Kaeo Road. Tel: 210 030. $$$

Ari-Rang (Korean), Star Inn Hotel, 36 Soi 4 Loi Kroh Road. Tel: 270 360. $$

Shere Shiraz (Indian/Muslim), 23-25 Charoen Prathet Road. Tel: 276 132. $$

European
Bier Stube (German), 33/6A Moonmauang Road (near Tapae Gate). Tel: 278 869. $
Café de Paris (French), 14-16 Kotchasan Road. Tel: 234 804. $$
Di-Dario's, off Sumonthewaraj Road, near hospital and airport. The only farang restaurant in town. Swiss-run. The Italian and Thai food gets rave reviews, but the restaurant is very difficult to find, especially at night. May be packed with locals. $
Haus Munchen (German), 115/3 Loi Kroh Road. Tel: 274 027. $$
Nan Phin Pub, 440 Sumonthewaraj Road, Amphur Muang. Tel: 772 640, 771 697. Ground floor of Nan Fa Hotel. Nightly folk music show, with traditional instruments. Arrive well before 9pm to avoid karaoke. $
Pensione La Villa (Italian), 145 Ratdamnern Road. Tel: 277 403. $
The Pub (English), Huay Kaeo Road, near the Rincome Hotel (Tel: 211 550), has English meals and a fireplace. $$

PATTAYA
Thai and Seafood
La Mer Grill, Montien Hotel, Pattaya 2 Road. Tel: 428 155/6. Maela Plaphao, Soi Siam Country Club. Tel: 716 181.
Thai House, 171/1 North Pattaya Road. Tel: 370 579/81.

Asian and Continental
Akamon (Japanese), 464/19 Pattaya 2 Road, North Pattaya. Tel: 423 727.
Chalet Swiss (Continental), 220 Beach Road. Tel: 429 255.
Diulio's (Italian), 192 Moo 9, Soi Foodland. Tel: 427 154.
Dolf Riks (Indonesian, Thai, Continental), 116/8 Pattaya-Naklua Road. Tel: 367 585.
Moon River Pub (Mexican), Thai Garden Resort, North Pattaya Road. Tel: 426 009.
Yamato (Japanese), Soi Yamato. Tel: 429 685.

PHUKET
Phuket Town
Ka Jok See, 26 Takua Pa Road. Tel: 217 903. Intimate dining in a delightful off-the-wall Thai restaurant. Newspaper table covers, household antiques and a porch with verdant potted plants create a raffish feel underscored by jazz music. $$
Mala, 5/72-73 Mae Luan Road. Tel: 214 201. Open-front restaurant decorated with vintage household artefacts. It also serves *kaow yam* mixed herbal dish good for your health. Tasty curries like masaman guy are made fresh each morning. $
Laem Thong, 31-39 Chana Charoen Road. Tel: 211 269. Large and urbane Chinese-Thai restaurant specializing in Thai seafood and Pekinese cuisine. Lobster, oyster, shark's fin and suckling pig draw dedicated gourmands. $$$
Le Café, Phuket Shopping Centre, Rasda Road. Tel: 215 563. French-style eatery in the town centre serving exotic coffees and teas by cup or pot. Reasonable selection of steaks, pizzas and ice creams. $$
Metropole Coffee Shop, Metropole Hotel, Montri Road. Tel: 215 050. Upmarket yet very good value lunch venue with a bountiful buffet spread of Thai cuisine from four regions of the country. Prompt table service. Thai classical music plays in the background. $$
Ocean Time Square, Tilok Uthit 1 Road. Tel: 213 213. Unremarkable modern shopping mall distinguished by very good Asian fast-food restaurants: the Noodle Garden and Joto Bar-B-Q (Chinese), Suan Mee Suki (Japanese), Uptown (Thai-Western). $$
The Rooftop, Pearl Hotel, Montri Road. Tel: 211 044. Exquisite Cantonese restaurant on the top floor of the hotel. Refurbished in classical Chinese style. Popular with local business community. Acclaimed by Gault Millault. $$$
Thai Naan, 16 Wichitsongkhram Road. Tel: 226 164/7. Mammoth teak-panelled Thai, Chinese and Japanese restaurant which claims to be the largest in South Thailand. Some small air-conditioned rooms. Live classical music. Good food and service despite size. Sumptuous Srivichai Room specializes in southern fare with show. $$$

Tung-ka Café, Top of Khao Rang Hill. Tel: 211 500. Romantic open-air Thai restaurant with sweeping views of Phuket town and the coast. Small selection of Japanese and Western dishes. Restaurant is at its best by night with views of the town lit up below. $$

Phuket Beaches
Bang Thao Ruen Thai, Dusit Laguna Resort. Tel: 324 320/9. Central Royal Thai cuisine served by waitresses in Thai classical costumes to the accompaniment of kim music. Romantic candlelit setting beside a lake. $$$
Tatonka, just outside Laguna Phuket. Tel: 324 349. Delicate and innovative fusion cuisine combining western, Thai, Mexican and Mediterranean influences in a café setting with wine bar. The kitchen is open for all to see. Surprisingly inexpensive. $$
Chalong Gan Eng 1, 9/3 Chaofa Road. Tel: 381 212, 381 323. Simple open-air restaurant on the waterfront. Popular with locals and tourists alike. Seafood dishes are a specialty. $$
Jimmy's Lighthouse, Moo 9 Chalong Bay. Tel: 381 709. Seafront maritime café popular with international yachtsmen. Ambitious menu successfully plunders the best of Europe and Asia. $$
Kamala Paul's Place, Kamala Beach Estate, Kamala Beach. Tel: 324 111. Trendy wooden Thai restaurant on stilts overlooking peaceful Kamala beach. Broad range of Thai dishes is served to the Chinese granite-top tables. Medium pricing. Good atmosphere from sunset onwards. Steak, pasta, schnitzel options too. $$
Karon Little Mermaid, 36/10 Patak Road. Tel: 396 628. Comfortable Scandinavian restaurant in the heart of Karon. The thoughtful menu allows diners to tick options like medium or rare for steaks, with fries or baked potato. $$
Old Siam, Thavorn Palm Beach Hotel. Tel: 396 116. A large restaurant with an emphasis on royal Thai traditions. Nightly kim classical music performances and

Thai dancing add ambience. Ask for one of the outdoor balcony tables with excellent views of Karon beach at sunset. $$

On the Rock, Marina Cottage Resort. Tel: 330 625. Very popular small restaurant on the rocks overlooking Karon Bay. Strong on Thai food, seafood and international items. Although a tad pricey, the superlative setting and taste compensate. Dinner bookings essential. $$$

The Terrace, Karon-Patong coast road. Tel: 286 030. Continental restaurant perched on a cliff overlooking Karon Bay. Specializes in dishes like tagliatelle alla vodka and Chateaubriand steaks. Thai menu too. $$$

Kata Boathouse Wine & Grill, The Boathouse, 2/2 Patak Road. Tel: 330 015/7. Refined Thai and European dining on a romantic terrace overlooking the sea. Large wine selection and set menus. $$$

Islanders, 6/3 Soi Tuey Ngam, Patak Road. Tel: 330 740. Busy open-air restaurant in south Kata. Diners are typically hotel residents going local. Seafood is the mainstay but Italian and Japanese fare also served. $$

Kampong Kata Hill, 112/2 Patak Road, opp. Kata Centre. Tel: 330 103. Steep flight of stairs leads to quaint Thai restaurant on a wooden balcony in what is effectively an Asian art gallery. Moderately priced food from all areas of Thailand and a few international dishes. $$

Nai Harn Regatta Bar & Grill, Royal Le Méridien Phuket Yacht Club. Tel: 381 156. Colonial feel to an opulent but understated Italian restaurant in one of Phuket's most exclusive hotels. Set menus or la carte. Eclectic wine list. $$$

Patong Ban Rim Pa, 100/7 Kalim Beach Road. Tel: 340 789, 341 768. Delightfully located romantic restaurant with views of Patong Bay. Refined central Thai dining by candlelight. Seafood, however, plays a minor role in the menu. Reservations are advisable. $$$

Bangla Seafood, 82/46 Soi Bangla, Patong Beach. Tel: 342 436. Place to go for excellent range of big

lobsters, grilled crabs, juicy prawns and crispy-fried fish. Easy to run up a big bill if you choose lobsters. Fast business-like service in street-side open air café. Great location for watching assorted characters walk by. $$

Kubu Restaurant, Muen Ngoen Road, Patong. Tel: 292 191. Delightful hill setting at southern end of Patong Beach matched by high finesse of the Thai dishes. You order 24 hours in advance. Ingredients are bought in the market next morning. You taste the benefit in the evening. Romantic and surprisingly affordable. $$

Navrang Mahal, Soi Patong Resort, off Soi Bangla. Tel: 292 280. All corners of Indian cuisine touched here, from succulent northern tandoori dishes to spicy southern curries. A tad pricey. $$$

No. 4, 82 Moo 3, Soi Bangla, Patong. Tel: 342 319. No-frills, brightly lit seafood room at end of a shopping lane. Price advantage does not compromise taste. Extensive Thai and seafood choice. Afterwards you can write your name on the graffiti wall. $$

Pizzeria Napoli, Soi Patong Post Office. Tel: 340 674. Indoor dining on a wide range of pizzas, pastas and other Italian specialties. $$

KRABI

Krabi Town

Ruen Mai, Maharat Road, Krabi town. Tel: 631 797. Shade-dappled outdoor restaurant set among native trees, a kilometer out of town. Exclusively Thai menu at competitive prices reflects country cooking from south, central and northeastern Thailand. Open all day. $$

Barn Thai Issara, Ruen Rudee Road, Krabi town. Tel: 620 373. Family-run café which serves a limited range of high-quality pastas, salads, pizza breads, shakes and coffees. Superlative homemade bread. Open daytime only. $$

Ao Nang

Sala Thai, behind Beach Terrace hotel, Ao Nang. No phone. Atmospheric beachside seafood

and Thai curry restaurant a little hard to find, but well worth seeking out. The unpretentious setting on bamboo tables beside lapping waves attracts hotel guests going local. Open all day. Moderately priced. $$

Gift's, Beach Road, Ao Nang. Tel: 637 193. Pleasant central rendezvous for all-day dining. Attentive informal service underpins consistently good Thai dishes. Pastas, cocktails and homemade bread are a bonus. $$

Drinking Notes

Many restaurants catering to western tastes whip up a delicious shake made of pureed fruit, crushed ice and a light syrup. Chilled young coconuts are delicious; drink the juice, then scrape out and eat the tender young flesh. Try Vitamilk, a health drink made from soya bean milk. For a refreshing cooler, order a bottle of soda, a glass of ice and a sliced lime. Squeeze the lime into the glass, add the soda and enjoy. Sip the very strong Thai coffee flavored with chicory. The odd orange Thai tea is sticky sweet but delicious. On a hot day, Chinese prefer to drink a hot, very thin tea, believing that ice is bad for the stomach. Try all three over ice anyway.

Beers include Kloster, Carlsberg, Amarit, Singha and Singha Gold. Carlsberg and Heineken are now brewed in Thailand. Of the many Thai cane whiskeys, Mekhong is the most popular. It is drunk on the rocks, with soda and lime or with a bit of honey added to it.

Attractions

Leisure Pursuits

COURSES
Community Services of Bangkok, 15/1 Soi 33, Sukhumvit Road, tel: 258 4998, 258 5652, fax: 260 3563. This volunteer organization runs different courses each month on a variety of diverse subjects. More expensive for non-members, but still reasonable.
Oriental Hotel Cooking School, Soi Oriental, Charoen Krung (New) Road. Tel: 236 0400/39. Offers five-day classes in Thai cuisine and vegetable-carving.

Buddhist Meditation
Studying Buddhism is not an uncommon pursuit for foreign visitors to Thailand. There are many venues for such study throughout the country, including the following. Telephone or write first since schedules change frequently and accommodation is often limited.

Bangkok
House of Dhamma, 26/9 Soi 15 (Soi Chompon), Lard Prao Road. Tel: 511 3549, 511 0439.
International Buddhist Meditation Centre, Wat Mahathat, Maharat Road, Tha Phra Chan. Tel: 222 6011.
World Fellowship of Buddhists, 33 Sukhumvit Road (between Soi 1 and 3). Tel: 251 1188.

Provinces
Wat Khao Tham, Ko Pha Ngan, Surat Thani Province 84280.
Wat Pah Nanachat, Ban Bung Wai, Amphur Warin, Ubon Ratchathani 34310.
Wat Ram Poeng, Tambon Suthep, Amphur Muang, Chiang Mai 50000. Tel: (053) 278 620.

Wat Suan Mokkh, Amphur Chaiya, Surat Thani 84110.

HEALTH SPAS
The Banyan Tree, Westin Banyan Tree Hotel, Thai Wah II Tower, 51st Floor, Sathorn Tai Road. Tel: 679 1200. Hydrotherapy, seaweed masks, Swedish massage. Fabulous view from the tallest building in Thailand.
Grande Spa and Fitness Centre, Sheraton Grande Hotel, 250 Sukhumvit Road. Tel: 653 0334/8, fax: 653 0400. Swedish massage, hydrotherapy, algae and mud wraps.
JW's Health Club and Spa, JW Marriott Hotel, 4 Soi 2, Sukhumvit Road. Tel: 656 7700, fax 656 7711. Offers a flight reviver massage in addition to aromatherapy, Swedish massage, and body polishing.
The Oriental Spa, opposite the Oriental Hotel, 48 Oriental Avenue. Tel: 439 7613/4, fax: 439 7587. Seaweed treatments, foot massage, aromatherapy, papaya body polish. Special program to relieve jet lag. Advance booking recommended.

Sightseeing

BANGKOK
After touring the famous attractions like the Grand Palace, Wat Phra Kaeo, Wat Po, and Wat Arun, visit these lesser-known sites:

See Buddhist monks on their morning alms round by visiting **Wat Benchamabophit** at about 6.30am. Here, Buddhists take food to monks waiting silently outside the gates of the temple.

Tour **Vimarnmek**, the world's largest golden teak palace, and its superb collection of crystal, gold and silver art objects. Open daily, 9.30am–4pm. Admission is 50 baht or free with an entrance ticket to the Grand Palace.

Early in the morning, wander through Bangkok's largest wet market, **Pak Khlong Talat**, near the foot of the Memorial Bridge. Then visit the flower market on nearby Chakraphet Road.

Enjoy a traditional Thai massage in the sala, or resting pavilion, near the eastern wall of the **Wat Po** compound and grounds.

Board the Chao Phraya river express from the Oriental Hotel or Tha Chang near the Grand Palace, and ride 45 minutes up river to Nonthaburi with its bustling market. Have a drink or a meal at the floating restaurant next to the beautiful old provincial office. Alternatively, take the boat downstream to the last stop near the Krung Thep Bridge.

Take a free guided tour of the **National Museum**, Wednesday–Sunday at 9.30am.

Enjoy the educational snake show (where cobras are milked) at the **Snake Farm** (formerly the Pasteur Institute) on Rama IV Road at 10.30am and 2pm on weekdays, 10.30am on weekends and holidays, admission 70 baht.

On Saturdays and Sundays, explore the **weekend market** at Chatuchak Park. Start early to avoid the midday heat.

Take the Chao Phraya river express to the **Tha Ratchawong** landing in Chinatown. Walk down Ratchawong Road and turn in either direction on Sampeng Lane for a staggering assortments of shops selling everything from gold jewelry to steel wool.

Stroll through a former century of gracious living at the **Jim Thompson House**, Soi Kasem San 2, Rama I Road, Monday to Saturday, 9am–5pm, admission 100 baht. Or visit the complex of old houses at **Suan Pakkad Palace**, Sri Ayutthaya Road (between Phaya Thai and Ratchaprarop Roads), Monday to Saturday, 9am–4pm, admission 150 baht.

Visit the **Ancient City** (Muang Boran in Thai) with its miniature replicas of the kingdom's chief architectural masterpieces.

Rent a private boat at the Oriental Hotel and cruise through Khlong Bangkok Noi, stopping at the **Royal Barge Museum**. Take the long route home, through the smaller canals to Khlong Bangkok Yai and back to the Oriental.

Attend a **Thai boxing** (*muay Thai*)

match at Ratchadamnern or Lumpini Stadium.

Watch a free *likay* performance at Lak Muang.

Make a wish and an offering at the **Erawan Shrine** at the corner of Ratchadamri and Ploenchit roads.

Take a stroll through **Bangrak Market** (on Charoen Krung (New) Road, behind the Shangri-La Hotel), to see the splendid and colourful array of cut flowers.

Get a traditional herbal cure from a pharmacy in **Chinatown**. Buy a love potion or a Buddhist amulet from the stalls in the covered lanes beside **Wat Ratchanadda**, off Ratchadamnern Road and across from the Golden Mount.

Try to locate the **gold leaf beater's shop** in a small soi behind Tanao Road in Banglampoo Market.

Visit the **monks' bowl neighbourhood** (Baan Baat), the only place in Bangkok where the bowls are still crafted by hand, in the small *soi* located behind the Golden Mount.

Stroll around the campus of **Chulalongkorn University**, between Henri Dunant and Phaya Thai Roads, which is surprisingly cool and peaceful in the midst of Bangkok. Ask someone where the bookstore is.

Go for a walk or jog in **Lumpini Park** at 6am. Watch the *taichi* exercises being performed.

Have cocktails in the rooftop bar at the **Dusit Thani**. Pay a visit to **Kamthieng House**, a folk art museum, at the Siam Society on Soi 21 (Soi Asoke), Sukhumvit Road. Open Tuesday to Saturday, 9am–5pm, admission 25 baht.

CENTRAL PLAINS

Take the train to the **Bridge on the River Kwai**. The State Railways of Thailand offers a day trip each Saturday. If you have several days, stay on one of the raft houses farther up the river.

Ride the *Oriental Queen* up the Chao Phraya River to Ayutthaya, visiting Bang Pa-In along the way.

Enjoy the water sports in **Jomtien** or the nightlife in **Pattaya**.

Take a bus to Phetchaburi to

explore **King Mongkut's palace and observatory** on top of the hill.

Drive to **Ratchaburi** to look at the beautiful ceramics crafted and sold there. Visit **King Narai's old palace** at Lopburi.

Take the train to Phitsanulok to see the Phra Buddha Chinaraj image in **Wat Mahathat**. Continue to Sukhothai to see Thailand's first capital city, then to Si Satchanalai for some quiet beauty. Complete the journey by dropping south to the walled city of Kamphaeng Phet before returning to Phitsanulok.

THE NORTH

Visit the hilltop temple of **Doi Suthep** at sunset for a panoramic view of Chiang Mai Valley.

Explore the **crafts studios** along the road to Borsang.

Drive the tree-lined road to Lamphun to visit **Wat Phra That Haripunchai** and **Wat Chamathewi**.

Take a trek to visit **hill tribes** outside of Chiang Mai or Chiang Rai. Attend the demonstration of elephant's skills in moving teak logs at the **Young Elephant's Training School** at Lampang or the **Chiang Dao Elephant Camp**.

Ride a longboat 3.5 hours down the **Kok River** from Tha Ton to Chiang Rai.

Visit Mae Sai on the Burmese border and then drive to the **Golden Triangle** where the borders of Laos, Thailand and Burma meet in the middle of the Mekong River.

THE NORTHEAST

Drive to the Northeast to see **Khmer temples** at Phimai, Phanom Wan, Phanom Rung and Muang Tham. Travel from Ubon along the **Mekong River** to Nong Khai. View Friendship Bridge at Nong Khai, linking Thailand and Laos.

THE SOUTH

Visit the islands of **Phang Nga Bay**.

Ride the train from Bangkok to **Penang** in Malaysia.

Roam the farm areas and coastal roads of **Phuket** in a rented jeep. Rent a motorcycle and visit all the beaches of **Ko Samui**. Cruise around Phuket on a **Chinese junk**.

Beach facilities range from the rustic to the well-developed, each attracting a different clientele. On a rating of 1–3 (1=basic facilities only; 2=adequate but not luxurious facilities; 3=first-class hotels with restaurants, sports, shopping and sightseeing facilities).

PATTAYA AND JOMTIEN

Plenty of water sports and activities, but unfortunately the ocean is reputedly none too clean, so fewer people are swimming here. Best bets for water lovers are nearby islands or in hotel swimming pools. Pattaya has extensive services and facilities, excellent restaurants, golf courses, cultural shows, and, of course, the tatty nightlife. (2/3)

EAST COAST

The long stretch of sandy, tranquil, tree-lined coast running east of Ban Phe to Laem Mae Phim has numerous quiet resorts and good hotels set in leafy gardens. Water activities are generally confined to swimming and trips to nearby islands. An ideal area for families and those wanting a quiet, relaxing vacation. (2)

Ko Samet

This beautiful island is still a backpacker's retreat with rustic bungalows along lovely beaches. There are a few slightly more upmarket hotels, at cheaper prices than on the coast, but the lack of connection with the mainland, other than scheduled ferry boats, means that the island attracts a hardier crowd. Water sports facilities are increasing, along with the accompanying noise of jet-skis. Nighttime entertainment involves a few discos, video shows and beachside restaurants. (2)

Ko Chang

The size of Phuket, this quiet outpost, whose name means Elephant Island, is still a tranquil, forested oasis. Simple huts are slowly being joined by more upmarket resorts, but Ko Chang is too far from major centers to see huge changes soon. Diving here is very rewarding with wonderful coral and gorgeous fish. Lovely forest walks add to the island's quiet but potent charm. (2)

HUA HIN AND CHA-AM
In former times, royalty gathered here, and there is still an air of grandeur to its wide beaches. The area generally attracts families and older vacationers, but there are young couples as well. Excellent for quiet relaxation, strolling the fishing docks, a leisurely round of golf, riding ponies on the beach, or just sitting in a beach chair. Several international-class hotels and golf courses. (3)

PHUKET
Combining natural beauty with a complete range of resort facilities, Phuket has turned into a magnet for Asians and Europeans alike. Gone are most of the budget accommodations, but there are still low-priced as well as luxury hotels. It has land and water sports, a golf course, cultural shows, nightlife, drives around the island, in short, a full-fledged beach resort. (3)

PHI PHI
For years, its natural attractions were muted by its remoteness so that only budget travelers stayed in its thatched bungalows. It is still bungalow accommodation for the most part, but it has begun to move upmarket. Superb snorkeling, limited water sports, virtually no land sports, little nightlife, trips to nearby islands, restaurants and surpassing beauty is what it offers. Becoming overcrowded. (1.5)

KRABI
The newest of Thailand's beach resorts now offers some first-class hotels but smaller places and bungalows remain the main option. Snorkeling on offshore islands. (2)

KO SAMUI
Wide beaches and a laid-back lifestyle formerly drew only budget travelers. An airstrip has made the island accessible and first-class hotels make it comfortable for better-heeled tourists. Some water sports and cultural activities. (2.5)

Trekking
It's called trekking, but a two- to seven-day hike in the northern Thai hills shouldn't conjure up daunting visions of the Nepali version. Thailand's tallest mountain, Doi Inthanon, is less than 2,600 meters (8,530 ft) in height. While you should be fit, you need not be excessively so. Retirees trek, and so do children as young as ten.

Seeing tribal people living and working in their natural settings is the primary reason most people take treks. For those who have been stuck in Bangkok, total immersion in clean air and green things may feel like a physical and mental necessity. Trekkers also tend to have interests in birdwatching, botany, agriculture, opium, herbal medicine or New Age ideas. For wildlife enthusiasts, there's a chance to spot small game, such as antelope, wild pigs, bats and, yes, large snakes.

Most of the walking is on level ground and well-worn paths. The going becomes tough only during the height of the hot season, from March to May. Even then, the nights are cool enough to require a blanket. The best season is from November to March. Second best may be in June and July, before the full onslaught of the rainy season.

No special equipment is required. You carry a change of clothing, toilet articles, a flashlight and mosquito repellent. The guide takes care of the rest, including food, water bottles and transportation. You pay for the optional toke of opium, which is, of course, illegal. Water purification tablets should be brought from home, but an adequate substitute, iodine, can be bought in Thailand (one drop to a liter). You can sleep on the hardwood floor of a villager's thatched house while pigs root in the open space below. It's spartan, but no hardship for anyone who is accustomed to camping.

GUIDES and TOURS
The difference between a terrific and a disastrous experience depends greatly on your guide. It's therefore risky to book a tour from a large agency in Bangkok. Besides, whenever you arrive in Chiang Mai or Chiang Rai, it's always possible to join a trek leaving the following day. The choice of trekking tours in the two cities is so huge that it's discouraging. Every agency will promise "new" areas, unjaded villagers, multilingual guides and zero encounters with other groups.

You can narrow the choices by talking to tourists who have just returned from treks. In either city, or anywhere in northern Thailand, it's easy to meet such people, and they will eagerly pass on their recommendations and warnings. Keep in mind that they will recommend an individual guide, not the particular company he or she works for.

This emphasis also runs through the books of glowing handwritten customer comments that every self-respecting outfit displays.

You're more likely to hit an uncongested area if you bypass Chiang Mai and Chiang Rai altogether. Start with a small one- or two-person agency in a smaller town, such as Mae Hong Son, Pai, Mae Sai or Mae Sariang. Guesthouses can always direct you to someone. Guides in these places usually have completed a government training course and have previously been employed at low wages by slicker companies. More important, they are often tribesmen themselves or local Thais truly fluent in several tribal languages. Tribal guides usually speak English as well as, or better than, urban Thai guides.

SIGNING ON
Before you sign for any tour, determine how many hours you will walk, what you will eat and which tribes you will visit. As a rule of thumb, treks north of Chiang Mai

offer more of the "colourful" tribes, the vividly adorned Akha and Hmong people. To the west, along the Pai river and close to Mae Hong Son, however, there's much less deforestation. Try to meet your companions the night before the trek. The optimum number is between six to ten. The trekking agency will store your luggage and valuables, but credit cards are safer on your person.

A portion, perhaps half, of the tour fee should be paid before setting out, but be skeptical of demands for full payment. If the agency doesn't deliver on the promises, there is no way you will get a refund. A basic three-day, two-night trek costs between 1,000 and 1,500 baht.

River rafting and an elephant ride can add an extra 500 baht. Elephant rides, it must be noted, become uncomfortable very quickly. And rafting means seeing fewer villages. But in the rainy season – from July to October – rafting is a welcome respite from midday heat and leeches.

GETTING ALONG

Many prospective trekkers worry that their presence will contribute to the disintegration of tribal cultures. There is merit in this view. The most zoo-like encounters take place at tribal villages close to major roads and at the chilling, artificial Ravan (Long Necks) villages outside Mae Hong Son. A tour bus will pull up on schedule. Exotically garbed tribal women will envelope the tourists, badgering them to buy clothing or trinkets. The tourists will snap photos for a price. When the bus departs, the women will replace their traditional dress with T-shirts and Thai sarongs.

With a good guide-cum-interpreter, trekkers can humanize interactions by asking villagers about their customs, history and legends. Show respect for their religious beliefs and ceremonies. Play with the children. Via sign language, ask people before taking their photos. Give only adults small gifts, such as soap, bandages and

sewing needles, which are the kinds of things for which they need money. It's certainly bad form to bargain for the clothing on a person's back, but it's hard to see why some tourists refuse to buy handwoven clothes or embroidered bags that have been made for sale. Such small sums may keep a village intact, and the purchase indicates a respect for the artisan's quality workmanship.

It also eliminates the much wealthier Thai middlemen who run the numerous tribal handicraft shops in Chiang Mai. Many tourists say they wouldn't mind overpaying for an item if the money reached the maker. You can maximize the amount that will reach the hill tribes by buying products marketed by charitable organizations, such as the Thai Hill-Crafts Foundation and Thai Tribal Crafts. Another way is to seek out the tribal vendors in Chiang Mai's night market. They are easily recognized by the colourful garments and jewelry they wear.

Nightlife

For years, Thailand has enjoyed a lusty reputation as a centre for sex of every persuasion and interest. While the reputation was not altogether undeserved, times and clienteles have changed. The American GIs of the 1960s and German and Arab sex tourists of the 1970s have been replaced by upmarket tourists, usually traveling as couples. Also common are Japanese men on packaged sex tours, sex included. Western pedophiles are a continuing problem, especially in Pattaya.

While there has been no diminution in the number of massage parlors and bars, there has been an increase in other activities to meet the needs of the new breed of travelers, most of them in the 20–50 age range.

Jazz clubs, videotheques, discos and open-air restaurants are the most popular form of entertainment in towns.

A sign of the drastic changes is that the queen of nighttime

activities in Bangkok is shopping. Night markets have sprung up along Sukhumvit and Silom roads. Even that wrinkled old harlot of a street, Patpong, has not been immune to the breezes of change. Vendors' tables choke the street, drawing more patrons than the bars with a wealth of counterfeit Rolex watches, Benetton shirts and cassette tapes.

The change has rubbed off on the bars as well. Many of Patpong's bars have metamorphosed into discos, which begin to throb, so to speak, with life after 11pm.

Upcountry, the scene is essentially the same. Chiang Mai's night bazaar on Chang Klan Road attracts more tourists than the bars along Chaiyaphum Road.

In Phuket, "barbeers" (a bar which serves beer) line the streets of Patong beach's Soi Bangla and similar areas of Karon and Kata; but the hard sex of Bangkok's yesteryear has never established a foothold there.

MASSAGES

Massages fall into two categories: regular and "special". Establishments billing themselves as "Traditional Thai Massage" and "Ancient Thai Massage" offer therapeutic services according to age-old traditions, in other words, a legitimate massage. The best place for this, however, is at Wat Po.

The "special" type of massage is sexual. You pick a woman, or sometimes a girl, from behind a one-way mirror and then spend the next hour getting a bath and whatever else you arrange.

BANGKOK

Bars

There are three key areas in Bangkok where the types of entertainment for which the city has become famous can be found.

Patpong describes three streets: Soi Patpong itself and Soi Patpong 2, which is a welter of bars and bright lights, and Soi Patpong 3, which is almost exclusively gay. **Soi Cowboy** is a somewhat downmarket version of Patpong. Here, the entertainment is more basic. Midway between the two in geographic and entertainment terms, is the **Nana Entertainment Plaza** off Soi 4, Sukhumvit Road.

Gay and Lesbian Scene
Bank Studio, Soi 6, between Silom and Suriwongse. Tel: 236 6385. Daily 10pm–2am.
Dance club, popular with Thais, women welcome. DJ Station, 8/6 Soi 2, Silom Road. Tel: 266 4029. Daily 10pm–2am.
Gay disco, crowded. Henry Club, 8/10-11 Soi 2, Silom Road (opposite DJ Station). Tel: 632 7223. Daily 8pm–2am. Nightly show at 1am.
Sphinx, 98-104 Soi 4, Silom Road. Tel: 234 7249. Daily 7pm–1am. Elegant bar and restaurant. Good food.
Telephone, 114/11-13 Soi 4, Silom Road. Tel: 234 3279. Daily 8pm–2am. Bar/restaurant, good location for watching Soi 4 happenings. Telephones on each table enable patrons to dial other tables.
Utopia, 116/1 Soi 23 (Soi Prasanmit), Sukhumvit Road (opposite Tia Maria). Tel: 259 9619. Daily noon–2am. Shop, gay/lesbian social centre and café. Pub upstairs, Women's Night, Fridays; Drag Show, Saturdays.

Discos
Patpong also offers discos, many of which continue to throb long after the bars have closed down. Here, there are no sexual solicitations or other expectations.

Hotel discos worthy of consideration include: **Bubbles** at the Dusit Thani, **Cabaret Nightclub** at the Asia Hotel, and **Spasso's** at the Grand Hyatt Erawan.

Other discos include **Narcissus**, Soi 23 (Soi Prasanmit), Sukhumvit Road, tel: 258 2549; **Rome Club**, Soi 4, Silom Road, tel: 233 8836; and **Taurus**, Soi 26, Sukhumvit Road, tel: 261 3991/4. Generally, these venues appeal more to Thais than to foreigners, but there is room for both.

Music Clubs
This is not the kind of music you will find in New York, London or Tokyo, but it is very pleasant, and some of it is very innovative. Jazz clubs proliferate along Soi Sarasin, Soi Lang Suan, and elsewhere. They differ from their murky, hostess-filled counterparts in being open – usually glass-fronted and with sidewalk tables – with the emphasis on good live music and good conversation.

Music clubs appeal as much to professional Thais as they do to Westerners. Among the most popular with mixed nationality crowds are **Brown Sugar**, 231/19 Soi Sarasin, tel: 250 0103; **Round Midnight**, 106/2 Soi Lang Suan, Ploenchit Road, tel: 251 0652; and **Saxophone Pub Restaurant**, 3/8 Victory Monument, Phaya Thai Road, tel: 246 5472.

If you like Dixieland jazz and a lively atmosphere, head to **Bobby's Arms**, Car Park Building, First Floor, Soi Patpong 2 (behind Foodland), tel: 233 6828, on Sunday evenings. The band is comprised of local residents who play for the fun of it. Bobby's offers good British cuisine and lots of beer in a convivially British setting.

Most of the more sophisticated nightclubs are found in firs-class hotels. Classy and classic, the Oriental Hotel's famed **Bamboo Bar** nightclub is for dressier occasions. The scene is chic, normally with jazz singers from the United States playing long-term engagements. You can also find imported acts at the Dusit Thani Hotel's **Tiara Lounge**. Most hotels have lounge bars with good musical acts.

For other nighttime activities, check the daily newspapers for announcements of concerts, art shows, lectures and other offerings around the city. The Sunday morning *Bangkok Post* and *The Nation* carry listings for the following week.

Bars
Bull's Head, Soi 33, Sukhumvit Road (near Villa Supermarket). Tel: 259 4444. Pleasant pub

atmosphere. Popular with foreigners.
Delaney's Irish Pub, 1-4 Sivadon Bldg., Convent Road. Tel: 266 7160. The only place in Bangkok which serves Guinness on tap. Live music some nights.
Front Page, 14/10 Soi 1, Sala Daeng Road. Tel: 233 6315. Low-key neighborhood bar.
Hard Rock Café, Soi 11, Siam Square, Rama I Road. Tel: 251 0792/4, 254 0831. Live rock most evenings.
Jool's Bar and Restaurant, 21/3 Soi 4 (Soi Nana Tai), Sukhumvit Road. Tel: 252 6413. Understated British-style pub.
Witches Tavern, Soi 55 (Soi Thong Lo), Sukhumvit. Tel: 391 9791. Live music on weekends.

Cigar Lounges
Private Cellar, Pavilion Y, RCA, New Phetburi Road. Tel: 203 0926/30. Many fine cigars, impressive vintage wines, excellent port and malt whiskeys, bistro-style snacks. Dress Code. Expensive.
Regent Lobby, Regent Hotel, 155 Ratchadamri Road. Tel: 251 6127. Daily 6pm–1am. Excellent selection of imported cigars, staggering assortment of single malt whiskeys, great jazz band. Dress Code.

Microbreweries
The Paulaner Bruhaus, President Park, end of Soi 24, Sukhumvit Road. Tel: 661 1210, 661 1111/5. Good German food, including Sunday brunch.
Royal Hofbruhaus, 5 Soi Sala Daeng Place Bldg., Soi Sala Daeng, Silom Road. Tel: 636 0015/8. Comprehensive German menu, many fine German wines and spirits. There is also a branch conveniently located at Don Muang International Airport (Terminal 2) and pleasant for unexpected delays.
Taurus Brew House, Soi 26, Sukhumvit Road. Tel: 661 3535. Daily 5pm–2am. American style microbrewery offering four beers.

CHIANG MAI
Chiang Mai nightlife is subdued by comparison to that of Bangkok.

Perhaps it is the fatigue induced by trekking, the calmer nature of the town, or simply the calmer nature of the traveler. But in the evenings, Chiang Mai is very quiet.

Music Clubs and Bars

The normal evening entertainment is to sit in a restaurant or pub and listen to local musicians sing soft tunes. **Riverside Restaurant** on Charoenrat Road and **Chiang Mai Tea House** on the Chiang Mai-Lamphun Road are two examples of this kind of entertainment. Bars along Chaiyaphum Road in the vicinity of Tapae Gate offer live and recorded music. The latter also have bargirls but not in the numbers of Bangkok or Pattaya.

During the dry season, most of Chiang Mai's evenings are spent in outdoor restaurants like **Antique House** on Charoen Prathet Road, **The Brasserie** on Charoenrat Road, the sidewalk café in front of the **Suriwongse Hotel**, the **Smiling Monkey** on Bamrungburi Road, and **Daret's House**, located on Chaiyaphum Road.

Massages

Traditional massages are available at **Diamond Hotel**, Charoen Prathet Road, or at **Rin Kaeo Phovej**, 183/4 Wua Lai Road (beside the Old Chiang Mai Cultural Centre). Tel: 234 565, 235 969. Open from 8am–midnight.

PATTAYA

Pattaya's nightlife is still somewhat in the old mold, with bars proliferating in the South Pattaya area. Here, the emphasis is on picking up bargirls and drinking. There are one or two music clubs, where one can sip a beer and listen to 60s rock and roll.

Hotels have lobby bands and bars with lounge singers. The Beach Road and Pattaya 2 Road are lined with beer bars, which differ little from their cousins in South Pattaya.

PHUKET

As Phuket has become sophisticated, so has its nightlife. In Patong, **Simon Cabaret** (342

114) has evolved into a highly professional showpiece with elaborate stage sets and a few comic laughs. The cast is exclusively, and rather deceptively, it seems, feminine. Shows: 7.30 and 9.30pm.

The **Safari Pub**, a kilometer up the hill from Simon, heats up around 11pm with the live band luring an unlikely mix of cocktail-compromised Thais and tourists to the dance floor. In downtown Patong, the dance scene revolves around the evergreen **Banana disco** on Beach Road, the newly opened **Shark Club**, and the Thai-oriented **Tin Mine**. The **Sports Pub** at the Shark shows live sports events via satellite. Dozens of beer bars with hostesses still provide the backbone of Patong's nightlife in and around Soi Bangla. A-go-go thrives at **Extasy**, **Firehouse** and **Rock Hard**. Massage houses are many. **Christin Massage** is the glossiest. The traditional version is available at **Hutavat** in Phra Baramee Road.

In Karon there are beer bars opposite **Crystal Beach Hotel** and massage at the **Blue Moon**. In Kata there are a few beer bars south of the Siam Commercial Bank, but the upscale **Islander Bar** is a better bet.

The live music at Phuket town's **Timber Rock club** in Yaowarat Road is the best in town. Ten-pin bowling at **Pearl Bowl** on Montri Road is a tradition. The slick Thai-style coffee shop, **Bua Luang**, on Pattana Road, is a Phuket institution.

Culture

Culture

Modern pop culture seems to have gained ascendancy over traditional Thai arts, despite government support for Thai arts and performers. Foreign culture is promoted by the respective country cultural organizations, but little is done to attract foreign performers in the manner of, say, Hong Kong's Art Centre and the annual Hong Kong Arts Festival.

The many museums in Bangkok and in major towns around the country are devoted to preserving the past and contain some superb specimens.

Exhibitions of modern art are arranged by private gallery owners, foreign cultural centers, or by corporate patrons, usually banks.

Museums

BANGKOK

The **National Museum** on Na Phra That Road, tel: 215 8173, next to Sanam Luang in the heart of the old royal city, is a repository of archaeological finds, Buddha images, old royal regalia, ceramics and art objects (usually Buddhist) from neighboring countries. The walls of the Buddhaisawan Chapel in the museum grounds are covered in some of the finest Buddhist murals in Thailand. The museum is open from 9am–4pm, Wednesday to Sunday. Last ticket sold at 3.30pm. Admission is 20 baht.

The National Museum offers free guided tours of Buddhist and other art, and conducts them in a number of languages. The schedule is: **English:** Buddhism (Wednesday); Thai art and culture (Thursday). **French:** Thai art (Wednesday).

German: Thai art and culture (Thursday). **Spanish:** By special arrangement for groups.

Tours start at 9.30am and last about two hours. For information call the museum volunteers at 215 8173. Whatever tour you take, be sure to visit the Buddhaisawan Chapel and the Cremation Chariot Hall (Hall 17) afterwards.

Almost every urban centre in Thailand has a branch of the National Museum.

CHIANG MAI

The **National Museum**, near Wat Jet Yot on Highway 11. Open 9am–4pm Wednesday–Sunday. Collections of Sawankhalok china and Buddha images are highlights.

The **Folk Art Museum**, near the junction of Thiphanet and Wualai roads. Open 10am–4pm Friday–Wednesday. Collection of household items housed in a traditional-style house.

The **Tribal Research Centre**, on Chiang Mai University campus. A small ethnographical museum with costumes and implements of hill tribes on display.

Art Galleries

The **National Gallery**, to the north of the National Museum in Bangkok, across the approach to the Phra Pinklao Bridge at 4 Chao Fa Road, tel: 281 2224, displays works by Thai artists and offers frequent film shows. Open Wednesday to Sunday from 9am–4pm. Exhibitions of paintings, sculpture, ceramics, photographs and weaving are varied and numerous. Check the *Bangkok Post* for details.

Silpakorn University, opposite the Grand Palace on Na Phralan Road, is the country's premier fine arts college. It frequently stages exhibitions of students' work. Other promoters of Thai art and photography are the British Council, the Goethe Institut and Alliance Francaise, all of which sponsor various exhibitions.

Art galleries seem more interested in selling mass market

and "tourist" works than in promoting experimental art; but one, **Visual Dhamma**, takes an active role in ensuring that talented artists exhibit their works. As its name implies, it is interested primarily in a new school of Thai art which attempts to re-interpret Buddhist themes. It is located at 44/28 Soi 21 (Soi Asoke), Sukhumvit Road. Tel: 258 5879.

Concerts

The Fine Arts Department periodically offers concerts of Thai music and dance/drama at the **National Theatre**. On Saturday afternoons at 2pm, programs of Thai classical dance are presented at the auditorium of the **Public Relations Building** on Ratchadamnern Klang Avenue opposite the Royal Hotel. Each Friday, Bangkok Bank offers traditional Thai music on the top floor of its **Pan Fah** branch (Ratchadamnern Avenue at the intersection with Phra Sumen Road) at 5pm.

Concerts of European music and dance are now regular events. The Bangkok Symphony Orchestra gives frequent concerts, as do groups from western countries. See *Bangkok Post's* Sunday magazine for details.

Theaters

The **National Theatre** presents Thai works and, occasionally, big-name foreign ensembles like the New York Philharmonic. For more experimental works, Thai or foreign, look to the **Thailand Cultural Centre**. The Centre, which is a gift of the government of Japan, is located on Ratchadapisek Road north of Bangkok, tel: 247 0028. Its three stages present everything from pianists to puppets. See the newspapers for announcements of forthcoming performances.

It is also possible to find Chinese opera performed as part of funeral entertainment or during the Vegetarian Festival each September in Chinatown. These performances

are normally not announced, but are an unexpected surprise one stumbles across when wandering back alleys. It is hard to miss; the clash of cymbals and drums and the screech of violins identify it.

Likay, the village version of the great *lakhon* and *khon* dance/dramas of the palace, was once staple fare at temple fairs. Alas, most of the fairs have faded away in the city and are found only in rural areas. Even there, likay performances are often given second billing to popular movies shown in the open air on big screens. About the only place one can see truncated likay performances is at Lak Muang, where successful supplicants pay a troupe to perform for gods of the heavens and angels of the city.

Movies

Bangkok movie theaters present Thai, Chinese and subtitled Western films. The Western films are either megahits or are filled with violence – gore being substituted for dialogue. Thai films are either based on a set theme (good versus evil, with pathos, rowdy humor, ugly villains and plenty of fisticuffs) that appeal only to provincial audiences (and indeed are made primarily with them in mind), or are silly comedies on the theme of young love. Only rarely does a film of social significance appear.

Libraries

For reading or reference, stop in at one of these libraries. All carry books in English on Thailand. **American University Alumni** (AUA), 179 Ratchadamri Road. Tel: 252 8170/3. The library, which is sponsored by the U.S. Information Agency, is open to non-members. In Chiang Mai: 24 Ratchadamnern Road. Tel: 211 973, 278 407. **Neilson Hayes**, 195 Suriwongse Road. Tel: 233 1731. Open from 9.30am–4pm Monday to Saturday; and from 9.30am–12.30pm on Sunday. The oldest English language library in Thailand, with

over 20,000 volumes.
Siam Society, 131 Soi 21 (Soi Asoke), Sukhumvit Road. Tel: 258 3491. Open from 9am–5pm on Tuesday–Saturday.

Bookstores

Bangkok has perhaps the best bookstores in Southeast Asia, with a wide selection of books for information and for entertainment. If you want to read about something you have encountered in Bangkok or just want a good, light read for the beach, try one of these bookshops. Alternatively, your hotel bookstore may have something you are looking for.
Asia Books, with branches at 221 Sukhumvit Road (between Soi 15 and 17); Peninsula Plaza (153 Ratchadamri Road); Landmark Plaza (138 Sukhumvit Road); Thaniya Plaza (next to Soi Patpong 2); Times Square; World Trade Centre (4 Ratchadamri Road); Seacon Square (Si Nakharin Road) and Siam Discovery Centre.
Bookazine branches can be found on Ploenchit Road (Sogo Department Store, 3rd Floor); Silom Road (CP Tower, 313 Silom Road, near Convent Road); and Sukhumvit Road (Robinson Department Store).
D.K. Books, branches at Siam Square (Rama I Road); Mahboonkrong (opposite Siam Square); Sukhumvit Road (near Soi 12) and Seacon Square (Si Nakharin Road).
Chulalongkorn University (Phaya Thai Road, south of Siam Square) also has a good bookshop with some esoteric titles in English.

Festivals

Festivals and Fairs

Temple fairs upcountry are great fun to attend. They are usually held in the evenings during the cool season to raise money for repairs to temple buildings. There are carnival rides, freak shows, halls of horror, *rumwong* dances, food vendors and deafening noise – the one element without which a fair would not be a fair. If you see one in progress, stop, park and enjoy yourself.

The dates for these festivals and fairs change from year to year. Check the exact dates by calling the TAT in Bangkok.

JANUARY
New Year's Day is a day of relaxation after the festivities of the night before. It is a public holiday.
Phra Buddha Chinarat Fair is held in late January or early February. Enshrined in Phitsanulok's Wat Phra Si Ratana Mahathat, Phra Buddha Chinarat is one of Thailand's most sacred and delicately-cast Buddha images of the Sukhothai style. The fair includes a display of giant birds made from straw, folk performances and various forms of entertainment.
Don Chedi Memorial Fair in Suphanburi (late January) commemorates the decisive battle won by King Naresuan at Don Chedi. The fair features historical exhibitions, entertainment and local handicraft stalls.
Bo Sang Umbrella Fair, in Bo Sang near Chiang Mai, is held in the main street and celebrates the traditional skill of making gaily painted umbrellas and other handicrafts.

FEBRUARY
Flower Festival is held in Chiang Mai during early February. This annual event features flower displays, floral floats, beauty contests and coincides with the period when the province's temperate and tropical flowers are in full bloom.
Dragon and Lion Parade is held annually between January and February in the central Thailand town of Nakhon Sawan, by people of Chinese ancestry. The Dragon and Lion procession is a traditional homage-paying rite to the golden dragon deity in gratitude for his benevolence to human beings. The lively parade includes marching bands, golden dragon and lion dances, and processions of deities.
Chinese New Year is not celebrated with the boisterousness of other Asian countries. The temples are a bit busier with wishes made for good fortune in the coming year, but otherwise there is nothing to mark the period. Shops close and, behind the steel grilles, private family celebrations go on for three or four days.
Magha Puja, a public holiday in Bangkok and a Buddhist holiday on the full moon night of February, marks the spontaneous gathering of 1,200 disciples to hear the Lord Buddha preach. In the evening, Thais gather at temples to hear a sermon by the chief monk of the wat. Then, when the moon is rising, they place their hands in a praying position before their faces and clasping candles, incense and flowers, follow the chanting monks around the bot of the wat three times before placing their candles and incense in trays at the front of the bot. It is a most solemn and moving ceremony.

MARCH
Kite flying is not a festival but it would be difficult to convince kite enthusiasts otherwise. They gather at Sanam Luang, in Bangkok, in the afternoons as the brisk winds haul their large kites aloft, filling the sky with bright colours.

Barred Ground Dove Festival.
Dove lovers from all over Asia come to Yala for this event. The highlight is a dove-cooing contest involving over 1,400 competitors.

APRIL

Chakri Day on 6 April celebrates the founding in 1782 of the dynasty that presently rules Thailand. It is celebrated in the palace, but there are no public ceremonies. An official holiday, most Thais celebrate it as a day off from work.

The **Phra Chedi Klang Nam Fair** in April is one of the larger temple fairs. It is celebrated at the wat on the river's edge at Phrapadaeng, 15 km (9 mi) south of Bangkok, on the Thonburi side of the river.

Songkran is a public holiday that, in the past, was the traditional Thai New Year – until royal decree shifted the official new year's to January 1. It most closely resembles the Indian festival of Holi which occurs at the same time. Songkran is a time of wild revelry, a chance for the normally placid Thais to let off steam. The central event is the sprinkling of water on one's friends to bless them, but this usually turns into a boisterous throwing of buckets of water on passers-by.

The celebration of Songkran in Bangkok is a little more subdued than in the north, and while it may be safe for visitors to ride in an open-windowed bus down the street, they are advised to be prepared when walking in the street, riding a tuk-tuk or visiting Bangkok's nightlife areas in Patpong, Nana Entertainment Plaza and Soi Cowboy.

To see Songkran at its most riotous, travel down the western bank of the Chao Phraya River to the town of Phrapadaeng. There, no one is safe, but in the April heat, who cares? Songkran in the north of Thailand, particularly in Chiang Mai, is fervently celebrated over several days and attracts many visitors from Bangkok.

Turtle Releasing Fair. At Nai Yang beach in Phuket, young turtles are released for their journey to the sea. The festival begins early in the morning with alms offered to monks and is accompanied by music, dancing, sports and food.

MAY

Labor Day (May 1) is a public holiday.

Coronation Day (May 5) is a private royal affair and a public holiday.

The **Rocket Festival** in Yasothon in the northeast of Thailand is held in early May. Well worth the trip to witness the launching of the locally made missiles of all shapes and sizes, some as tall as a person.

The **Ploughing Ceremony** is a colourful ancient tradition celebrated only in Bangkok. Held at Sanam Luang, it is presided over by King Bhumibol and marks the official start of the rice planting season. Crimson-clad attendants lead bullocks, drawing an old-fashioned plough, around a specially prepared ground. The lord of ceremonies, usually the minister of agriculture, follows behind, scooping rice seed out of baskets held by pretty maidens and sowing it in the furrows left by the plough, all to the accompaniment of blaring conch shells and drums.

Visakha Puja is a public holiday on the full moon night of May that commemorates the birth, enlightenment and death of Buddha. The three things are all said to have happened on the same day. Visakha Puja is celebrated like Magha Puja, with a triple circumambulation around the temple as the moon is rising.

Fruit Fairs. There are annual fairs in Chiang Mai, Rayong, Chanthaburi, Trat and several other locations throughout Thailand to celebrate the harvest of lychees, durian, mangosteen, rambutan, jack fruit and zalacca. Besides stalls selling the produce of the surrounding orchards, there are beauty pageants, cultural shows and local entertainment.

JUNE

Sunthorn Phu Day. This annual celebration in late June commemorates the birth of the Thai poet Sunthorn Phu. The festivities include dramatic performances and puppet shows depicting his literary works, poetry recitals and folk entertainment.

JULY

Asalaha Puja on the full moon night of July is the third most important Buddhist holiday and marks the occasion when Buddha preached to his first five disciples. It is celebrated on the full moon night in similar manner to Magha Puja and Visakha Puja. It also marks the beginning of the three-month Lenten season. Tradition says that Buddha was approached by farmers who asked that he bar monks from going on their morning alms rounds for a period of three months, because they were trampling on the rice shoots they had just planted. They offered instead to take food to the monks at the temple during this period, a practice which has been followed ever since.

Khao Phansa is celebrated almost immediately following Asalaha Puja and marks the commencement of the annual three-month Rains Retreat.

Candle Festival takes place during Khao Phansa in the northeast town of Ubon. It celebrates the commencement of Khao Phansa with a lovely spectacle where some beautifully embellished beeswax candles are ceremoniously paraded before being presented to temples.

AUGUST

Queen Sirikit marks her birthday (August 12) by religious ceremonies and private celebrations. It is a public holiday.

SEPTEMBER

On the first day of the eighth lunar month, Chinese celebrate the **Moon Festival**. They place small shrines laden with fruit, incense and candles in front of their houses to honor the moon goddess. It is a lovely festival, the highlight of which are the utterly scrumptious cakes shaped like a full moon. They are specially prepared, often by chefs flown in from Hong Kong, and found no other time of the year.

Phichit Boat Races. A regatta featuring long-boat races. Similar events are held in Phitsanulok and all over Thailand at this time of year. The low-slung, wooden boats are raced with great gusto.

Taan Khuay Salak. A series of races on the Nan River, northern Thailand, in long, narrow "dragon" boats propelled by 50 oarsmen. Mid-September to mid-October.

OCTOBER

The **Chinese Vegetarian Festival**, held in mid-October, is a subdued affair in Bangkok by comparison with the firewalkers of Phuket. Enormous amounts of vegetarian food, Chinese operatic performances and elaborate offerings are made at various Chinese temples around the city. A superb photographic opportunity. Only those wearing all-white attire are allowed in the area of the altar, so dress appropriately.

Ok Phansa marks the end of the three-month Lenten season, and the beginning of the Kathin season when Buddhists visit wats to present monks with new robes and other necessities. Groups will rent boats or buses and travel long distances to spend a day making gifts to monks of a particular wat. If you are invited, by all means go, because it is a day of feasting and fun as well.

Chulalongkorn Day (October 23) honors King Rama V (1868–1910), who led Thailand into the 20th century. On this public holiday, students lay wreaths before his statue in the plaza at the old National Assembly building during an afternoon ceremony.

Lanna Boat Races. If you miss the Phichit Boat Races, this regatta is just as exciting.

The **Buffalo Races** held in late October in Chonburi rival the excitement of the Kentucky Derby.

NOVEMBER

Golden Mount Fair, held the first week of November in Bangkok, is one of the noisiest of temple fairs. Carnival rides, food concessions, variety performances and product stalls are the main attractions.

The **Little Royal Barge Festival** at Wat Nang Chee in Phasi Charoen early in November is a smaller version of the grand Royal Barge procession, but it is marked by more gaiety in small towns.

Loy Krathong, one of the most beautiful festivals anywhere in Asia, is on the full moon night of November. It is said to have been started in Sukhothai in the 13th century. A young queen, Nang Nopamat, is said to have floated a small boat laden with candles and incense downstream past the pavilion where her husband was talking with his friends. Whatever the origins, it has grown to be one of the country's most enchanting festivals, a night when Thais everywhere launch small candle-laden boats into the rivers and canals to ask blessings. The tiny dots of light and shimmering water are mesmerizing.

Long-boat races have become increasingly popular in the past few years, and it is not unusual to open a newspaper during November and find that yet another race is being staged somewhere in Thailand. They are colourful and exciting and provide superb photo opportunities.

The **Elephant Round-Up** in Surin is held in mid-November and attracts visitors from all over Thailand and elsewhere.

The **Phra Pathom Chedi Fair** at the world's biggest chedi, in Nakhon Pathom, is another temple fair, and is regarded as one of the most exciting.

Khon Kaen Silk Fair. Silk weaving demonstrations and a chance to buy lustrous silk in a major centre of production.

River Kwai Bridge Week. A sound-and-light presentation recaptures this dark period of recent history when Asians and Europeans died in the thousands at the hands of the Japanese to build the infamous Death Railway during World War II.

Sunflower Fair. The photogenic sight of Mexican sunflowers in bloom is best seen in the hills of Doi Mae U-Khor, as Mae Hong Son holds a three-day festival of ox-carts decorated with the beautiful flowers. When the flowers finally fade, the seeds are used to make organic insecticides.

DECEMBER

Trooping of the Colours (December 3). The royal regiments dressed in brilliantly-coloured costumes pass in review before the king. Held on the plaza before the old National Assembly building, the Trooping of the Colours is the most impressive of martial ceremonies.

King Bhumibol celebrates his birthday (December 5) with a ceremony at Wat Phra Kaeo only for invited officials and guests and with a private party. It is a public holiday.

King's Cup Regatta. Long-distance yacht racing from Nai Harn Bay in Phuket with entries from around the world.

Constitution Day (December 10) is a public holiday in Thailand.

Christmas may soon be a Thai holiday if the merchants have any say in the matter. If endless repetitions of Christmas carols in department stores bludgeon everyone into acceptance, it may not be long before it becomes an official holiday.

But **New Year's Eve** on December 31 is indeed a public holiday.

Shopping

General

Whatever part of your budget you have allocated for shopping, double it or regret it. Keep a tight grip on your wallet or you will find yourself being seduced by the low prices and walking off with more than you can possibly carry home. If you cannot resist, see the "Export" section for an inexpensive way to get souvenirs home.

Over the years, there have been two major changes in the shopping picture. First, there have been subtle design alterations to make the items more appealing to foreign buyers. The purists may carp, but the changes and the wider range of products have found welcome reception by shoppers. At the same time, new products have been introduced which have found popular reception among visitors.

The other change is that while regional products were once found only in the towns that produced them, there has been a homogenization of distribution, so that it is now possible, for example, to buy Chiang Mai umbrellas in Phuket. The widest range of items are found in Bangkok and Chiang Mai, but if you never have a chance to leave Bangkok, do not despair; nearly everything you might want to buy in provincial towns can be found in the capital.

Export

SHIPPING

Most shops will handle documentation and shipping for your purchases. Alternatively, the General Post Office on Charoen Krung (New) Road, near the Oriental Hotel, offers boxes and a packing service for goods sent by sea mail. Packages can be shipped from most post offices. Post offices in most towns also sell cardboard boxes specially created for shipping packages and freight.

Thai Airways in Bangkok also offers a special service called THAIPAC that will air freight your purchases (regardless of the mode of transportation or the airline you are using) to the airline's destination closest to your home for 25 percent of the normal rate. Just take your goods to the airline's office at 485 Silom Road. They must fit into a special box and weigh no more than 33 kg (73 lbs) per box.

Thai Airways will also handle the documentation and customs clearance for a small charge.

EXPORT PERMITS

The Fine Arts Department prohibits the export of all Thai Buddha images, images of other religious deities and fragments (hands or heads) of images dating from before the 18th century.

All antiques and art objects, regardless of type or age, must be registered with the Fine Arts Department. The shop will usually do this for you. If you decide to handle it yourself, take the piece to the Fine Arts Department at the National Museum on Na Phra That Road, across from Sanam Luang, together with two postcard-sized photos of it. The export fee ranges from between 50 and 200 baht, depending on the antiquity – and authenticity – of the piece.

Fake antiques do not require export permits, but airport customs officials are not art experts and may mistake it for a genuine piece. If it looks authentic, clear it at the Fine Arts Department to avoid problems later.

Complaints

The customer is (nearly) always wrong might be the most candid way of putting it. Except for very large shops, expect that once you have paid for an item and left the store, or that unless the defect is very glaring and there is no possible way you could have caused it, the moment you walk out the door, that's it. You can report the shop to the Tourist Police, but they are not usually interested. Shop carefully. *Caveat emptor.*

Shopping Areas

BANGKOK

If you cannot find it in Bangkok, you will not be able to find it anywhere else in the country. Aside from the traffic problems, Bangkok is the most comfortable place to shop. Shopping venues range from huge air-conditioned malls to tiny hole-in-the-wall shops to crafts sections of large department stores.

Queen Sirikit's Chitralada stores sell the rare crafts she and her organization, SUPPORT, have worked so diligently to preserve by teaching the arts to village women. There are branches at the Grand Palace, in Oriental Plaza and the Hilton International Hotel, and at the airport, as well as in Pattaya.

Note that Nancy Chandler's Map of Bangkok, widely available in bookstores and hotels, is an invaluable reference for serious shoppers. It is not the best map for finding specific street addresses in Bangkok, but for pointing you in the direction of the top shopping areas, restaurants and sights, it is unparalleled. Also, the brightly coloured, hand-lettered map makes a wonderful souvenir to take home.

CENTRAL BANGKOK

World Trade Centre, 4 Ratchadamri Road. The flagships of this huge 8-floor shopping complex are Zen Central and Isetan, two well-regarded department stores. Other attractions include a **Duty Free Shop** on the seventh floor (passport and ticket must be presented), many fast-food outlets and bistro-type restaurants, and a wealth of small boutiques selling nearly everything imaginable.

Narayana Phand, the government handicraft centre, 127 Ratchadamri Road (across the street from the

World Trade Centre), is the very best place to go to see the whole range of Thai crafts, particularly if your time is limited. Wood carvings, bencharong, jewelry, pewter, ceramics, silk, handmade paper, textiles, and clothing can all be found at reasonable (and fixed) prices here. Pleasant restaurant on the second floor. The market in the basement beneath Narayana Phand is the best place in town for inexpensive blue jeans; leather goods, casual jewelry, videos and T-shirts are also available here.

Siam Square, Rama I Road (between Henri Dunant and Phaya Thai Roads), home to 7 movie theaters, several bookstores and innumerable Western and Asian fast-food outlets, also has many small shops selling clothing, electrical goods and gift items. Investigate the vendors along the central laneways. Popular, particularly with teenagers.

Across Phaya Thai Road, **Mahboonkrong** is a multi-level shopping complex offering a variety of items including leather goods, clothing, jewelry, audio tapes and CDs at mid-range prices.

Gaysorn Plaza, at the intersection of Ploenchit and Ratchadamri Roads, and Peninsula Plaza, 153 Ratchadamri Road, are two chic shopping malls with designer fashion outlets and a variety of small boutiques. **Amarin Plaza**, Ploenchit Road (near Erawan Shrine), is the place to go for up-market shoes and jewelry.

Pratunam Market, at the intersection of Phetburi and Ratchaprarop Roads, is a huge, bustling warren of stalls which caters less to tourists than to Thais. It is somewhat difficult to locate, but a good place to absorb lots of local colour. There are many street vendors along Ratchaprarop Road outside the market.

SUKHUMVIT ROAD

There are many craft shops in soi off the Sukhumvit corridor.

Among the best for a variety of items are these:
Gifted Hands, 172/18 Soi 23 (Soi Prasanmit), Sukhumvit Road. Tel: 258 4010. Handcrafted silver beads, necklaces, earrings.
Lao Song Handicrafts, 2/56 Soi 41, Sukhumvit Road. Tel: 261 6627. Village handicrafts, non-profit.
L'Arcadia, 12/2 Soi 23 (Soi Prasanmit), Sukhumvit Road. Tel: 259 9595. Thai and Burmese wood and lacquer items.
Nandakwang, 108/3 Soi 23 (Soi Prasanmit), Sukhumvit Road. Tel: 258 1962. Cotton table/bed linens and clothing.
Nature's Touch, 87 Soi 5, Sukhumvit Road. Tel: 251 6086/7. Khon masks, other papier masks items and pottery.
Rasi Sayam, 32 Soi 23 (Soi Prasanmit), Sukhumvit Road. Tel: 258 4195. High-quality handicrafts.
Siamraj Marketing, 160/4-6 Soi 55 (Soi Thong Lo), Sukhumvit Road. Tel: 391 8367, 392 4066. Silk flowers, bencharong and other ceramic items.
Vilai, 731/1, Soi 55 (Soi Thong Lo), Sukhumvit Road. Tel: 391 6106. Excellent fabrics.

Street vendors are common, particularly after dark, along both sides of Sukhumvit Road, between Soi 3 and 11. Perhaps the most useful items they sell are suitcases in a variety of sizes, handy to get all the extra shopping home.

CHAROEN KRUNG ROAD

River City, 23 Trok Rongnamkaeng, Yota Road (on the river, a little north of the Royal Orchid Sheraton). Tel: 237 0777/8, ext. 618. Daily 10am–8pm. Fashionable shopping arcade, the top two floors of which are devoted entirely to antiques. The merchants there are not fond of bargaining, but it can be done, particularly if you have some time to devote to the endeavor.
Oriental Plaza, Soi Oriental, Charoen Krung (New) Road, is another stylish shopping complex with a wide variety of top quality merchandise.
Bangrak Market, Charoen Krung (New) Road, between the Oriental and Shangri-La hotels, something of a contrast to the more sophisticated shopping complexes in the area, sells Indian spices, fresh fruit and cut flowers, and a variety of household goods. **Street vendors** are common along Charoen Krung (New) Road between Silom and Suriwongse Roads.

SILOM ROAD

Soi Patpong hosts a bustling night market each evening from about 6pm. Provided you aren't bothered by the occasional flash of skin through the open club doors, or by the touts doing their best to lure you inside, it can be an enjoyable experience. Silver jewelry, audio and video tapes, T-shirts, dresses, ties, leather goods and watches are common here, and along Silom Road just outside Patpong. Bargain for everything.

Soi Lalai Sap, Soi 5, Silom Road (beside Bangkok Bank). Vendors offering a variety of inexpensive food, flowers, leather goods, watches and clothing line this small soi on weekdays only, until about 3pm. Interesting shops include:
Choisy, 9/25 Suriwongse Road. Tel: 233 7794. Haute couture in Thai silk.
Jim Thompson's Thai Silk, 9 Suriwongse Road (near Rama IV Road). Tel: 234 4900. Daily 9am–9pm. Staggering array of silk items; expensive but top quality.
Motif, 296/7 Silom Road. Tel: 233 1203. Export quality silk and cotton fabrics, handmade paper, paper flowers and a splendid range of cloth items.
Shinawatra Thai, at the intersection of Sathorn Tai Road and Soi Suan Plu. Tel: 286 9991/4. Large assortment of silk and cloth items, including table linen, cushion covers and lingerie.
Silom Village Trade Centre, 266 Silom Road (near Soi 24). An attractive complex of small shops offering a variety of leather goods, wood carvings, handmade paper products, Burmese lacquerware, jewelry and cloth goods. The coffee shop at the entrance is a good place to people watch.
Thaniya Plaza, Thaniya Road, off Silom Road. Small shopping

complex with boutiques, book stores, a coffee shop, and one or two small gift shops. Legend on the 3rd floor has a good selection of handicrafts, including celadon, teak and baskets.

CHINATOWN

Even if you don't have any use for a dozen hand towels, six large rolls of gift wrap or entire bolts of cloth, a stroll down Sampeng Lane in the heart of **Chinatown** is a delightful, if somewhat sense-assaulting, way to pass several hours. There are many small soi leading off Sampeng which are jammed with shops selling fabrics, herbal remedies, toys, clothes, paper items and household goods.

Follow **Sampeng Lane** up to the canal and cross over into Pahurat, an adjoining market with a strong Indian flavour. This is the place to find batik and other textiles, sewing notions and a wide range of spices. North of Pahurat you will find **Old Siam Plaza**, a market with an old world ambiance. The gun shops will likely be of little interest to the average tourist, but there are many handicrafts to be found here, as well as decent restaurants and coffee shops.

Beyond **Old Siam**, follow Charoen Krung (New) Road away from the river to reach **Thieves Market** (Nakhon Kasem in Thai). Brass, porcelain, antiques, musical instruments and amulets are among the items for sale in these narrow streets lined with old wooden houses.

Pak Khlong Talat is a huge, crowded riverside market at the northwestern edge of Chinatown. It is at its most atmospheric around 2 or 3 in the morning when large quantities of fresh flowers and vegetables are unloaded from the boats and made ready for sale the following morning.

BANGLAMPOO AREA

Banglampoo Market, a sprawling area beside the river northeast of Sanam Luang, caters more to the budget traveler than to the one with gold cards. This is a good market

for inexpensive clothing, audio tapes and second-hand books; there are a few craft shops along Khao San Road as well. Shops offering hair braiding and beading are a common sight in this area. Thai musical instruments can be purchased at **Duriyabanna**, 151 Tanao Road, and gold leaf beating takes place at 321 Phra Sumen Road (eastern edge of Banglampoo Market, before Prachatipatai Road) from 9am–3pm, Monday–Friday. There is also a bookstore with a good selection of Buddhist books next door.

On the other side of **Democracy Monument**, the markets at Tha Phra Chan and Wat Ratchanadda sell love potions and amulets to protect one from every conceivable misfortune. On Friday and Saturday, investigate the night market at Democracy Monument, mostly offering second-hand goods without a lot of the traditional tourist fare, but entertaining nevertheless.

CHATUCHAK MARKET

By far the most challenging (and often most rewarding) shopping experience is the huge weekend market at **Chatuchak Park** on Phaholyothin Road. Over 8,500 vendors ply their wares here on Saturday and Sunday; it's best to come early to avoid the heat. Antiques, clothing, jewelry, wood carvings, brassware, masks, baskets, handmade paper, and other crafts from around Southeast Asia can be found here, in addition to the usual fruit, vegetables, plants and animals.

Bargaining adds to the fun of a day at **Chatuchak**, and when energy levels start to flag, there are many food stalls, and even a coffee shop or two, to offer sustenance. If you're not content just to wander aimlessly through the many alleyways, the aforementioned Nancy Chandler map is essential to help you find your way to a particular area of the market.

Finally, no matter which area you find yourself in, most major department stores have special handicrafts sections carrying a wide selection of items. Try **Central** (branches at 1691 Phaholyothin Road; 306 Silom Road; and 191 Silom Road), **Robinson** (branches at 1 Phaholyothin Road; intersection of Silom and Rama IV Roads; and Soi 19, Sukhumvit Road), **Sogo** at Amarin Plaza, **Tokyu** at Mahboonkrong, and **Zen Central** at the World Trade Centre.

OUTSIDE BANGKOK

Chiang Mai also has air-conditioned department stores that sell household and personal products. Handicrafts can be found at studios along the 9-km (6-mi) road to Borsang and along Wua Lai Road. For fake antiques, you must travel farther, to Baan Tawai on the highway to Chom Thong. The famous Night Bazaar on Chang Klan Road and the vendors along Tapae Road are also places to pick up bargains.

Pattaya has malls like Mike's Shopping Mall, Big C, Royal Garden Shopping Plaza and Thai Pan, but most of the casual items are found on the Beach Road. Shops sell a good selection of casual wear.

Phuket offers fewer shopping areas, and most are concentrated on Highway 402 between the airport and Phuket town. Thai Village (km 2.5), Native Handicraft Centre (km 8.5), Shinawatra (km 9) and Cheewa (km 10.6) offer both local handicrafts and those imported from other regions of Thailand. Thai Village has workshops where you can watch the artisans at work. For casual wear, check the shops and vendors along Patong's Beach Road and Soi Bangla, and in Kata and Karon. In Phuket town, browse vendors and shops along Ranong Road.

What to Buy

REAL/FAKE ANTIQUES

Wood, bronze, terra cotta and stone statues from all regions of Thailand and Burma can be found in Bangkok and Chiang Mai. There are religious figures and characters from classical literature, carved wooden angels, mythical animals, temple bargeboards and eave brackets. Note that most fake antiques passed off as real are crafted in Chiang Mai and surrounding villages.

Although the Thai government has banned the export of Buddha images, there are numerous deities and disciples which can be sent abroad. Bronze deer, angels and characters from the *Ramakien* cast in bronze do not fall under the export ban. It is also possible to buy and export Burmese Buddha images.

Chiang Mai produces beautiful wooden replicas modeled on antique sculptures. Sold as reproductions, with no attempt to pass them off as genuine antiques, they make lovely home decor items. Animals, Buddha's disciples and dozens of items range in size from small to life-sized.

Chiang Mai also produces a wide range of beautifully crafted wooden furniture. Cabinets, tables, dining room sets, elephant *howdah*, bedroom sets or simple items like wooden trays are crafted from teak or other woods and carved with intricate designs.

BASKETS

Thailand's abundant bamboo, wicker and grasses are transformed into lamps, storage boxes, tables, colourful mats, handbags, letter holders, tissue boxes and slippers. Wicker and bamboo are turned into storage lockers with brass fittings and furniture to fill the entire house. Shops can provide the cushions as well.

Yan lipao, a thin, sturdy grass, is woven into delicate patterns to create purses and bags for formal occasions. Although expensive, the bags are durable, retaining their beauty for years.

CERAMICS

Best known among the distinctive Thai ceramics is the jade green celadon, which is distinguished by its finely glazed surface. Statues, lamps, ashtrays and other items are also produced in dark green, brown and cobalt blue hues.

Modeled on its Chinese cousin, blue-and-white porcelain includes pots, lamp bases, household items and figurines. Quality varies according to the skill of the artist, and of the firing and glazing.

Bencharong (meaning five colours) describes a style of porcelain derived from 16th-century Chinese art. Normally reserved for bowls, containers and fine chinaware, its classic pattern features a small religious figure surrounded by intricate floral designs. The whole is rendered in five colours – usually green, blue, yellow, rose and black.

Earthenware includes a wide assortment of pots, planters and dinner sets in a rainbow of colours and designs. Also popular are the big, brown glazed Shanghai jars bearing yellow dragons, which the Thais use to hold bath water and which visitors use as planters. Antique stoneware includes the double-fish design plates and bowls originally produced at Sawankhalok, the kilns established near Sukhothai in the 13th century.

Some of the best ceramics come from Ratchaburi, southwest of Bangkok. The wide variety makes a special trip there worthwhile.

DECORATIVE ARTS

Lacquerware comes in two styles: the gleaming gold-and-black variety normally seen on temple shutters, and the matte red type with black and/or green details, which originated in northern Thailand and Burma. The lacquerware repertoire includes ornate containers and trays, wooden figurines, woven bamboo baskets and Burmese-inspired Buddhist manuscripts.

The pieces may also be bejeweled with tiny glass mosaics and gilded ornaments.

Black lacquer is also the base into which shaped bits of mother-of-pearl are pressed. Scenes from religious or classical literature are rendered on presentation trays, containers and plaques.

Beware of craftsmen who take shortcuts by using black paint rather than the traditional seven layers of lacquer. On these items, the surface cracks, often while the item is still on the shelf.

FABRICS AND CLOTHES

Thai silk is perhaps Thailand's best-known craft. Brought to world attention by American entrepreneur Jim Thompson, Thai silk has enjoyed enduring popularity. Sold in a wide variety of colours, it is characterized by the tiny nubs which, like embossings, rise from its surface. Unlike sheer Indian silks and shiny Chinese-patterned silks, Thai silk is a thick cloth that lends itself to clothes, curtains and upholstery. It is more popular as blouses, ties and scarves. It is also used to cover purses, tissue boxes and picture frames. Lengths printed with elephant, bamboo, floral and dozens of other motifs are turned into decorative pillowcases to accent rooms.

Mudmee is a northeastern silk whose colours are somber and muted. A form of tie-dyed cloth, it is sold both in lengths and as finished clothing or accessories.

Cotton is popular for shirts and dresses, since it breathes in Thailand's hot, humid air. Although available in lengths, it is generally sold already cut into frocks and shirts. Southern Thailand is a batik centre and offers ready-made clothes and batik paintings.

Burmese in origin and style, *kalaga* wall hangings depicting gods, kings and mythical animals have gained increasing popularity in the past few years. The figures are stuffed with *kapok* to make them stand out from the surface in relief.

GEMS AND JEWELRY

Thailand is one of the world's exporters of cut rubies and sapphires. The rough stones are mostly imported from Cambodia and Burma, as local mines are not able to meet the demand. Customers should patronize only those shops that display trade's official emblem: a gold ring mounted with a ruby, which guarantees the dealer's integrity.

Thailand is now regarded as the world's leading cutter of gemstones, the "Bangkok cut" rapidly becoming one of the most popular. Thai artisans set the stones in gold and silver to create jewelry and bejeweled containers. Artisans also craft jewelry that satisfies an international clientele. Light green Burmese jade (jadeite) is carved into jewelry and art objects. The island of Phuket produces international standard natural, cultured Mob (teardrop) and artificial pearls (made from pearl dust glued to form a globule). They are sold as individual items or are set into gold jewelry.

Costume jewelry is a major Thai business with numerous items available. A related craft which has grown rapidly in the past decade is that of gilding Thai orchids for use as brooches.

HILL-TRIBE CRAFTS

Northern hill tribes produce brightly coloured needlepoint work in a wide variety of geometric and floral patterns. These are sold either as produced, or else incorporated into shirts, coats, bags, pillowcases and other items.

Hill-tribe silver work is valued less for its silver content (which is low) than for the intricate work and imagination that goes into making it. The genre includes necklaces, headdresses, bracelets and rings the women wear on ceremonial occasions. Enhancing their value are the old British Indian rupee coins that decorate the women's elaborate headdresses.

Other hill-tribe items one might consider include knives, baskets, pipes and gourd flutes that look and sound like bagpipes.

METAL ART OBJECTS

Although Thai craftsmen have produced some of Asia's most beautiful Buddha images, modern bronze sculpture tends to be of less exalted subjects and execution. Minor deities, characters from classical literature, deer and abstract figures are cast up to 2 m (7 ft) tall and are normally clad with a brass skin to make them gleam. Bronze is also cast into handsome cutlery and coated in shiny brass.

Silver and gold are pounded into jewelry items, boxes and other decorative pieces; many are set with gems. To create nielloware boxes and receptacles, a design is incised in silver or gold. The background is cut away and filled with an amalgam of dark metals, leaving the figures to stand in high relief against the black background.

Tin, mined near Phuket, is the prime ingredient in pewterware, of which Thailand is a major producer. Items range from clocks and steins to egg cups and figurines.

PAINTINGS

Modern Thai artists paint everything from realistic to abstract art, the latter often a weak imitation of Western art. Two areas at which they excel are depictions of everyday village life and of new interpretations of classical Buddhist themes. Artists can also work from live sittings or photographs to create superb charcoal or oil portraits. A family photograph from home can be transformed into a painting. The price depends on size: a 40 cm x 60 cm (16" x 24") charcoal portrait costs around 1,000 baht. There are several street-side studios in Bangkok, Phuket and Pattaya that specialize in this art.

THEATRE ART OBJECTS

Papier mâché khon masks, like those used in palace dance/drama, are painted and accented with lacquer decorations and gilded to create superb works of art.

Shadow puppets cut from the hides of water buffaloes and displayed against backlit screens in open air theaters tell the Ramakien story. Check to be sure the figure is actually cut from hide and not from a sheet of black plastic.

Bright coloured shadow puppets cut from buffalo hide make excellent wall decorations.

Inspired by the Ramakien, craftsmen have fashioned miniature models of chariots and warriors in gilded wood or glass sculpture. These two materials are also employed to create reproductions of the famous Royal Barges.

UMBRELLAS

Chiang Mai produces lovely umbrellas and fans made from silk or sa paper, a fine parchment often confused for rice paper but made from pounded tree bark.

Sport

Thailand has developed its outdoor sports facilities to a considerable degree and air-conditioned the ones played indoors. Nearly every major hotel has a swimming pool and a fitness centre; some have squash courts and jogging paths.

DEEP-SEA FISHING

For deep-sea fishing, go to Phuket or to Bang Saray south of Pattaya. At Bang Saray, marlin, king mackerel, cobia, yellow jack, barracuda, bonito, giant groupers, red snapper, rays and black tip sharks lurk among submerged rocks. Boats, tackle and guides are available for very reasonable fees. There are small hotels in Bang Saray, but most fishermen spend the night in Pattaya and head out early in the morning. Fishing trips can be arranged by calling Bang Saray Fishing Lodge at its Bangkok office. Tel: 233 7719, 234 3094.

The waters off Phuket offer numerous challenges to deep-sea fishermen. Sailfish, barracuda, albacore, marlin, wahoo, tuna and king mackerel are just a few of the varieties awaiting a baited hook near Raja islands, east of Phuket.

The **Travel Company** on Patong Beach near Soi Patong Post Office, tel: (032) 321 292, offers daily cruises aboard converted Thai fishing trawlers equipped with fixed sockets to hold the rods. The price for one day is around 6,000 baht for charter, usually with food and drink. No minimum number of persons is required and the cruise is offered year-round. Travel Company also offers night fishing tours that leave Patong at 4pm and return at 9am the following day.

FITNESS CENTERS

In Bangkok, the Asia-wide **Clark Hatch** has a branch in the Thaniya Plaza, off Silom Road. Tel: 231 2250. **Fitness International** is located in the Dusit Thani Hotel. Part-time membership is available. All the top hotels in Bangkok have well-equipped fitness centers.

In Phuket, there is a **Clark Hatch Fitness Centre** in Le Méridien Hotel, tel: 321 480/1, ext. 1428, that is open from 7am–8.30pm. The **Holiday Inn** in Patong also has a fitness centre. The **Pattaya Fitness Centre**, with weights, gym and a sauna, is near the Regent Marina Complex.

FITNESS PARKS

One corner of Bangkok's **Lumpini Park** boasts a fitness park. In Chiang Mai, there is a free fitness park on **Nimmanhaemin Road** that is open from 5am–10pm. In Pattaya, the fitness park is located on the slopes of **Pattaya Hill**; in Phuket, it sits atop **Rang Hill** in the middle of Phuket town.

GOLF

Thais are great golfing buffs, going so far as to employ some of world golfing's stellar architects to design international-class courses. The best courses are in Bangkok, Phuket and Pattaya, with other courses in Chiang Mai, Khao Yai and Hua Hin. Greens fees range from 500–1,000 baht per round on weekends, and it is generally not difficult to reserve a time.

Among Bangkok's courses is the **Navathanee Golf Course** (22 M.1, Sukhapiban 2 Road. Tel: 376 1020) designed by Robert Trent Jones Jr. It is open from 6am–6pm. The **Army Golf Course** at 459 Ram Intra Road, tel: 521 1530, is open from 5am–9.30pm. The **Railway Training Centre Golf Course**, on Phaholyothin Road, tel: 271 0130, west of the Hyatt Central Plaza Hotel, opens at 6am, closes at 8pm. The **Krungthep Sports Golf Course**, 522 Hua Mark Road, tel: 379 3732, opens at 5am, closes at 5pm.

In Chiang Mai, the **Lanna Golf Course** on Chotana Road, tel: 221 911, is open 6am–6pm.

In Pattaya, try the **Siam Country Club Golf Course** 10 km (6 mi) east of town in rolling hills.

Phuket has excellent, if pricey, golf courses at the **Banyan Tree** (324 350), **Blue Canyon** (327 440), the **Phuket Country Club** (321 365, 321 038) and **The Century** (321 329).

HORSE RIDING

There are no public horse-riding facilities in Bangkok, but in Chiang Mai there is a stable on Chotana Road near the new provincial hall. It is open on Saturday and Sunday from 6am–noon and the cost is 200 baht per hour. Telephone 247 478 for more information.

In Phuket, ride at **Crazy Horse Club** at 17 Moo 2, 1 km (0.6 mi) down the back road connecting Kakata Inn with H 4028. Instructors accompany riders through rice fields and down the beach. Morning rides into the jungle are also offered. During the dry season, owners take riders on 2-hour trips into the hills.

ICE SKATING

Undoubtedly one of the more unusual tropical pursuits, ice skating has a certain popularity in Bangkok. Try it at the **World Ice Skating Centre**, World Trade Centre, 8th Floor, 4 Ratchadamri Road. Tel: 255 9500. Monday–Friday and Sundays: 10am–2.45pm and 4–9pm, Saturdays: 8.30am–4pm and 5–9pm.

JOGGING

Two jogging sites for those wise enough not to challenge Bangkok's traffic for right-of-way are in **Lumpini Park** and **Chatuchak Park**. The Siam-Intercontinental, Hilton and Ambassador hotels, among others, have jogging paths.

In Chiang Mai, joggers run up the hill to **Doi Suthep** and catch a mini-bus back. In Pattaya, jog up **Pattaya Hill**. In Phuket, try **Rang Hill**, a 1.3 km (0.8 mi) jaunt. There is a fitness park at the top.

SNOOKER

Thailand has produced some excellent snooker players who are nipping at the heels of world champions in international competitions. As a result, parlors have sprung up everywhere in Thailand as budding aspirants focus their eyes on complex shots and potential riches. In Bangkok, there are numerous snooker parlors around the city. The "Rooks" chain is the most popular and dozens of its snooker parlors can be found.

SCUBA DIVING

Shops in Pattaya and Phuket's Patong beach provide comprehensive courses leading to internationally-recognized PADI or NAUI certification. In Pattaya, try **Seafari** and **Dave's Divers Den**, both on the Beach Road.

Ko Tao is popular with experienced and first-time divers alike; the many placid bays and leeward shores are perfect for the beginner. The visibility is generally exceptional in the pristine waters off this tiny island, and sightings of spotted rays, trigger fish, whale sharks and even giant clams are not uncommon.

There are upwards of 20 diving schools on Ko Tao with 100 or more professional instructors, including **Buddha View Dive Resort**, tel: (01) 229 3948, (01) 229 4466; **Gecko Divers**, tel: (01) 229 5515, (01) 725 0711; **Samui International Diving School/Planet Scuba**, tel: (077) 231 242, in Bangkok, tel: (02) 253 8043.

In Pattaya, **Seafari Sports Centre** on the Beach Road. (Tel: 419 060), and **Dave's Divers Den** at Soi 6 on the Beach Road offer PADI and NAUI courses and diving trips to the outer islands. The water in the bay is murky and visibility is limited.

In Phuket, **Fantasea** (340 088), **South East Asia Liveaboards** (340 406), **Santana** (340 360), **Sea Bees** (381 765) and **Marina Divers** (330 272), among others, have a good reputation. Shop around and you can find scuba trips aimed at German, Scandinavian, French, Thai and Japanese customers. For beginners, the four-day **PADI Open Water course** costs around 8,500 baht, including classroom theory, shallow water introduction, and four dives, usually in Phi Phi, Shark Point or Raja Island.

Day trips for divers with an Open Water card typically visit **Phi Phi**, **Shark Point** or the two **Raja islands**. Day trips average 1,500 baht, plus 500 baht for full equipment rental.

There is a trend towards live-aboard trips to the high visibility dive sites at the **Similan** and **Surin islands**, and even into Burma. These places offer a better chance of seeing large turtles, whale sharks, manta rays and the like. Depending on the vessel, which can be basic or luxurious, trips run 2,500–6,000 baht per person per day. Trips last 2 to 7 days.

Spectator Sports

Despite the hot climate, Thai men and women are avid sports enthusiasts, actively playing both their own sports and those adopted from the West according to international rules.

The king of foreign sports is soccer and is played by both sexes. Following a close second is badminton, with basketball, rugby, track and field, swimming, marksmanship, boxing, tennis and golf trailing only a short way behind. Check the English-language newspapers for schedules.

The principal sports venues in Bangkok are the National Stadium, on Rama I Road just west of Mahboonkrong Shopping Centre; the Hua Mark Stadium, east of the city next to Ramkhamhaeng University; and the Thai-Japanese Sports Centre, at Din Daeng near the northern entrance to the expressway.

In Chiang Mai, games are played at the Chiang Mai Stadium and at Chiang Mai University; in Phuket, at the Phuket Stadium on Vichaisongkhram Road.

Thailand has also created a number of unique sports and these are well worth watching as much for the grace and agility displayed as for the element of fun that pervades every competition.

KITE FIGHTING

The heat of March and April is relieved somewhat by breezes that the Thais use to send kites aloft. **Sanam Luang** in Bangkok and open spaces everywhere across the country are filled with young and old boys clinging to kite strings.

The Thais have also turned it into a competitive sport, forming teams sponsored by major companies. Two teams vie for trophies. One flies a giant star-shaped male *chula* kite nearly 2 m (6.5 ft) high. The opposing teams (there may be more than one) fly the diminutive diamond-shaped female *pakpao* kites. One team tries to snare the other's kite and drag it across a dividing line. Surprisingly, the odds are even and a tiny female pakpao stands a good chance of pulling down a big chula male. Teamwork and fast action make for exciting viewing. Competitions at Bangkok's Sanam Luang start at 2pm.

TAKRAW

With close relatives in the Philippines, Malaysia and Indonesia, *takraw* employs all the limbs except the hands to propel a woven rattan ball (or a more modern plastic ball) over a net or into a hoop. In the net version, two three-player teams face each other across a head-high net, like that used in badminton. As the match heats up, it is not unusual for a player to turn a complete somersault to spike a ball across the net.

In the second type, six players form a wide circle around a basket-like net suspended high in the air. Using heads, feet, knees and elbows to keep the ball airborne, they score points by putting it into the net. A team has a set time period in which to score as many points as it can, after which it is the opposing team's turn.

Tournaments are held at the **Thai-Japanese Sports Centre** (Tel:

465 5325 for dates and times) four times a year; admission is free. Competitions are also held in the northwest corner of Bangkok's **Sanam Luang** during the March–April kite contests. Free admission. During the non-monsoon months, wander into a park or a temple courtyard anywhere in the country late in the afternoon.

THAI BOXING (MUAY THAI)

One of the most exciting and popular Thai sports is Thai boxing. In Bangkok, **Ratchadamnern Stadium** on Ratchadamnern Nok Avenue offers bouts on Monday, Wednesday, and Thursday at 6pm and on Sunday at 4.30 and 8.30pm. The Sunday matinee at 4.30pm is recommended, as it has the cheapest seats. Ticket prices run between 500 and 1,000 baht for ringside seats (depending on the quality of the card), running downwards to 100 baht.

Lumpini Boxing Stadium, on Rama IV Road, stages bouts on Tuesday and Friday at 6.30pm and on Saturday at 1 and 6.30pm. Ticket prices are the same as at Ratchadamnern. As above, weekend afternoon matinees are the cheapest.

There are also televised bouts on Saturday and Sunday, and at 10.30pm on some week nights. For many visitors this will be sufficient introduction to the sport. The **Rose Garden** and Phuket's **Thai Village** offer short demonstrations of Thai boxing, but these are played more for laughs than for authenticity.

Thai boxing bouts in Chiang Mai can be seen at the Dechanukrau boxing ring, on Bumrungrat Road, on the weekends. Bouts are staged each Friday at 8pm at the **Phuket Boxing Stadium** at Saphan Hin (to the right of the tin dredge memorial where Phuket Road meets the sea). Most large rural towns have their own boxing gyms and stage weekly bouts by young hopefuls.

Language

Origins and Intonation

For centuries, the Thai language, rather than tripping from foreigners' tongues, has been tripping them up. Its roots go back to the place Thais originated from, in the hills of southern Asia but overlaid by Indian influences. From the original settlers come the five tones which seem designed to frustrate visitors, one sound with five different tones to mean five different things.

When you mispronounce, not only are you saying the word incorrectly, chances are you're saying another word entirely.

It is not unusual to see a semi-fluent foreigner standing before a Thai running through the scale of tones until suddenly a light of recognition dawns on his companion's face. There are misinformed visitors who will tell you that tones are not important. These people do not communicate with Thais, they communicate at them in a one-sided exchange that frustrates both parties.

Thai Names

From the languages of India have come polysyllabic names and words, the lexicon of literature. Thai names are among the longest in the world. Every Thai first name and surname has a meaning. Thus by learning the meaning of the name of everyone you meet, you would acquire a formal, but quite extensive vocabulary.

There is no universal transliteration system from Thai into English, which is why names and street names can be spelled three

different ways. For example, the surname Chumsai is written Chumsai, Jumsai and Xoomsai depending on the family. This confuses even the Thais. If you ask a Thai how you spell something, he may well reply "how do you want to spell it?" Likewise, Bangkok's thoroughfare of Ratchadamnern is also spelled Rajdamnern and Ratchadamnoen. Ko Samui can be spelled Koh Samui. The spellings will differ from map to map, and book to book.

Phonology

The way Thai consonants are written in English often confuses foreigners. An "*h*" following a letter like "*p*", and "*t*" gives the letter a soft sound; without the "*h*" the sound is more explosive. Thus, "*ph*" is not pronounced "*f*" but as a soft "*p*". Without the "*h*", the "*p*" has the sound of a very hard "*b*". The word Thanon (street) is pronounced "tanon" in the same way as "Thailand" is not meant to sound like "Thighland". Similarly, final letters are often not pronounced as they look. A "*j*" on the end of a word is pronounced "*t*"; "*l*" is pronounced as an "*n*". To complicate matters further, many words end with "*se*" or "*r*" which are not pronounced; for instance Suriwongse, one of Bangkok's main thoroughfares, is simply pronounced "Suriwong."

Vowels are pronounced like this: **i** as in *sip*, **ii** as in *seep*, **e** as in *bet*, **a** as in *pun*, **aa** as in *pal*, **u** as in *pool*, **o** as in *so*, **ai** as in *pie*, **ow** as in *cow*, **aw** as in *paw*, **iw** as in *you*, **oy** as in *toy*.

In Thai, the pronoun "*I*" and "*me*" use the same word but it is different for males and females. Men use the word *phom* when referring to themselves; women say *chan* or *diichan*. Men use *khrap* at the end of a sentence when addressing either a male or a female i.e. *pai* (f) *nai, khrap* (h) (where are you going? sir). Women add the word *kha* to their statements as in *pai* (f) *nai, kha* (h).

To ask a question, add a high

tone *mai* to the end of the phrase i.e. *rao pai* (we go) or *rao pai mai* (h) (shall we go?). To negate a statement, insert a falling tone *mai* between the subject and the verb i.e. *rao pai* (we go), *rao mai pai* (we don't go). "Very" or "much" are indicated by adding *maak* to the end of a phrase i.e. *ron* (hot), *ron maak* (very hot).

Listed below is a small vocabulary intended to get you on your way. The five tones have been indicated by appending letters after them viz. high (h), low (l), middle (m), rising (like asking a question) (r), and falling (like suddenly understanding something as in "ohh, I see") (f).

Useful Phrases

NUMBERS

1/*Nung* (l)
2/*Song* (r)
3/*Sam* (r)
4/*Sii* (l)
5/*Haa* (f)
6/*Hok* (l)
7/*Jet* (l)
8/*Pat* (l)
9/*Kow* (f)
10/*Sip* (l)
11/*Sip* (l) *Et* (l)
12/*Sip* (l) *Song* (r)
13/*Sip* (l) *Sam* (r) and so on
20/*Yii* (f) *Sip* (l)
30/*Sam* (r) *Sip* (l) and so on
100/*Nung* (l) *Roi* (h)
1,000/*Nung* (l) *Phan* (m)

DAYS OF THE WEEK

Monday/*Wan* (m) *Jan* (m)
Tuesday/*Wan* (m) *Angkan* (m, m)
Wednesday/*Wan* (m) *Phoot* (h)
Thursday/*Wan* (m) *Pharuhat* (m, h, l)
Friday/*Wan* (m) *Sook* (l)
Saturday/*Wan* (m) *Sao* (r)
Sunday/*Wan* (m) *Athit* (m, h)
Today/*Wan* (m) *nii* (h)
Yesterday/*Mua* (f) *wan* (m) *nii* (h)
Tomorrow/*Prung* (f) *nii* (h)
When/*Mua* (f) *rai* (m)

GREETINGS AND OTHERS

Hello, goodbye/*Sawasdee* (a man then says "*khrap*"; a woman says "*kha*"; thus, *sawasdee khrap* or *sawasdee kha*)

How are you?/*Khun sabai dii, mai* (h)
Well, thank you/*Sabai dii, Khapkhun*
Thank you very much/*Khapkhun Maak*
May I take a photo?/*Thai roop* (f) *noi, dai* (f) *mai* (h)
Never mind/*Mai* (f) *pen rai*
I cannot speak Thai/*Phuut Thai mai* (f) *dai* (f)
I can speak a little Thai/*Phuut Thai dai* (f) *nit* (h) *diew*
Where do you live?/*Khun yoo thii* (f) *nai* (r)
What is this called in Thai?/*An nii* (h), *kaw riak aray phasa Thai*
How much?/*Thao* (f) *rai*

DIRECTIONS AND TRAVEL

Go/*Pai*
Come/*Maa*
Where/*Thii* (f) *nai* (r)
Right/*Khwaa* (r)
Left/*Sai* (h)
Turn/*Leo*
Straight ahead/*Trong pai*
Please slow down/*Cha cha noi*
Stop here/*Yood thii* (f) *nii* (f)
Fast/*Raew*
Hotel/*Rong raam*
Street/*Thanon*
Lane/*Soi*
Bridge/*Saphan*
Police Station/*Sathanii Dtam Ruat*

OTHER HANDY PHRASES

Yes/*Chai* (f)
No/*Mai* (f) *chai* (f)
Do you have...?/*Mii ... mai* (h)
Expensive/*Phaeng* (m)
Do you have something cheaper?/*Mii arai thii thook* (l) *kwa, mai* (h)
Can you lower the price a bit?/*Kaw lot noi dai* (f) *mai* (h)
Do you have another colour?/*Mii sii uhn mai* (h)
Too big/*Yai kern pai*
Too small/*Lek kern pai*
Do you have bigger?/*Mii arai thii yai kwa mai* (h)
Do you have smaller?/*Mii arai thii lek kwa mai* (h)
Hot (heat)/*Ron* (h)
Hot (spicy)/*Phet*
Cold/*Yen*
Sweet/*Waan* (r)
Sour/*Prio* (f)
I do not feel well/*Mai* (f) *sabai*

Further Reading

General

Amranand, Pimsai. **Gardening in Bangkok**. Bangkok: Siam Society. Good work on plants though could do with more photos.
Cooper, Robert and Nanthapa. **Culture Shock: Thailand**. Singapore: Times Books, 1990. Very useful look at Thai customs and how to avoid faux pas. Written and illustrated in highly amusing manner.
Gray, Denis, et al., **National Parks of Thailand**. Bangkok: Industrial Finance Corporation of Thailand, 1994.
Hollinger, Carol. **Mai Pen Rai**. Boston: Houghton Mifflin. Expatriate life in the 1950s.
Ingram, J.C. **Economic Change in Thailand 1830–1970**. Palo Alto, California: Stanford University Press, 1971.
Segaller, Denis. **Thai Ways**. Bangkok: Thai Wattana Panich, 1979. Collection of columns on Thai customs by a longtime resident.
Siam Society, Culture and Environment in Thailand. Siam Society: Bangkok, 1989.
Sternstein, Larry. **Thailand: The Environment of Modernisation**. Sydney: McGraw-Hill, 1976. Excellent geography text.
Stockmann, Hardy. **Thai Boxing**. Bangkok: D.K. Books, 1979. Excellent, well illustrated book on the basics of Thai boxing.
Warren, William. **The Legendary American**. Boston: Houghton Mifflin. The intriguing story of American Thai silk king Jim Thompson.

History

Chakrabongse, Prince Chula. **Lords of Life**. London: Alvin Redman, 1960. A history of the Chakri kings.

Kasetsiri, Charnvit. *The Rise of Ayudhya*. London: East Asian Historical Monographs, 1976. A narration of the history of early Ayutthaya.

Coedes, George. *The Indianized States of Southeast Asia*. Trans. Susan Brown Cousing. Ed. Walter F. Vella. Honolulu: East-West Centre Press, 1968. Well written scholarly work.

Hall, D.G.E. *A History of South-east Asia*. 3rd ed. London: Macmillan, 1968. The classic text.

Hutchinson, E.W. *1688: Revolution In Siam*. Hong Kong University Press. The events leading to the expulsion of the foreigners from Ayutthaya.

McCoy, Alfred W. *The Politics of Heroin in Southeast Asia*. New York: Harper & Row, 1973. The pioneering work. Readily found in Bangkok.

Moffat, Abbot Low. *Mongkut, the King of Siam*. Ithaca, New York: Cornell University Press, 1961. Superb history of one of Asia's most interesting 19th century men.

Phongpaichit, Pasuk and Chris Baker. *Thailand's Boom!* Chiang Mai: Silkworm, 1997. Two academics give a lively, popular account of the forces that fueled a decade of rapid economic growth. Some portents of the collapse.

Van Beek, Steve. *Bangkok Only Yesterday*. Hong Kong: Hong Kong Publishing, 1982. Anecdotal history of Bangkok illustrated with old photos.

Vella, Walter F. *Chaiyo!* Honolulu: University of Hawaii Press, 1979. The life and times of King Vajiravudh (1910–1925).

Wright, Joseph. *The Balancing Act: A History of Modern Thailand*. Oakland: Pacific Rim Press, 1991. Accessible and detailed history of modern Thailand.

Wyatt, David K. *Thailand: A Short History*. Bangkok/London: ThaiWattana Panich/Yale University Press, 1984. Concise and well-written.

People

Aylwen, Axel. *The Falcon of Siam*. London: Methuen, 1988. A fictionalized story of Constant Phaulkon, Greek adventurer in Siam in the late 1600s.

Collis, Maurice. *Siamese White*. London: Faber, 1965. Fictionalized account of a contemporary of Constant Phaulkon in 1600s Siam.

Ekachai, Sanitsuda. *Behind the Smile, Voices of Thailand*. Thailand. Thai Development Support Committee, 1990. Well-written and informative portraits of Thai life by local journalist.

Lewis, Paul and Elaine. *Peoples of the Golden Triangle*. London: Thames and Hudson, 1984. Excellent text and photos on the hill tribes.

Seidenfaden, Erik. *The Thai Peoples*. Bangkok: Siam Society, 1967. Solid work by long-time resident.

Skinner, G. William. *Chinese Society in Thailand*. Ithaca, New York: Cornell University Press, 1957. Gives an insight into an important segment of Bangkok's history.

Religion

Bunnag, Jane. *Buddhist Monk, Buddhist Layman*. Cambridge: Cambridge University Press, 1973. Gives an insight into the monastic experience.

Nivat, Prince Dhani. *A History of Buddhism in Siam*. Bangkok: Siam Society, 1965. One of Thailand's most respected scholars.

Rahula, Walpola. *What the Buddha Taught*. New York: Grove Press, 1974. Comprehensive account of Buddhist doctrine; other editions available.

Art and Culture

Diskul, M.C. Subhadradis. *Art in Thailand: A Brief History*. Bangkok: Silpakorn University, 1970. Dean of the Fine Arts University.

Klausner, William J. *Reflections on Thai Culture*. The Siam Society: Bangkok, 1987. Observations of a longtime resident anthropologist.

Rajadhon, Phya Anuman. *Essays on Thai Folklore*. Bangkok: D.K. Books. A description of Thai ceremonies, festivals and rites of passage.

Van Beek, Steve & Tettoni L.I. *The Arts of Thailand*. London, Thames & Hudson, 1991. Lavishly illustrated, includes the minor arts.

Warren, William. *The House on the Klong*. Tokyo: Weatherhill. The story of the Jim Thompson House.

Wray, Joe, Elizabeth Wray, Clare Rosenfeld and Dorothy Bailey. *Ten Lives of the Buddha; Siamese Temple Paintings and Jataka Tales*. Tokyo: Weatherhill, 1974. Well illustrated, valuable for understanding Thai painting and the Tosachat (Jataka Tales).

Natural History

Gray, Dennis, Collin Piprell and Mark Graham. *National Parks of Thailand*. Bangkok: Industrial Finance Corp. of Thailand, 1991. Accommodation information is very unreliable. Otherwise, this is a useful survey of the natural assets of many national parks.

Lekagul, Boonsung and Philip D. Round. *A Guide to the Birds of Thailand*. Bangkok: Saha Karn Bhaer, 1991. The standard handbook.

Rabinowitz, Alan. *Chasing the Dragon's Tail: The Struggle to Save Thailand's Wildcats*. New York: Doubleday, 1991. Well-told tales from a zoologist.

Stewart-Cox, Belinda and Gerald Cubitt. *Wild Thailand*. Bangkok: Asia Books, 1995. A coffee-table book with a solid text and a sobering tone.

ART & PHOTO CREDITS

Apa 20, 205
Bowden, David 17, 66/67, 69, 87, 91, 110, 182, 185, 194, 222, 230, 232, 255, 257, 298, 308, 314
Compost, Alain 60/61, 65, 301
Evrard, Alain 59, 79
Henley, David/CPA 262
Höfer, Hans 38, 40L/R, 48, 55, 84/85, 105, 122/123, 154R, 265, 282, 284, 286, 287, 299, 304/305, 317
Jezierski, Ingo 325
Karnow, Catherine 12/13, 70, 71, 72, 73, 74, 75, 76, 104, 106/107, 116, 117, 118, 155M, 268/269
Photobank 6/7, 8/9, 18/19, 22/23, 24, 26, 27, 28, 30, 34, 41, 56, 57, 68, 96, 108, 114/115, 124/125, 128/129, 134/135, 136, 152, 156, 158/159, 160, 169R, 190/191, 197L/R, 202L, 203M, 219, 245R, 257M, 260M, 275, 283M, 285, 302M, 306
Rangsit, M.C. Piya 42/43, 45, 53, 94/95
Smith, Marcus Wilson 58, 100, 102, 144, 144M, 145M, 149M, 150M, 154L, 155, 161, 162M, 163, 164M, 167, 171, 172, 172M, 185M, 186, 188, 207M, 220, 220M, 227M, 231M, 234, 234M, 235L/M, 237, 243, 243M, 270/271, 272, 274, 276L/R, 279, 299M, 307, 310M, 319M, 321, 329M, 330, 330M, 331
Sreedhavan, Slim (WWF) 187L
Strange, Morten 311, 332
Suwanarungsi, Duangdao 62, 63, 189
Tackett, Larry P. 310
Tettoni, Luca Invernizzi 1, 10/11, 14, 21, 25, 29, 31, 32/33, 35, 36, 37, 39, 44, 46, 47L/R, 49, 50/51, 52, 77, 78L/R, 80, 81, 86, 88, 89, 90, 97, 98, 99, 101, 103, 109, 111, 119, 120, 121, 126/127, 130, 140, 141, 142L/R, 145L/R, 147, 148, 149, 150, 151L, 153, 157, 162, 164, 165, 166, 168, 169L, 170, 173, 176, 179M, 180, 181, 183, 184, 195, 198/199, 200, 201, 202R, 203, 204, 206, 208, 209, 210, 211, 212, 213, 214/215, 218, 221, 222M, 223, 224, 225, 226, 228, 229, 231, 233, 235R, 239, 240, 241, 242, 244, 245L, 246, 247, 250/251, 254, 256, 259, 261, 263, 264, 267, 280, 281, 283, 290/291, 292, 294, 295, 296R, 300, 302, 303, 309, 312, 315, 316, 318, 319, 320, 323, 324, 326L/R, 328, 329, 333, 334
Tsuji, Atsuo 64, 174/175, 177, 238, 266
Van Beek, Steve 151R, 278M, 296L

Picture Spreads

Pages 82/83: All pictures by Michael Freeman except main picture Oliver Hargreave/CPA.
Pages 92/93: Top row from left to right: Jeremy Horner/Panos Pictures, James Davis Travel Photography, Marcus Wilson-Smith. Centre row: James Davis Travel Photography. Bottom row from left to right: John Hulme/Eye Ubiquitous, Jex Cole/Eye Ubiquitous, Jex Cole/Eye Ubiquitous, James Davis Travel Photography.
Pages 112/113: Top row from left to right: Micheal Freeman, Marcus Wilson-Smith, David Henley/CPA. Centre right: Marcus Wilson-Smith. Bottom row from left to right: Michael Freeman, Michael Freeman, Michael Freeman.
Pages 248/249: Top row from left to right: James Davis Travel Photography, James Davis Travel Photography, Nigel Blythe/Cephas. Centre row: Graham Wicks/Cephas. Bottom row from left to right: Marcus Wilson-Smith, James Davis Travel Photography, John Heinrich/Cephas.
Pages 288/289: Top row from left to right: John Sims/The Anthony Blake Photo Library, Gerrit Buntrock/The Anthony Blake Photo Library, Nigel Blythe/Cephas. Centre row from left to right: A Collison/The Anthony Blake Photo Library, John Sims/The Anthony Blake Photo Library. Bottom row from left to right: Graham Kirk/The Anthony Blake Photo Library, John Sims/The Anthony Blake Photo Library, Gerrit Buntrock.

INSIGHT GUIDE Thailand

Maps **Polyglott Kartographie**
Berndtson & Berndtson Publications
Cartographic Editor **Zoë Goodwin**
Production **Caroline Low**
Design Consultants
Klaus Geisler, Graham Mitchener
Picture Research **Hilary Genin**

Index

The Insight Approach

The book you are holding is part of the world's largest range of guidebooks. Its purpose is to help you have the most valuable travel experience possible, and we try to achieve this by providing not only information about countries, regions and cities but also genuine insight into their history, culture, institutions and people.

Since the first Insight Guide – to Bali – was published in 1970, the series has been dedicated to the proposition that, with insight into a country's people and culture, visitors can both enhance their own experience and be accepted more easily by their hosts. Now, in a world where ethnic hostilities and nationalist conflicts are all too common, such attempts to increase understanding between peoples are more important than ever.

Insight Guides:
Essentials for understanding
Because a nation's past holds the key to its present, each Insight Guide kicks off with lively history chapters. These are followed by magazine-style essays on culture and daily life. This essential background information gives readers the necessary context for using the main Places section, with its comprehensive run-down on things worth seeing and doing.

Finally, a listings section contains all the information you'll need on travel, hotels, restaurants and opening times.

As far as possible, we rely on local writers and specialists to ensure that information is authoritative. The pictures, for which Insight Guides have become so celebrated, are just as important. Our photojournalistic approach aims not only to illustrate a destination but also to communicate visually and directly to readers life as it is lived by the locals. The series has grown to almost 200 titles.

Compact Guides:
The "great little guides"
As invaluable as such background information is, it isn't always fun to carry an Insight Guide through a crowded souk or up a church tower. Could we, readers asked, distil the key reference material into a slim volume for on-the-spot use?

Our response was to design Compact Guides as an entirely new series, with original text carefully cross-referenced to detailed maps and more than 200 photographs. In essence, they're miniature encyclopedias, concise and comprehensive, displaying reliable and up-to-date information in an accessible way. There are almost 100 titles.

Pocket Guides:
A local host in book form
However wide-ranging the information in a book, human beings still value the personal touch. Our editors are often asked the same questions. Where do *you* go to eat? What do *you* think is the best beach? What would *you* recommend if I have only three days? We invited our local correspondents to act as "substitute hosts" by revealing their preferred walks and trips, listing the restaurants they go to and structuring a visit into a series of timed itineraries.

The result: our Pocket Guides, complete with full-size fold-out maps. These 100-plus titles help readers plan a trip precisely, particularly if their time is short.

Exploring with Insight:
A valuable travel experience
In conjunction with co-publishers all over the world, we print in up to 10 languages, from German to Chinese, from Danish to Russian. But our aim remains simple: to enhance your travel experience by combining our expertise in guidebook publishing with the on-the-spot knowledge of our correspondents.

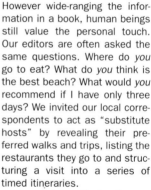